The Cancer of Colonialism

The Cancer of Colonialism

W. Alphaeus Hunton,
Black Liberation, and the *Daily Worker*, 1944-1946

Edited and with an Introduction by

Tony Pecinovsky

Foreword by Vijay Prashad

INTERNATIONAL PUBLISHERS
New York

THIS PRINTING, 2021
ISBN-10: 0-7178-0881-5   ISBN-13: 978-0-7178-0881-6
Typeset by Amnet Systems, Chennai, India

COVER IMAGE: Alphaeus Hunton, Dorothy Hunton, Paul Robeson, and W.E.B. Du Bois (December 1951: photo by Inge Hardison), New York Public Library / Schomburg Center for Research in Black Culture; Hunton Portrait Collection

Table of Contents

*He sharpened his pencils on the lies
of the U.S. government*

By Vijay Prashad

In 1946, the Council on African Affairs held a meeting at the Abyssinian Baptist Church in New York City. The purpose of the meeting was for people in the United States of America to build international solidarity with the struggles of the people of South Africa against the United Party's segregationist and racist policies that would shape the apartheid system two years later. At the meeting, the 4,500 people in attendance collected 10 tons of canned food as well as cash in small notes. Paul Robeson captured the mood: "Freedom for the oppressed black peoples of South Africa is inseparable from the struggle for freedom everywhere – in China, or India, or our own South." Robeson's pithy statement, linking the struggles of people in South Africa with the people of the U.S. South, was axiomatic to the work of the CAA's main intellectual and organizer, Alphaeus Hunton.

Seven years later, in 1953, Hunton authored a postscript to the CAA's key pamphlet, *Resistance Against Fascist Enslavement in South Africa*, written now after the United Party had established a formal apartheid state. Here, he reflected on the links between fascistic tendencies in South Africa and in the United States. "There are some who may say that we have enough to do in cleaning up *our own* backyard; it is perhaps not quite as ugly as South Africa, but still surely bad enough. True. There IS a big job to be done in defending and winning our rights here at home." But, asked Hunton rhetorically, "can we separate the problem of Jim Crow in America from the problem of Apartheid in South Africa? Can the octopus of racism and fascism be killed by simply cutting off *one* menacing tentacle?" The answer was clear: no, of course not, because racism and fascism needed to be confronted everywhere.

It was not enough to confront this octopus without understanding what it emerged out of, namely the swamp of ancient hierarchies that had been reshaped and modernized through capitalist social relations. Race, the invention of Europe's early modern period, drew from earlier forms of xenophobia, mapped itself onto national distinctions, entangled itself with patriarchal norms, and emerged on the floor of the factory and the field of the farms in the contorted forms of class struggle. It took work to understand how the antagonism of class was refracted through the mess of inherited hierarchies, distinctions which the Marxist tradition – which gripped Hunton – had always condemned. In *Capital, Volume 1*, Marx wrote, "Labour in white skin cannot emancipate itself where the black skin is branded." That is the clarity at the foundation of the Marxist tradition, carried forward into the rest of the tradition in V.I. Lenin's writings on national self-determination (and his crisp denunciation in 1913 of the structure of Jim Crow in the United States). It is this clarity that is found in the writings of José Carlos Mariátegui on Andean socialism and of E.M.S. Namboodiripad on the Indian revolution, with indigenousness and caste as an integral part of their respective analyses. Marxism appealed to those of us in the darker nations because it did not neglect or evade the enormity of the national and social question as well as the wretchedness of social hierarchies inherited from past histories into the present structures.

There is a straight line from the 1919 Manifesto of the Communist International to Hunton's 1940s writings in the *Daily Worker* – collected in this splendid volume. Communists, inspired by the bright light of the October Revolution, understood immediately that their revolutionary path had to confront social hierarchies as vigorously as they built organizations of the working class to advance class conflict. There would have been no revolution in the Tsarist empire if women had not marched down the streets in Russia and there would have been no possibility for the revolution to have sustained itself if the colonized minorities from Dagestan to Uzbekistan had not joined the revolutionary wave.

The commitment to social revolution meant a commitment to the aspirations of subjugated peoples, whether their subjugation was conducted along racial or national lines. Nothing one reads here from Alphaeus Hunton would come as a surprise to Communists in Africa, Asia, or Latin America – at the very least – and certainly not those who built the Communist International into an important force for the propagation of world revolution.

Hunton was part of a global struggle that emerged out of a range of prior movements for emancipation. There is no singular point of origin for the histories that wrapped themselves around Hunton. These histories include generations of struggle by African Americans against the hideousness of enslavement and Jim Crow, facts of life for a family that would leave Georgia – where Hunton was born – and travel to Brooklyn – where he was raised. They include cascading histories of working class and peasant struggle that would culminate in the October Revolution and give buoyancy to the Communist movement into which Hunton went as a young man. These two threads – anti-racism and anti-capitalism – were woven into the worldview of Hunton and helped shape his commitment to anti-racism, anti-capitalism, and anti-imperialism. The adversaries that faced Hunton were fierce, and their power meant that he would find himself under attack throughout his life, attacks that disturbed him (as when he was expelled from Ghana), but which did not deter his confidence and motivation to remain engaged in the struggle against imperialism.

Hunton's concerns in these *Daily Worker* columns show us how clear was his perspective of the iron hold of imperialism. One day he writes about the U.S. base system that had maintained the Pacific islands in colonial subjugation; another day he writes about the U.S. government support for the hideous apartheid regime. Each of these columns, drips with Hunton's basic assertion that humanity is more important than the exercise of power through military force and through the warped legality of racist state systems. Not for Hunton the illusion that the United States did not have colonies; Jim Crow in his native Georgia was easily identified both in the U.S. failure to condemn the trusteeship system in the United Nations and to condemn South Africa's establishment of apartheid. This was a Communist who did not allow illusions to be easily spread. He sharpened his pencil on the lies of the U.S. government.

It was not enough for Hunton to reveal the mendacity of the colonial powers – including the United States – as they sought to undermine the Atlantic Charter and the United Nations Charter in their quest to retain their colonies. He had to make clear that the USSR stood with the national liberation movements, fighting for them in the United Nations and elsewhere. On September 23, 1960, the USSR put forward a resolution for immediate decolonization. This resolution was opposed by the entire Western bloc, led by the United States. A few months later, 43 countries from Africa and Asia affirmed the Bandung principles and put forward their own resolution. Eventually, on December 14, the UN General Assembly adopted a resolution, *Declaration on the Granting of Independence to Colonial Countries and Peoples*. This was the resolution originally put forward by the USSR, then reshaped by African and Asian states. Eighty-nine countries – including the USSR – voted for it; no one voted against it, but nine countries abstained; these nine countries were Australia, Belgium, Dominican Republic, France, Portugal, Spain, Union of South Africa, United Kingdom, and the United States of America. Hunton's country, the USA, stood with the old colonial powers and South Africa against a statement that read, "the process of liberation is irresistible and irreversible." In several of his *Daily Worker* columns, Hunton wrote of how the USSR stood for anti-colonialism while the USA stood with colonialism; this clarified the difference between socialism and capitalism. It is no wonder that Hunton remained a Communist right through to the end of his life. It was the only way for a man with his fierce commitment to end racism and to end colonialism to live with himself.

An era has elapsed since these columns were written. Hunton's assessment of imperialism is virtually unchanged, the structure manifest in the attempt to shape the world to benefit the capitalist class and to subjugate aspirations for the realm of freedom. There is a more sophisticated apparatus to extract surplus value from the workers of the world, and there are now more U.S. military bases in the world than there were in 1946. What is different, however, is that clarity over this structure of imperialism is not so widely acknowledged. Too many people, in too many communities, are caught in the fog of liberal propaganda, unable to harness Hunton's precision. Reading Hunton in these times, when hybrid wars suffocate countries from Venezuela to Iran, provides lessons about the world in his times, and to learn how to understand our own world. And then, like Hunton, act to change things.

Acknowledgements

This book, like any long term project, was a collective endeavor. As such, I am thankful for the encouragement and insight, feedback and comments, of a small cohort of friends and colleagues – all deeply invested in making the monumental life and work of W. Alphaeus Hunton available to researchers and general readers.

Historian Gerald Horne, whose voluminous scholarly works mirror that of W.E.B. Du Bois and Alphaeus Hunton, is an inspiration. Without his example and dedication to the historiography of the globalization of the struggle for equality and liberation, this book would not be possible.

Denise M. Lynn and C.J. Atkins both offered thoughtful and constructive feedback on the manuscript, suggestions for clarification, and a few helpful additional sources. Their editing skills made the finished product more informative and readable. As a historian and author, Lynn is challenging the dominant, though spurious, narratives that were used to justify Red Scare political repression directed against activists like Hunton. As managing editor of the *People's World* (the *Daily Worker*'s great-grandchild), Atkins is continuing in the radical journalistic footprints of Hunton. Scholar Charisse Burden-Stelly shares my excitement and enthusiasm for the life and work of Hunton; her focus on the "Tradition of Radical Blackness," of which Hunton was a key personality, is helping to shed much needed light on oppressed peoples and their liberating efforts. Timothy V Johnson was an early supporter of this project; additionally, as head librarian at New York University's Tamiment Library (now retired), he accommodated my research schedule there; as editor of the peer reviewed journal *American Communist History*, he encouraged me to submit my presentations to the 2019 Organizations of American Historians and the 2021 Working Class Studies Association annual conferences, respectively, the most recent paper on Alphaeus Hunton.

Vijay Prashad's excellent and concise Foreword helps to frame this volume. He places Hunton and his *Daily Worker* columns in global and historical context. Like Gerald Horne, Prashad is redefining the role of the scholar – through his many books and various projects (i.e., *The Tricontinental* and LeftWord Books). For this, I am thankful.

I also want to appreciate *People's World* and *Longview Publishing, Co., Inc.*, the owner of the *Daily Worker* archives, for granting me permission to reproduce Hunton's columns. Additionally, Gary Bono at International Publishers saw early potential in this project; I am thankful to him for bringing *"The Cancer of Colonialism": W. Alphaeus Hunton, Black Liberation, and the* Daily Worker, *1944-1946* to print. The St. Louis Workers Education Society also supported this project; I am indebted to my WES mentors Zenobia Thompson and Don Giljum, and my friend Al Neal for their support.

While working on the cover design for this book, I came across a photo Dorothy Hunton published in her excellent biography, *Alphaeus Hunton: Unsung Valiant.* Unfortunately, she did not attribute credit to the photographer. This same photo was republished in the volume *No Easy Victories: African Liberation and American Activists over a Half Century, 1950-2000*, edited by William Minter, Gail Hovey, and Charles Cobb, Jr. It was noted that the photo was reproduced from Dorothy Hunton's 1986 biography. In my research, I came across this same photo, though Du Bois was cropped out, in the January 1952 issue of Paul Robeson's newspaper *Freedom*. This time, fortunately, the photo was credited to Inge Hardison.

The photo of Alphaeus Hunton, his wife Dorothy, Robeson, and Du Bois, which graces the cover of this book, was taken at LaGuardia Airport in New York shortly after Alphaeus was released from a six month prison sentence for refusing to divulge the names of Civil Rights Congress bail fund contributors. I mention this to acknowledge and appreciate Inge Hardison. Though she would by the 1960s become a fixture of the Black arts and culture movement, primarily as a sculptor, like Lorraine Hansberry she found early opportunity at *Freedom*, and it was her work as a photographer that enables us to capture this historic moment when Hunton rejoined his comrades in the struggle for African American equality, Black liberation, and socialism.

If this project helps to shed a little light on the life and work of W. Alphaeus Hunton, I will consider it a huge success. This book is dedicated to my daughter Ida. All errors are mine and mine alone.

Abbreviations

African National Congress – ANC
American Federation of Labor – AFL
American Peace Mobilization – APM
Black Lives Matter – BLM
Black Panther Party – BPP
Brotherhood of Sleeping Car Porters – BSCP
Civil Rights Congress – CRC
Communist Party, USA – CPUSA
Communist University of the Toilers of the East – KUTV
Congress of American Women – CAW
Committee / Congress of Industrial Organizations – CIO
Council on African Affairs – CAA
Daily Worker – DW
House Un-American Activities Committee – HUAC
International Labor Defense – ILD
International Workers Order – IWO
National Alliance Against Racist and Political
    Repression – NAARPR
National Anti-Imperialist Movement in Solidarity with African
    Liberation – NAIMSAL
National Association for the Advancement of Colored
    People – NAACP
National Maritime Union – NMU
National Negro Labor Council – NNLC
National Negro Congress – NNC
Sojourners for Truth and Justice – STJ
South African Communist Party – SACP
Southern Negro Youth Congress – SNYC
Women's International Democratic Federation – WIDF
World Federation of Trade Unions – WFTU

The Cancer of Colonialism

Introduction

Excising the tumor – colonial anti-communism and mass murder

By Tony Pecinovsky

It is well-known that cancer not only affects the individual. While it can disfigure physically and emotionally, leaving individual scars and wounds, it also impacts family members and friends, loved ones and partners who all experience in their own way the sadness, anxiety, anger, and hopelessness that a cancer diagnosis brings. While many do recover, tragically cancer often leads to chemotherapy, radiation sickness, other debilitating treatments, and eventually death. The pain touches all of us in some way.

The old colonial empires were very similar. Colonial subjugation and repression not only affected the individual subjects. It not only disfigured them physically and emotionally, leaving scars and wounds, seen and unseen. It impacted family members and friends, loved ones and partners. Like tumors metastasizing in the human body, colonialism also affected the body politic on a global scale. It not only led to individual death. It led to mass murder, to tens of millions of deaths. Further, it led to moral and spiritual death; to torture chambers, mutilation, starvation, assassination; to the dehumanization, brutal sexualization, and rape of entire peoples; to racism and apartheid. The pain of colonialism touched and continues to touch all of us in some way.

This analogy comes to us from one of the more astute critics of 20th century colonialism, the African American scholar-activist W. Alphaeus Hunton. In the October 19, 1944 issue of the Communist Party, USA's newspaper, the *Daily Worker*, Hunton analyzed the "social and economic ailments from which the world

3

at present suffers" and noted that "the cancer of colonialism is one of the gravest."[1] The personal agonies inflicted upon individual colonial subjects, as well as the impersonal, mass suffering inflicted upon nameless millions in all colonized nations endeared Hunton to a worldwide movement predicated upon liberation and socialism, a movement given substantial aid by the Soviet Union.

Hunton cut his political teeth as a leader of the Washington, D.C. area National Negro Congress and spent 1943 to 1955 with the Council on African Affairs, the domestic linchpin of a global movement for national liberation. He helped the CAA build cross-Atlantic solidarity between African Americans fighting for equality and Africans fighting for liberation.[2] Hunton's regular columns in the *Daily Worker*, from July 20, 1944 to January 19, 1946, showcase and foreshadow many insights, his analysis that would be more fully fleshed-out in the pages of the CAA's newsletters *New Africa* and *Spotlight on Africa*, as well as in the pages of Paul Robeson's newspaper *Freedom*, magazines such as *Masses & Mainstream* and *Political Affairs*, and later *Freedomways*. Hunton's "activism, movement building, organizing, and militant journalism" is part of what Charisse Burden-Stelly calls the "Tradition of Radical Blackness," a tradition that includes "efforts to imagine and bring into being liberating possibilities for all oppressed peoples."[3] Of course, Hunton wrote numerous press releases and pamphlets, and gave countless speeches during this time. All of these sources hold value to anyone interested in the evolution of 20th century resistance to domestic Jim Crow and colonial subjugation. After the CAA's forced dissolution in 1955, a tragic victim of Red Scare anti-communism, Hunton published a major anti-colonial contribution, the 1957 book *Decision In Africa: Sources of Current Conflict*, a project W.E.B. Du Bois, Hunton's co-worker

1. Alphaeus Hunton, "Today's Guest Column: How World Economic and Social Council Would Work," *Daily Worker*, October 19, 1944, 7. Tragically, Hunton died of cancer on January 13, 1970, at the age of 66.

2. For a brief introduction to Hunton's work in the CAA, see: Tony Pecinovsky, *Let Them Tremble: Biographical Interventions Marking 100 Years of the Communist Party, USA* (New York: International Publishers, 2019), Chapter 6. An expanded version of that essay is included in this volume.

3. Dorothy Hunton, *Alphaeus Hunton: Unsung Valiant* (New York: International Publishers, 2021). From Burden-Stelly's Foreword to the new edition.

and friend, called a "brilliant exposition of the structure of the new imperial order in Africa and of the role of American capital, private and public, in underwriting it."[4]

As an introduction to Hunton's Marxist worldview, his *Daily Worker* columns provide a glimpse, a window into a particular moment in time. Hunton wrote with clear, concise prose, with purpose, and with passion. Sometimes intellectual in tone, at others alternatingly biting and humorous, sarcastic and witty, Hunton wrote with a larger goal in mind – unity. Written with urgency, his *Daily Worker* columns encapsulate the final year of World War II, as well as the emerging global systems of power sharing, namely the United Nations. With humanistic compassion, the columns repeatedly call for "collective security"; they acknowledge and describe the devastation and destruction inflicted by the war, as well as the optimism that the war-time alliance between the United States, Great Britain, and the Soviet Union would persist into the post-war world. The hope that the Allied powers would fulfill promises made in, for example, the Atlantic Charter in the colonies – where blood was also shed in the fight against fascism – is also initially evident in Hunton's columns. For Hunton, progressive labor had an important role to play, as well. From fall 1944 into summer 1945, as fascism was decisively defeated and WWII ended, Hunton increasingly shifts his focus to the question of national liberation from colonial subjugation and oppression, and to the mechanisms by which colonial peoples could gain independence. This became the dominant theme for the remainder of Hunton's tenure as a columnist for the *Daily Worker*. The activist-scholar, Hunton also joined the *Daily Worker* in organizing a conference on "world security, and the role of the press," among other activities.[5] As an NNC, CAA, and CPUSA leader, Hunton has been eclipsed by his better known peers.

---

4. Alphaeus Hunton, *Decision In Africa: Sources of Current Conflict* (New York: International Publishers, 1957), 9

5. "Councilmen At Press Parley," *Daily Worker*, April 20, 1945, 4. This was not the only time CPUSA activists addressed the role of media in democracy. For an interesting essay on how Black Communists, particularly Black women Communists such as Claudia Jones, utilized journalism as "a tool for speaking back to power" and "resist[ing] dominant political discourses," see: Cristina Mislan, "Claudia Jones speaks to 'half the world': gendering Cold War politics in the *Daily Worker*, 1950-1953," *Feminist Media Studies*, Vol. 17, No. 2 (2017), 281-196

The current volume is a modest attempt to share his life and work with a new generation.

*   *   *

It is a pleasure and an honor to bring Hunton's *Daily Worker* columns to publication for historians and general readers. *"The Cancer of Colonialism": W. Alphaeus Hunton, Black Liberation, and the* Daily Worker, *1944-1946* consists of three overlapping, mutually reinforcing parts.

The first part, this Introduction, gives readers a brief overview of 20th century colonialism, the role of Communists in anti-colonial, national liberation struggles, the impact reflexively violent anti-communism had on these struggles, as well as the role of U.S. imperialism and militarism in bolstering some of the most horrific mass murder campaigns in modern history. To provide a complete picture, the Introduction will go significantly beyond Hunton's life and work. As we will see, while the tumor was eventually excised, it came at a bloody cost. Unfortunately, if recent headlines are any indication, the cancer may have evolved as we potentially enter a new, 21st century Red Scare.[6] If this is

_____

6. A few examples should suffice: David A. Graham, "Trump's New Red Scare," *The Atlantic*, February 20, 2019; Alan Neuhauser, "Russia, China and the New Red Scare," *U.S. News & World Report*, June 19, 2018; Ana Swanson, "A New Red Scare Is Reshaping Washington," *New York Times*, July 20, 2019; Peter Waldman, "As China Anxiety Rises in U.S., Fears of New Red Scare Emerge," *Bloomberg*, December 31, 2019; Courtney Weaver, Lauren Fedor, and Katrina Manson, "Joe Biden's socialism problem with Latinos," *Financial Times*, November 4, 2020; "The new red scare on American campuses," *The Economist*, January 2, 2020; David Smith, "'America vs. socialism': conservatives rage against the left and plot new red scare," *The Guardian*, March 1, 2020; Angel Bermudez, "US election 2020: How the ghost of 'socialism' is dividing Venezuelan vote," *BBC News*, October 16, 2020; Ben Weingarten, "Communist China Is Preparing To Eat Joe Biden's Lunch," *Newsweek*, January 5, 2021; Nicholas Goldberg, "Column: In Georgia, the GOP tried to revive fears of a 'red menace.' Are we back in 1952?," *Los Angeles Times*, January 6, 2021. Of course, President Trump's use of terms, such as "China virus" and "Commie virus," in reference to the COVID-19 pandemic, as well as attempts to paint then-candidate Joe Biden as a Stalinist served to aggravate tensions; recall, armed right-wing militias storming state capitols in Michigan, and elsewhere, and conspiracy theorists at Florida townhall meetings likening face mask regulations to so-called "communist dictatorships," among other examples, which signal a turn toward dangerous

the case, I hope it is less bloody than the one my parents and grandparents witnessed. The Introduction also provides a brief overview of some of Hunton's *Daily Worker* columns.

The second part of this volume consists of a short biography of Alphaeus Hunton. This is an expanded version of an essay originally published in 2019; like that essay, this biography does not provide much background on Hunton's familial or personal life, on his relationship with his third wife, Dorothy. This is intentional, as Hunton's was a political life. As such, this biography is divided into the three major chapters of Hunton's political life; his time with the National Negro Congress (starting in 1936); his leadership of the Council on African Affairs (from 1943 to 1955); and finally, the publication of *Decision In Africa*, as well as his time in Guinea and Ghana, until his death in Zambia (from 1957 to 1970). Of course, given the limitations of this short biography, I only touch on key moments and topics. The primary focus, however, is on Hunton's time with the CAA. A number of major African American personalities coalesce in this narrative, primarily Paul Robeson and W.E.B. Du Bois, Hunton's closest co-workers and friends at the CAA. Though Hunton joined the CPUSA in 1936 and remained a member the rest of his life, he was not

---

absurdity. Perhaps unsurprisingly, the right-wing, Proud Boy, "Stop the Steal" racists who stormed the Capitol on January 6, 2021, hoping to nullify the outcome of the November 2020 Presidential elections, were somehow (through the same intellectual somersaults used to justify the Capitol assault) compared to the 1948 Smith Act indictments of the top leadership of the CPUSA by CNN's Eliott C. McLaughlin; another example of an emerging Red Scare. Fortunately, dozens of prominent historians and academics penned an open letter to CNN challenging their characterization of the CPUSA as coup plotters. Gerald Horne wrote, "Not only is CNN's characterization dangerous, it's outrageous. CNN's characterization is dangerous because it flips facts on their head. Far from plotting a coup attempt, Communists in 1948 were in fact the victims of a government plot to deny democratic rights – the right of association, the right to speak, the right to their beliefs." See: Eliott C. McLaughlin, "With coup label, Capitol rioters join communist party in plotting against USA, university project says," *CNN*, February 3, 2021; "Historians say CNN wrong to compare Communists to Trump's coup plotters," *People's World*, February 12, 2021; Tony Pecinovsky, "Is CNN jumping on the red-baiting bandwagon?," *People's World*, February 4, 2021; and Pecinovsky, "Missouri's COVID-19 lawsuit against China another effort to distract from Republican failure," *People's World*, April 23, 2020. This author was intimately involved in the effort to circulate and publicize the open letter.

intimately involved in internal party politics[7]; as such, this is not a major theme of the biography. Hunton wrote extensively; I rely heavily on this material, though other primary and secondary sources, personal correspondences, and letters are used.

The third part of this volume reprints for the first time since their original publication Hunton's *Daily Worker* columns from July 1944 to January 1946. The columns are reprinted here as he wrote them and as the *Daily Worker* published them. Where appropriate, though sparingly, short comments have been inserted into the text. Where needed, more detailed explanatory notes have been added at the bottom of the page. Misspellings, typos, and other errors have not been corrected; they reflect the pace in which Hunton wrote, as well as the varied and monumental demands placed on him as a leader of the NNC, CAA, and CPUSA, as well as other organizations. It is unclear why Hunton stopped writing regular *Daily Worker* columns so abruptly, without notice. Likely, his CAA work became too overwhelming, and he simply could no-longer maintain regular contributions. Fortunately, Hunton left these columns, a treasure trove of content for historians and general readers interested in the struggle against Jim Crow and colonial subjugation.[8] A selected bibliography is at the end of the book, providing an easily accessible list of titles readers will find useful for further research.

*　*　*

It is not an exaggeration to say that 20th century colonial subjugation and repression covered the world with corpses. Colonial

---

7. Penny M. Von Eschen, *Race Against Empire: Black Americans and Anticolonialism, 1937-1957* (New York: Cornell University Press, 1997), 60

8. Volumes similar to this one appear periodically, though they take different forms. A collection of Richard Wright's *Daily Worker* articles was published in 2016. See: Earle V. Bryant (ed), *Byline, Richard Wright: Articles from the DAILY WORKER and NEW MASSES* (Columbia: University of Missouri Press, 2016). More frequent are biographical accounts, such as the recently published monograph on Michael Gold. See: Patrick Chura, *Michael Gold: The People's Writer* (Albany: State University of New York Press, 2020). Of course, Communists publish their own collections, too. See: James E. Jackson, *The View From Here: Commentaries on Peace and Freedom* (New York: Publishers New Press Co., Inc., 1963); Virginia Brodine, *Red Roots, Green Shoots* (New York: International Publishers, 2007); and Ellen Perlo, Staley Perlo, Arthur Perlo (eds), *People Vs. Profits – Columns of Victor Perlo: Volume 1: The Home Front* (New York: International Publishers, 2003), among other examples.

subjects were often butchered, and their horrific deaths were meant as an example, as a gruesome reminder of what would befall anyone who resisted so-called colonial masters.

Scholars have rightfully used the word "genocide" to describe atrocities associated with colonialism.

In the early years of the 20th century, German soldiers in South-West Africa (present-day Namibia) presided over the slaughter of the Herero people, who dared to fight for control of their land. According to Dennis Laumann, it is "estimated that more than eighty percent of the Herero died during the genocide, either directly murdered by the Germans or indirectly through starvation and disease." The German general staff, in an official history, concluded that the goal was "annihilation of the Herero people." They were to be eradicated. In the Belgian Congo, known today as the Democratic Republic of the Congo, "the entire population of the territory was conscripted in the collection of wild rubber, with unrealistic quotas." Armed gangs were sent into villages to kidnap women and children. If the men did not collect enough rubber, Belgian officers, or African soldiers forcibly conscripted, "not only beat, tortured, and raped Africans but also chopped off the limbs of men, women, and children as punishment…[and] Belgian district officers proudly produc[ed] baskets of hands and feet [for] their superiors as evidence" that the indigenes would be compliant, and thereby produce wondrous profits for King Leopold II. It is estimated that 20 to 50 percent of the population of the Congo Free State, "or ten million people [died] as a result of famine, outbreak of disease, and depopulation" due to Belgian colonialism.[9] In 1963, the African American CPUSA leader James E. Jackson noted, there "were 30 million people in the Congo in 1884. Today there are but 13 million." Where did they go, he asked? His answer: The Belgians "murdered them by the millions." In short, the "history of the Belgian colony of the Congo is *the* classic horror story of colonialism," Jackson explained.[10] As such, many more examples could easily be cited.

As Laumann writes, colonialism "generally refers to the seizure and occupation of territory (colonization) belonging to one

---

9. Dennis Laumann, *Colonial Africa, 1884-1994* (New York: Oxford University Press, 2013), 48-50 and Tim Harford, "The horrific consequences of rubber's toxic past," *BBC News*, July 24, 2019, https://www.bbc.com/news/business-48533964

10. Jackson, *The View From Here…*, Ibid., 3-4. *Italic* added.

group of people (the colonized) by another group of people (the colonizer)."[11] Though different colonial governments, magistrates, administrators, and soldiers balanced competing interests and constituencies in differing way, all sought stability and control, to suppress opposition to colonial rule, and were dependent upon indigenous labor for their wealth and survival. Extreme violence was an integral component of colonial governance. This remained true throughout much of the 20th century.

After the 1917 Bolshevik revolution in Russia, communism became the favored global scapegoat for colonial powers' brutality. Portrayed as a threat to freedom and democracy, communism instead provided "an alternative system that promised self-determination and equality" to subject peoples.[12] Additionally, it did not have any imperial possessions of its own, which further attracted millions of followers. Communism's mass appeal, among colonial peoples and their allies in more developed nations,[13] frightened colonial magistrates and administrators; they chose barbaric cruelty in the guise of anti-communism to conceal their colonial interests. Anti-communism became the dominant repressive political ideology of the 20th century, a doctrine so ingrained and reflexive, so emotionally resistant to reason and rational debate, that some have labeled it "the most powerful political force in the world."[14]

Further, as Charisse Burden-Stelly argues, anti-communism served to sever post-war domestic discourses on civil rights

---

11. Laumann, *Colonial Africa…*, Ibid., xi

12. Laumann, Ibid., 70

13. For example, see: Philip S. Foner (ed), *The Bolshevik Revolution: Its Impact on American Radicals, Liberals, and Labor* (New York: International Publishers, 2017)

14. For an interesting discussion on repressive, reflexive anti-communism, see: American Friends Service Committee (ed), *Anatomy of Anti-Communism* (New York: Hill & Wang, Inc., 1969); Nick Fisher, *Spider Web: The Birth of American Anti-communism* (Urbana: University of Illinois Press, 2016); and Michael Parenti, *The Anti-Communist Impulse* (New York: Random House, 1969). As Parenti notes, "Thousands of volumes have been written about the ideology, history, and evils of communism, but not very much about anti-communism. Yet anti-communism is the most powerful political force in the world. Endowed with an imposing ideology, and a set of vivid images and sacred dogmas, it commands the psychic and material resources of the most potent industrial-military arsenal in the history of mankind…Our fear that communism might someday take over most of the world blinds us to the fact that anti-communism already has. If America has an ideology, or a national purpose, it is anti-communism." Parenti, 4

from the "Radical Black Peace Activism" of Du Bois, Robeson, Claudia Jones, and others, who made the "inexorable interconnection" between disarmament, equality, national liberation, and "the eradication of capitalist exploitation." The "Cold War state apparatus" responded to Du Bois, Robeson, and Jones "by weaponizing anticommunism"; this repressive ideology was used to "curb internationalism, promote militarism, undermine economic justice, justify the expansion of neocolonialism and corporate imperialism, and rationalize racialized inequality."[15] Hunton, of course, was part of this cohort of increasingly marginalized Black activists. As a result, we cannot discuss colonialism and the struggle against it without also discussing anti-communism. This is especially true in the inter-war and post-World War II period; it is also true of WWII as well, though to a lesser extent.[16] Interestingly, Hunton's first *Daily Worker* column addresses the "widespread and genuine appreciation...[for] those aspects of Soviet life which form the basis of her national strength." To Hunton and other anti-colonial activists, and to millions of colonial peoples, "the way in which, within a quarter of a century, many millions of people of different races, creeds and cultures, illiterate, impoverished and degraded victims of exploitation under the old Russian Empire, were raised to full social, economic and political equality with the most advanced section of the population," was evidence of communism's commitment to equality and liberation. To the old colonial empires, as well as the U.S. ruling class – which emerged at the helm of a post-war world power – this was a cataclysmic, frightening shift, one with the potential to realign world power. In the same article, Hunton chastised British Prime Minister Winston Churchill, who did not support African self-government as "reasonable or useful to foresee." However, he

---

15. Charisse Burden-Stelly, "In Battle For Peace During 'Scoundrel Time,'" *Du Bois Review*, December 23, 2019, https://www.cambridge.org/core/journals/du-bois-review-social-science-research-on-race/article/in-battle-for-peace-during-scoundrel-time/F81265698C05F13CE8B852BF54014461

16. It has been argued that anti-colonialism was absorbed and overshadowed by anti-fascism during the Popular Front and WWII period among Communists, socialists, and progressives generally. See: John Munro, *The Anticolonial Front: The African American Freedom Struggle and Global Decolonization, 1945-1960* (Cambridge University Press, 2020), 15-36. Of course, anti-communism was less potent during this time as well.

added that "the people in British Asia, Africa and the Caribbean, as well as an increasingly large section of the British public itself, have a different outlook."[17] To Hunton, the colonized and their allies – not Churchill – were the final authority on colonial self-rule.

*   *   *

Several recent works, such as Vijay Prashad's *Washington Bullets: A History of the CIA, Coups, and Assassinations*,[18] Vincent Bevin's *The Jakarta Method: Washington's Anticommunist Crusade and the Mass Murder Program that Shaped Our World*,[19] Kristen Ghodsee's *Second World, Second Sex: Socialist Women's Activism and Global Solidarity during the Cold War*,[20] and Gerald Horne's *White Supremacy Confronted: U.S. Imperialism and Anti-Communism vs. the Liberation of Southern Africa from Rhodes to Mandela*,[21] among others, are excellent examples that confront international anti-communism as a repressive global ideology designed to maintain colonial power, as an ideology that left tens of millions dead. Of course, anti-communism was used domestically against the allies of anti-colonial movements as well, though with less lethal results. Penny M. Von Eschen's *Race Against Empire: Black Americans and Anticolonialism, 1937-1957*,[22] Nicholas Grant's *Winning Our Freedoms Together: African Americans & Apartheid, 1945-1960*,[23] Lindsey R. Swindall's *The Path To The Greater, Freer, Truer World: Southern Civil Rights and Anticolonialism, 1937-1955*,[24] as well as, John Munro's

---

17. Alphaeus Hunton, "Today's Guest Column: Textbook for Conference On Colonial Freedom," *Daily Worker,* July 20, 1944, 7

18. Vijay Prashad, *Washington Bullets: A History of the CIA, Coups, and Assassinations* (New York: Monthly Review Press, 2020)

19. Vincent Bevins, *The Jakarta Method: Washington's Anticommunist Crusade & the Mass Murder Program that Shaped Our World* (New York: Public Affairs, 2020)

20. Kristen Ghodsee, *Second World, Second Sex: Socialist Women's Activism and Global Solidarity during the Cold War* (Durham: Duke University Press, 2019)

21. Gerald Horne, *White Supremacy Confronted: U.S. Imperialism and Anti-Communism vs. the Liberation of Southern Africa from Rhodes to Mandela* (New York: International Publishers, 2019)

22. Von Eschen, *Race Against Empire...*, Ibid.

23. Nicholas Grant, *Winning Our Freedoms Together: African Americans & Apartheid, 1945-1960* (Chapel Hill: University of North Carolina Press, 2017)

24. Lindsey R. Swindall, *The Path To The Greater, Freer, Truer World: Southern Civil Rights and Anticolonialism, 1937-1955* (Gainesville: University Press of Florida, 2014)

The Anticolonial Front: The African American Freedom Struggle and Global Decolonization, 1945-1960,[25] all also confront – to varying degrees – the ways in which anti-communism attempted to sever anti-colonial and anti-capitalist critiques of U.S. foreign policy from the civil rights movements of the 1950s and 1960s.

As we will see below, the specter of communism was time-and-time again used to justify support for truly wretched, horrid colonial magistrates or indigenous military despots who did the bidding of colonial masters, would-be dictators who betrayed their own people for power and profit. Anti-communism was used as a pretext to stifle women's rights, workers' rights, pro-democracy, and national liberation movements globally, while simultaneously nearly breaking the back of a once vibrant and expansive domestic Communist Party, USA with deep roots in the Black community. As I have written elsewhere, the domestic post-war anti-communist hysteria and the growing right-wing fear of an emerging Black militancy comfortable with red allies, can be considered symptoms emanating from a general crisis of capitalism, a crisis spurred by socialism's advances globally.[26] That Black luminaries, such as Robeson and Du Bois – Hunton's CAA co-workers – chose to align with Communists despite the repression they faced, complicates our discourses on the permissible boundaries of Black civil rights; that Robeson, Du Bois, and Hunton – among others – also sought and found allies internationally, particularly in the socialist camp, adds another layer of nuance.[27]

Of course, post-war colonial anti-communist repression was not a new phenomenon. As Vijay Prashad argues, Washington's repressive bullets were "shinned by the bureaucrats of the world order who wanted to contain the tidal wave that swept from the October [Bolshevik] Revolution of 1917 and the many

25. John Munro, *The Anticolonial Front...*, Ibid.

26. Pecinovsky, *Let Them Tremble...*, Ibid., 13

27. African American artist Ollie Harrington is an interesting example; he spent the last four decades of his life in the German Democratic Republic due to political repression domestically. See: Rachel Rubin and James Smethurst, "The Cartoons of Ollie Harrington, the Black Left, and the African American Press During the Jim Crow Era," in Tony Pecinovsky (ed), *Faith In The Masses: Essays Celebrating 100 Years of the Communist Party, USA* (New York: International Publishers, 2020)

waves that whipped around the world to form the anti-colonial movement."[28] From its inception the young Soviet government sought to build a global anti-colonial movement and Communists throughout the world were instrumental in this effort. From the period directly after World War I and then again after World War II, Communists supported liberation struggles with ideological, cultural, organizational, financial, and military aid.

The Soviet Union, and later the Eastern European states and Cuba, subsidized international anti-colonial movements, peace conferences, world youth festivals,[29] training schools, trade union confederations, women's congresses, educational seminars, friendship tours, cultural exchanges, travel, and rest,[30] as well as countless Marxist journals, newspapers, and books in multiple languages,[31] among numerous other examples. This ideological

---

28. Prashad, *Washington Bullets…*, Ibid., 18

29. Even after socialism's collapse in Eastern Europe, the world youth festival movement persisted. The World Federation of Democratic Youth (WFDY), founded in 1945 as an international non-governmental organization with consultative status with the United Nations, was presented the Peace Messenger Award by the United Nations General Secretary in 1987 and has since its founding held 19 world youth festivals. This author attended the 16th world youth festival in Venezuela in 2005 along with 15,000 other youth and was part of the U.S. NPC (national preparatory committee), which mobilized 700 U.S. youth to attend. For more on WFDY, see: https://www.wfdy.org/about

30. In summer 1990, as socialism was collapsing and the Communist Party of the Soviet Union was losing its "leading status," CPUSA leader William Pomeroy candidly wrote to his comrade Marilyn Bechtel lamenting the loss of "free travel," "hospitality facilities," and "quotas for rest." By simply providing travel, leisure, and rest, a reprieve from the often harsh conditions of revolutionary life, the Soviet Union aided Marxist movements throughout the world. Often free medical care was provided as well. NYU, TAM 132, Box 63, Folder 9: Letter from Pomeroy to Bechtel, August 12, 1990

31. One of the more ambitious Communist cultural-educational initiatives connected to anti-colonial struggles was Progress Publishers. As Rossen Djagalov writes, "In the history of publishing, there has probably never been a press so linguistically ambitious." In 1931, its first year, Progress published in 10 West European, seven East European, and five Asian languages; 30 years later, the number of Eastern languages had increased to 28. By 1980, the Indian section was producing more titles than the English one. "Throughout this period, books in the colonial languages – English, French, Spanish, and Portuguese – were also being sent to Africa, Asia, and Latin America" to further anti-colonial struggles. By 1991, Progress Publishers "was a behemoth publishing yearly close to 2,000 new titles with a print run approaching 30 million copies." Similar Foreign

and material support, as historian Julia Mickenberg noted, nurtured and reinforced global "networks of hope."[32]

To fully understand the barbarity of 20th century colonial repression and why anti-communism became such a reflexively violent, ideological component of the maintenance of colonial rule, it is imperative to also understand the role of Communists in the various anti-colonial movements. As such, Hunton, the CAA, and the *Daily Worker*, as well as the various global movements for liberation, did not exist in a vacuum. They were inevitably shaped by – and shaped – an ascending world movement for socialism.

*   *   *

The new Soviet government's 1917 proclamation granting the right of self-determination to colonial peoples of the Russian Empire was empowering and transformative; this was true outside of Russia's borders, as well. The new revolutionary government stood for the "liberation of peoples subjected to direct or indirect colonial oppression, which then afflicted almost all of Asia and Africa." Indeed, the Russian Revolution itself was seen, in part, as "a revolt of Asiatic peoples oppressed by tsarism." After consolidating power, the Bolsheviks quickly took the initiative. By 1919, after the formation of the Communist International (the Comintern), the First Congress of the Peoples of the East in Baku, Azerbaijan was organized with 2,000 delegates from Central Asia and the Middle East attending. In 1922, a similar conference was held for the Far East. The International Red Aid and the League Against Imperialism were soon founded; support for striking workers in China fighting against British colonial magistrates, as well as Syrian rebels revolting against a

---

Language Publishing Houses were established throughout Eastern Europe and China. These books, coupled with Marxist magazines, journals, and newspapers, subsidized by socialist states and disseminated throughout the decolonizing world in dozens of languages, nurtured the rise of the global left for much of the 20th century. See: Vijay Prashad (ed), *The East Was Read: Socialist Culture In The Third World* (New Delhi: LeftWord Press, 2019), 83-84

32. Tony Pecinovsky, "Historians: History is more than an academic exercise," *People's World*, April 21, 2015, https://www.peoplesworld.org/article/historians-history-is-more-than-an-academic-exercise/

French massacre of 10,000 Arabs, are two early examples of the international solidarity that emerged. Red Aid became "a genuine force in the political life of the colonial powers." Communists also helped establish anti-colonial, workers' rights movements throughout Central and South America,[33] and the Caribbean,[34] as well as in Japan, Korea, Indonesia, Australia, and the Philippines, through the Pan-Pacific Trade Union Secretariat, a division of the Red International of Labor Unions (the Profintern), founded in 1921.[35] The 1927 Soviet initiated International Congress Against Imperialism and Colonialism, organized by the German Communist Willi Munzenbuerg and held in Brussels, attracted intellectual luminaries such as Albert Einstein. Though it only lasted a few years, the League Against Imperialism was initially a broad-based representative gathering, a "first attempt to structure international anti-colonial unity." It included delegates from South Africa, Algeria, Indonesia, Palestine, Iran, India, China, Peru, and the United States; future Indian Prime Minister Jawaharlal Nehru attended.[36] As Robin D. G. Kelley asserts, "the League marked an important step toward coordinating various struggles for national liberation in the colonies and 'semi-colonies,' and it served as an intermediary between the Communist International and the anti-colonial movement."[37]

These initiatives, among others, had a profound global impact, and set the tone of Soviet support for anti-colonial, and national

---

33. John Riddell, Vijay Prashad, Nazeef Mollah (eds), *Liberate the Colonies: Communism and Colonial Freedom, 1917-1924* (New Delhi: LeftWord Books, 2019) and Riddell, "The League Against Imperialism (1927-37): An early attempt at global anti-colonial unity," *Monthly Review*, July 20, 2018, https://mronline.org/2018/07/20/the-league-against-imperialism-1927-37-an-early-attempt-at-global-anti-colonial-unity/

34. Margaret Stevens, *Red International And Black Caribbean: Communist In New York City, Mexico And The West Indies, 1919-1939* (London: Pluto Press, 2017)

35. Josephine Fowler, *Japanese and Chinese Immigrant Activists: Organizing in American and International Communists Movements, 1919-1933* (New Brunswick: Rutgers University Press, 2007)

36. Odd Arne Westad, *The Cold War: A World History* (New York: Hachette Book Group, Inc., 2019), 279; Vijay Prashad, *The Darker Nations: A People's History of the Third World* (New York: The New Press, 2007), 21, 22; and Riddell, "The League Against Imperialism…," Ibid.

37. C.L.R. James, *A History Of Pan-African Revolt* (Oakland: PM Press, 2012), 8. Quote in Kelley's Introduction.

liberation struggles throughout much of the 20th century. Prashad added, "the radical energy" of 1917 and the formation of the Comintern "brought together the peoples of the world"[38] into a global anti-colonial front,[39] a first of its kind.

*   *   *

Communists expanded their concept of colonialism to not only include the global south – Africa, Asia, and Latin America – but to also include the southern United States. Soviet indictment of U.S. racism, particularly in the southern states, stretched back to the Comintern's First Congress, but found concrete organizational form in 1922 with the creation of a "Negro Bureau" and the formulation of a "Thesis on the Negro Question." This document articulated the Comintern's "support of all black liberation movements that helped undermine imperialism." By 1928, the Comintern declared African Americans to be "an oppressed nation with the right to national self-determination," a designation, according to Meredith L. Roman, that "anointed them the vanguard among colonized nations." Regardless of the merit of what was called the "Black Belt Thesis," which was continually debated within the CPUSA, this declaration "encouraged the elevation of antiracism to a priority policy" by the late-1920s and early-1930s, a designation that would lead Communists to promote the struggle for equality internally and externally.[40] As Gerald Horne argues, "despite its flaws, the party was probably unparalleled in not just fighting racism in society

---

38. Riddell, Prashad, Mollah (ed), *Liberate the Colonies…*, Ibid., 13.

39. Though focused on the 1945-1960 period, Munro uses this term to describe an anti-colonial "political bloc" in opposition to U.S. imperial power and Western European imperialism; the term "front" is used as "a site of political engagement and as a loose affiliation of shared ideas." Though there "was no uniform position on imperialism…there was broad interest and opposition." See: Munro, *The Anticolonial Front…*, Ibid., 3, 36

40. Meredith L. Roman, *Opposing Jim Crow: African Americans And The Soviet Indictment Of U.S. Racism, 1928-1937* (Lincoln: University of Nebraska Press, 2012), 4-8

but within the ranks as well,"[41] though, some have argued campaigns against "white chauvinism" went too far.[42]

Of course, this was not the first time U.S. Communists raised the questions of African American equality, national liberation, or the linkages between to two. The earliest mention of what was then called the "Negro question" was in the Communist Party of America's founding program of 1919, which like those of the Socialist Party and the Industrial Workers of the World did not recognize the special oppression of people of color. The program noted, "The racial oppression of the Negro is simply the expression of his economic bondage and oppression...The Communist Party will carry on agitation among the Negro workers to unite them with all class-conscious workers."[43]

By 1921, this perspective had begun to change. The United Communist Party, founded after a merger of the Communist Labor Party and the CPA, noted in its 1921 program and constitution that African Americans were "the most exploited people in America." The party's task, it added, was "to break down the barrier of race prejudice that separates and keeps apart the white and the Negro workers, and to bind them into a union of revolutionary forces for the overthrow of their common enemy." This was a dramatic shift in analysis, partly due to the Comintern's prodding.

Shortly thereafter, this emphasis began to show dividends. Communists worked with numerous African American-led working class organizations, including the African Blood Brotherhood and the American Negro Labor Congress, which sought to break down Jim Crow barriers within the conservative American Federation of Labor. Additionally, Black Communists such as Otto Huiswood, Cyril Briggs, and Lovett Fort-Whiteman, and

41. Gerald Horne, *Black Liberation / Red Scare: Ben Davis and the Communist Party* (Newark: Associated University Presses, 1994), 71

42. Robert W. Cherny, "The Party's Over: Former Communist Party Members in the San Francisco Bay Area," in Vernon L. Pedersen, James G. Ryan, and Katherine A.S. Sibley (eds), *Post-Cold War Revelations and the American Communist Party: Citizens, Revolutionaries, and Spies* (London: Bloomsbury Academic, 2021), 237. Cherny cites Dorothy Healey, who argued, "A legitimate concern turned into an obsession." She estimated the Los Angeles CP in the late 1940s expelled 200 members on charges of white chauvinism, "usually on the most trivial of pretexts."

43. Timothy V Johnson, "The Communist Party and the African American Question," in Pecinovsky (ed), *Faith In The Masses...*, Ibid., 151-179

those close to Communists such as Claude McKay, discussed the domestic application of the national/colonial question with the Comintern. By 1925, special party schools were established, and literature was produced to improve the recruitment of African Americans; party organizers were sent into the southern Black Belt; and a subcommittee of the CPUSA's Central Executive Committee was created to oversee work in the Black community.[44]

Communists also played a leading role in the Harlem Renaissance. Cotton Club dancer and CPUSA organizer Howard 'Stretch' Johnson later recalled, "75 percent of Black cultural figures" during this time were either party members or "maintained regular meaningful contact" with the party. While this is an exaggeration, as William J. Maxwell argues, Johnson was not wrong by much.[45] The CPUSA was the only organization on the left to make African American equality and colonial liberation a centerpiece of its work. The defense of the Scottsboro Nine, the organizing of the Sharecroppers Union,[46] a turn toward Popular Front politics, and the emergence of groups like the National Negro Congress and the Southern Negro Youth Congress,[47] as well as multi-racial Communist-led unions in the CIO, gave the CPUSA a level of respect and prestige only dreamed of a decade earlier. Hard-won acceptance resulted in a number of African American activists,

---

44. Johnson, "The Communist Party...," Ibid.

45. William J. Maxwell, *New Negro, Old Left: African-American Writing and Communism Between the Wars* (New York: Columbia University Press, 1999), 1 and Howard Eugene Johnson with Wendy Johnson, *A Dancer in the Revolution: Stretch Johnson, Harlem Communist at the Cotton Club* (New York: Fordham University Press, 2014)

46. For example, see: Robin D.G. Kelley, *Hammer And Hoe: Alabama Communists During The Great Depression* (Chapel Hill: University of North Carolina Press, 1990); Mary Stanton, *Red, Black, White: The Alabama Communist Party, 1930-1950* (Athens: University of Georgia Press, 2019); and Gerald Horne, *Black Revolutionary: William Patterson and the Globalization of the African American Freedom Struggle* (Chicago: University of Illinois Press, 2013)

47. For example, see: Erik S. Gellman, *Death Blow To Jim Crow: The National Negro Congress and the Rise of Militant Civil Rights* (Chapel Hill: University of North Carolina Press, 2012); Sara Rzeszutek Haviland, *James and Esther Cooper Jackson: Love and Courage in the Black Freedom Movement* (Lexington: University Press of Kentucky, 2015); and David Levering Lewis, Michael Nash, Daniel J. Leab (eds), *Red Activists And Black Freedom: James and Esther Jackson and the Long Civil Rights Revolution* (New York: Routledge, 2010)

including W. Alphaeus Hunton,[48] joining the Communist Party. The work of Communists globally had a domestic impact.

*   *   *

By the late 1920s and early 1930s, the world Communist movement and the CPUSA had taken ambitious steps to elevate the struggle for African American equality and colonial liberation. One vital initiative was the assigning of cadre to study in the Soviet Union. A modest number of Black Americans attended the KUTV, the Communist University of the Toilers of the East, and the International Lenin School in Moscow. African Americans studying in the Soviet Union "negotiated the power, promise, and limitations of Soviet antiracism." They "consistently invoked Soviet antiracism, demanding the freedom from racism it promised them." At least some of these students, such as Harry Haywood, the first African American enrolled in the Lenin School in 1927, returned to the United States and took on CPUSA organizing assignments in the South; in Haywood's case, in Birmingham, Alabama.[49] Others, such as William L. Patterson, returned from Moscow "redder than a rose" and led the legal defense of the Scottsboro Nine, and later the Civil Rights Congress, of which Hunton was a trustee.[50]

Hundreds of students from China, India, Indonesia, Korea, and other Asian or Pacific island nations attended the KUTV during this time; a smaller number came from Africa.[51] It is estimated

---

48. Hunton's perspectives on Marxism, African American equality, and Black liberation were shaped, in part, by the Communists he met and worked with while at Howard University, New York University, with the NNC, and the CAA; Edwin Berry Burgum, a member of *Science & Society*'s editorial board had an early impact on Hunton, too. See: Von Eschen, *Race Against Empire*..., Ibid., 59

49. Roman, *Opposing Jim Crow*..., Ibid., 8, 156-158, and Gwendolyn Midlo Hall (ed), *A Black Communist in the Freedom Struggle: The Life of Harry Haywood* (Minneapolis: University of Minnesota, 2012)

50. Horne, *Black Revolutionary*..., Ibid. and Denise Lynn, "Louise Thompson and the Black and White Film," *Black Perspectives*, April 15, 2021, https://www.aaihs.org/louise-thompson-and-the-black-and-white-film/

51. Irina Ivanovna Filatova, "Indoctrination or Scholarship? Education of Africans at the Communist University of the Toilers of the East in the Soviet Union, 1923-1937," *Paedagogica Historica, International Journal of the History of Education* (Brussels), vol. XXXV (1999), No. 1 January, 41-66

that roughly 3,500 students from 59 countries "passed through" the Lenin School from 1926 to 1938, when it closed. The impact of cadre trained at the KUTV was immense. Many future leaders of national liberation movements, such as Ho Chi Minh, learned valuable lessons, and built a network of international contacts through the KUTV and Lenin School. They also gained organizational and military know-how. Some KUTV graduates later distanced themselves from or became critical of Soviet socialism; a handful became government witnesses or FBI informants and helped in the persecution of U.S. Communists.[52] But the "vast majority" of KUTV and Lenin School students "remained committed anti-imperialists," including George Padmore and Kenya's Jomo Kenyatta.[53]

Padmore,[54] head of the International Trade Union Committee of Negro Workers and editor of *The Negro Worker* from 1931 to 1934,

---

52. Tuomas Savonen, *Minnesota, Moscow, Manhattan: Gus Hall's Life and Political Line Until the Late 1960s* (Helsinki: The Finnish Society of Sciences and Letters, 2020) (academic dissertation, University of Helsinki), 63, 78-81

53. Rossen Djagalov, "The Communist University for Toilers of the East (KUTV)," *Global South Studies: A Collective Publication with The Global South,* August 28, 2020, https://globalsouthstudies.as.virginia.edu/key-moments/communist-university-toilers-east-kutv

54. Apparently, Padmore's displeasure with the Comintern's focus on defeating fascism – its "attenuation of anticolonialism," as Munro put it – precipitated his decision to leave the organization and become an independent Marxist; to his credit, Padmore was able to work with Communists and non-Communists alike, nor did he turn to anti-Sovietism. See: Munro, *The Anticolonial Front...,* Ibid., 49, 51-52. Though the CAA did report on Padmore's 1945 Manchester Pan-African Congress, it "did not mention Padmore, and it seems likely that Hunton and [Max] Yergan ignored him because of his expulsion from the Comintern." Apparently, Padmore had misgivings about the CAA as well, though he did agree to work with it. See: Von Eschen, *Race Against Empire...,* Ibid., 53. Swindall notes that the Manchester Congress "was not listed among the annual review of important events in African affairs for the previous year" in the January 1946 *New Africa.* She also remarks that the CAA "did not want to acknowledge the Pan-African Congress because they were affiliated with the Communist left, and there was tension with Padmore..." Though DuBois, who attended the Congress, "remained a crucial link between the Council on African Affairs and the Pan-African Federation." See: Swindall, *The Path To The...,* Ibid., 102. Brenda Gayle Plummer argues, "Communists in the Council on African Affairs particularly detested Padmore, an apostate. Hunton was not permitted to link the council with any project associated with him." See: *Rising Wind: Black Americans And U.S. Foreign Affairs, 1935-1960* (Chapel Hill: University of North Carolina Press,

helped organize an International Conference of Negro Workers
in Hamburg, Germany in July 1930. It included delegates from
British Guiana, Trinidad, Jamaica, several West African countries,
and South Africa, as well as a number of African American delegates, including CPUSA leader James W. Ford. The conference
"called for complete independence for all colonies and the recognition of the right of self-determination for all nations." Most
delegates also attended the Congress of the Red International of
Labor Unions in Moscow.[55] According to Holger Weiss, the "ideological legacy" of *The Negro Worker* was "more tangible and
longer-lasting" than the ITUCNW as an organization. The journal
was "widely distributed and read throughout the African Atlantic, raising awareness of the exploitation of Black workers...and
disseminating radical political ideas about the common cause of
the Black toilers." Though no more than 5,000 copies of a single issue were ever printed,[56] C.L.R. James[57] noted that *The Negro*

1996), 158. I find Plummer's language – that Hunton was "not permitted" –
troubling. Hunton does not strike me as the type of person to simply be told; I
find it more plausible that he likely agreed with his CPUSA and Comintern comrades and as a result did not press the issue.

55. Stevens, *Red International...*, Ibid., and Susan Campbell, "The Negro
Worker: A Comintern Publication of 1928-1937 – An Introduction," Marxist.org,
https://www.marxists.org/history/international/comintern/negro-worker/
index.htm

56. Holger Weiss, "Between Moscow and the African Atlantic: The Comintern Network of Negro Workers," *Dans Monde(s)*, (2016)/2, No. 10, https://www.
cairn.info/revue-mondes-2016-2-page-89.htm. Weiss notes, circulation of *The
Negro Worker* peaked at around 5,000 copies per-issue by the end of 1932; however, by spring 1934 the print run shrunk to 2,000 copies to cut costs. Despite
its small numbers, the publication was "the first such journal ever to circulate
among Africans and although the British colonial authorities tried their best to
prevent its distribution in Africa," it grew a readership and radicalized "indigenous political attitudes in Africa."

57. James would spend from 1938 to 1953 in the U.S. loosely affiliated with
one Trotskyist group or another; he produced a steady stream of works during
this time. As Munro put it, "By calling out the crimes taking place under Soviet
domination, James inferred the ultimate unavailability of this form of Marxism
for liberation Movements." Though incorrect, James had no way of knowing
what the future would hold nor what role the Soviet Union and the Eastern
European states would play in national liberation movements in the coming
decades. Munro correctly notes James' relative isolation; CPUSA leaders James
and Esther Cooper Jackson recall, as Munro writes, that James was absent from
"mass proletarian and Black struggles of the period," at least while in Michigan.

Worker "gave 'hundreds of thousands of active Negroes and the millions whom they represented' access to the world,"[58] thereby inspiring militant action far beyond Communist ranks.

Kenyatta later led the Kenya African Union, which had 100,000 members and was considered Kenya's "main liberation front." In spring 1953, he was jailed as part of an "increasingly brutal" crackdown by British authorities. This assault, "through [the] courtroom and machinegun," had the "same objective: to destroy the KAU...behead the leadership...and decimate all Africans who continue to display the slightest resistance to the pitiless exploitation of the tiny minority of white settlers." Kenyatta was sentenced to "seven years at hard labor." Within "one week" an additional 7,000 Kenyans were arrested. Known as the Mau Mau uprising, years of war with the British followed. Hunton's CAA fundraised for the Kenyatta Defense Fund and sought to help build a "nationwide Kenya Aid Committee"; six years earlier Kenyatta had signed the NNC petition to the UN charging the U.S. with "severe human rights abuses against African Americans."[59] The links between African American equality and Black liberation in Africa were multifaceted and reciprocal, and often centered around Communist-led initiatives dating back to relationships forged in or through Moscow.

Officially, the British claimed 11,000 Mau Mau rebels were killed, including 1,090 who were hanged; just 32 white settlers

---

The Jacksons on the other hand, were deeply entrenched and developed a number of relationships with Black leaders who would go on to play key roles locally and nationally in the emerging civil rights movements; for example, National Negro Labor Council leader and future Detroit Mayor Coleman Young, James Jackson's "buddy," was mentored by the Jacksons and shared a house with them. See: Munro, *The Anticolonial Front...*, Ibid., 31-36; Lewis, Nash, and Leab (eds), *Red Activists...*, Ibid. 71; Dayo F. Gore, *Radicalism at the Crossroads: African American Women Activists in the Cold War* (New York: New York University Press, 2011), 36; and Jarvis Tyner and Sam Webb, "James E. Jackson an appreciation," *People's World*, September 14, 2007, https://www.peoplesworld.org/article/james-e-jackson-jr-an-appreciation/

58. Vijay Prashad, *Red Star Over The Third World* (New Delhi: LeftWord Book, 2017), 70

59. "British Jail Kenyatta," *Freedom*, April 1953, 1, 4; John H. Jones, "African Council Says U.S. Foreign Policy Hinders Drive of Africans for Freedom," *Freedom*, April 1954, 3; and Gerald Horne, *Mau Mau In Harlem: The U.S. And The Liberation Of Kenya* (New York: Palgrave Macmillan, 2009), 89, 116

were killed during eight years of fighting. The Kenya Human Rights Commission, however, claims 90,000 Kenyans were executed, tortured, or maimed, with an additional 160,000 detained in concentration camps, where they were beaten and "subjected to appalling sexual abuse." In 2011, the British High Court threw out a claim brought by elderly Kenyans, victims of British colonial officers. It was claimed "Kenya had its own legal colonial government, which was responsible for the camps."[60] In every corner of the globe, colonialism and anti-communism worked in tandem to constrain a rising tide of liberation. Often, extreme, depraved forms of violence accompanied them.

Regardless, Comintern initiatives were global in scale and Communists saw themselves as internationalists committed to building anti-colonial, workers' rights solidarity wherever they happened to physically be. The Indian revolutionary M.N. Roy became a founder of the Mexican Communist Party, white the Chilean socialist Luis Emilio Recabarren became a founder of the Argentinian Communist Party. Dada Amir Haidar Khan, from Pakistan become a leader of the CPUSA, then went to the KUTV, which sent him to India. The Kansas-born CPUSA leader Earl Browder helped to build the Chinese Communist Party. The Japanese Communist Sen Katayama helped build the Communist Party in Mexico, Canada, and the United States. The list could go on. As Prashad notes in *Red Star Over The Third World*, "From one end of the planet to the other, Comintern agents...carried instructions and methods, wondering how best to help along the revolutions," of which national liberation was a key component.[61]

This internationalism partly explains why the Jamaican-born CPUSA leader and second in command of the National Maritime

60. "Maul Mau uprising: Bloody history of Kenya conflict," *BBC*, April 7, 2011, https://www.bbc.com/news/uk-12997138 and "Mau Mau case: UK government cannot be held liable," *BBC*, April 7, 2011, https://www.bbc.com/news/uk-12994190

61. Prashad, *Red Star...*, Ibid., 71. For more on Roy, Recabarren, Haidar Khan, Browder, and Katayama, see: Kris Manjapra, *M.N. Roy: Marxism and Colonial Cosmopolitanism* (New York: Routledge, 2010); Maria Alicia Rueda, *The Educational Philosophy of Luis Emilio Recabarren* (New York: Routledge, 2021); Hassan N. Gardezi, *Chains To Lose: Life and Struggles of a Revolutionary – Memoirs of Dada Amir Haider Khan* (University of Karachi, 2007); James G. Ryan, *Earl Browder: The Failure of American Communism* (Tuscaloosa: University of Alabama Press, 1997); and Fowler, *Japanese and Chinese Immigrant Activists...*, Ibid.

Union, Ferdinand Smith, would later be seen as a threat and deported; he and his maritime comrades fostered a global solidarity network not constrained by the requisite chains of domestic Jim Crow and colonial subjugation.[62] Like the Trinidad-born Claudia Jones, who was also deported,[63] Smith's internationalism helped to bolster links between the NMU, the CAA, the CRC, and their global counterparts.

Though Communists provided material support – organizational, financial, and ideological – the psychological impact of Comintern training cannot be ignored. "Perhaps the most important influence" the KUTV and Lenin School, among others, had on students–who were "often the lowest of the low in their countries of origin" – stemmed "from the fact that they were looked upon, treated and taught as future political leaders," which many eventually became. They received "formal instruction" in mass mobilization and organization and were introduced to skills "only taught by Comintern universities at that time." These institutions "helped students develop a genuine self-respect and self-assertiveness" they then took back to their home countries, an empowering and transformative process. Moses Kotane, who served as secretary general of the South African Communist Party from 1939 until 1978, recalled that the Lenin School "broadened his horizons" and "helped him to believe in himself," taught him "to think politically."[64] At the very least, inter-war Communist initiatives re-energized and reframed anti-colonial struggles as part of a global campaign against capitalism and provided institutional support and resources for fledgling movements and their leaders. In return, these movements and leaders provided aid in the fight against fascism and led liberation struggles in the post-war period. Like other Communists, Hunton saw the Soviet Union through this prism, as his *Daily Worker* columns indicate.

* * *

62. Gerald Horne, *Red Seas: Ferdinand Smith and Radical Black Sailors in the United States and Jamaica* (New York: New York University Press, 2005)

63. Carole Boyce Davies, *Left Of Karl Marx: The Political Life Of Black Communist Claudia Jones* (Durham: Duke University Press, 2008)

64. Filatova, "Indoctrination or Scholarship?...," Ibid.

Though the war-time alliance between the United States, Great Britain, and the Soviet Union was uneasy, many – including Hunton – were initially optimistic it would continue in the post-war period. Unfortunately, this proved not to be the case. U.S. policy makers were just as preoccupied with Asia and the Pacific as they were with Europe and the old colonial empires. China, India, Korea, and the Philippines soon become major focal points in the early Cold War. Though the Comintern no longer existed, during the post-war period Communists still saw revolutionary potential in anti-colonial movements and hoped to establish coalition governments that would at the very least maintain neutrality – or perhaps, be supportive of the Soviet Union in the long-term conflict between the capitalist West and the socialist East. John Munro writes, "World war was over. And wars of politics, culture, ideology, and violence, all in the name of empire and decolonization, were resumed."[65] However, the United States and the Soviet Union also hoped to avoid direct military confrontation, especially after the advent of the atomic bomb. As Prashad argues, "once the USSR (1949) and China (1964) tested their nuclear weapons no direct war would be possible. The battlefield moved from along the Urals and the Caucasus into Central and South America, into Africa, and into Asia – into, in other words, the South."[66] This shift proved fateful. The colonial powers devastated by WWII could no longer afford to govern the colonies in the old way, and the colonial peoples themselves refused to be governed by outsiders.

Communists who "resisted fascism and colonialism earliest and most forcefully around the world – gave it [the Soviet Union] global prestige in 1945," Vincent Bevins notes. Additionally, Communist-led guerrilla movements in Western Europe, particularly in Greece, Italy, and France – where they had led the underground anti-fascist resistance – seriously contested for political power at war's end. In Iran, the Communist-led Tudeh Party was the "largest and best organized political group in the country." And by 1949, the Chinese Communist Party had defeated the Nationalists; Hunton's CAA helped organize a rally "for American friendship with New China." Further, in India,

---

65. Munro, *The Anticolonial Front...*, Ibid., 43
66. Prashad, *Washington Bullets...*, Ibid., 18

the Philippines, and Indonesia Communist Parties had built alliances with anti-colonial movements distrustful of the old colonial empires and the United States. Bevins adds, "leaders of Third World independence movements associated the United States with its Western European imperialist allies; others believed the Soviet Union was an important friend in the struggle against colonialism."[67] Unfortunately, the U.S. government repeatedly turned its back on independence movements and used anti-communism to stifle anti-colonial, national liberation struggles throughout the region. As Bevins documents, mass murder became one method by which U.S. policy makers shaped the world in which we now live.

For example, in the Philippines the Hukbalahap (the National Anti-Japanese Army) and Communists would be early victims as the battlefield shifted South. The Huk (as they were known) and the Philippine Communist Party had been instrumental in the guerilla war against Japanese occupation. After the war, they expected to be full participants in a nationalist coalition government. The creation of the Democratic Alliance, which consisted of peasant and worker organizations, Huk militants, and Communists, coupled with the "promise of independence by 1946," provided early hope that a peaceful pathway to post-colonial democracy would be achieved. However, after six Democratic Alliance congressmen won seats in the House of Representatives, but were ousted "arbitrarily and without cause," those hopes were dashed. Shortly thereafter, the Philippine armed forces, with the support of the U.S. military, began a campaign of "indiscriminate killings, murder, torture, mass arrest, and wholesale razing of villages." Additionally, the PKP and the peasant and trade union organizations it led were outlawed. Around the world, Communists, and those aligned with Communists, called

---

67. Bevins, *The Jakarta Method...*, Ibid., 12-16, 21. Re CAA solidarity with "New China," see: "Rally Tonight Backs New China," *Daily Worker*, June 15, 1946, 7. Re India, see: "One Hundred Years of the Communist Movement in India," *Tricontinental*, September 1, 2020, https://www.thetricontinental.org/dossier-32-communist-movement-in-india/. It is estimated that Britain "stole $45 trillion from India" from 1765 to 1938. See: Jason Hickel, "How Britain stole $45 trillion from India – And lied about it," *Aljazeera*, December 19, 2018, https://www.aljazeera.com/opinions/2018/12/19/how-britain-stole-45-trillion-from-india. Indonesia and the Philippines are discussed below.

for solidarity as the Huk and PKP fought to survive. Due to increased repression, by 1948 the aboveground nationalist movement for democratic independence turned into an underground struggle for national liberation led by the Hukbong Mapagpaiaya ng bayan (the National Army of Liberation) and the PKP. Though the Huk rebellion would continue for years, by the early 1950s it was militarily defeated and exhausted, with many leading cadre dead or imprisoned. According to William Pomeroy, a U.S. Communist stationed in the Philippines during WWII who joined the Huk and the PKP, the "principal factor in the setback of the Huk movement was ruthless military suppression, carried out with vast quantities of U.S. military aid, by an army equipped, trained and supervised by an American military advisory group."[68]

Despite this setback, Soviet supported anti-colonial initiatives continued. The Women's International Democratic Federation is an excellent example. Through WIDF, the Indian Communist Gita Bannerji helped to organize the 1949 Asian Women's Conference in Beijing, where women from around the world came together to denounce colonialism. As Elisabeth Armstrong argues, the 1949 conference laid the groundwork for future anti-colonial struggles and "consolidated a transversal strategy for women's internationalism" in the fight against colonialism: one strategy, for women from colonized (and recently independent) countries, and another for women in imperialist countries. While the strategies converged in many ways, the key distinction was that women from Asia, Africa, Latin America, and the Caribbean, where women fought colonialism and imperialism, should organize "the masses of women…[to] defend their basic rights," while women in "imperialist countries" should refuse to be "accomplices in murder" in Vietnam, Indonesia, and Korea. According to Armstrong, this strategy "dispensed with allies in struggle to create accomplices in the fight against colonialism, fascism, and racism."

---

68. William J. Pomeroy, *Guerrilla & Counter-Guerrilla Warfare: Liberation and Suppression in the Present Period* (New York: International Publishers, 1964), 59-66 and "Demand release Of Labor Leader In Philippines," *Freedom*, May 1951, 5. Also, see: Pomeroy, *The Forest: A personal record of the Huk guerrilla struggle in the Philippines* (New York: International Publishers, 1963) and Vina A. Lanzona, *Amazons of the Huk Rebellion: Gender, Sex, and Revolution in the Philippines* (Madison: University of Wisconsin Press, 2009)

After the U.S. invasion of North Korea in April 1950, Bannerji – along with her friend, WIDF co-worker, and CPUSA leader Betty Millard – helped to lead the "Hands Off Korea" campaign and issue the fact finding study, *We Accuse! Report of the Commission of the Women's International Democratic Federation in Korea, May 16 to 27, 1951*. The report, "galvanized women's organizations around the world to oppose the U.S. military occupation of Korea." More broadly, Armstrong added, WIDF provided "centrifugal energy as an international organization," though its "creativity and vitality came not from the central offices…but from the varied struggles waged in colonialized, post-colonial and imperial contexts. International organizations like WIDF meant little without the bullets taken by its members, and the campaigns launched by its affiliated women's groups – campaigns that were won and lost and won again."[69]

In February 1951, Paul Robeson's *Freedom* newspaper published excerpts from a "passionate message" released by the Union of Democratic Women of Korea, a WIDF affiliate, "to all the women of the world." It was both "an unanswerable charge against the American warmakers and a mighty demand for peace." The statement vividly articulated the "unheard-of suffering…[as] the barbarians drop their incendiary bombs and flaming liquid," now known as napalm; it is estimated that the U.S. military dropped 32,557 tons on napalm on North Korea during the war. "American aerial pirates now devote themselves solely to murder and destruction," the statement continued. Rape and sexual assault were also documented: "…The air is filled with the groans and curses of our sisters violated by the Americans and their Korean mercenaries. Many of our sisters could not bear the shames inflicted on them. Such was their hatred of the enemy that they committed suicide."[70] These were the horrid extremes to which U.S. imperialism and militarism coupled with anti-communism would descend.

---

69. Elisabeth Armstrong, "Gita, Betty, and the Women's International Democratic Federation: An Internationalist Love Story," in Pecinovsky (ed), *Faith In The Masses…*, Ibid., 313-336

70. "Korean Women Accuse 'Aerial Pirates,'" *Freedom,* February 1951, 6 and Tom O'Connor, "What War With North Korea Looked Like in the 1950s and Why It Matters Now," *Newsweek,* May 4, 2017, https://www.newsweek.com/us-forget-korean-war-led-crisis-north-592630

Domestically, Claudia Jones, the Congress of American Women and Sojourners for Truth and Justice,[71] as well as Hunton's CAA,[72] among others, protested the military occupation – and all the barbarity that came with it – and called for an immediate ceasefire. Jones asked why men of color should fight and die, "often wantonly killed by white American U.S. troops," in a faraway land, while African Americans were still being lynched at home. Like other Communists, she viewed the "conflict as an unjust war against a people of color fighting for national liberation...[and an attempt] to suppress the world socialist revolution."[73] Calls for peace were then considered subversive, especially when made by a Black woman Communist.

At least one young Communist, the African American leader of the Labor Youth League Roosevelt Ward, Jr., was court martialed under "phony 'draft evasion' charges"; authorities claimed Ward "failed to report a change of address" to the draft board. As William L. Patterson put it, Ward was "framed" because he did not want to "murder and pillage...colored peoples of the world."[74] Ward told reporters, he was humbled and "a little surprised" to be part of "such a select group...[of] militant Negro leaders," including Robeson, Du Bois, and Patterson who were all "under one sort of persecution or another." However, the experience helped him "begin to see my own connection, not only with the Negro youth but with the youth all over the world in relation to this whole fight today for peace – for the right to live a decent, happy life," as he put it.[75] At least 250 million people around the world shared Ward's desire for peace and showed their support by signing the Stockholm Peace Appeal.[76]

---

71. For more on Jones and STJ, see: Gore, *Radicalism at the Crossroads...*, Ibid.

72. Pecinovsky, *Let Them Tremble...*, Ibid., 308

73. Erik S. McDuffie, "'For a New Antifascist, Anti-imperialist People's Coalition': Claudia Jones, Black Left Feminism, and the Politics of Possibility in the Era of Trump," in Pedersen, Ryan, and Sibley (eds), *Post-Cold War Revelations...*, Ibid., 193

74. "Group To Defend LYL Leader," *Daily Worker*, July 4, 1951, 3 and Denise Lynn, "Silencing Black Radicalism Since the Cold War," *Black Perspectives*, December 3, 2020, https://www.aaihs.org/silencing-black-radicalism-since-the-cold-war/

75. Roosevelt Ward, "'I Feel a Quiet Confidence,'" *Freedom*, October 1951, 7

76. Vincent J. Intondi, *African Americans Against The Bomb: Nuclear Weapons, Colonialism, And The Black Freedom Movement* (Stanford: Stanford University Press, 2015), 35

Armstrong's emphasis on multifaceted international women's organization is essential and touches on the importance of intersectionality decades before it became part of the academic lexicon. As Carole Boyce Davies notes, intersectionality is "a laudable Black feminist position" that presupposes "intersecting oppressions." However, she adds that triple oppression – the exploitation of Black women based on their race, class, and gender – as argued by Claudia Jones in 1949, differs from intersectionality in the sense that the "super-exploitation of Black women" is layered within "the context of a Marxist labor framework as opposed to meeting at an intersection." This is an important distinction, one that centers the struggle for equality and liberation with the most exploited section of the working class, Black women and other women of color.[77] Further, though much of the history of 20th century anti-colonial, national liberation struggles have been masculinist,[78] new research is shedding much needed light on the role of women and women's organizations like WIDF.[79] As Kristen Ghodsee argues, "although the U.S. tried to delegitimize anything socialist…the activism of Eastern Bloc women and their state socialist allies in the Global South did increase attention to international women's issues in the capitalist West." This increased attention "proved productive for the creation of new international conventions to protect social and economic rights." For example, while U.S. policy makers supposedly supported

77. Claudia Jones, "An End To The Neglect Of The Problems Of The Negro Woman!," *Political Affairs,* June 1949 and Charisse Burden-Stelly, "Claudia Jones Research and Collections: Questions of Process & Knowledge Construction [interview with Carole Boyce Davies]," *The Journal Of Intersectionality - Claudia Jones: Foremother Of World Revolution,* Vol. 3, No. 1 (Summer 2019), 4-9

78. Compare, for example, the number of volumes written about prominent male revolutionaries, such as Che Guevara, and the dearth of literature on prominent female revolutionaries, such as Gita Bannerji or the WIDF. Historians are rightly challenging the male dominant narratives of the domestic struggles for civil rights; similar efforts regarding the struggles for national liberation are needed.

79. See: Yulia Gradskova, *The Women's International Democratic Federation, the Global South and the Cold War: Defending the Rights of Women of the 'Whole World'?* (New York: Routledge, 2020) and Elisabeth Armstrong, *Gender and Neoliberalism: The All India Democratic Women's Association and its Struggle of Resistance* (New Delhi: LeftWord, 2021). The All India Democratic Women's Association today has 10 million members and plays an important role fighting for working class women's rights.

women's "basic needs," such as water, shelter, education, and access to healthcare, Soviet and Eastern European countries argued that "basic needs" were meaningless in a society that lacked racial and sexual equality. As Ghodsee told this author, by connecting seemingly disparate issues, Communists "were intersectional before it was cool." Further, despite "failing to live up to all of their promises, Marxist-Leninist parties, wherever revolutionary governments came to power granted women full legal equality, expanded literacy campaigns, promoted education and professional training, and encouraged full labor force participation." Of course, this "resulted directly from ideological commitments to women's emancipation and the state's empowerment of women's organizations to achieve these aims."[80]

Ghodsee's analysis of women's anti-colonial solidarity between Second World socialist nations, such as Bulgaria, and newly independent nations in the Third World, such as Zambia, resurrects the international solidarity first given concrete, tangible form with the creation of the Comintern in 1919. It suggests that the Soviet Union, and later the Eastern European states and Cuba, stretched their meager resources to support colonial liberation precisely at a time when the old colonial empires were most dependent on the United States. Far from retreating in the post-war period, over the next four decades Communists sought to establish themselves as legitimate partners to decolonizing movements and newly independent nations.

*   *   *

Whereas the Comintern provided financial, organizational, and ideological support directly to Communist parties and their organizational initiatives prior to WWII, after the war with a growing world socialist community of nations, the Soviet Union and the Eastern European states increasingly also provided aid directly to newly independent nations.[81] In June 1959, Haile Selassie visited

---

80. Ghodsee, *Second World, Second Sex…*, Ibid., 17, 25, 50 and Tony Pecinovsky, "Intersectional before it was cool": The women's movement under state socialism," *People's World*, October 3, 2019, https://www.peoplesworld.org/article/intersectional-before-it-was-cool-the-womens-movement-under-state-socialism/

81. For an interesting discussion on the socialist Council for Mutual Economic Assistance and economic collaboration, development, construction, and trade

Moscow and praised the USSR as "the world's greatest power." In return, Selassie was praised as a representative of "the whole African liberation movement." Ultimately, Selassie's visit and the Soviet Union's "extension of high-impact economic projects" in Ethiopia, represented a step forward for anti-colonial, national liberation forces on the continent, as well as a "curb" on Western initiatives; the visit also helped to foster "a positive image [of the USSR] as an international partner."[82] Shortly after gaining independence from Great Britain in 1964, Zambia established diplomatic ties with the Eastern Bloc nations, resulting in "trade, aid, and cultural cooperation." From 1964 to 1979, Zambia received $15 million in direct aid from the USSR, and an additional $60 million from the Eastern European states. Additionally, hundreds of Zambian youth were sent to socialist countries for education and training.[83] It is estimated that "50,000 international students completed their education at the universities and colleges of the GDR," tuition free.[84] By the mid-1960s, the USSR had diplomatic relations with dozens of newly independent African nations. Between 1953 and 1964, Soviet development projects in the Third World grew to an estimated 6,000. In Guinea, during this time the Soviet Union constructed an airport, a cannery, a sawmill, a refrigeration plant, a hospital, a technical school, a hotel, and carried out geological surveys, as well as other research projects.[85] Hunton, who had emigrated to Guinea in 1960, was well aware of these initiatives. Black liberation in Africa, buoyed by ascendant socialism,

---

with newly independent African and Asian nations, see: Ondrej Belicek, "How Eastern Bloc Architects Shaped Cities Across the Third World: An Interview With Lukasz Stanek," *Jacobin*, September 15, 2020, https://www.jacobinmag.com/2020/09/soviet-architecture-global-socialism-stanek. Stanek notes, even if Eastern Bloc architects did not necessarily see themselves as building socialism in newly independent nations (in Ghana, for example), "the politics of architecture is not the politics of its architects…"; Stanek recalled a Ghanaian architect who "remembers very well these Eastern European architects, because it was the first and the last time that a white man had an African boss in Ghana."

82. Radoslav A. Yordanov, *The Soviet Union and the Horn Of Africa during the Cold War: Between Ideology and Pragmatism* (Lanham: Lexington Books, 2016), 16-18

83. Ghodsee, *Second World, Second Sex…*, Ibid., 126

84. Vijay Prashad, "Move underway to rescue East Germany from anti-communist historian," *People's World*, May 3, 2021. Also, see: "Risen from the Ruins: The Economic History of Socialism in the German Democratic Republic," *Tricontinental*, April 20, 2021, https://thetricontinental.org/studies-1-ddr/

85. Christopher Andrew and Vasili Mitrokhim, *The World Was Going Our Way: The KGB and the Battle for the Third World* (New York: Basic Books, 2005), 6

was advancing on multiple fronts – or so it seemed. In Guinea, Hunton proclaimed, the "day is past where the poorer nations, for lack of any other source of aid, must obey the dictates of imperialist countries." Further, he felt as if he were in the "mainstream not only of African liberation forces but what was progressive globally." [86] Unfortunately, his optimism was soon tempered.

The counter-force of anti-communism continued to have a devastating impact. During much of the 1950s, the CPUSA's top leadership was either in jail, on trial, underground, or deported.[87] Communist-led organizations, such as the Civil Rights Congress,[88] the International Workers Order,[89] the National Negro Labor Council,[90] the Jefferson School of Social Science,[91] Sojourners for Truth and Justice, and the Council on African Affairs,[92] among others, were forced to dissolve. During the 1960s, Communists continued to be spied on, harassed, infiltrated, and called before investigative committees.[93] Across the globe – in Iran, Guatemala,

---

86. Mike Newberry, "A Talk With Editor Of 'Freedomways,'" *The Worker,* June 18, 1961, 9 and Dorothy Hunton, *Alphaeus Hunton: The Unsung Valiant* (self-published, 1986), 114

87. For an excellent discussion of the Smith Act indictments, see: John Somerville, *The Communist Trials and the American Tradition: Expert Testimony on Force and Violence, and Democracy* (New York: International Publishers, 2000). Also, see: Scott Martelle, *The Fear Within: Spies, Commies, and American Democracy on Trial* (New Brunswick: Rutgers University Press, 2011). John J. Abt's memoir (with Michael Myerson), *Advocate and Activist: Memoirs of an American Communist Lawyer* (Urbana: University of Illinois Press, 1995), is also an important source.

88. See: Horne, *Communist Front: The Civil Rights Congress, 1946-1956* (Associated University Presses, 1988), Ibid. and Horne, *Black Revolutionary...,* Ibid.

89. See: Robert M. Zecker, *"A Road to Peace and Freedom": The International Workers Order and the Struggle for Economic Justice and Civil Rights, 1930-1954* (Philadelphia: Temple University Press, 2018)

90. For more on the NNLC, see: Gore, *Radicalism At The Crossroads...,* Ibid.

91. For more on the Jefferson school, see: Marvin E. Gettleman, "'No Varsity Teams': New York's Jefferson School of Social Science, 1943-1956," *Science & Society,* Vol. 66, No. 3 (Fall 2002), 336-359

92. For more on STJ and CAA, see Gore, Ibid. and Von Eschen, *Race Against Empire...,* Ibid.

93. It should be noted, despite the CPUSA's ongoing persecution and declining membership, Communists took a number of important initiatives throughout the 1960s, including the formation of the W.E.B. Du Bois Clubs; were active leaders in the various campus free speech movements, including the Berkeley Free Speech Movement; and held leadership positions in key peace organizations including New Mobe and Student Mobe. See: Pecinovsky, *Let Them Tremble...,* Ibid.

Indonesia,Kenya,Ghana,SouthAfrica,Cuba,Chile,[94] andVietnam[95] – anti-communism, continued to leave death and destruction in its wake; like colonialism and fascism, victims were dehumanized, killed indiscriminately, reflexively, and without remorse, a point U.S. Communists, and their allies sought to publicize.[96]

As Lorraine Hansberry, by then a CPUSA member,[97] reported in April 1952, in "the Americas, some people have already been murdered, scores have been tortured, thousands have been imprisoned and thousands more have fled their homelands in

94. The suppression of (even moderate) national liberation movements and U.S. complicity in or support of atrocities in Guatemala, Indonesia, Kenya, Ghana, and South Africa are briefly discussed below. U.S. intervention in Cuba and Chile are well known. For more on Iran, see: Roham Alvandi and Mark J. Gasiorowski, "The United States Overthrew Iran's Last Democratic Leader," *Foreign Policy*, October 30, 2019, https://foreignpolicy.com/2019/10/30/the-united-states-overthrew-irans-last-democratic-leader/ and Mark J. Gasiorowski and Malcolm Byrne, *Mohammad Mosaddeq and the 1953 Coup in Iran* (New York: Syracuse University Press, 2004)

95. While about 58,000 U.S. soldiers died during the Vietnam War, a staggering one-to-three million Vietnamese were killed. See: Charles Hirschman, Samuel Preston, and Vu Manh Loi, "Vietnamese Casualties During the American War: A New Estimate," *Population Development Review*, Vol. 21. Issue 4 (December 1995). For more on the My Lai massacre, see: Howard Jones, *My Lai: Vietnam, 1968, and the Descent into Darkness* (New York: Oxford University Press, 2017). Conversely, the socialist nations aided liberation by sending "machinery, experts, weapons, and food at various points during the consecutive wars against France and then the United States...within this they were often keen to prove that they weren't just giving *charity*, but something more concrete: *solidarity*." During the late 1970s, the GDR also assisted in the construction of the Quang Trung estate, a 74-acre social housing complex, providing shelter to thousands of Vietnamese. See: Owen Hatherley, "International Solidarity Rebuilt Postwar Vietnam," *Jacobin*, May 17, 2021, https://jacobinmag.com/2021/05/international-solidarity-postwar-vietnam-vinh-socialist-housing; Christina Schwenkel, "Spectacular infrastructure and its breakdown in socialist Vietnam," *American Ethnologist*, Vol. 42, No. 3, 520-534; and Schwenkel, *Building Socialism: The Afterlife of East German Architecture in Urban Vietnam* (Durham: Duke University Press, 2020)

96. For one prominent example, see: Herbert Aptheker, *Mission to Hanoi* (New York: International Publishers, 1966). After returning from Vietnam, Aptheker embarked on a national tour speaking with thousands of students on college and university campuses across the country helping to build the anti-Vietnam War peace movement. See: Gary Murrell, *"The Most Dangerous Communist in the United States": A Biography of Herbert Aptheker* (Amherst: University of Massachusetts Press, 2017)

97. Joel Whitney, "Lorraine Hansberry Was an Unapologetic Radical," *Jacobin*, December 16, 2020, https://www.jacobinmag.com/2020/12/lorraine-hansberry-raisin-in-the-sun-playwright

exile. Throughout Latin America, the interventionist policy of the United States Government has made the very word PEACE illegal." Hansberry was reporting first-hand on her trip to the Inter-Continental Peace Congress in Montevideo, Uruguay. She noted, "In Brazil a young woman was murdered in the streets; a young boy had instruments of torture placed under his gums, because he collected signatures for peace. In Argentina, no one may organize for peace without fear of imprisonment." Though "all nations and all peoples need it so desperately, peace in the America's is illegal," she added. "[O]fficially banned," the Conference, "called by the representatives of 179 million people who suffer some of the worst colonial exploitation of any area of the world," included 250 delegates from nine countries: Paraguay, Brazil, Venezuela, Argentina, Puerto Rico, Chile, Columbia, Uruguay, and the U.S.; delegates from the West Indies, Mexico, Canada, Peru, and Panama "had been stopped in their own countries in some cases and held at foreign borders in others." Delegate after delegate described the plunder of their nation and the violence inflicted upon anti-colonial movements. The delegates also linked national liberation and peace in the Americas to the war raging in Korea. One delegate from Brazil, a member of the WIDF international women's commission that investigated atrocities in Korea spoke with Hansberry. She said, "I can tell you about 10-year old children who have been raped. I can tell you about whole forests and fields which have been burned so that people will starve to death…What I have seen in Korea is not war at all. It is the extermination of a people." Hansberry, who went to the conference in place of Paul Robeson whose passport had been revoked, "slyly obtained a passport under the pretense" that she would be "vacationing in Europe." Shortly after her return, however, her passport was also confiscated.[98]

Just two years later, Guatemala became another example of the violence inflicted upon liberation struggles that dared to challenge the dictates of colonialism and U.S. imperialism. When the Guatemalan President Jacabo Arbenz implemented a "New Deal-style

---

98. Lorraine Hansberry, "Inter-America Peace Congress - 'Illegal' Conference Shows Peace Is Key to Freedom," *Freedom*, April 1952, 3 and Imani Perry, *Looking for Lorraine: The Radiant And Radical Life Of Lorraine Hansberry* (Boston: Beacon Press, 2018), 57-59

economic program" and expropriated "with full compensation" uncultivated United Fruit Company land, while legalizing the Communist Party – "unacceptable acts" from Washington's "vantage point" – he was overthrown by the CIA. According to Greg Grandin, Arbenz fell "because the [Guatemalan] military refused to defend him, fearing Washington's wrath if it repelled the mercenaries," not because he wasn't supported by the people; in fact, Arbenz had a mandate for progressive change.[99] In an interview with Grandin, it was emphasized that the collapse of the Soviet Union and the Eastern European states served to embolden – rather than constrain – U.S. military adventures in Latin America, and throughout the world. As Grandin put it, "for the first time in half a century [the U.S.] didn't face a rival superpower to check its ambitions, to check its arrogance."[100] As one 1954 *Freedom* columnist put it, "There is no limit to the lengths to which imperialism is prepared to go in horror and mass murder when the exploited peoples concerned are of dark skin. Hand butchery for the black people of Africa and the southern U.S. and the less personal atom bomb, flame thrower, and napalm for the yellow and brown people. So far, in Guatemala, it has been regular bombs, straight machine-gunning, and jails – jails – jails."[101] In short, anti-communism was just a convenient scapegoat, a pretext, a violent reflex turned dogma used to justify the unjustifiable – the mass murder of colonial peoples. Bevins approvingly quotes historian John Coatsworth, who estimates that "the number of victims of US-backed violence in Latin America 'vastly exceeded' the number of people killed in the Soviet Union and the Eastern Bloc over the same period of time [1960-1990],"[102] contrary to the dominant, though persistent, myth.

---

99. Greg Grandin, *Empire's Workshop: Latin America, the United States, the Rise of the New Imperialism* (New York: Metropolitan Books, 2006), 42-44

100. Tony Pecinovsky, "Latin America, the U.S., and the New Imperialism: Talking with Greg Grandin," *Political Affairs*, February 7, 2007, http://www.politicalaffairs.net/latin-america-the-u-s-and-the-new-imperialism-talking-with-greg-grandin/

101. Adam Brand, Jr., "White Supremacy & Search for Super Profits Merged in Guatemala," *Freedom*, August 1954, 4-5

102. Bevins, *The Jakarta Method...*, Ibid., 228 and Grace Blakeley, "Remembering Capitalism's Crimes," *Jacobin*, June 10, 2020, https://jacobinmag.com/2020/06/jakarta-method-vincent-bevins-indonesia-anticommunism

Around the globe, the post-war "mass murder program" continued unabated. Bevins' book *The Jakarta Method* documents the indiscriminate slaughter of at least one million Indonesian civilians starting in October 1965 engineered by the U.S. According to Bevins, throughout the late 1950s and early 1960s the U.S. government "prodded the [Indonesian] military to adopt a stronger position and take over the government, knowing full well that the method being employed to make this possible was to round up hundreds of thousands of people around the country, stab or strangle them, and throw their corpses into rivers. The Indonesian military officers understood very well that the more people they killed, the weaker the left would be, and the happier Washington would be." As Bevins concludes, "Up to a million Indonesians, maybe more, were killed as part of Washington's global anticommunist crusade." For what reason were the Communists and their allies tortured and killed? As Bevins argues, the anti-communist strategy of mass murder was employed "not because [the Indonesian Communist Party] was seizing power undemocratically, but because it was popular." The PKI was the third largest Communist Party in the world outside of the Soviet Union and China. Like popular Communist parties aligned with anti-colonial movements elsewhere, the PKI's real crime, the crime for which it was exterminated, was that it was not beholden to U.S. capitalist interests. As one State Department official recalled when asked about the massacre, "No one cared... as long as they were Communists, that they were being butchered."[103] As Michael Parenti argues, anti-communism became the "most powerful political force in the world."[104] As such, the reflexive mass murder that it engendered did not have to be justified nor was it questioned.

Indonesia had proudly hosted the 1955 Bandung Afro-Asian Conference representing about 1.5 billion of the world's then 2.8 billion people. It was, as President Sukarno defiantly declared, the "first intercontinental conference of colored peoples in the history of mankind," the birthplace of the nascent non-aligned movement. Ten years later, Indonesia was now a "quiet, compliant partner" of the United States in a growing Cold War

103. Bevins, *The Jakarta Method...*, Ibid., 157-158
104. Parenti, *The Anti-Communist Impulse...*, Ibid.

world. All it took was the "annihilation" of the PKI and its allies, the "fall of the founder of the Third World movement," and the establishment of a "fanatically anticommunist military dictatorship."[105] In his "heartfelt greetings," Robeson – who was still unable to travel due to State Department confiscation of his passport – noted, "the hopes of mankind were centered" on the Conference. The "very fact of the convening…will be recorded as an historic turning point in all world affairs," he added. Though the participants "have long been subjected to colonial serfdom and foreign domination," Bandung signals "the power and the determination of the peoples…to decide their own destiny, to achieve and defend their sovereign independence, to control the rich resources of their own lands, and to contribute to the promotion of world peace and cooperation." Robeson also pointed to the Soviet Union as a beacon. "The possibility and practicability of such rapid social advancement have been attested by those who have objectively examined the history of the Soviet Union since 1917 and developments during the last decade in the countries of Eastern Europe, in China, and in newly emancipated Asian countries such as India," he continued. Characteristically, Robeson did not mince words. He took direct aim at the enemy; "imperialist enslavement…[and] imperialist terror has been unleashed in an attempt to keep freedom-aspiring peoples in subjection." The massacre ten years later created a bloody tidal wave, a "tsunami that reached [into] almost every corner of the globe," Bevins concludes.[106]

Though less bloody[107] than the Indonesian massacre, similar events were unfolding thousands of miles away in Ghana, the first Sub-Saharan nation to gain independence. In February 1966, Kwame Nkrumah the independent socialist first president of

---

105. Bevins, Ibid., 159 and Prashad, *The Darker Nations…*, Ibid., 31-50. Also, see: Christopher J. Lee, *Making A World After Empire: The Bandung Moment And Its Political Afterlives* (Athens: Ohio University Press, 2019)

106. Paul Robeson, "Greetings to Bandung: Afro-Asian Conference Represents a Turning Point in World Affairs," *Freedom,* April 1955, 1, 7, and Bevins, Ibid., 159

107. It is estimated at least 1,600 people died during the coup, while "scores more were injured." See: "How did a fateful CIA coup – executed 55 years ago this February 24 – doom much of sub-Saharan Africa?," *Monthly Review,* February 25, 2021, https://mronline.org/2021/02/25/how-did-a-fateful-cia-coup-executed-55-years-ago-this-february-24-doom-much-of-sub-saharan-africa/

Ghana – where Hunton had resided since 1962 – was ousted by a CIA-backed military coup; in one scenario, which was apparently *not* approved, CIA operatives "were to wear blackface and attack the Chinese Embassy during the Coup," kill everyone there, and steal as much material as possible from the Embassy's code room.[108] Nkrumah was in Beijing at the time, about to depart for Hanoi, where Ho Chi Minh and the Vietnamese Communists were fighting for liberation. Within a week of the coup, the new Ghana regime had "ousted 620 Soviet technicians, teachers and advisers, working in schools, state farms, research institutes and government ministries." By late March, Major General Joseph Arthur Ankrah, the coup leader, wrote a "personal message" to President Lyndon Johnson vowing to "remove all traces of alien ideological [Communist] influence." He also asked for improved relations with the West, along with aid, food, and credit to "avoid economic disaster." As Natalia Telepneva writes, U.S. officials "were predictably happy with the outcome of the coup." The new Ghanaian leaders were "pathetically pro-Western," it was added. As a result, they were handsomely rewarded; food and other aid was quickly dispatched. Harvard economist Gustav Papanek, "fresh from a stint in Indonesia," became an economic advisor to the new regime.[109] Nine years earlier, on March 6, 1957, Nkrumah had addressed a "massive, rapturous crowd" declaring Ghana's independence from Britain. In that speech, he connected Ghana's and Africa's independence and declared, "Our independence is meaningless unless it is linked up with the total liberation of Africa."[110] Though the Soviet Union and Czechoslovakia, along with Nkrumah loyalists, made some attempts at a counter-coup in 1968 – codenamed Operation ALEX – it was unsuccessful, and Nkrumah spent the rest of his life in Guinea, a guest of President Sekou Touré. However, the "practical lesson" Communists took from the coup "was their underestimation of the importance of the army in Africa." Henceforward, "Moscow

---

108. Seymour M. Hersh, "C.I.A. Said to Have Aided Plotters Who Overthrew Nkrumah in Ghana," *New York Times*, May 9, 1978

109. Natalia Telepneva, "Saving Ghana's Revolution: The Demise of Kwame Nkrumah and the Evolution of Soviet Policy in Africa, 1966-1972," *Journal of Cold War Studies*, Vol. 20, Issue 4 (Fall 2018), 4-25 and "How did a fateful CIA coup…," Ibid.

110. Laumann, *Colonial Africa…*, Ibid., 62

would try to compensate by providing increasing amounts of training and equipment for the military and security service personnel of friendly regimes" on the continent.[111] Of course, this solidarity extended to non-state actors, fraternal parties, and allied organizations as well, such as the South African Communist Party and the African National Congress in its struggle against apartheid, a struggle Hunton would lend nearly 30 years of his life to.

In Guinea, Nkrumah pondered the prospects of furthering the African revolution. He wrote, "while still concentrating its main effort on the destruction of imperialism, colonialism and neo-colonialism, [it] is aiming at the same time to bring about a radical transformation of society." To Nkrumah, the question of pursuing a capitalist or "non-capitalist path" was moot. To him, the "choice has already been made by the workers and peasants of Africa. They have chosen liberation and unification; and this can only be achieved through armed struggle under socialist direction."[112]

* * *

U.S. Communists grappled with the question of armed struggle against repressive violence as well. In spring 1966, CPUSA Negro Commission chair Claude Lightfoot told reporters, Communists support "self-defense for Negroes…[but] we are not advocates of violence." He elaborated: African Americans had a right to "use violence to achieve change…[when] channels for democratic change are closed to them." Additionally, he continued, Communists argued that African Americans should be able to "police their own communities," due to racist police terror. To Lightfoot and other CPUSA members, the question was not "violence in the Negro community but the increasing violence being directed at it." In short, "armed self-defense, if necessary" was a legitimate tactic when all other avenues for democratic change were closed. Regarding self-defense, African Americans "not only

---

111. Telepneva, Ibid. It was noted by a coup leader in 1967 that "it is quite probable that President Nkrumah and the CPP would command the support of a majority of the electorate…in genuinely free elections." See: "How did a fateful CIA coup…," Ibid.

112. Kwame Nkrumah, *Class Struggle In Africa* (New York: International Publishers, 1984), 84

have the right but the responsibility to defend their persons, their homes and their communities." In another interview, Lightfoot concluded that African American equality and Black liberation must go beyond "the norms of bourgeois legality."[113] This was an important clarification, as the CPUSA sought to distinguish itself from some 1960s Black Power movements that they saw as adventurist and counter-productive. As Beth Slutsky argues, throughout the late-1960s and early-1970s some Communists "compared the oppression of minorities in the United States with colonized peoples in the Third World." To them, the 1965 Watts uprising, for example, was "comparable to a colonial area occupied by an invading armed force…subject to the constant pressures of that invading army." As Slutsky notes, this argument was later adopted by Third World Left organizations and the Black Panther Party,[114] an organization that benefited from the insight of both Black and white Communists, such as William L. Patterson and Herbert Aptheker.[115] As Slutsky adds, this dynamic "amounted to more than a power struggle and violation of civil liberties, according to the party. Instead, the eruption of violence – and the police and city government response to this violence – signaled a colonial struggle between an oppressed nation and its colonizers."[116]

However, local Communists, such as Dorothy Healey and William Taylor, saw the Watts uprising through less romantic lenses; further complicating their analysis was the fact that the National Guard was welcomed by some in the Black community.

113. Peter Kihss, "U.S. Communist Party Supports Negro Violence," *New York Times,* October 23, 1967, and "Reds in U.S. Urged to Give More Support to Negroes," *New York Times,* May 5, 1969. Note the horribly misleading title of Kihss' article.

114. Beth Slutsky, "American Communism in a Time of Détente," in Pedersen, Ryan, and Sibley (eds), *Post-Cold War Revelations…*, Ibid., 208-210

115. See: Horne, *Black Revolutionary…*, Ibid., and Murrell, *"The Most Dangerous Communist…,"* Ibid. For example, Patterson provided BPP leaders with legal advice and Aptheker spoke to 4,000 people at a BPP sponsored National Conference for a United Front Against Fascism in July 1969. See: Herbert Aptheker, "Racism and the Danger of Fascism in the United States," in *Racism and Reaction in the United States: Two Marxist Studies* (New York: New Outlook Publishers, 1971). Of course, there was considerable disagreement within the CPUSA as to the role of the BPP; it was often accused of classlessness, petty bourgeois left-adventurism, etc. Murrell, 271-273

116. Slutsky, Ibid., 209-210

"We were very surprised by this, taken aback," Healey said, "because our first reaction had been to oppose the calling-out of the National Guard. It was the Black comrades in Watts who kept saying, 'You just don't know what you're talking about.'" Additionally, Communists were criticized for not providing public "leadership to this mass upsurge," though, according to Gerald Horne, "the nationalism of the revolt" impacted the party and gave "impetus to the slogan of 'Nationalist in Form, Anti-Imperialist in Content,'" a throwback to the Black Belt Thesis and the right to self-determination. Additionally, some Communists saw the uprising as a "spontaneous upheaval" made up of "individual acts which were not preceded by political actions and demands," which they argued would lead to cynicism. Further, the counter-force of anti-communism used the Watts events to its own advantage; staunch anti-communist Ronald Reagan won the California governorship in 1966 on an anti-civil rights platform.[117]

African American CPUSA national chairman Henry Winston denigrated the "internal colony" theory as a "pseudo-radical concept." To Winston, a "Black liberation strategy here must differ from an anti-colonial strategy aiming for political independence... [because the] ghettos of the United States, despite the intensity of their oppression, are economically and politically different from colonies." To him, "this difference can be traced to their origins: Ghettos are the descendants of the old Southern slave quarters and are no more economically viable than were their plantation forerunners." Additionally, Winston argued that "to apply the 'internal colony' theory [domestically]...is to overlook the nature of the colony...[which] has a common territory and economy, and is usually separated geographically from the 'mother' country." Further, "to speak of a colonial economy means to speak of the raw materials – diamonds, oil, silver, cocoa, sugar, coffee, tin, jute, gold, uranium, bananas, spices, copper – that are the source of countless billions for imperialism's super-profits. But the raw materials for industry and agriculture found in colonies are missing from ghettos – whose streets are lined not with gold

---

117. Gerald Horne, *Fire This Time: The Watts Uprising and the 1960s* (Charlottesville: University Press of Virginia, 1995), 271-275. Interestingly, a store owned by Healey's "cousin by marriage" was burned down during the uprising; Healey was less than concerned, though, as there were, apparently, "credit rackets of all kinds" taking place on the premises. Horne, 271

and oil, or any other raw material, but only rubble."[118] Winston was challenging Stokely Carmichael, earlier a high school friend of Gene Dennis (son of CPUSA leader Eugene Dennis) and regular at Young Communist League meetings[119]; Carmichael would become a leader of the Student Nonviolent Coordinating Committee. According to Winston, Carmichael "distorted the meaning of Black power." Winston continued, "people who live in a colony earn their living *only* within that colony. But this is not true of the majority in Harlem, Chicago's South Side, Watts and Bedford Stuyvesant. These ghettos are geographically separated and economically detachable only in the view of those who confuse segregation with geography and economy." Unlike a colony, the ghetto did not have the potential to offer "full economic, social and political development for the people on its territory." Therefore, to Winston, the "internal colony" concept confused more than it clarified.[120]

These ideological disagreements coupled with a smaller membership (than its 1930s and 1940s peak) would have crippled other organizations. The CPUSA, however, still had a considerable "bureaucratic infrastructure that provided the financial and administrative backing for revolutionaries" and it remained an important international gatekeeper able to connect domestic activists to global anti-colonial struggles aided by ascendant socialism. This enabled Communists in the 1960s and 1970s – like the International Labor Defense in the 1930s and Civil Rights Congress in the 1950s – to reestablish their "value as an entity that constructed coalitions of leftists," such as with the campaign to free Angela Davis. Communists "did what they do best," Slutsky added, "provide support and build campaigns for key trials and campaigns." Through the National United Committee to Free Angela Davis, they employed "race and class-based connections to build bridges" with, for example, the Southern Christian Leadership Conference.[121] This was a strategic approach, one Winston expanded upon in his book *Strategy for a Black Agenda.* He argued that while oppression "would first be unleashed against

118. Henry Winston, *Class, Race and Black Liberation* (New York: International Publishers, 1977), 123-125.

119. Munro, *The Anticolonial Front…*, Ibid., 284

120. Winston, *Class, Race and Black Liberation*, Ibid. *Italic* in original.

121. Slutsky, "American Communism…," Ibid., 207-212

Black people, [it] would not end there." Therefore, individual "militancy" was not enough to stop racism and reaction; "armed self-defense," he added, created a "false choice diverting [activists] from mass unity and struggle." To him, "It is clear that the people want to challenge the oppressor on the ground *they* choose, not on those chosen by their enemy. They want to engage the class enemy where he is most vulnerable . . . [in] the arena of mass struggle." To Winston, the domestic taking up of arms was a "defensive strategy...[the] idea of an elite few acting for the masses." This concept excludes the people, primarily African Americans, "from their own liberation struggle." Winston juxtaposed the "defensive strategy" of armed action with the "offensive strategy" of mass action offered by Dr. Martin Luther King, Jr. The Montgomery bus boycott, the Poor People's Campaign, and support for striking sanitation workers in Memphis, Tennessee: These were his examples of an "offensive strategy." Additionally, Winston centered his analysis on the working class. "No fundamental change – or even a challenge to the monopolists – can occur without the working class," he wrote. In short, to Winston, organizing and mobilizing a broad-based working class movement, not domestic armed struggle, was key to Black liberation.[122]

In 1973, this strategic formulation coupled with the successful campaign to free Angela Davis evolved to become the National Alliance Against Racist and Political Repression headed by CPUSA leader Charlene Mitchell; the NAARPR became one of the most important civil rights organizations of the 1970s and early-1980s. Of course, Communists had also been active in the anti-Vietnam war peace movement as well. In 1966, as the war escalated U.S. Communists – two of the Fort Hood Three – refused to deploy to Vietnam and were court martialed, thereby helping to spark the genesis of the organized GI anti-war movement, attacking imperialism where it was most vulnerable, among working class soldiers of color.[123]

---

122. Henry Winston, *Strategy for a Black Agenda: A Critique of New Theories of Liberation in the United States and Africa* (New York: International Publishers, 1973) and Tony Pecinovsky, "A forthright stand": Communists in the struggle for Black lives," August 10, 2020, https://www.cpusa.org/article/a-forthright-stand-communists-in-the-struggle-for-black-lives/. *Italic* in original.

123. Pecinovsky, *Let Them Tremble...*, Ibid. Regarding J.J. Johnson and Dennis Mora's membership in the CPUSA (two of the Fort Hood Three): Author

In 1964, Winston published *New Colonialism: U.S. Style*, which was printed abroad as *The Challenge of U.S. Neo-Colonialism*, but was barred by U.S. customs. This pamphlet, a stinging critique of U.S. imperialism, situated Winston as a foremost working class intellectual of international Black liberation and foreshadowed his leadership of the National Anti-Imperialist Movement in Solidarity with African Liberation, which he helped found roughly ten years later. In *New Colonialism* Winston outlined the emerging contest between U.S. imperialism and ascendant socialism in relation to national liberation. He wrote that, while imperialism could act through "open, direct coercion, domination and conquest," it could also employ "concealed and more cunning forms of exploitation." To Winston, these new, concealed forms were "introduced because of the powerful sweep of the national liberation movements and the aid given them by the socialist countries," an illustration of capitalism's retreat. Jim Crow and colonialism both had to contend with "New World Realities," he added, and a "distinction must be drawn between the appetite of U.S. imperialism and the practical possibilities for satisfying it." The modern empire was "doomed to remain a pipe-dream," he concluded, due to "changes in the world balances of forces in favor of socialism, democracy and peace."[124]

Domestically and internationally, throughout the 1960s, 1970s, and 1980s, Communists fought for liberation. They debated theories on internal colonies and colonial liberation. They challenged New Left, armed struggle concepts. They discussed and critiqued Frantz Fanon, Regis Debray, and Herbert Marcuse.[125] They "succeeded in

---

interview with Elena Mora, long-time Party leader and niece of Dennis Mora while in Chicago at a CPUSA National Board meeting, May 29-31, 2015; author interview with Marc Brodine while in Chicago at a CPUSA Marxist Strategy and Tactics conference, February, 18, 2017: Brodine attended Party School with Johnson; and author interview with Tim Wheeler, a fellow *Daily World* reporter who worked with Johnson in the *DW* New York office, October 2, 2017. Also, see: *The Fort Hood Three: The Case Of The Three G.I.'s Who Said "No" To The War In Vietnam* (Fort Hood Three Defense Committee, 1966). For obvious reasons (anti-communism) Johnson and Mora denied membership in the CPUSA. See: Martin Arnold, "3 Soldiers hold News Conference to Announce They Won't Go to Vietnam," *New York Times*, July 1, 1966

124. Henry Winston, *New Colonialism: U.S. Style* (New York: New Outlook Publishers, 1965)

125. See: Winston, *Class, Race and Black Liberation*, Ibid.; Winston, *Strategy for a Black Agenda*, Ibid.; and Jack Woddis, *New Theories of Revolution: A commentary on*

injecting a consistent anti-imperialist content to the then-developing movements with African liberation," as Angela Davis put it in 2012.[126] While the struggle was difficult with many casualties, in South Africa as Nkrumah indicated armed struggle coupled with international pressure proved to be the path to liberation.

*   *   *

As Gerald Horne argues in *White Supremacy Confronted*, in many ways "obdurately incoherent apartheid was its own gravedigger." Correspondingly, the brutally suppressed Black majority in South Africa "became more susceptible to the blandishments of Communists." While Pretoria and Washington may have been more concerned about Moscow's support of the SACP and the ANC, many among the latter were keen to also point to the aid they received from U.S. Communists and their allies; from Robeson, Hunton, and the CAA, and later, in the 1970s, from Winston, Davis, Anthony Monteiro, and the National Anti-Imperialist Movement in Solidarity with African Liberation. One ANC leader noted in 1976, "for our purposes there is [no] support group whose loyalty and dedication to the ANC can...surpass that of the Communist Party, USA." Of course, the links forged between the ANC-SACP and the CAA-CPUSA in the 1940s and 1950s, and later with NAIMSAL, undoubtedly caused consternation and angst in the "two citadels of white supremacy."[127] Hunton was one of the most vocal early critics of South Africa. In a December 6, 1945, *Daily Worker* column he wrote, South Africa "must

---

the *views of Frantz Fanon, Regis Debray and Herbert Marcuse* (New York: International Publishers, 1972). Though Woddis was a member of the Communist Part of Great Britain, where he served as secretary of the International Department, his views were apparently shared by the CPUSA. For Fanon, Debray, and Marcuse, See: Frantz Fanon, *The Wretched of the Earth* (New York: Grove Press, 1963); Regis Debray, *Revolution in the Revolution* (New York: Grove Press, 1967); and Herbert Marcuse, *One-Dimensional Man: Studies in the Ideology of Advanced Industrial Society* (Boston: Beacon Press, 1964). Also, see: Albert Memmi, *The Colonizer and the Colonized* (Boston: Beacon Press, 1965)

126. Remarks by Davis at the Henry Winston 100th Anniversary Tribute Program held on February 19, 2012, at the Henry Winston Unity Hall (CPUSA offices), 235 W. 23rd St., NY.

127. Horne, *White Supremacy Confronted...*, Ibid., 11, 19, 586 and Pecinovsky, *Let Them Tremble...*, Ibid., 201-208

be classed with Spain and Argentina as one of the places where the job of liquidating fascism remains to be accomplished." He added, "women and children" are routinely "shot down for protesting." He also called attention to the "acute starvation" facing the Black majority, as undernourishment and disease, "which go along with poverty, have stalked the indigenous population… ever since the coming of the European."[128]

South Africa was then considered "one gigantic concentration camp," and the hated Pass Laws restricting "freedom of movement" were akin to regulations used by Nazis "against the Jews of Europe." In another *DW* column, Hunton refers to the "Pass system" as a "badge of serfdom." To him, this was a less-than-subtle means of "maintaining a supply of cheap African labor," a way of maintaining racist subjugation and oppression, as well as creating exorbitant profits. The Pass Laws created a panopticon effect, a feeling of constant, all-consuming, ubiquitous control. For starters, Black South Africans had to use an identification pass, which "must be renewed monthly and costs two shillings (40 cents)." To leave the segregated "reserve" a trek pass and a travel pass were required. "That makes three of these things to start with," though the District Commissioner could "simply refuse to grant these passes." Then "our African friend must immediately register" and get a six-day special pass, "the fourth pass, which allows him to seek work." After finding work, the "young African must acquire his fifth and sixth passes to prove that he has a job," a service contract pass and a daily laborer's pass. Both must be renewed monthly. "If he wants to visit someone who lives in another area…he must have his seventh and eighth passes," the one-day special pass and the location visitor's pass. If he is out past curfew, 9 p.m. for Africans, he must have a night special pass, the ninth pass. Additionally, he must also acquire a lodger's pass and a poll tax receipt pass. "That makes 11 of these dog tags," Hunton concluded.[129] With many among South Africa's ruling class having been sympathetic to Nazi

128. Alphaeus Hunton, "Today's Guest Column: Hunger, Disease, Fascist Repression – South Africa," *Daily Worker*, December 6, 1945, 7

129. Alphaeus Hunton, "Today's Guest Column: 11 Badges of Serfdom In South Africa," *Daily Worker*, December 20, 1945, 7

Germany, it is little wonder they employed Nazi-style tactics to systematically suppress the Black majority.

Though relatively small compared to Communist Parties in other de-colonizing lands (the Communist Party of South Africa then had about 2,500 members), the CPSA was outlawed in 1950. Anti-communism was a "convenient and up-to-date political ideology around which South Africa's domestic racial policies could be justified to the outside world"; further, anti-communist ideology was malleable enough to encapsulate both white supremacy and vague free world proclamations. Reconstituted in 1953 as the SACP, most Communists throughout the 1950s poured themselves into the ANC and the South African Congress of Trade Unions, and were considered "the most disciplined single bloc," within the Congress Alliance, helping to draft the Freedom Charter, organize marches and protests, and build international solidarity.[130]

The March 1960 Sharpeville Massacre, where 69 Black men, women, and children were killed, and 200 were wounded,[131] "further unmasked Pretoria as the heir to Nazi barbarism"; the massacre, however, also had another effect, as the NAACP later invited ANC leader Oliver Tambo to that organization's convention, thereby fostering a degree of international solidarity thought destroyed with the dissolution of Hunton's CAA. Further, Dr. Martin Luther King, Jr., noted that the massacre "should serve as a warning signal" for the type of violence that could potentially erupt if domestic white supremacy was not confronted. King would later confer in London with Adelaide Tambo – spouse of the ANC leader – further highlighting a growing concern among the ruling class that they "risked losing ground globally unless Jim Crow was subdued." It was not lost on Washington nor Pretoria that "anti-racism was propelled by the mass action of

130. Stephen Ellis and Tsepo Sechaba, *Comrades against Apartheid: The ANC & the South African Communist Party in Exile* (Bloomington: Indiana University Press, 1992), 23-24, 27 and Grant, *Winning Our Freedoms Together...,* Ibid., 35. For more on the SACTU, see: Ken Luckhardt and Brenda Wall, *Organize...or Starve: The History of the South African Congress of Trade Unions* (New York: International Publishers, 1980)

131. William Pomeroy, *Apartheid Axis: United States & South Africa* (New York: International Publishers, 1971), 25. Also, see: Pomeroy, *Apartheid, Imperialism and African Freedom* (New York: International Publishers, 1986) and *African Communists Speak: Articles and Documents from "The African Communist"* (Moscow: Nauka Publishing House, 1970)

Negroes [with the] avid support of national liberation forces and the socialist camp," which is partly why they reacted "by tarring the most militant activists...as unrepentant Communists."[132] Unfortunately, not everyone in the emerging civil rights movement was as farsighted as King, who kept a copy of Du Bois' application to join the CPUSA in his desk drawer.[133] King's support of domestic Communists, such as Benjamin Davis, Jr., Winston, and Du Bois,[134] as well as his links to one-time Communist Jack O'Dell and likely Communist Stanley Levison, were concerning – at least to the FBI, who kept tabs on both King and Communists.[135] That reds were then making somewhat of a comeback, packing college and university auditoriums with tens of thousands of students,[136] often discussing national liberation struggles aided by Soviet socialism, added to the FBI's paranoia. Regardless, Communists continued to make the links between domestic capital and apartheid. Writing in *The Worker*, James E. Jackson argued, "Behind South Africa's white supremacy policies of Apartheid, behind the bloodletting, is the gold-getting greed of far-flung industrial and financial empires with home offices in Wall Street."[137] Of course, the inverse was true as well; the apartheid government "deliberately played up the threat of the Soviet Union in ways that associated anti-apartheid protest with communist subversion." It used the "language of anticommunism" to justify "oppressive racial policies" and violence, like the Sharpeville massacre. As Nicholas Grant argues, "Operating transnationally, anticommunist ideology represented a powerful tool that could be used to stifle black

---

132. Horne, *White Supremacy Confronted...*, Ibid., 309, 311, 320

133. Du Bois officially applied to join the CPUSA in 1961. Re King keeping a copy of Du Bois' CPUSA application, see: Michael K. Honey, *Going Down Jericho Road: The Memphis Strike, Martin Luther King's Last Campaign* (New York: W.W. Norton & Co., 2007), 287-288

134. See: Horne, *Black Liberation/Red Scare...*, Ibid.; Horne, *Black & Red: W.E.B. Du Bois and the Afro-American Response to the Cold War, 1944-1963* (Albany: State University of New York Press, 1986); Munro, *The Anticolonial Front...*, Ibid., 166; and Pecinovsky, *Let Them Tremble...*, Ibid., 176

135. Honey, *Going Down Jericho Road...*, Ibid., 90-91

136. Tony Pecinovsky, "Far From Marginal: The CPUSA in the early 1960s and 1970s," in Pecinovsky (ed), *Faith In the Masses...*, Ibid., 337-372

137. Jackson, *The View From Here...*, Ibid., 1

protest on both sides of the Atlantic."[138] Domestic civil rights and anti-colonial solidarity were both seen as subversive.

By mid-1961 the ANC had started debating the question of armed struggle. Once established, ANC and SACP members joined the armed underground Umkhonto we Sizwe "in large numbers." That December, it successfully attacked numerous strategic locations and "over the next 18 months…carried out some 200 attacks," a precursor of events to come. As Stephen Ellis and Tsepo Sechaba argue, the decision to build a guerilla organization and to declare war on the government "greatly increased the Party's weight in its alliance with the ANC." The Communists had several "valuable assets"; they had "experience of working in underground conditions," "could draw on an international experience…and they could secure the backing of a superpower."[139] The seeds planted by the Comintern in the 1920s and 1930s, were still reaping considerable fruit in the struggle for liberation.

Additionally, post-WWII Communist initiatives such as WIDF brought international pressure to bear against apartheid through the United Nations. As WIDF President Freda Brown noted, apartheid is "the policy of institutionalized racist domination and exploitation imposed by [the] minority regime in South Africa…It rests on the dispossession, plunder, exploitation and social deprivation of the African people." Brown's remarks were part of a WIDF roundtable held in Luanda, Angola in 1978 in partnership with the Angolan Women's Organization as part of the 1978 Anti-Apartheid Year. The Angolan roundtable itself was part of a larger UN Decade Against Racism, Racial Discrimination and Apartheid; that May, WIDF held a leadership meeting in Moscow, which "adopted a statement sharply condemning the racist South African regime." Leslie O. Harriman, UN Chairman of the Special Committee Against Apartheid, extended greetings to the Luanda participants; she noted, the "struggle for freedom…has reached a critical stage. Faced with great advances of the national liberation movements, the apartheid regime and its friends are resorting to brutal repression." Brown, WIDF, and their ANC and SACP comrades were not deterred by the violence, though. As Brown put it, "Despite all the brutal fascist terror of the minority regime in South Africa, the

138. Grant, *Winning Our Freedoms Together…*, Ibid., 10-11, 61
139. Stephen Ellis and Tsepo Sechaba, Ibid., 33-35

women and the people, even the children, are daily demonstrating their courage, their determination, and their willingness to die in the fight for freedom." She added, South Africa "was only able to continue its regime of murder and plundering because of the support it receives from its western trading partners," primarily the United States, Britain, and France.[140]

Like KUTV cadre decades earlier, SACP and ANC leaders traveled to the Soviet Union, East Germany, and other socialist countries for training. This sometimes hot, sometimes cold conflict[141] continued into the 1980s, when Cuba sent tens of thousands of soldiers and massive amounts of military equipment to defend Angola from a South African invasion, eventually defeating the South African army in the Angolan city of Cuito Cuanavale. This defeat foreshadowed the end of apartheid. Just a few years later the ANC and SACP were legalized, and Nelson Mandela was elected President. As Laumann rightly notes, "it was fitting... that the army defending the last bastion of European rule on the continent...was defeated by forces comprising diasporic Africans from a socialist country."[142] Of course, without the dedication and sacrifice of indigenous Communists like Moses Kotane, Joe Slovo, and Ruth First, among others, this victory would not have been possible.[143]

As Stephen Ellis and Tsepo Sechaba wrote, "it is impossible to separate completely" the histories of the SACP, the ANC, and the organization "formed by both in 1961 under the command of Nelson Mandela, the guerrilla army Umkhonto we Sizwe." While the relationship between these organizations is "not a simple one," and while they were indeed separate organizations, in the "circumstances of the underground struggle the identity of all three became blurred. The Party, the ANC and Umkhonto we

140. *Women in Action – for the elimination of apartheid, for freedom and full human rights for the people of southern Africa* (Berlin, GDR: Women's International Democratic Federation, 1978)

141. For more on the hot conflict in Southern Africa during the Cold War, see: Vladimir Shubin, *The Hot "Cold War": The USSR in Southern Africa* (London: Pluto Press, 2008)

142. Laumann, *Colonial Africa...*, Ibid., 72-75

143. For more on Kotane, Slovo, and First, see: Brian Bunting, *Moses Kotane, South African Revolutionary* (London: Inkululeko Publications, 1975) and Alan Wieder, *Ruth First and Joe Slovo in the War Against Apartheid* (New York: Monthly Review Press, 2013)

Sizwe merged to the point that it became difficult to define the three separately."[144]

Ellis and Tsepo's comment is profound. Not only does it complicate our understanding of the specific histories of the SACP, ANC, and Umkhonto we Sizwe. In many ways, it also complicates our understanding of the history of 20th century colonial liberation in general, a movement so deeply and intrinsically, so fundamentally and innately supported by Communists that it is difficult – if not impossible – to disentangle. Similarly, the alliances between the old colonial empires, U.S. imperialism, and the repressive ideology of reflexively violent anti-communism is just as difficult to separate. Add into the mix the mass murder documented above, and we get a peek, a passing glimpse, into the horrific barbarity inflicted upon countless millions who sought liberation from colonial subjugation.

This partly explains why in 1991, as socialism was collapsing in the Soviet Union, Nelson Mandela hosted a reception for CPUSA leaders Angela Davis and Charlene Mitchell, to Washington's chagrin. At that reception, the future Nobel Peace Prize recipient told his comrades: "We will never permit our enemies to tell us who our friends should be."[145] This passing comment is important. Mandela was articulating a strategic formulation some today seem incapable of learning as the repulsive stench of reflexive anti-communism still lingers. Regardless, when "the cancer of colonialism" was finally excised, Mandela was keen to acknowledge who his friends were; for example, he profusely embraced Communists like Fidel Castro who supported the long struggle for Black liberation in Africa.[146] Further, as John Riddell accurately argues, Comintern efforts to "forge unity against imperialism scored important victories and contributed to the demise of direct colonial rule *almost everywhere* by the end of the century."[147] This admission, linked with what some have

144. Stephen Ellis and Tsepo Sechaba, *Comrades against Apartheid...*, Ibid., 6

145. "Home from South Africa: Angela Davis, Charlene Mitchell plan national report-back tour," *Daily World,* September 21, 1991, 2

146. Sean Jacobs, "To so many Africans, Fidel Castro is a hero. Here's why," *The Guardian,* November 30, 2016, https://www.theguardian.com/commentisfree/2016/nov/30/africa-fidel-castro-nelson-mandela-cuba

147. John Riddell, "Toward a global strategic framework: The Comintern and Asia 1919-25 (Part 1)," https://johnriddell.com/2018/01/04/

asserted was "the greatest geo-political catastrophe of the 20th century," the collapse of socialism in Eastern Europe, tells us a lot.[148] Communism and anti-communism indelibly shaped our world. Like other Communists, W. Alphaeus Hunton chose sides. He fought for African American equality, Black liberation, and socialism. His *Daily Worker* articles foreshadow decades of unflinching commitment during a time of tumultuous change.

*   *   *

It was announced in the July 20, 1944, issue of the *Daily Worker* that Alphaeus Hunton would for the "next few work weeks" replace Max Yergan,[149] his co-worker at the CAA, as a guest columnist. Hunton's first *DW* column appeared that same day. By way of introduction, it was added that Hunton was the educational director of the CAA "in charge" of its publications, "on the faculty of the Jefferson school and a member of the national board of the National Negro Congress."[150] A few weeks turned into almost two years. Hunton continued writing guest columns until January 19, 1946, publishing 70 semi-regular "Today's Guest Column" articles.

Throughout all of Hunton's columns his sympathies for the Soviet Union are clear. Not only was he a Communist, but the Soviets were a war-time ally in the fight against fascism and they had a record of support for colonial liberation movements, a record of which Hunton was undoubtedly well aware. Additionally, even many non-communists then held the USSR in high regard. However, Hunton, as his columns indicate, was primarily

---

toward-a-global-strategic-framework-the-comintern-and-asia-1919-25/.   *Italic* added, T.P.

148. Gerald Horne, "Rethinking the History and Future of the Communist Party," *People's World*, April 6, 2007, https://www.peoplesworld.org/article/rethinking-the-history-and-future-of-the-communist-party/

149. Yergan had embarked upon an extensive speaking tour. For more on Yergan, see: David Henry Anthony III, *Max Yergan: Race Man, Internationalist, Cold Warrior* (New York: New York University Press, 2006). Prior to Hunton taking responsibility for writing the column, Yergan would occasionally send financial contributions to the *Daily Worker* as well. See: "Yergan Sends Column – Cash," *Daily Worker*, June 30, 1944, 9

150. "Dr. Hunton Writes Guest Column," *Daily Worker*, July 20, 1944, 3 and Gettleman, "No Varsity Teams...," Ibid.

concerned with how "the people of Africa themselves" viewed the Soviet Union. In August 1944, he noted a Soviet Friendship Congress held in Johannesburg, as well as a parade in Accra of African troops honoring Red Army victories, among other examples. He wrote, "As the war has made the whole world smaller, so it has brought Africa closer to the great land of the Soviets, as well as to America." With the "increasing knowledge of the Soviet Power, African leaders are more frequently citing the contrast between the failure of the European colonial administration...and the remarkable success of the Soviet government," which had raised its people out of a "state of colonial serfdom comparable to that of the most 'backward' Africans," he continued.[151] The CAA helped to foster this knowledge, and Hunton emphasized the links between the domestic struggle "for full rights in this country" and "the struggles of other oppressed peoples." However, he also criticized "narrow racial nationalism... [as] a fertile field in which to sow [the] seeds of division and discord." These "defeatist forces," as he called them, "must be nullified." Like other Communists, Hunton saw the "separatist 'Back-to-Africa' movement [as] a reactionary pipe dream," advocated by the anti-Semitic America First Party presidential candidate Gerald L.K. Smith, the racist Senator Theodore Bilbo of Mississippi, as well as the conservative African American journalist George S. Schuyler. To Hunton, this was "cynical defeatism" during a time of cataclysmic war. Just "as the struggle here will be won through the close collaboration and unity of the progressive forces in every section of the population," he continued, "so the liberation and progress of the African people and other colonial subjects must come through the concerted efforts of the United Nations, first in winning a decisive victory over fascism and, second in building a new world of equality, justice and peace."[152] Hunton's optimism shined, despite the war-time conditions.

Also, appearing in Hunton's columns are numerous calls to action. While he was indeed a scholar, Hunton was also an activist, intent on organizing and mobilizing. He complicates and

151. Alphaeus Hunton, "Today's Guest Column: People of Africa Learn From the USSR," *Daily Worker*, August 3, 1944, 7

152. Alphaeus Hunton, "Today's Guest Column: Negro People Concerned With Africa's Future," *Daily Worker*, August 24, 1944, 7

challenges arguments that Communists sidelined the struggle for equality and liberation during WWII.[153] In particular, regarding British colonies, Hunton wrote, "some of the American critics are better haters of Britain than they are friends of the colonial people." He added, "what is needed now is not further protestations of good intentions, but deeds." And he criticized the "extremely limited and piecemeal" efforts of the British Colonial Office to "promote social and economic development in the various colonies." Unsurprisingly, he supported "an entirely new approach," perhaps "a 20-year plan on the Soviet model" advocated by Labour Party politician Dr. Haden Guest while speaking in the British House of Commons. The international impact of domestic elections was front and center in his mind, too. He asked if the "present administration's policies are [to be] upheld by the American people" and wondered if "arguments of 'economy' and 'states rights' [were being] used by the reactionary congressional coalition to knife the administration's reconversion plans" just as "arguments of 'national self-interest' and 'national sovereignty' [could wreck] world security proposals based on international collaboration." Hunton proved to be insightful on this point. Regardless, he concluded, "Americans have their job cut out for them in the coming elections."[154]

---

153. For example, see: Henry Winston, *Old Jim Crow Has Got To Go!* (New York: New Age Publishers, 1941); *Communists In The Struggle For Negro Rights* (New York: New Century Publishers, 1945). This pamphlet includes excerpts from speeches given by CPUSA leaders James W. Ford, Benjamin Davis, Jr., William L. Patterson, and Earl Browder based on a round-table symposium "Have the Communists Quit the Fight for Negro Rights" sponsored by *Negro Digest*. George S. Schuyler and Horace Cayton participated in the symposium and took the affirmative side. Also, see: Thelma Dale, "Reconversion And The Negro People," *Political Affairs*, October 1945. Numerous Black and white Communists, such as Claude Lightfoot, James Jackson, and Herbert Aptheker, among others, challenged racist policies within the military as well. See Murrell, "*Most Dangerous Communist…,*" Ibid.; Haviland, *James and Esther Cooper Jackson…*, Ibid.; and Claude Lightfoot, *Chicago Slums To World Politics: Autobiography of Claude M. Lightfoot* (New York: New Outlook Publishers, no date). It is estimated that 15,000 Communists served in the armed forces during WWII; a detailed study documenting efforts by Communists inside the armed forces to challenge racist policies would be welcomed.

154. Alphaeus Hunton, "Today's Guest Column: Role of U.S. Elections In Future of Colonial People's," *Daily Worker*, September 14, 1944, 7

As a Communist Hunton devoted considerable attention to organized labor and its role in a post-war world. "Labor must," he wrote, "simultaneously concern itself with domestic issues and questions of foreign policy as part of one common task." While India was a "pivotal problem for winning the war," to Hunton, "Africa represents a key question in winning the peace." As proved to be the case, that "great continent, the least developed in all the world, is fraught with dangers of imperialistic conflicts." In his columns, Hunton sometimes straddled the fence, though. He noted, it was "yet uncertain" if post-war development "will be to the advantage of the African people and in the interest of world-wide prosperity," or to the benefit of the old colonial empires and U.S. imperialism. He was cautiously optimistic that the war-time alliance would hold. Again, domestic concerns were merged with international affairs. "The task of American labor, working in close cooperation with the democratic labor forces of all countries, is to exert maximum influence toward the shaping of a world which will no longer be one-third free and two-thirds slave." Hunton continued, the "time for American labor to apply itself to that task is now."[155] Unfortunately, by the late 1940s the careful alliances U.S. Communists had forged with unions, particularly in the CIO, would be broken; Communist-led unions then representing roughly one million workers were purged.[156]

Hunton was deeply concerned with unions and workers' rights in colonial lands. As a Marxist, he saw how war-time production had "even in the least economically developed countries...meant a quickening of the tempo of production and the development of new industries. Supplying the new manpower needs means, especially in colonial or semi-colonial regions, shifting people from a primitive agricultural economy into an entirely new way of life." Correspondingly, this shift in the means and relations of production called for a shift in worker organization, collective identity, and class consciousness. As Hunton saw it, the "new urban and industrial environment produces new social attitudes which supplant the old. The basis for working class organization

---

155. Alphaeus Hunton, "Today's Guest Column: American Labor and the Colonial Postwar World," *Daily Worker,* September 21, 1944, 7

156. See: Judith Stepan-Norris and Maurice Zeitlin, *Left Out: Reds and America's Industrial Unions* (Cambridge: Cambridge University Press, 2003)

and ideals is established." He also noted, the "milestone" meeting in Nigeria of "representatives of 36 trade unions [who] met in the first convention of the Nigerian Trades Union Congress," as well as the second meeting of "over 300 delegates representing 64 trade unions" and 500,000 workers. He proudly referenced a letter sent by the secretary of the Nigerian TUC to the CAA; it said in part, "To know that we have friends at the other end of the Atlantic is comforting and inspiring in our struggle for freedom from want and heartless exploitation."[157] Hunton helped build these types of alliances throughout his life. "That the Negro worker in South Africa," Hunton added in another column, "has been able to achieve any labor organization whatever is a remarkable fact" given the "fetish of racialism" by the white minority who are "even now still openly pro-Nazi." Hunton likened the racists in South Africa to "our poll-taxers and [Herbert] Hoover-[Thomas] Dewey Republicans [who] are the enemy of both black and white workers in that country."[158]

Though wide-ranging, Hunton's writing was always focused on Black liberation. For example, he wrote about the CAA and NNC sponsoring African American representation at the World Trade Union Congress,[159] as well as the formation of global systems of power sharing. He briefly analyzed the Dumbarton Oaks conference and the formation of the United Nations.[160] He challenged journalists Walter Lippmann and George S. Schuyler on "the Colonial problem" and "made-in Berlin [red-baiting] propaganda," respectively.[161] He also analyzed the February 1945 World Labor Conference held in London, which led to the formation of the World Federation of Trade Unions. Always, though, he connected his columns to the struggles of colonial peoples for

157. Alphaeus Hunton, "Today's Guest Column: Trade Unionism in Nigeria," *Daily Worker*, September 28, 1944, 7

158. Alphaeus Hunton, "Today's Guest Column: South African Labor Movement Growing," *Daily Worker*, October 5, 1944, 7

159. Alphaeus Hunton, "Today's Guest Column: The Negro's Stake in World Labor Congress," *Daily Worker*, October 4, 1945, 7

160. Alphaeus Hunton, "Today's Guest Column: How World Economic and Social Council World Work," *Daily Worker*, October 19, 1944, 7 and Hunton, "Today's Guest Column: San Francisco, 1945 And Paris, 1919," *Daily Worker*, April 26, 1945, 7

161. Alphaeus Hunton, "Today's Guest Column: The Westbrook Pegler Of Negro Journalism," *Daily Worker*, March 8, 1945, 7 and Hunton, "Today's Guest

liberation. He called for "a New Deal for colonial and dependent peoples." He called for freedom from "imperialist bondage." To Hunton, colonialism "is a synonym for social stagnation because colonies can only be profitable to a minority of foreign investors or immigrant settlers under conditions which are socially and economically disadvantageous to the native inhabitants." He also reminded *Daily Worker* readers that at "one time Negro slaves represented the most profitable export commodity; later it was such things as gold, diamonds, copper, oil and rubber." Essentially, colonialism was "shortsighted and selfish production for profit"; those were the "inevitable, essential characteristics of colonialism," he concluded.[162]

In his first column of 1945, Hunton again emphasized "that many millions of colonial peoples all over the world are thinking...not only of the end of the war but of the time when they can be free from imperialist domination." However, he added, they understand "liberation depends in the first place upon the defeat of the fascist enemy," though this "will not of itself solve their problems." As the war was nearing its end, he criticized colonial administrators who were "notoriously lacking in specific goals and plans for the advancement of their governed subjects." This was a systemic flaw, based on the "stagnant character of the colonial regime." He called for a United Nations colonial independence policy centered on "specific goals...within specific time limits." If such a policy could be won, he argued, "it will mean a real New Year and New Deal for the hundreds of millions of colonial peoples."[163]

To Hunton, the "annihilation of fascism and the continued effective functioning of the United Nations coalition, strengthened by a united world labor movement," was then the route to liberation. He was hopeful that the Atlantic Charter, with its promise that "men in all the lands may live out their lives in freedom from fear and want," would be applied to the colonies; he also emphasized the Charter's third principle: "the right of all

---

Column: Lippmann Sees Colonies Through Col. Blimp's Glasses," *Daily Worker,* March 29, 1945, 7

162. Alphaeus Hunton, "Today's Guest Column: A New Deal for Colonial And Dependent Peoples," *Daily Worker,* November 23, 1944, 7

163. Alphaeus Hunton, "Today's Guest Column: Colonial Peoples Look Forward as 1945 Opens," *Daily Worker,* January 4, 1945, 7

peoples to choose the form of government under which they will live." By reminding *Daily Worker* readers that slavery in the U.S. was defeated, in part, with international support, Hunton articulated his internationalism in action. "The Abolitionist forces in America, looked to England for help in their struggle, and they received much practical support, financial and otherwise," he wrote. Just as Frederick Douglass, and others, looked abroad to England, Hunton, Robeson, Du Bois, as well as Benjamin Davis, Jr., William L. Patterson, Claudia Jones, Ferdinand Smith, and later Angela Davis and Charlene Mitchell, looked abroad to the Soviet Union and Eastern Europe; others looked to China. Hunton's observation was astounding. He wrote, "never before have the Negro and other oppressed peoples had such strong manifold allies as today,"[164] allies that are now, in the post-Cold War world, gone.

In April 1945, Hunton raised what on the surface appeared to be a "rather academic" question. He asked whether it would be possible for "the colonial peoples of Africa...to leap the stage of capitalist development and advance rapidly from feudalism to socialism." However, as he noted, "Africans themselves" were discussing this very question. Hunton cited the *West African Pilot*, the "most widely circulated" Nigerian newspaper, as evidence. The paper reported on a recent lecture ("The New Russia") at an evening school in Lagos. It was said: "We have every reason to feel that nothing but the complete socialization of our services and institutions can save us from the economic ruin we seem to be heading for at the moment. Colonialism and imperial exploitation are political and economic tenets that will have no place in our vocabulary of tomorrow. And if we are to benefit from the new Russia, if we are to obtain maximum

---

164. Alphaeus Hunton, "Today's Guest Column: Crimea Conference Heightens Role of Negro History Week," *Daily Worker*, February 15, 1945, 7 and Hunton, "Today's Guest Column: Self-Determination and Colonial Policy," *Daily Worker*, April 19, 1945, 7. For more on African Americans looking abroad for allies, see: Horne, *Black Liberation/Red Scare...*, Ibid.; Horne, *Black Revolutionary...*, Ibid.; Horne, *Black & Red...*, Ibid. Also, re China, see: Robeson Taj Frazier, *The East Is Black: Cold War China In The Black Radical Imagination* (Durham: Duke University Press, 2015). After the collapse of Eastern European socialism Horne asked, "Who Lost the Cold War?" His answer: "Africans and African Americans." And he cautioned against creating "what could well be called a 'Richard Pryor School of History' that causes us to celebrate what should be mourned." See: Horne, "Who Lost the Cold War? Africans and African Americans," *Diplomatic History*, Vol. 20, No. 4 (Fall 1996)

efficiency in the socialization of our institutions, the sooner we have the reins of administration of our country in our own hands the better."[165] Hunton read the colonial press voraciously; he devoured the information and compiled it into useful tidbit for his *Daily Worker* columns and the CAA's newsletters.

By May, Hunton was discussing another topic that would take on increasing importance after WWII and amid the emergence of the Cold War: the question of "U.S. control of island bases" in the Pacific. As he noted, if "this kind of discussion is not soon squelched, it will of course, result in side-tracking agreement on any effective plan of international action for bringing progress and freedom to colonial peoples for the sake of world security." Instead, it will lead to "renewed imperialist rivalries."[166] U.S. imperialism coupled with reflexively violent anti-communism in the region had devastating, horrific consequences in the Philippines, Korea, Indonesia, Vietnam, and elsewhere.[167]

In some columns, Hunton uses third-person dialogue.[168] In others sarcasm and humor, mockingly creating fictitious dialogue among British aristocrats as they boasted about Malayan rubber profits. "I say, Smithers, bring me a brandy," Hunton mirthlessly joked.[169] He also referenced other Marxist authors, such as R. Palme Dutt.[170] National and local politics were always on his mind; in November 1945, he wrote a letter to President Truman.[171] He wrote about the

---

165. Alphaeus Hunton, "Today's Guest Column: Perspectives For Africa's Development," *Daily Worker,* April 5, 1945, 7

166. Alphaeus Hunton, "Today's Guest Column: Colonial Issues Won't Be solved By Strategic Bases," *Daily Worker,* May 17, 1945, 7

167. The impact of reflexively violent anti-communism in the Philippines, Korea, Indonesia, Vietnam, and elsewhere, is briefly discussed above. For an examination of how the U.S. has created the world's largest collection of foreign military bases, which have led to millions of deaths, see: David Vine, *The United States of War: A Global History of America's Endless Conflicts, from Columbus to the Islamic State* (Oakland: University of California Press, 2021)

168. Alphaeus Hunton, "Today's Guest Column: Conversation In the Colonies," *Daily Worker,* May 31, 1945, 7

169. Alphaeus Hunton, "Today's Guest Column: Col. Blimp Counts His Rubber Profits," *Daily Worker,* October 11, 1945, 7

170. Alphaeus Hunton, "Today's Guest Column: Value of Rereading Dutt's 'World Politics,'" *Daily Worker,* July 26, 1945, 7

171. Alphaeus Hunton, "An Appeal for Cacchione and Baker in Brooklyn," *Daily Worker,* October 18, 1945, 7 and Hunton, "Today's Guest Column: A Letter to The President," *Daily Worker,* November 1, 1945, 7

initial optimism of the British Labour Party victory in 1945 and the hopeful outlook in India, British Africa, and the British West Indies; he also wrote about how those hopes were dashed rather quickly.[172] In another column he made a point of highlighting the *Chicago Defender*'s interview of the Chinese Communist Tung Pi-wu, who was "sharply critical of the weak stand taken by the Kuomintang delegates on various critical issues during the earlier sessions of the [San Francisco UN] conference." According to Hunton, Pi-wu's pressure on the Chinese delegates "is believed to have influenced the gradual strengthening of the Chinese stand on colonial trusteeship." Even at this early juncture, signs were already appearing that the U.S., Britain, and other colonial powers were beginning to "side against the Soviet Union and China" and hinder peaceful, democratic pathways toward colonial independence.[173]

Hunton, however, was clear that the "weaknesses" in the World Charter drafted at the UN conference "should not be permitted to weaken the Negro's support" for the document as a whole. "We must keep the larger perspective clear," he added. The Charter "is not the end but merely the beginning of United Nations' planning for world security and peace," and in this regard a step forward. Hunton emphasized the importance of potential U.S. post-war collaboration with emerging colonial independence movements and leaders and noted that the "key test will be right here…[as] this country holds the decisive power" to support or hinder liberation movements globally. As discussed, unfortunately, the latter proved to be the case. Hunton again raised the issue of "unilateral control of 'strategic' areas in the Pacific…as though the U.S. alone had the job of maintaining world peace." This, of course, was a "thinly disguised program of imperialist expansion," which would cost tens of millions of lives in the coming decades. Hunton also recognized that the "European powers will take their cue as to their colonial policies from the United States." This also proved to be the case. Domestically, he urged "the most alert progressive elements in this country

172. Alphaeus Hunton, "Today's Guest Column: Colonies Await Action By British Labor Cabinet," *Daily Worker*, August 2, 1945, 7, and Hunton "Today's Guest Column: Laborites' Statement On Colonial Policy," *Daily Worker*, August 9, 1945, 7,

173. Alphaeus Hunton, "Today's Guest Column: Chinese Communist Interviewed by Negro Press," *Daily Worker*, June 7, 1945, 7

to recognize and live up to their responsibility for mobilizing public opinion so that our government will throw its influence on the side of self-determination and independence for all colonial peoples, as demanded by the Soviet Union and all anti-imperialist states."[174]

In the August 16, 1945, issue of the *Daily Worker*, Hunton makes a passing remark about the "breath-taking sequence of events during this historic month, bringing the Japanese fascists to their knees," but does not elaborate; in fact, he quickly pivots to continue a weeks-long discussion of the British Labour Party's policy toward the colonies.[175] To anyone in 1945, Hunton's inference would have been obvious. However, to readers today it may not be clear. Hunton is writing about the dropping of the atomic bombs on Hiroshima (August 6) and Nagasaki (August 9), in which it is estimated that a combined 210,000 people perished, mostly civilians.[176] Hunton's passing remark is troubling and in many ways contradicts his life-long dedication to the liberation of peoples of color. Written during a time of cataclysmic war, today we cannot fully comprehend the death and destruction brought by both the Allied and Axis powers, nor can we minimize the horrendous loss of life due to the dropping of the atomic bombs on Hiroshima and Nagasaki.[177]

---

174. Alphaeus Hunton, "Guest Column: The Charter and the Colonial Countries," *Daily Worker,* July 3, 1945, 12. No reason is given in the *DW* as to the slight change in column title and page number.

175. Alphaeus Hunton, "Today's Guest Column: Laborites' Colonial Policy Can Be Changed," *Daily Worker,* August 16, 1945, 7. In the same issue as Hunton's column at least one *Daily Worker* reader considered the development and use of atomic weapons a "Great Advance." To him, the "harnessing of atomic energy is the natural development – for progress of a changing society." See: "Atomic Bomb, Great Advance," Dan Davis (letter to the editor), *Daily Worker,* Ibid.

176. The first major reference to the hundreds of thousands of dead, dying, and wounded civilians in Japan in the *Daily Worker* was in the August 23 issue, which reprinted a United Press report. See: "500,000 Casualties From Atomic Bombs, Tokyo Says," *Daily Worker,* August 23, 1945, 8

177. Early *Daily Worker* reportage on the use of atomic bombs was mixed. Some articles tried to explain the science; others boasted of the contributions of Communists and workers to the development of the technology; still other articles expressed awe, cautioned that the "war is not over," that the "atombomb [sic] didn't win the war," and that the technology was too important for "private ownership." See: J.B.S. Haldane, "2 French Communists Pioneered in Atomic Energy" and "American Labor Contributed Its Share in Creating Atombomb [sic]," *Daily*

By late-August, the *Atlanta Daily World*, the *Chicago Defender*, and the *Baltimore Afro-American*, among other leading African American publications, had denounced the dropping of the atomic bombs; many wondered why the bombs had been used on the Japanese – a people of color – and not on Germans? Langston Hughes and Du Bois quickly joined the chorus of protest; even the otherwise moderate NAACP seemed to be ahead of Hunton in criticizing the use of atomic weapons.[178] By early-September, first-hand reports were published describing the horror. Wilfred Burchett's account ("The Atomic Plague") was published in the London *Daily Express* on September 5.[179] By mid-September, Hunton would have been aware of this article. Significantly, Hunton does not analyze the horrific toll the bombs took on Japanese civilians, nor does he provide a deeper analysis of the potential impact the use of atomic weapons might have on U.S. or Soviet geo-politics in the region in his remaining *Daily Worker* columns, though he did question the validity of "retaining exclusive knowledge of how to make atomic bombs and other weapons" in his letter to Truman.[180] The August-September CAA *New Africa* newsletter also neglects to mention the dropping of the atomic bombs and their impact.[181]

As is well-known, U.S. Communists were not immune to anti-Japanese jingoism and were also silent about the internment of Japanese Americans during the war, including the internment of

---

Worker, August 8, 1945, 4; "Challenge to Humanity – Your Future and Atomic Power," *Daily Worker*, August 8, 1945, 6; "Humanity's Future And Atomic Power," and "Private Ownership Can't Be Trusted With Atombomb [sic]," *Daily Worker*, August 12, 1945, 3; "Scientists Ask Security Body Control Atombomb [sic]," *Daily Worker*, August 13, 1945, 5; "Fur Dyers Urge United Nations Own Atombomb [sic]," *Daily Worker*, August 14, 1945, 9; and "'Atombomb [sic] Didn't Win War,'" *Daily Worker*, August 17, 1945, 2

178. Intondi, *African Americans Against The Bomb…*, Ibid., 12-16, 22

179. For an analysis of Wilfred Burchett's first-hand account (as the first Western journalist to reach Hiroshima), see: Richard Tanter, "Voice and Silence in the First Nuclear War: Wilfred Burchett and Hiroshima," *The Asia-Pacific Journal*, Vol. 3, Issue 8 (August 2005) and George Burchett and Nick Shimmin (eds), *Rebel Journalism: The Writings of Wilfred Burchett* (Cambridge: Cambridge University Press, 2007)

180. Hunton, "A Letter…," Ibid.

181. See: *New Africa*, Vol. 4, No. 8 (August-September 1945)

Japanese Communists.[182] Some Communists argued, the "atomic bomb hit Japan on the 'head' with a terrific impact. But aside from its 'head,' Japan still has a mighty big 'belly' on the continent of Asia. This 'belly' is practically immune to atomic bombs," hence the need for Soviet mobilization in the region.[183] A *Daily Worker* letter to the editor published at the end of August and written by "Just Another Army Wife," urged readers to "start remembering Pearl Harbor" and asked: "Don't the 'despicable barbaric' crimes of the Japanese against our own American boys worry you any? Have you ever seen our casualty list?" Apparently, this *DW* reader had little sympathy for dead and dying Japanese civilians. "As far as the atomic bomb is concerned…thank your lucky stars that Tokyo didn't discover the bomb first," she concluded.[184] As Gerald Horne has documented, there were considerable attempts to create pro-Japanese sentiment, especially among African Americans, before and during the war[185] – a sentiment at odds with Hunton and the CPUSA's win-the-war-at-all-cost line. Communists attempted to counter these overtures; one pamphlet from 1938 published by the CPUSA's Negro Commission, asked "Is Japan the Champion of the Colored Races?," while highlighting the "latest crime[s] of the Japanese war lords" in China.[186] Nothing can be said to excuse the CPUSA's appeasement of

---

182. For example, see: Tim Wheeler, "Karl Yoneda and Elaine Black – star-crossed lovers in a class war," *People's World*, November 19, 2020, https://www.peoplesworld.org/article/karl-yoneda-and-elaine-black-star-crossed-lovers-in-a-class-war/ and "Obituaries: Elaine Black Yoneda, 81: 'The Red Angel' of the 1930s," *Los Angeles Times*, May 30, 1988. It should be noted, despite the treatment he received (from the U.S. government and the CPUSA) Karl Yoneda still served with honor in the armed forces as an intelligence officer in the Pacific during WWII.

183. A Veteran Commander, "This Is the Payoff," *Daily Worker*, August 9, 1945, 2

184. Just Another Army Wife, "Thank Our Stars U.S. Had Bomb," *Daily Worker*, August 30, 7. It should be noted, there is a disclaimer at the bottom of the page that reads: "The opinions expressed in these letters are those of the readers and not necessarily of the paper…" It should also be noted, the *DW* was at this time read by a much more diverse array of people, not necessarily Marxists; its readership likely included people less refined in the tactful language of Marxism-Leninism, which the editors saw as reflecting its then growing status and appeal.

185. See: Gerald Horne, *Race War!: White Supremacy and the Japanese Attack on the British Empire* (New York: New York University Press, 2004) and Horne, *Facing The Rising Sun: African Americans, Japan, and the Rise of Afro-Asian Solidarity* (New York: New York University Press, 2018)

186. Theodore Bassett, A.W. Berry, Cyril Briggs, James W. Ford, Harry Haywood, and the Negro Commission of the National Committee of the Communist

racism. By August 13, CPUSA leader William Z. Foster declared the dropping of the atomic bombs "precipitated upon the world a major political problem. This has to do with the control of this new, almost fantastic instrument of power." While he warned that "such a terrific power cannot be left in the hands of reactionaries," he did not mention the incredible loss of civilian life in Japan.[187] By November, Robeson was quoted in the *Daily Worker* as saying, "Reliance upon might, armaments, military bases and atomic bombs will not help us toward [the] goal" of a world of "peace and security."[188] By December, a *DW* reader suggested starting a petition to ban the manufacture of atomic bombs.[189] By January 1946, Hunton, along with CPUSA leader James S. Allen, among others, spoke on "Japan and the Colonies" at a Jefferson School of Social Science sponsored event[190]; it is unclear if he spoke out against the loss of civilian life at this event, though. At this point, we can only speculate on Hunton's silence in the *DW* regarding the use of atomic bombs in Japan. His reticence on this, as well as the Khrushchev revelations documenting Stalin's crimes against socialism and the Soviet people,[191] complicate our understanding of him as a person. More research (of unpublished personal correspondences, etc.)[192] may shed light on

Party, USA, *Is Japan the Champion of the Colored Races? The Negro's Stake in Democracy* (New York: Workers Library Publishers, August 1938)

187. William Z. Foster, "The Politics of the Atombomb [sic]," *Daily Worker,* August 13, 1945, 5

188. Paul Robeson, "'No Real Minorities in USSR' – Paul Robeson," *Daily Worker,* November 22, 1945, 7

189. Mrs. J. Fenster, "Suggest Petition Against Making of Atomic Bomb," *Daily Worker,* December 13, 1945, 7

190. "An Institute on America and the Far East Program...[advertisement]," *Daily Worker,* January 20, 1946, 13. It is unclear if Hunton spoke on the use of atomic bombs in Japan and their devastating impact.

191. For example, Hunton published *Decision in Africa* in 1957, after Khrushchev's so-called "secret speech." Perhaps unsurprisingly (since the book was published by International Publishers, a publisher closely aligned with the CPUSA), he does not mention human rights abuses in the Soviet Union; he also welcomes an invitation to travel to Eastern Europe in the late 1950s and early 1960s, apparently without hesitation.

192. While I have read some of Alphaeus and Dorothy Hunton's personal correspondences, they are primarily about the publication of *Decision in Africa* and/or from the mid-1960s while they were living in Ghana and Alphaeus was working on the *Encyclopedia Africana* at DuBois' invitation. A future project will explore Hunton's personal correspondences in more detail.

the question of whether Hunton had unexpressed, hidden feelings regarding this loss of life.

In his August 23 column Hunton continues to hammer away at a familiar theme, U.S. "control over a vast chain of islands in the Pacific, including 'specific and substantial rights' to American bases on islands belonging to other Allied powers as well as outright domination of Japanese-owned and mandated islands." These plans, he wrote, "have been brewing in Washington for a long time." Again, with keen insight, he noted, "progressive forces in America have paid far too little attention to this aspect of our foreign policy,"[193] a foreign policy that would have devastating consequences. Hunton's next column continued to expand on this theme. He ominously noted, a House Naval Affairs Sub-Committee report declared that the U.S. "should take outright the Japanese mandated islands" and secure "full title" to bases on other Pacific islands now owned by Great Britain, France, Australia, New Zealand, Portugal, Chile, and the Netherlands. Of course, "this policy of U.S. domination in the Pacific" was asserted "for the protection of the United States…[and] those who yell loudest for American expansion in the Pacific" are the same people who "say that we 'cannot trust the Soviet Union.'"[194] Again, Hunton's insights foreground decades of U.S. foreign policy in the region.

By summer 1945, as it became increasingly clear that Truman had no intention of continuing Roosevelt's approach to the Soviet Union and the colonies, the tone in Hunton's *DW* columns shifts dramatically.[195] Gone is the optimism that the war-time alliance would hold. Gone is the hope that the principles set forth in the Atlantic Charter would create a democratic pathway to independence for the colonies. Also, as mentioned earlier, the British Labour Party failed to live up to Hunton's initial optimistic view. Regarding India, "the touchstone of colonial independence in the

---

193. Alphaeus Hunton, "Today's Guest Column: Handling of Colonies Will Be Key Test," *Daily Worker*, August 23, 1945, 7

194. Alphaeus Hunton, "Today's Guest Column: Danger's in U.S. Pacific Policy," *Daily Worker*, August 30, 1945, 7

195. Hunton's monthly *New Africa* "Editorial" took a similar turn. He writes, "The hope and faith which the people of Africa and Asia had in America when Roosevelt was alive is now at low ebb," though he was still hopeful that the U.S. could still "regain its position of leadership in the cause of world-wide democracy…" See: Alphaeus Hunton, "Editorial," *New Africa*, Vol. 4, No. 7 (July 1945)

east, a very disturbing and disappointing prospect is provided by the British Labor [sic] government's stupidity and effrontery," as it betrayed early hopes for a different colonial policy. Additionally, Hunton noted the "infamous policy of Gen. [John R.] Hodge in permitting Japanese authorities to continue the administration of affairs in Korea." Further, "Japanese tanks and machine guns last week" were allowed to surround "a mass rally of 10,000 people who raised the demand for the freedom of Java," a precursor of the horrors to come in Indonesia. Hunton did not mince words. "The time is now for action, and the first step in getting action – so far as this country is concerned – is for the American people to demand a clear and forthright statement from their government as to what it plans to do about the future of the colonial peoples of Asia and the Pacific."[196]

Expanding on the "dastardly British slaughter of Indonesians" in Java, Hunton asked why "should Americans and the people of every other country be concerned." His answer: "[T]hat island is today the test of whether the imperialist powers have any solution other than brute force," other than mass murder. Hunton continued, the "struggle of the Indonesians is the same as that of colonial peoples throughout Asia and Africa. The degree of intensity of the struggle varies in these countries, but the fundamental issue at stake is the same everywhere – freedom, freedom to live and order their own lives."[197]

At the heart of this collection is the belief that colonial peoples – with the aid of Communists – shared this one desire, freedom, a desire that was often thwarted by the reflexively violent, barbaric, brutal ideology of anti-communism.

Three years after Hunton's columns end, the *Daily Worker* published a letter by Hunton and Louis Burnham, a fellow Communist and leader of the Southern Negro Youth Congress.[198] The letter dated August 9, 1949, expresses solidarity with the indicted Smith Act defendants, "the Twelve" top leaders of the CPUSA. This letter is significant for what it tells us about how Hunton saw Communists in the fight for African American equality in

---

196. Alphaeus Hunton, "Today's Guest Column: The East Is Fed Up With Promises," *Daily Worker,* September 27, 1945, 7

197. Alphaeus Hunton, "Today's Guest Column: Fate of Indonesia Signpost Of Future – It's Up to the People," *Daily Worker,* November 15, 1945, 7

198. Kelley, *Hammer And Hoe...,* Ibid., 221-222

the struggle for democracy. They note, the "record will show that the fight for the freedom of the Communists is a fight for their right to fight for the rights of Negroes." This neglected statement is profound. Though not explicit, like other Communists Hunton saw African Americans as part of a national minority brutally oppressed by the ruling class. As such, he and Burnham focus on the "odious legal proceedings," reminiscent of the "lynch-dominated court which daily convict Negroes in the South of 'crimes' they have never committed."[199] To them, Communists and African Americans both were convicted without ever having committed actual crimes. In this they shared a common persecution. As a result, they also shared a common struggle and a common enemy, a partial explanation for Hunton's decision to join the CPUSA in 1936.

*   *   *

This year marks an important moment for Alphaeus Hunton and his legacy. The appearance of the present volume, *"The Cancer of Colonialism": W. Alphaeus Hunton, Black Liberation, and the* Daily Worker, *1944-1946*, coincides with the republishing of Dorothy Hunton's *Alphaeus Hunton: Unsung Valiant,*[200] as well as Hunton's *Decision In Africa: Sources of Current Conflict*[201] – all from International Publishers. Together, they signal a renewed interest in Hunton and his role in the struggle for African American equality, Black liberation, and socialism. It could not come at a better time. With a new generation of activists taking to the streets demanding an end to police violence and terror[202]; with Black Lives Matter

199. Louis Burnham and Alphaeus Hunton, "They Second Ben Gold's Motion: 'Fight for 12 is Fight for Negroes.'" *Daily Worker,* August 9, 1949, 5

200. This volume includes a new Foreword by scholar Charisse Burden-Stelly. See: Dorothy Hunton, *Alphaeus Hunton: Unsung Valiant* (New York: International Publishers, 2021)

201. This volume includes both a new Foreword and Afterword by historians Timothy V Johnson and David Henry Anthony III, respectively. See: Alphaeus Hunton, *Decision In Africa: Sources of Current Conflict* (New York: International Publishers, 2021)

202. Not only are a new generation of activists taking to the streets, but as the *New York Times* reports "Black Lives Matter May be the Largest Movement in U.S. History." Larry Buchanan, Quoctrung Bui, and Jugal K. Patel, July 3, 2020. They note, it is estimated that "about 15 million to 26 million people in the United

activists, such as Congresswoman Cori Bush (MO-1),[203] winning elections; with racists statues and monuments being torn down and replaced; and with an increased interest in socialism,[204] now is a perfect time to explore the life of W. Alphaeus Hunton, a towering figure[205] in the struggle for African American equality, Black liberation, and socialism.

July 2021

States have participated in demonstrations over the death of George Floyd and others in recent weeks."

203. It should be noted that now-Congresswoman Cori Bush is no stranger to the question of socialism. In August of 2018, she joined a panel discussion with this author and Maria Svart, national director of Democratic Socialists of America, among others on "What Is Socialism?" at the St. Louis Workers' Education Society, a non-profit education organization and community center. Also, in fall 2019, Bush endorsed this author, a national leader of the CPUSA, in the St. Louis (Ward 14) Aldermanic elections, despite red-baiting and anti-communism, as did the now-Mayor of St. Louis Tishaura Jones, the first African American women to hold the position; I lost by only 52 votes. Perhaps, as St. Louis native Gerald Horne has argued, anti-communism remains less impactful among people of color who have fewer options for allies.

204. When *Teen Vouge* is writing positively about socialism, you know a sea change has taken place. Additionally, DSA's membership is now hovering around 100,000, something unseen since the CPUSA's 1930s-1940s peak; while CPUSA membership has grown, it has not increased as dramatically; according to a recent report, there are currently 75 functioning CPUSA clubs. The CPUSA's daily online publication, the *People's World*, today reaches roughly 3.2 million readers annually, a significant accomplishment given the history of anti-communism in the U.S. See: Samuel Arnold, "What Is Democratic Socialism and Why Is It Growing More Popular in the U.S.?," *Teen Vouge*, May 1, 2020; "DSA Recruitment Drive: Kickoff and 100K Pledge Training," Tuesday October 6, 2020, https://www.dsausa.org/calendar/dsa-100k-recruitment-drive-kickoff-and-training-2/; Rossana Cambron, "Org Dept Report to the National Committee (outline) rev 4/12/21"; and Chauncey Robinson, "3 MILLION REACHED! – PW website traffic 2020," internal reports in author's possession.

205. Hunton was considered "lanky," "tall, gaunt, and handsome" by some. See: Horne's "Foreword," in Pecinovsky, *Let Them Tremble...*, Ibid. and David Levering Lewis, *A Biography: W.E.B. Du Bois* (New York: Holt Paperbacks, 2009), 9

W. Alphaeus Hunton

The National Negro Congress, the Council on African Affairs, and Black Liberation – a short biography

By Tony Pecinovsky

It was early 1966. A coup led by a group of reactionary military leaders determined to stoke ethnic rivalries and build their "financial empires,"[1] had recently deposed Kwame Nkrumah, the charismatic socialist first president of the independent African nation Ghana. As an international leader of a "new, more militant generation of Pan-Africanists," Nkrumah was "determined to disprove those who doubted the ability of Africans to govern themselves."[2] This was a goal revolutionary leaders throughout the continent strove toward. The coup, backed by imperialist powers and supported by the CIA,[3] was a setback for independence in Africa, an attempt to roll back the gains then being made by national liberation movements throughout the world – with the aid of ascendant socialism.[4]

---

1. W. J. Tettey, K. P. Puplampu and B. J. Berman (eds), *Critical Perspectives in Politics and Socio-Economic Development in Ghana* (Leiden: Brill, 2003), 120

2. Laumann, *Colonial Africa…*, Ibid., 62-65

3. George B. Murphy, Jr., "William Alphaeus Hunton: His Roots In Black America," *Freedomways*, Vol. 10, No. 3, 249

4. For example, see: Horne, *White Supremacy Confronted…*, Ibid. For an analysis of Soviet and China competition to win over national liberation movements, see: Jeremy Friedman, *Shadow Cold War: The Sino-Soviet Competition for the Third World* (Chapel Hill: University of North Carolina Press, 2015). For an analysis of Cuban solidarity with African national liberation movements, see: Piero Gleijeses, *Conflicting Missions: Havana, Washington, and Africa, 1959-1976* (Chapel Hill: University of North Carolina Press, 2002)

In an "effort to attack notions of white superiority and black inferiority,"[5] Nkrumah – in late 1961 – invited the Pan-African intellectual and now Communist Party, USA member W.E.B. Du Bois to Ghana to oversee the "major work" of the *Encyclopedia Africana*. This was "a project Du Bois had contemplated and longed for for at least fifty years," and was considered by some to potentially be "the crowning achievement of his long life," a life full of tremendous accomplishments. As "head of a new Negro Encyclopedia," Du Bois was "provided funds, a home and an office," a secretary and "at least five" research assistants.[6] However, Du Bois – now 94 years old – needed more help with the monumental task, which is why in early 1962 he invited his friend the activist-scholar William Alphaeus Hunton to join him in Ghana. By July 1962, Du Bois' health had declined dramatically, requiring hospitalization. He left Hunton in charge of the *Encyclopedia* as its Secretariat,[7] a position he would hold until the 1966 coup.

According to Hunton, Nkrumah and Du Bois both saw the *Encyclopedia* "as a powerful instrument for the African peoples' achievement of their cultural renaissance." Additionally, there "was a spreading consciousness that the liberation of Africa was not simply a matter of political emancipation but entailed also freeing the African mind from an ideology that fostered servitude and dependence," of which the *Encyclopedia* could play an integral role. Hunton clarified: This was not to be a "universal encyclopedia like the *Britannica* or *Collier's*." Rather, it was "frankly Afro-centric...concerned with the African continent, but at the same time giving due attention to Africa's relationship to the outside world." Hunton saw the *Encyclopedia* as "the welding of real economic and political unity, the one thing that spells the salvation of Africa."[8]

5. Clarence G. Contee, "W.E.B. Du Bois and the Encyclopedia Africana," *The Crisis*, November 1970, 379

6. Gerald Horne, *Black & Red...*, Ibid., 344; Murphy, Jr., Ibid.; and Contee, Ibid.

7. Herbert Aptheker (ed), *The Correspondence of W. E. B. Du Bois: Volume III Selections, 1944-1963* (Amherst: University of Massachusetts Press, 1997), 458, 459

8. W. Alphaeus Hunton, "Recapturing A Buried Past," *World Magazine* (reprinted in *Daily World*), February 21, 1970, M-3

He poured himself into the project. Within days of arriving in Ghana, while his "permanent lodging" and contract were still being finalized, Hunton was already working. He interviewed scores of office assistants, stenographers, and typists. Apparently, there was a minor drama regarding the *Encyclopedia* letter-head. "I imagine Shirley [Graham Du Bois] will tell you the story," Hunton wrote to his friend and mentor. "Suffice to say that I told Prof. [Ernest A.] Boateng that I had instructions from you to print the letter-head in the form you had prepared, and that is the way it is being done." Hunton then informed Du Bois of his plans for the "next two or three weeks," which included compiling a list of guests to be invited to "our conference" in Accra, writing "on your behalf to those persons in Africa who responded to your letters with concrete offers of cooperation" on the *Encyclopedia*. He hoped to "inform them of the establishment of the Secretariat...[see] what steps can be taken by them toward organizing research units where they are," and inform them "that they will shortly be advised of plans for an initial conference in Accra." Hunton wanted to pull together "historians, anthropologists, and other scholars resident in Africa...to exchange views on and plan collectively the preparatory work" for the *Encyclopedia*. "These things, together with getting the office prepared and in operation, will keep me occupied, I imagine, until you come home – an event which all of us here await with eagerness."[9]

In short, Hunton did the unglamorous grunt work. He built "the conceptual, human and material framework" for the projected ten volume *Encyclopedia*. He interviewed and organized the staff, created lists of entries, recruited contributors, and launched a monthly bulletin to keep interested partners and contributors informed on the progress of the work. Due to Du Bois' declining health, Hunton was primarily responsible for getting the project up and running. The *Encyclopedia* project had a home before Hunton did. In another letter to Du Bois, Hunton noted that an "Office Assistant (Typist-Stenographer)" had been hired; that the office had "been completely re-painted inside and out, and looks very nice...[though] no telephones have yet been installed." Hunton also reported on office furniture, desks, typewriters, a

---

9. UMass-Amherst, Special Collections, W.E.B. Du Bois Papers, Box 155: Series 1, 1A: Letter from Hunton to Du Bois, April 15, 1962

mimeograph machine, filing cabinets, and "miscellaneous office supplies." He had lunch with Professor Thomas Hodgkin, director of the Institute of African Studies; they discussed initial plans for the Accra Conference and the forming "of a small group... [to] lay the basis, in terms of broad sponsorship and ideas on the scope, form, etc., of the proposed *Encyclopedia*."[10] Hunton was a work horse, resolute, focused.

Even as his mentor's health deteriorated, Hunton worked tirelessly. Shortly after Du Bois' death – in August 1963 – he "embarked on an exhausting continental tour to organize corresponding secretariats" in other African nations.[11] Hunton envisioned a project embraced and supported by the entire African diaspora. He told *Freedomways* readers, "We of course had to start from zero, nothing comparable to what we planned ever having been published."[12] Unfortunately, as Hunton was working relentlessly, busily planning content entries and organizing a "committee of specialists from various parts of Africa,"[13] the coup ousted his patron Nkrumah and dashed his dream of completing Du Bois' last and most ambitious work.

Writing from Ghana, Hunton's wife Dorothy told her friend Esther Cooper Jackson,[14] "A [Alphaeus] and I are both adjusting to

---

10. Apparently, the minor drama surrounding the letter-head was resolved prior to Hunton gaining "permanent lodging." The letter to Du Bois was dated May 1; as Hunton indicated, a "bungalow for our residence has been made available" and we will "probably be moving later this week or next," i.e., mid-May, "luckily" with a working phone. There also seemed to still be some lingering disagreements regarding the terms of Hunton's employment and the name "Encyclopedia Africana Project" instead of "Secretariat." See: UMass-Amherst, Special Collections, W.E.B. Du Bois Papers, Box 155: Series 1, 1A: Letter from Hunton to Du Bois, May 1, 1962, and James T. Campbell, *Middle Passages: African American Journeys to Africa, 1787-2005* (New York: The Penguin Group, 2007), 341

11. Campbell, *Middle Passages...*, Ibid., and *William Alphaeus Hunton Papers, 1926-1967*, New York Public Library Archives & Manuscripts: Biographical / Historical Information, http://archives.nypl.org/scm/20646

12. W. Alphaeus Hunton, "Recapturing A Buried Past," *World Magazine* (reprinted in *Daily World*), February 21, 1970, M-3

13. Campbell, Ibid., 359 and Contee, Ibid., 379

14. Esther Cooper Jackson was a leader of the Southern Negro Youth Congress in the 1940s; she married James E. Jackson, a CPUSA leader; in 1961, she also helped co-found and became the managing editor of *Freedomways*, the quarterly journal of Black liberation, in which Hunton was an associate editor. See: Haviland, *James and Esther Cooper Jackson...*, Ibid.

our new way of life since the coup." She noted that many of their friends had left. "[O]ur circle has become a mere dot," she added dejectedly. "However, we are carrying on, hoping conditions will improve." Research on the *Encyclopedia* was progressing at a much "slower pace," she added. "A is [now] only an area editor, and his new contract is for only one year, an unpleasant situation, but he's making the best of it."[15] Of course, Hunton had no way of knowing how things would soon change – for the worse. "Right now I'm in a very depressed mood," she continued to Esther Cooper. "Three days ago the [Ghanaian] C.I.D. [Criminal Investigation Department] had a warrant to search our house. First they made a search of A's office and then came here…looking for what, I don't know." Somewhat jokingly Mrs. Hunton added, "it would take them weeks to go through all the [research] material we have," not the mere hours they spent rummaging through papers.

Reflecting on the persecution they had experienced in the United States during the McCarthy era – a partial reason for accepting DuBois' invitation to relocate to Ghana – Dorothy commented, "I thought we were through with that when we left the states, but one never knows." With Nkrumah's ousting Hunton became subversive, though "we have done nothing but mind our business and work."[16] That their work supported national liberation and socialism branded them enemies of U.S. imperialism and by default the post-coup Ghanaian ruling class. That fall, Mrs. Hunton was writing Esther Cooper again, "a hurried note to let you know that we have been deported." Alphaeus and Dorothy, in a "mad scramble," packed. Due to Alphaeus' health, they were faced with the "nerve racking suspense" of jail or, hopefully, becoming passengers on a passing freight ship. Ghanaian officials quickly ordered a Farrell Lines freighter, the appropriately named *African Lightening*, to take them on. "So ended our nearly five years in Ghana," Dorothy concluded. Reeling from the trauma, she added, "We are still a bit numb from the experience,"[17] an

15. NYU, TAM 347, Box 8, Folder 5: Letter from Dorothy Hunton to Cooper-Jackson, no date (c. early 1966)

16. NYU, TAM 347, Box 8, Folder 5: Letter from Dorothy Hunton to Cooper-Jackson, August 28, 1966

17. NYU, TAM 347, Box 8, Folder 16: Letter from Dorothy Hunton to Cooper-Jackson, December 8, 1966

experience not unlike the political repression Alphaeus Hunton faced throughout his political life.

Dorothy Hunton would later recall the deportation as a "despicable, humiliating, unwarranted act from which Alphaeus never recovered...Stunned and deeply hurt, denied the opportunity to continue his life's work for which he had given his all, he closed up. That was the beginning of the end for my beloved Alphaeus," she noted at a 1980 Trans-Africa event honoring Hunton.[18]

After a month long voyage, they made their way to Staten Island where Alphaeus was interviewed by the *New York Times*. He called the expulsion "unnerving and humiliating," but optimistically added that the *Encyclopedia* "was a pan-African project, not a Ghanaian one," which he hoped to continue working on. At the time of the coup, he continued, "articles were already being collected for the first volume" and the "board had hoped to enlarge the staff from 11 to 55." Hunton had asked the Nkrumah government to "double the $40,000 budget." However, since the coup funding had increasingly become a point of contention.[19] According to Nkrumah, who had been in China during the coup, the *Encyclopedia* was "being deliberately broken up because of the principles and ideology which inspired it,"[20] namely, Black liberation and socialism, ideas Hunton had committed himself to three decades earlier. Hunton and Nkrumah, then a leader of the African Student Association, first met in April 1944 at a New York Council on African Affairs conference titled "Africa – New Perspectives,"[21] an "important precursor" to the 1945 Manchester Pan-African Congress. As a "vital connector" to earlier conferences and movements,[22] their meeting foreshadowed a coalescence of forces that resulted in a global campaign for African American equality, Black liberation, and socialism.

*   *   *

18. Dorothy Hunton, "African-studies pioneer honored," *Daily World*, July 3, 1980, 16

19. Alan S. Oser, "African Encyclopedia Still Alive, Scholar Ousted by Ghana Says," *New York Times*, January 29, 1967

20. Contee, "W.E.B. Du Bois and...," Ibid.

21. Hunton, *Alphaeus Hunton...*, Ibid., 58 and Campbell, *Middle Passages...*, Ibid., 337. For more on the CAA Conference, see: "Conference Urges International Action For African Progress," *New Africa*, Vol. 3, No. 5 (May 1944)

22. Swindall, *The Path To The...*, Ibid., 90

William Alphaeus Hunton, born in Atlanta, Georgia[23] on September 18, 1903, was a scholar-activist and life-long member of the Communist Party, USA. While still young he moved with his family to Brooklyn, where he finished high school.[24] He graduated from Howard University in 1924 and Harvard in 1926; afterward, he taught English at Howard and led the effort to organize that university's faculty into the American Federation of Teachers Local 440. While at Howard, he also studied for and received his Ph.D. from New York University in 1938.[25] After the Howard union victory, he urged the union and its members to engage in Washington, D.C.'s larger movements for social and economic justice. According to fellow Howard professor and Communist Doxey A. Wilkerson, Hunton not only helped to organize the union, but also "fought to sustain [it] as a viable instrument for academic and social progress." Wilkerson added, the activities of the union "extended far beyond the campus, in support of working men's struggles in many places," an indication of Hunton's leadership.[26]

*   *   *

23. As Swindall argues, "...Hunton's family had deep southern roots that had impacted his intellectual and political development." Like Robeson, and the Communists Councilman from Harlem Benjamin Davis, Jr., among others, slavery, abolitionism, and radical Republican traditions shaped Hunton's family, childhood, and adult activism. See: Swindall, *The Path To The...*, Ibid., 87-88 and Horne, *Black Liberation/Red Scare...*, Ibid.

24. For a brief overview of Hunton's family and early life, see: Von Eschen, *Race Against Empire...*, 57-60.

25. *William Alphaeus Hunton Papers...*, Ibid.; Von Eschen, *Race Against Empire...*, Ibid., 60; James Hunter Meriwether, *Proudly We Can Be Africans: Black Americans and Africa, 1935-1961* (Chapel Hill: University of North Carolina Press, 2002), 61; and Paul Finkelman (ed), *Volume 1 – Encyclopedia Of African American History, 1896 To The Present: From The Age Of Segregation To The Twenty-First Century* (New York: Oxford University Press, 2009), 475

26. Gellman, *Death Blow to Jim Crow...*, Ibid, 115 and Doxey A. Wilkerson, "William Alphaeus Hunton: A Life That Made A Difference," *Freedomways*, Vol. 10, No. 3 (Third Quarter, 1970), 254. In 1954, Ralph Bunche would accuse Hunton and Wilkerson of using "unfair tactics, involving a technicality," to keep his name off of the 1940 AFT Convention ballot; Bunche was running for National Vice President (against Wilkerson, the incumbent) on an anti-communist slate. See: Ralph Bunche, "Report denying Communist Party affiliation," Dept. of Special Collections / UCLA Library, Online Archive of California, https://oac. cdlib.org/view?docId=hb967nb7pm&chunk.id=div00001&brand=oac4&doc. view=entire_text

In 1936, Hunton attended the founding convention of the National Negro Congress in Chicago. Along with 800 delegates representing 550 organizations and roughly three million people, Hunton helped build what eventually became "a broad federation of some 3,000 civic, religious and fraternal organizations" committed to social, cultural, political, and economic equality for African Americans.[27]

Born out of a 1935 Howard University meeting between prominent African American leaders, including Socialist A. Phillip Randolph and Communist James W. Ford, the Congress reflected a "growing convergence of outlook between Communists and activist black intellectuals."[28] This was a convergence powerful enough to shake U.S. capitalism and its foundational cornerstone, white supremacy, to its core. Consequently, after the 1935 meeting Howard University was put in the government's crosshairs. Anti-communists attempted to "silence and actually shut down the university."[29] John P. Davis, head of the Joint Committee for National Recovery and the person primarily responsible for sponsoring the initial conference, had been a CPUSA member since at least the fall of 1935 and possibly "for longer than generally believed."[30] This added fuel to the government's investigative fire, especially, as he was "really [the person] running the National Negro Congress," not Randolph, the titular president.[31] While at a meeting in the "citadel of the Party's Negro policies – the Central Committee's Negro Commission," Davis "characterized the building of a broad NNC as 'a paramount task of the Party.'" That Davis was the only full-time NNC staff person with Communist secretaries, likely raised additional investigative eyebrows, as did his 1937 visit to the Soviet Union,[32] a tour that served to highlight

27. Mark Solomon, *The Cry Was Unity: Communists and African Americans, 1917-1936* (Jackson: University Press of Mississippi, 1998), 304 and *William Alphaeus Hunton Papers...*, Ibid.

28. Mark Naison, *Communists in Harlem during the Depression* (Chicago: University of Illinois Press, 2005), 177-178

29. Jonathan Holloway, *Lecture 12 – Depression and Double V* (continued) [February 17, 2010], Open Yale courses, http://oyc.yale.edu/transcript/111/afam-162

30. Glenda Gilmore, *Defying Dixie: The Radical Roots of Civil Rights, 1919-1950* (New York: W.W. Norton & Co., 2008), 308 and Solomon, Ibid., 303

31. Holloway, Ibid.

32. Solomon, Ibid., 303; Naison, Ibid., 183; and Gellman, Ibid., 155

socialism's role in bolstering African American equality. As the Chicago area African American party leader Claude Lightfoot wrote, "The Communist Party threw all of its forces at the national and local levels to help him [Davis] put it [the NNC Convention] together," including mundane, organizational tasks such as securing the Convention hall.[33]

Despite government harassment, the NNC organized for workers' rights, against fascism, and used "mass-protest tactics to challenge racial discrimination." Communists helped create a movement and organization "of national significance whose constituency and leadership extended considerably beyond the Party's ranks." Hunton was proud of the NNC's work, which he spent his life attempting to duplicate. As Mark Naison points out in *Communists in Harlem During the Depression*, while the NNC was not "promoted as a Communist initiative…[reds] played a significant, and possibly determinative role in setting the stage for the congress's creation."[34] Communists, like Hunton – who officially joined the party around this time[35] – "did not stand out politically." At the Congress' founding convention the keynote argued, "the Negro must combine with white labor and overthrow the existing order in order to wrest their common rights from capitalism which exploits them both," a sentiment shared by Communists who focused on grunt work. They "arranged meetings, handled correspondences and organized fund raising." In short, the CPUSA maintained a "low-keyed Party presence." And the NNC became "the embodiment" of the party's Popular Front strategy, and quite possibly, as party member Harry Haywood later recalled, "the greatest Black united front movement of the period."[36]

According to James W. Ford, the NNC "was conceived… [as a] rallying center for the Negro people to fight off greater oppression." It was an organizational center with the potential to align all "groupings among the Negro people," conservative, "middle-of-the-roaders," and leftists, including Communists. "We want, to the fullest extent," Ford continued, "to help make

33. Claude Lightfoot, *Chicago Slums…*, Ibid., 70

34. Naison, Ibid., 177-178

35. Von Eschen, *Race Against Empire…*, Ibid., 60 and Meriwether, *Proudly We Can…*, Ibid.

36. Naison, *Communists In Harlem…*, Ibid.; Horne, *Black Revolutionary…*, Ibid., 87; and Mildo Hall (ed), *A Black Communist…*, Ibid., 224

the [NNC] movement something that represents the broadest sections of the Negro people, an instrument for combatting the many evils which face the Negro people…We are interested in working with all who, like us want to reach the same goal," namely African American equality and Black liberation. For example, every Communist organization in Harlem, "from the Young Liberators, to the Unemployed Council to the ILD," helped to build the NNC,[37] while simultaneously organizing others – churches, fraternal groups, the YMCA, and NAACP – around a Popular Front platform. In a letter to Ford, the Indian Marxist and Comintern leader R. Palme Dutt called the Congress' founding "enormously encouraging and important." He wrote, that "a really representative Negro Congress, based in the U.S. and with wide international connections, could exercise a big and badly needed influence in world opinion." Front and center on Dutt's mind, and many of the NNC's leader's, was "the struggles of the peoples of Ethiopia against the foreign invader."[38]

Strategically, the Popular Front was understood to mean that Communists should embrace anyone willing to fight for workers' rights and African American equality. Advancing socialism was not then the main strategic goal. As a result, the party's acceptance among non-communists "reached unprecedented heights."[39] They had become a legitimate part of a shared political universe. Within five months of its founding, NNC councils existed in 26 cities and 70 chapters had been formed across the country.[40] Many African Americans like Hunton simultaneously joined the NNC and CPUSA and served to bolster an emerging Red-Black alliance less susceptible to anti-communism.

Hunton quickly ascended to NNC leadership. As a member of its national executive board, he led the Washington, D.C. chapter

---

37. Gunnar Myrdal, *An American Dilemma, Volume 2: The Negro Problem and Modern Democracy* (Harper & Row, Publishers / Transaction Publishers, 2009 / 1996), 817 and Naison, Ibid., 179-180

38. "R. Palme Dutte [sic] Greets Negro Congress in U.S.," *Daily Worker,* January 11, 1936, 6

39. Solomon, *The Cry Was…,* Ibid., 304

40. *The John P. Davis Collection: The Forgotten Civil Rights Leader*: Rare Pamphlets: John P. Davis Collection: General Rare Pamphlets Collection, http:// www.collection.johnpdaviscollection.org/

and chaired the Labor Committee; his comrade Wilkerson chaired the Civic Affairs Committee. An "astute political journalist," Hunton also joined the editorial board of the NNC's journal, *Congress View*. He led campaigns to "Blast Jim Crow Out of Washington" and, as he put it, "make the district budget serve the human needs of the community" through boycotts, pickets, demonstrations, petitions, and strikes. Hunton also "worked untiringly to bring Black workers into the trade unions."[41] The NNC directly challenged employment discrimination and police brutality and are part of a larger Black radical tradition that helped to inspire today's Black Lives Matter movement.

* * *

To many, it seemed like a new day with the birth of the NNC. A vibrant and energized organization was systematically exposing police violence and abuse, something Communists would continue to do through 1955 and then again into the 1970s and 1980s with William L. Patterson's Civil Rights Congress[42] and Charlene Mitchell's National Alliance Against Racist and Political Repression,[43] respectively. For example, when in late August 1936 Leonard Basey was shot dead by D.C. police officer Vivian H. Landrum, the NNC rallied and called for an indictment. The *Baltimore Afro-American* screamed *"KILLER-COP FREE."* It was reported that Basey was "the fortieth colored person shot to death by Metropolitan police since 1925" and that every officer involved "has been exonerated." The *Daily Worker* published a list of the murdered African Americans – "The Toll of Negro Dead Slain by Washington Police." The district attorney was apparently unbothered, telling Adam Lapin, *Daily Worker* Washington bureau chief, he was "not interested in the case." By November, the officer was retired with a pension. The D.C. NNC was enraged. They saw the early retirement as a slap in the face to the Black community, and perhaps a reward to the officer for

---

41. *William Alphaeus Hunton Papers…*, Ibid.; Wilkerson, "William Alphaeus…," Ibid.; Finkelman (ed), *Volume 1…*, Ibid., 475; and Hunton, *Alphaeus Hunton…*, Ibid., 47, 49

42. Gerald Horne, *Communist Front…*, Ibid. and Horne, *Black Revolutionary…*, Ibid.

43. Pecinovsky, *Let Them Tremble…*, Ibid., 75-116

maintaining the then prevailing racial order. The NNC lobbied for a House sub-committee investigation and formed the Joint Committee for Civil Rights in the District of Columbia, which sponsored a series of weekly radio broadcasts. Like the latter day BLM movement, Hunton and the NNC dramatically brought public pressure to bear against institutionalized racism and the misuse and abuse of police power. They organized a "public trial" condemning the killer cops and used "theatrics" to garner public attention and support.[44]

"Washington sets the pattern of discrimination against the Negro people," Hunton wrote. Its laws "establish the nation's unwritten laws by unofficial endorsement of, or passive indifference to practices of discrimination, segregation and brutal oppression."[45] Basey's murder was a case in point. That the "nation's unwritten laws" included a racial hierarchy designating African Americans as targets wasn't lost on Hunton or other Communists, who sought allies abroad powerful enough to compel concessions away from Jim Crow and police terror.[46] As Wilkerson would later recall, "there was one period of two or three months in which a Negro was shot by police on the average of once a week, usually in the back, and never with any punishment for the offending officers."[47] According to Adam Lapin, Basey "was murdered in cold blood because he was a Negro." To him, the "evidence proves beyond the shadow of a doubt the existence of a police reign of terror against the Negro people,"[48] a terror reminiscent of the assault inflicted daily upon Black lives still today.[49]

---

44. Wilkerson, "William Alphaeus…," Ibid., 255; Adam Lapin, "Capital Cops Kill 40 Negroes…Every Killer Has Gone Free," *Daily Worker,* October 13, 1936, 3; and Craig Simpson, "Shootings by DC Police Spark Fight Against Brutality, 1936-41," *Washington Area Spark,* http://washingtonspark.wordpress.com/tag/national-negro-congress/

45. Hunton, *Alphaeus Hunton…,* Ibid., 47

46. For example, see: Horne, *Black Revolutionary…,* Ibid., and Robeson Frazier, *The East Is Black…,* Ibid.

47. Wilkerson, "William Alphaeus…," Ibid.

48. Lapin, "Capital Cops Kill 40 Negroes…," Ibid.

49. This author lives just miles from Ferguson, Missouri where in August 2014 Michael Brown was shot and killed by police officer Darren Wilson; shortly after the killing of Brown massive protests erupted and the St. Louis Workers Education Society opened its doors to the National Lawyers Guild (as an intake center)

Shortly after the Basey shooting, the NNC with the aid of local Communists led several marches and organized a conference of more than 100 organizations at the Lincoln Temple Congregational Church. There, Hunton outlined several demands and announced a forthcoming mass meeting. The demands: removal of the police superintendent; denial of pension to the officer who shot and killed Basey; suspension and trial of other officers involved in recent shootings and police terror; and compensation for the victims. The next day, at least 1,200 people rallied.[50] As Erik S. Gellman argues in *Death Blow to Jim Crow: The National Negro Congress and the Rise of Militant Civil Rights*, Hunton "played an essential behind-the-scenes role in the police brutality campaign," and helped to build a broad-based, Black and white movement for social and economic justice.[51] Wilkerson, added, "Alphaeus was in the thick of all these and related campaigns…He generally worked quietly, sensing and doing what needed to be done, seldom making big speeches, and never seeking the headlines; but those of us who worked with him knew very well that he was the mainstay of the struggle."[52]

In October 1937, the second NNC Convention was held in Philadelphia. Nearly 1,200 delegates attended. The NNC's dramatic growth in the Black community centered on issues like police brutality and workers' rights and paralleled the growth of Black unionism generally; from 1936 to 1940 Black union

---

where they documented the police misconduct and abuse that took place during the protests; WES also housed nonviolent civil disobedience trainings. It should be noted, though small in number, CPUSA members were very much a part of the marches and protests, primarily through their unions: the Service Employees International Union, the Missouri State Workers Union, and the Coalition of Black Trade Unionists, all of which had Communists in the leadership and/or on staff at that time. Communists in other parts of the country continued in Hunton and the NNC's footsteps as well, which is partly why Samaria Rice – mother of slain African American youth Tamir Rice – was proud to speak at the CPUSA's 2019 National Convention in Chicago. See: Michelle Zacarias, "CPUSA encourages building unity from ground up in anti-oppression panel," *People's World*, June 26, 2019, https://www.peoplesworld.org/article/cpusa-encourages-building-unity-from-the-ground-up-in-anti-oppression-panel/

50. Wilkerson, "William Alphaeus…," Ibid., and Simpson, "Shootings by…," Ibid.

51. Gellman, *Death Blow to Jim Crow…*, Ibid., 130

52. Wilkerson, Ibid.

membership increased from 100,000 to 500,000.[53] The NNC and CPUSA were major factors in this upsurge. In early 1937, they – along with the IWO, the Urban League, and the Workers Alliance, among others – convened a "conference of Negro civic and fraternal leaders together with Negro organizers on the staff of the Steel Workers Organizing Committee." The conference's goal; to put "the entire Negro community behind a last minute spurt to complete the S.W.O.C. drive." Ford noted that the drive in steel was "important to the entire Negro people, and that its success would immeasurably aid the organization of Negro workers in other industries."[54] It was noted in the 1937 NNC convention *Official Proceedings* that the "past few months have witnessed the steady march forward of thousands of Negro workers into the progressive trade union movement," namely the Congress of Industrial Organizations, which has "won new victories." As a result, "tens of thousands" have now "gained increased pay, shorter hours at work and improved living conditions."[55] The party-led NNC and the Southern Negro Youth Congress were in the vanguard of this movement.

The SNYC, which the NNC helped found earlier in 1937, was led by Communists James E. Jackson, Esther Cooper,[56] Edward Strong, Thelma Dale, and James Ashford, among others. Additionally, the NNC off-shoot was working class in character and eager to engage racism in the workplace, "adding a class content to the struggle for Black liberation."[57] In fact, SNYC members went directly "from the founding meeting" in Richmond, Virginia "to organizing local black tobacco workers into a new union – the Tobacco Stemmers and Laborers

---

53. Myrdal, *An American Dilemma...*, Ibid., 818, and Gilmore, *Defying Dixie...*, Ibid., 308

54. Adam Lapin, "Negro Leaders Meet to Speed Union Drive in Steel Mills: To Issue Call to 100,000 in Industry," *Daily Worker*, January 11, 1937, 3. On the same page as Lapin's article was an excerpt from William Z. Foster on "Methods of Organization Vital to Winning Strike," indicative of the CPUSA's efforts to educate, organize, and mobilize.

55. NYU, TAM 132, Box 110, Folder 19: Official Proceedings: Second National Negro Congress, October 15-17, 1937 (NNC, 1937)

56. Plummer, *Rising Wind...*, Ibid., 190; Haviland, *James and Esther Cooper Jackson...*, Ibid.; Lewis, Nash, Leab (eds), *Red Activists And Black Freedom...*, Ibid.; and Swindall, *The Path To The...*, Ibid.

57. Lightfoot, *Chicago Slums...*, Ibid., 73

Industrial Union," a CIO affiliate of more than 5,000 Black female tobacco stemmers, organized and led by CPUSA member Christopher Alston.[58] After a three day strike, employers agreed to their demands, invigorating the industrial union movement. Workers in other industries joined the CIO after SNYC's success.

One observer went so far as to call the Communist-led CIO-SNYC campaign, "the most significant thing that had happened to Richmond Negroes since Emancipation." Seven factories signed union contracts shortly thereafter. "For the first time, southern blacks would have a vehicle to take action and bring about change," Johnetta Richards wrote. "Nearly all of the established black civil rights organizations supported the creation of the SNYC," including "black newspapers, prominent clergy, and educational leaders." At its peak, the SNYC counted more than 115 local councils, many engaged in similar workers' rights campaigns and unionization drives.[59] SNYC held seminars to "generate new progressive leadership in the South." They tried to have racist Mississippi Senator Theodore Bilbo impeached. They worked with the Highlander Folk School "to train union representatives about the challenges of organizing in Dixie." They also "initiated voter registration drives and fought against discrimination in the armed forces and on public transportation." Further, as John Munro argues, in the post-war period SNYC combined "anti-colonial sensibility" with Popular Front "expectations that ran high in the aftermath of fascism's defeat." In short, the "courage of the SNYC activists was breathtaking."[60]

African American reds like Hunton agreed with the Comintern: Communists were "a guiding force...in every phase of its [the NNC's] activities."[61] The same could be said about the SNYC,

58. Elizabeth Davey and Rodney Clark (eds), *Remember My Sacrifice: The Autobiography Of Clinton Clark, Tenant Farm Organizer And Early Civil Rights Activist* (Baton Rouge: Louisiana State University Press, 2007), Introduction; Lewis, Nash, Leab (eds), Ibid., 26; and Robin D. G. Kelley, "Christopher Columbus Alston: Organizer, Fighter and Historian," Marxist Internet Archive, https://www.marxists.org/history/etol/newspape/atc/2514.html

59. Lewis, Nash, Leab, (eds), *Red Activists And Black Freedom...*, Ibid, 23-27 and Davey and Clark (eds), *Remember My Sacrifice...*, Ibid.

60. Munro, *The Anticolonial Front...*, Ibid., 78-79

61. Gilmore, *Defying Dixie...*, Ibid., 309

the NNC's "youth section," which was said to be "dominated by CP activists."[62]

In April 1940, the NNC held its third convention, which Hunton "was chiefly responsible" for organizing. At that convention, held in D.C. and attended by more than 1,300 people, Hunton helped draft the NNC constitution and "delivered a major address," *Negroes and the War*, to a national radio audience.[63] Greeting were sent by several religious denominations and trade unions, including the 40,000 members of the AFL affiliated Hotel and Restaurant Workers International Alliance and Bartenders League of America,[64] a sign of the NNC's stature even among more conservative AFL unions.

Unfortunately, unity was fractured when A. Philip Randolph – who was becoming increasingly "not happy" about the growing and respected public Communist Party influence in the NNC – attacked the party from the podium for its "policies...program tactics and strategy," calling them "fitful, changeful and unpredictable," just like "the foreign policy and line of Moscow." Randolph was then "basically booed off the stage"[65] by the large Communist and CIO delegations. As Gellman wrote, perhaps Randolph "felt like a second act" to John L. Lewis, head of the CIO who was then embracing Communists. That the CPUSA and the CIO helped fund the NNC

---

62. Waldo Martin, *"A Dream Deferred": The Southern Negro Youth Congress, The Student Nonviolent Coordinating Committee, And The Politics Of Historical Memory* (self-published pdf), and Martin Duberman, *Paul Robeson: A Biography* (New York: The New Press, 1995), 258

63. Finkelman (ed), *Volume 1...*, Ibid., 475 and *William Alphaeus Hunton Papers...*, Ibid.

64. "AFL Hotel Union Endorses Nat'l Negro Congress," *Daily Worker*, March 19, 1940, 3

65. Gilmore, *Defying Dixie...*, Ibid., 310 and Holloway, Ibid. According to Ralph Bunche, "an embarrassing silence and no applause" followed Randolph's remarks. Bunche, in 1954, blamed Communists for the NNC's demise and noted that it "died with the actions of the Third Congress..." See: Bunche, "Report denying Communist Party affiliation," Ibid. Apparently, the *Daily Worker* and the CPUSA were unaware of Randolph's turn toward vocal anti-communism. The *DW* approvingly published a photo of Randolph with John P. Davis and Kathryn Lewis, daughter of John L. Lewis, at a NNC testimonial dinner roughly one month prior to the 1940 Convention. See: "Honor Leaders of the National Negro Congress," *Daily Worker*, March 19, 1940, 3

probably irked Randolph, too[66]; he relied on the generosity of the conservative – perhaps, reactionary – leadership of the American Federation of Labor to subsidize his Brotherhood of Sleeping Car Porters, which it was said, was "likely to disappear" without funds from the AFL. After Randolph's departure, Max Yergan, whose life would negatively intersect with Hunton's in 1948, was elected the NNC's next president.[67]

Differing perspectives on the emerging war in Europe was not the only issue driving a wedge between Randolph and the CP/CIO-led NNC. Also, of concern were differing views on how to organize workers, especially African Americans, into unions and the role of Communists in this upsurge.

Even though Randolph paid lip-service to industrial unionism and the work of the CIO, he chose to stay in the AFL – known for its craft union traditions, lily white composition, and segregated locals[68] – rather than join the CIO. In 1929, when the AFL begrudgingly agreed to charter the BSCP it was only as second-class, separate federal locals under the "authority of the national AFL leadership," not as a single international union. This maneuver "effectively subordinated organized black workers under the AFL's white leadership." Further, it would not be until June of 1936 – just months after the NNC's founding – that the AFL granted an international charter to the BSCP.[69] In short, it was the NNC, the Communist left-flank, and the surging CIO

---

66. Gellman, *Death Blow To Jim Crow…*, Ibid., 151, 155-156 and Robert Parmet, *The Master of Seventh Avenue: David Dubinsky and the American Labor Movement* (New York: New York University Press, 2012), 154. According to Parmet, Lewis approached the CPUSA "first by granting an exclusive interview to the *Daily Worker*. Talks with party leaders produced an agreement that opened the CIO to the Communists…[CPUSA member] Len De Caux [was hired] to be the CIO's publicity director…In exchange, the Communists gave Lewis organizers – loads of them."

67. Andrew Kersten, *A. Phillip Randolph: A Life in the Vanguard* (Roman & Littlefield Publishers, Inc., 2007), 44

68. Philip Yale Nicholson, *Labor's Story In The United States* (Philadelphia: Temple University Press, 2004); Gilbert Jonas, *Freedom's Sword: The NAACP and the Struggle Against Racism in America, 1909-1969* (London: Routledge, 2005); Robert H. Zieger, *For Jobs And Freedom: Race And Labor In America Since 1865* (Lexington: University Press of Kentucky, 2007); and Philip S. Foner, *Organized Labor & The Black Worker, 1619-1981* (New York: International Publishers, 1981)

69. Robert L. Allen, *The Brotherhood of Sleeping Car Porters: C.L. Dellums and the Fight for Fair Treatment and Civil Rights* (Paradigm Publishers, 2015), 47-48, 58

that won concessions for African Americans from the AFL, not Randolph. Viewed in isolation, Randolph's decision to align with the AFL seems odd. The CIO was a bastion of party activity since its founding and not nearly as resistant to Communist influence as the AFL,[70] and as a result considerably more welcoming to people of color, which Randolph well knew.

Curiously, as the AFL's loyal opposition, Randolph's ideological summersaults justifying the continued subordinate role assigned to most Black AFL union members was largely based on his anti-communist alliance with the AFL's conservative white leadership – a leadership that begrudgingly gave him a platform and an audience,[71] while taking great pains to attempt to isolate the then ascendant red influence, an influence championing Black leadership. It was this racist status quo that Randolph was financially dependent upon as head of an African American union in the white AFL, hence a partial explanation for his resistance to Communist overtures, especially those made by Black Communists. Further, Randolph's stature as a prominent Black labor leader was not preordained. Arguably, several Communists could have eclipsed him as the foremost domestic Black labor leader. Ferdinand Smith, the Jamaican-born Communist and leader of the National Maritime Union, would for a time cast somewhat of a red shadow over Randolph and be considered by many the most influential person of color in the U.S. labor movement. That Smith led a union that was majority white – the opposite of Randolph's BSCP – added to his considerable influence. As

---

70. For example, see: Stepan-Norris and Zeitlan, *Left Out…*, Ibid.; Clarence Taylor, *Reds At The Blackboard: Communism, Civil Rights, and the New York City Teachers Union* (New York: Columbia University Press, 2011); Bruce Nelson, *Workers on the Waterfront: Seaman, Longshoremen, and Unionism in the 1930s* (Chicago: University of Illinois Press, 1990); Roger Keeran, *The Communist Party and the Auto-Workers' Union* (New York: International Publishers, 1986); Rosemary Feurer, *Radical Unionism In The Midwest, 1900-1950* (Chicago: University of Illinois Press, 2006); James L. Lorence, *The Unemployed People's Movement: Leftists, Liberals, And Labor In Georgia, 1929-1941* (Athens: University of Georgia Press, 2011); Gerald Horne, *Fighting In Paradise: Labor Unions, Racism, And Communists In The Making Of Modern Hawaii* (Honolulu: University of Hawaii Press, 2011); Horne, *Class Struggle In Hollywood, 1930-1950: Moguls, Mobsters, Stars, Reds, & Trade Unionists* (Austin: University of Texas Press, 2001); Michael Dennis, *Blood On Steel: Chicago Steelworkers And The Strike Of 1937* (Baltimore: Johns Hopkins University Press, 2014)

71. Zieger, *For Jobs And Freedom…*, Ibid., 90

the tide turned toward the Red Scare, Smith was unceremoniously ousted from the NMU in 1948 and eventually deported.[72]

Additionally, Randolph's AFL – unlike Smith's CIO – refused to participate in international trade union conferences initiated and led by the World Federation of Trade Unions, a body less hostile to Communists that was founded in fall 1945.[73] The WFTU connected Pan-Africanism to the growing trade union movement and socialism.[74] This put the CIO – not the AFL – in the mainstream of the then expanding international upsurge in workers' rights struggles backed by the Soviet Union. Randolph's rejection of the WFTU was curious, as he was supposedly championing the defeat of racism, domestically and internationally. It would not be until December 1949 that the International Confederation of Free Trade Unions – an anti-communist competitor of the WFTU – was founded.[75] In short, Randolph's anti-communism effectively limited his and his union's avenues for international solidarity. Even the otherwise staid NAACP noted in spring 1944, that the USSR had "the most advanced policy in the world with regard to minority peoples."[76] And State Department labor specialist, George McCray, no friend of the Communists, remarked that Randolph's shunning of the WFTU was "particularly stupid" considering that organization's considerable representation among unions in the decolonizing nations of Africa.[77] Further, it would be a Communist, Hunton, who would have decisive

---

72. Horne, *Red Seas…*, Ibid.

73. Adolf Sturmthal, "Discussions And Communications: The Crisis of the WFTU," *ILR Review*, Vol. 1, No 4 (July 1948), 630. For a brief history of the WFTU, see: World Federation of Trade Unions, 1) The Founding Congress, http://www.wftucentral.org/history/. Also see: Anthony Carew, *Labour under the Marshall Plan: The politics of productivity and the marketing of management science* (Manchester: Manchester University Press, 1987), 60, 70. Ironically, it would be a former Communist Jay Lovestone who would be the "biggest contributor to the molding of postwar AFL international policy." Lovestone eventually became a paid CIA informant. See: Kevin K. Gaines, *Black Expatriates and the Civil Rights Era: American Africans in Ghana* (Chapel Hill: University of North Carolina Press, 2006), 97

74. Von Eschen, *Race Against Empire…*, Ibid., 47-53 and Munro, *The Anticolonial Front…*, 54-56

75. R.F., "The International Confederations of Free Trade Unions," *The World Today*, Vol. 9, No. 1 (January 1953)

76. Munro, *The Anticolonial Front…*, Ibid., 142

77. Gerald Horne, *The Rise & Fall Of The Associated Negro Press: Claude Barnett's Pan-African News and the Jim Crow Paradox* (Chicago: University of Illinois Press, 2017), 86

influence on Du Bois regarding union-based Pan-Africanism,[78] which likely served to further bruise Randolph's ego. In short, disdain for Communists weakened Randolph's union domestically, while also serving to isolate it internationally.

The well-known Communist councilman from Harlem, Benjamin Davis, Jr., later call Randolph a "sheep in wolf's clothing...a pathological red-baiter, Soviet baiter and Wall Street bootlicker... constantly starting out like a lion and ending like a lamb."[79] Like Davis, Hunton grew increasingly frustrated with red-baiting, especially when scare tactics were used to divide the CP/CIO-led NNC coalition, a decisive moment for the National Negro Congress that proved difficult to recover from.

In 1943, John P. Davis resigned as NNC national secretary; his reasons were complicated. Ties with other prominent Communists had been strained due to the party's multiple shifts in foreign policy. Davis also felt "politically compromised" and did not want his CPUSA connections to "sabotage the NNC's need to reinvent itself."[80] While the NNC remained active,[81] the D.C. office closed, which "made the task of carrying on the Council's work extremely difficult and...a burden on Alphaeus," Dorothy Hunton recalled. In 1947, after "years of consistent struggle and effective work...[the] beleaguered and harassed Congress" merged into the Civil Rights Congress, which itself had been created after a merger of the party-led ILD and National Federation of Constitutional Liberties.[82] The CRC was led by the well-known African American Communist William L. Patterson, who had spearheaded the party's defense of the Scottsboro Nine.[83] Hunton would serve as a trustee of the CRC bail fund, a position for which he would be harassed and eventually jailed.

*   *   *

78. Von Eschen, *Race Against Empire...*, Ibid., 51-52

79. Gerald Horne, *Black Liberation / Red Scare...*, Ibid., 201

80. Gellman, *Death Blow to Jim Crow...*, Ibid., 143-144

81. "Plan Lobby to End Jim Crow in Army: Negro Congress Asks Legal Ban On Race Bias," *Daily Worker,* October 11, 1943, 3. For example, the NNC organized 100 national leaders to lobby in Washington, D.C. to discuss the "abolition" of Jim Crow in the armed forces.

82. Hunton, *Alphaeus Hunton...*, Ibid., 55, 82

83. Horne, *Black Revolutionary...*, Ibid.

During the early-1940s Hunton also worked with the American Peace Mobilization, which the House Committee on Un-American Activities called, "one of the most seditious organizations which ever operated in the United States."[84] This was a bold proclamation apparently only reserved for organizations led by Communists.[85] Of course, the Soviet Non-Aggression Pact with Germany signed in summer 1939, as well as the Communist Party's "ideological whiplash," as Gellman called it, two years later after the German invasion of the Soviet Union, complicated matters.[86] Still anti-war sentiment was wide-spread; many Americans did not want to be entangled in another European war. In May 1940, for example, 700 Bostonians gathered to hear Yergan "warn that the Negro people have nothing to gain from either side of the war."[87] Italian-American New York Congressman Vito Marcantonio was not shy about solidarity with APM, while merging discrimination against African Americans with demands for peace. He called "the Jim Crow situation in America today a national disgrace" and noted that discrimination in the armed forces was an expression of "the shallowness of our pretensions that this war is a war for democracy." A special St. Patrick's Day appeal was made by the author and poet Shaemas O'Sheel to Irish-American activists to attend an APM sponsored American People's Meeting.[88] Regardless, the party's dramatic political shift justifying the Non-Aggression Pact was proof to some – like Randolph – that the CPUSA was compromised and worked at the behest of a foreign power. Further, reds were often accused of trying to bring unions representing defense industry workers "under [the] leadership of the Communist party,"[89] an accusation that would soon be hurled at Hunton. Nonetheless,

---

84. Paul Kengor, *The Communist* (New York: Threshold Editions/Mercury Ink, 2012), 81

85. For more on the persecution of "Radical Black Peace Activists," see: Burden-Stelly, "In Battle For Peace During 'Scoundrel Times,'" Ibid.

86. Shawn Gude, "When Fighting Racism Meant Fighting Economic Exploitation [Gellman interview]," *Jacobin*, March 12, 2019, https://www.jacobinmag.com/2019/03/national-negro-congress-jim-crow-gellman

87. "Yergan Demands U.S. Stay Out of the War," *Daily Worker*, May 24, 1940, 4

88. "Marcantonio To Speak at APM Rally," and "Irish Urged to Back APM People's Rally," *Daily Worker*, March 17, 1941, 2

89. For example, see: "1941 Cabal Of Reds In Ohio Described," *New York Times*, July 13, 1950

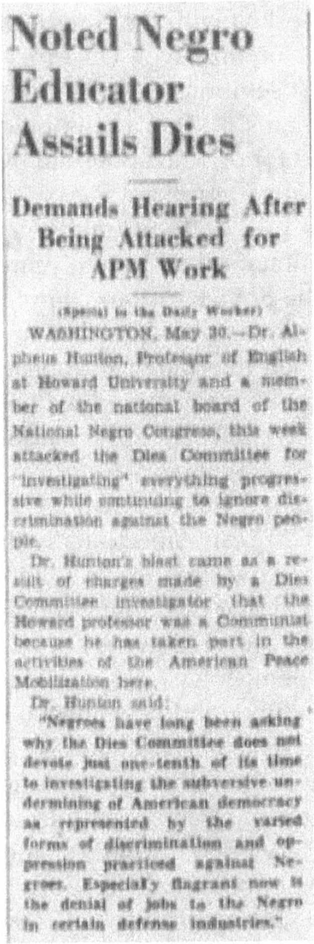

Noted Negro Educator Assails Dies

Demands Hearing After Being Attacked for APM Work

(Special to the Daily Worker)

WASHINGTON, May 30.—Dr. Alpheus Hunton, Professor of English at Howard University and a member of the national board of the National Negro Congress, this week attacked the Dies Committee for "investigating" everything progressive while continuing to ignore discrimination against the Negro people.

Dr. Hunton's blast came as a result of charges made by a Dies Committee investigator that the Howard professor was a Communist because he has taken part in the activities of the American Peace Mobilization here.

Dr. Hunton said:

"Negroes have long been asking why the Dies Committee does not devote just one-tenth of its time to investigating the subversive undermining of American democracy as represented by the varied forms of discrimination and oppression practiced against Negroes. Especially flagrant now is the denial of jobs to the Negro in certain defense industries."

IMAGE 1: *Daily Worker*, May 31, 1941. Courtesy of *People's World*.

"preventing U.S. entry into [World War II]" was then considered "seditious," as Hunton personally found out when he and other peace activists were "assaulted" by "soldiers, sailors and marines" while picketing in front of the White House.[90] Hunton was part of an APM sponsored "perpetual peace vigil" that included religious, community, and labor leaders. APM administrative secretary Marion Briggs noted at the vigil: "Our picket line is America's life line!"[91]

In spring 1941, the FBI opened a file on Hunton; agents followed him around, watched his mail, and spread word that he was subversive.[92] That May, he was called to testify before the Dies Committee due to his APM activism (image 1), a foreshadowing of the trials and travails that would hound Communists by 1948. Hunton called the committee's actions "reprehensible" and noted that he "knew absolutely nothing about the charges against me prior to reading about them in the papers." He responded to the inquiry by asking why the committee "does not devote just one-tenth of its time to investigating the subversive undermining of American democracy…[through] the varied forms of discrimination and oppression practiced against Negro citizens," especially the

90. Gilmore, *Defying Dixie…*, Ibid., 314, 351

91. "White House Peace Vigil In 48th Hour," *Daily Worker*, May 12, 1941, 1

92. Stephen L. Carter, "Why I Support Dissent: My Great-Uncle Who Wouldn't Name Names," *Bloomberg Opinion*, August 12, 2016, https://www.bloomberg.com/opinion/articles/2016-08-12/why-i-support-dissent-my-great-uncle-who-wouldn-t-name-names.

"flagrant...denial of jobs to Negroes in certain defense industries." He added, "I see nothing subversive" in an organization, the APM, "dedicated to the maintenance of peace and democracy," a sentiment then shared by most Americans. "You cannot make something bad by merely calling it a name," Hunton concluded. Though he denied being a Communist, he demanded "the right to testify" and to face his accusers – political cowards and sycophants who would later report that they were glad to have found nothing indicating Hunton "engaged in any activities...characterized as subversive or disloyal to our government." FBI Director J. Edger Hoover later placed Hunton on a list, along with other Communists, who were to be put under "preventive detention" in internment camps in the advent of war with the Soviet Union. That Hunton "spearheaded the fight for 'all-out defense of democracy' in defense industry – right here at home," specifically by fighting for African Americans jobs at the Glenn L. Martin Aircraft Plant in Baltimore, precipitated the inquisition.[93] The Dies Committee went so far as to claim that the "infiltration of Negro Communist workers" from the Washington NNC intended to "sabotage" the plant.[94] Hunton had "urged full ballot rights" for Communists, chaired a Citizens Conference on Jobs and Welfare (a precursor to the Glenn L. Martin campaign),[95] and was part of an American Youth Congress delegation that met with Vice President Henry Wallace[96] during the preceding 12 months, added to the government's ire. By March 1941, NNC leaders charged the aircraft company with "conducting a 'sit-down strike' against the Negro people." They found that Glenn L. Martin employed "not a

---

93. "Noted Negro Educator Assails Dies," *Daily Worker*, May 31, 1941, 5; Hunton, *Alphaeus Hunton...*, Ibid., 51-52; and Carter, "Why I Support Dissent...," Ibid. For more on the establishment of internment camps, see: C.P. Trussell, "Truman Won't Sign Subversive Curb; Red Roundup Ready," *New York Times*, September 8, 1950, and "6 Camps For Reds Set Up, The Closed," *New York Times*, May 5, 1962

94. "Negro Congress Answers Dies' Stooge Charges," *Daily Worker*, May 28, 1941, 5

95. "Prominent Negroes Urge Ballot Rights For Communists," *Daily Worker*, September 23, 1940, 4 and "Parley Hits Anti-Negro Bias on Defense Work," *Daily Worker*, November 13, 1940, 5.

96. "Fight Capital Jim Crow 'Town Meeting,'" *Daily Worker*, February 7, 1941, 1 and 3

single Negro" among its 18,000 workers.[97] Hunton's comrade, the fellow Communist George Meyers, led the campaign to unionize and integrate the plant, which would grow to employ 37,000 workers. It was argued Communists were strategically positioned to cripple an industry essential for national security. Hunton and Meyers' goal, however, was less conspiratorial; they and other Communists helped to break down racist hiring practices at the plant, leading to 7,000 jobs for African American workers,[98] bolstering an alliance less susceptible to anti-communism, an alliance the entire weight of the U.S. government would soon try to destroy.

In addition to his peace activism, Hunton's NNC organizing did not let up. For example, he was at the center of a Washington NNC and United Federal Workers of America report documenting cases of myositis among the mostly women workers at the machine tabulation division of the United States Census Bureau. The NNC report documented Jim Crow hiring practices, a sexist, piece-work wage scale, and speed-ups – all partial causes for the myositis. The May 28, 1941, edition of the *Daily Worker* includes a photo of Hunton interviewing Miss Virginia Allen (image 2), a Census Bureau worker. The report noted, "20 Negro and white girls [sic] employed as card punchers in this division of census work had been stricken with this disease and face the prospects of never again being able to earn a living at the same type of work." The NNC and union also outlined a "5-point program" to "eliminate the disease hazard."[99]

During the mid-1940s, Hunton also served as a director of the George Washington Carver School, the Harlem branch of the party's flagship adult education institution, the Jefferson School of Social Science.[100] Nearly 2,000 people attended classes and lectures at the Carver School during its first year with an additional 2,500 people attending the "I Am an American Day" meeting. It was noted that classes were "organized frequently

97. "Negro Congress Fights for Jobs in Martin Aircraft Co.," *Daily Worker*, March 17, 1941, 2

98. Frederick N. Rasmussen, "George Aloysius Meyers, 86, Communist Party member," *Baltimore Sun*, October 21, 1999, http://articles.baltimoresun.com/1999-10-21/news/9910210183_1_communist-party-meyers-party-members

99. "Speed-up in Washington: Census Bureau Girls Contract Disease Caused by Heavy Work," *Daily Worker*, May 28, 1941, 5

100. Gettleman, "No Varsity Teams…," Ibid.

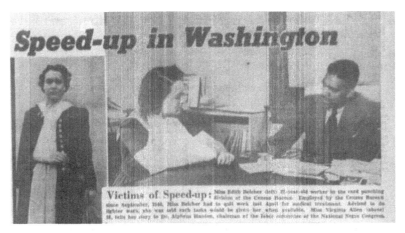

IMAGE 2: *Daily Worker*, May 28, 1941. Courtesy of *People's World*.

because of community demands." The "practical experience of
the instructors" was stressed, while the educational program was
designed to foster racial unity and to create "several opportunities for increased knowledge of people with varied racial and
national backgrounds."[101]

Like other Communists, after the German invasion of the
Soviet Union and the Japanese bombing of Pearl Harbor, Hunton
quickly shifted gears and threw himself into support of the war
effort. One lecture before the Lincoln Douglass Club of the Communist Political Association[102] in December 1944, dealt with the
"struggle for the liberation of Europe and the Negro people."[103]
Earlier that month, the Carver School, the Jefferson School, and
People's Voice sponsored a five-day course on "The Negro and the
Nation," which Hunton and Wilkerson participated in.[104] Hunton
also focused on electoral politics, and encouraged African Americans "to vote for men, regardless of party label, who by their

101. "Carver School Opens Tonight," *Daily Worker*, October 2, 1944, 11
102. In May 1944, the CPUSA officially dissolved under the leadership of
Earl Browder and chartered as the Communist Political Association. However,
in 1945, shortly after the conclusion of World War II, the CPA was itself
dissolved and the CPUSA was reconstituted. Browder was expelled. See: Ryan,
Earl Browder..., Ibid.
103. "Alphaeus Hunton To Speak Tonight," *Daily Worker*, December 12, 1944, 5
104. Doxey Wilkerson, "Toward Freedom," *Daily Worker*, December 4, 1944, 7

record, have been on the right side of our war effort" and have shown "concern for the rights of Negroes and the vast majority of the American people."[105]

*   *   *

Constrained by an increasingly restrictive political environment, Hunton resigned from Howard University in summer 1943; his comrade Wilkerson resigned earlier to work fulltime for the CPUSA. Soon thereafter, Hunton became the educational director of the Council on African Affairs, the domestic linchpin of the international Black liberation movement.[106] The council militantly promoted independence for African colonies and "the full freedom of colored peoples throughout the world."[107] The CAA began as the International Committee on African Affairs in 1937, partly funded by Paul Robeson and run by Max Yergan. Functioning primarily as an educational organization, the ICAA consisted of prominent Black lawyers, educators, and artists. Reorganized in 1942, the CAA was "distinctly different" and "explicitly anticolonial." It was more adversarial than its predecessor with an emphasis on "militant black international diaspora consciousness" and "independent black leadership" with a Marxist-based analysis embracing anti-imperialist and anti-capitalist politics. During World War II and the immediate post-war period, the CAA was part of "a second incarnation" of the Communist-led Popular Front, which endured through the early Cold War.[108] Illustrative of their influence, Hunton and other CAA leaders met regularly with officials of the U.S. State Department's Division of African Affairs, providing insight and analysis.[109] Though, as Martin Duberman argues, the CAA fused "anticolonial and

---

105. "Says GOP No Friend of Negro," *Daily Worker*, April 16, 1944, 6

106. Finkelman (ed.), *Volume 1...*, Ibid., 475; Wilkerson, "William Alphaeus...," Ibid., 255; and "Negro, White Leaders Honor Wilkerson," *The Worker*, August 8, 1943, 2

107. Paul Robeson, Jr., *The Undiscovered Paul Robeson: Quest for Freedom, 1939 – 1976* (Hoboken: John Wiley & Sons, Inc., 2010), 10

108. Von Eschen, *Race Against Empire...*, Ibid., 17-21 and Munro, *The Anticolonial Front...*, Ibid., 34-35

109. Hunton, *Alphaeus Hunton...*, Ibid., 58

pro-Soviet sentiments" domestically,[110] a perspective held by its principal leaders and one at odds with U.S. imperialism once Hitler and the Axis powers were defeated and the war-time alliance with the Soviet Union was broken.

According to Gerald Horne, the CAA was "the vanguard organization in the U.S. campaigning against colonialism."[111] Penny M. Von Eschen referred to it as "vital and important,"[112] providing the connective tissue that brought together African Americans struggling for equality with Africans struggling for Black liberation, particularly in South Africa. Eric Arnesen termed the CAA, "hard-nosed and partisan in an emerging Cold War that rendered the Third World a crucial ideological and political battle-field."[113] In short, the CAA brought together African Americans fighting for equality with Black liberation movements in Africa while both sought allies with ascendant socialism.[114] In 1958, Hunton reflected on the CAA and its leading role: It "stood alone as the one organization in the United States devoting full-time attention to the problems and struggles of the peoples of Africa," he wrote, a stance for which it would eventually be punished.[115]

Hunton joined CAA chairman (and perhaps, secret Communist) Paul Robeson[116] and later W.E.B. Du Bois, who would become

---

110. Duberman, *Paul Robeson...*, Ibid., 258

111. Gerald Horne, *Paul Robeson: The Artist as Revolutionary* (London: Pluto Press, 2016), 258

112. Von Eschen, *Race Against Empire...*, Ibid., 20

113. Eric Arnesen, "Civil Rights and the Cold War At Home: Postwar Activism, Anticommunism, and the Decline of the Left," *American Communist History*, Vol. 11, No. 1 (April 2012), 5-44

114. For an example of how African Americans and Africans built cross-Atlantic alliances and sought allies with the socialist world, see: Horne, *White Supremacy Confronted...*, Ibid.

115. Paul Robeson, *Here I Stand* (Othello Associates, Inc., 1958), 127. Some disagree with Hunton's assessment. Arnesen argues, the CAA's "demise did not spell the silencing of anticolonial discourse. Just as the CP-oriented unions and fronts were never alone in promoting an economic agenda, neither too was the CP-oriented CAA the sole voice of anticolonialism..." See: Arnesen, "Civil Rights and the Cold War At Home...," Ibid.

116. Re Robeson and the CPUSA, see: Gus Hall, "Paul Robeson: An American Communist," Communist Party, USA (text of a centennial tribute speech delivered on May 31, 1998, at the Winston Unity Auditorium, CP national office, 235 W. 23rd St., New York, NY), 3, 6, 8. Later reprinted, Gus Hall, "Paul Robeson: Artist, Freedom Fighter, Hero, American Communist," *Political Affairs*, July 1998.

vice chair – "the CAA troika"[117] – as they collectively articulated and fought for "radical internationalism" and "black nationalism, with [an] emphasis on racial consciousness and unity." As editor of the CAA's publications, *New Africa* and later *Spotlight on Africa*, and through countless articles, pamphlets, and booklets distributed globally, Hunton promoted "connections with Africa and concern for its problems." He placed the anti-colonial struggle in historical context and as part of a "worldwide political economy." The CAA and Hunton were "in the vanguard of educating the general public about imperialism and its devastating effects on Africa."[118] Press releases, conferences, and countless demonstrations, boycotts, and marches highlighted domestic solidarity with Black liberation. Under Hunton's leadership, the CAA also "functioned as a press service," providing content to organizations, newspapers, and journals, content largely unavailable elsewhere. *New Africa* was increasingly influential, too, and by 1950 it was banned in South Africa, Kenya, and Belgian Congo.[119] In addition to the CAA's newsletters, Hunton also provided content and analysis to 62 international and 67 U.S. newspapers; further, the council acted as "a liaison agency between the U.N. and the public, here and abroad...particularly in Africa." As Hunton noted, the CAA's "prime objective was to provide a sound basis

---

Hall writes: "My own most precious moments with Paul were when I met with him to accept his dues and renew his yearly membership in the CPUSA. I and other Communist leaders, like Henry Winston...met with Paul to brief him on politics and Party policies and to discuss his work and struggles." Also, see: Vijay Prashad, "Comrade Robeson: A Centennial Tribute to an American Communist," *Social Scientist*, Vol. 25, No. 7/8 (Jul.-Aug. 1997), 40-41. Prashad, however, quotes from the above. Gerald Horne wondered if Robeson had been a member of the Communist Party of Great Britain, which was "more of a likelihood than U.S. membership." See: Horne, *Paul Robeson: The Artist as Revolutionary* (London: Pluto Press, 2016), 6. Martin Duberman notes that Robeson offered to publicly join the CPUSA in 1951 out of solidarity with his beleaguered comrades and friends; the proposal was rejected by the CPUSA's leadership. See: Duberman, *Paul Robeson: A Biography* (New York: The New Press, 1989), 420. While Robeson's membership in the CPUSA is contested, it is clear he did not hesitate to align himself with the CPUSA, its leadership, and its policies.

117. Horne, *Black & Red...*, Ibid., 184

118. Meriwether, *Proudly We Can Be Africans...*, Ibid., 61-62 and Finkelman (ed.), *Volume 1...*, Ibid., 475-476

119. Campbell, *Middle Passages...*, Ibid., 337 and Von Eschen, *Race Against Empire...*, Ibid. 60, 122

of accurate information so that the American people might play their proper part in the struggle for African freedom."[120]

"Just as labor and the liberal forces of England recognized 180 years ago that their own interest lay in the overthrow of American slavery," Hunton told a reporter on his first day at the CAA office, "so today it is necessary for Americans and all people of the anti-axis [sic] world to realize that their future security and peace must ultimately depend upon the abolition…of imperialism in Africa and throughout the world."[121] The CAA became the "central point of interaction between Africans' and African Americans' struggles for liberation."[122] Unfortunately, in the postwar period international solidarity, especially with Black liberation in Africa, became subversive; in 1947, Attorney General Tom Clark placed the CAA on the list of organizations that it claimed threatened to subvert U.S. democracy.[123] Even Du Bois assumed the CAA was "financed by the Communists[,] which is probably true," he added.[124]

Though Max Yergan was then still the CAA's executive director,[125] it was widely acknowledged that Hunton "single-handedly

---

120. Hunton, *Alphaeus Hunton…*, Ibid., 62, 65, and Robeson, *Here I Stand…*, Ibid., 127

121. Hunton, *Alphaeus Hunton…*, Ibid., 57

122. James Pope, "Exploring the Parallels Between the U.S. Civil Rights Movement and the African Liberation Movement," *Poverty & Race*, May/June 2010, http://www.prrac.org/full_text.php?text_id=1269&item_id=12371&newsletter_id=111&header=Race+%2F+Racism&kc=1

123. Carol Anderson, *Eyes Off The Prize: The United Nations and the African American Struggle for Human Rights, 1944-1955* (Cambridge: Cambridge University Press, 2003), 163 and Von Eschen, Ibid., 115

124. Munro, *The Anticolonial Front…*, Ibid., 71: Du Bois letter to Padmore, July 12, 1946. Du Bois did not join the CAA staff until 1948 and likely only had a vague awareness of the CAA's internal funding in 1946; his comment is speculation, not condemnation. Stephen Carter notes that a HUAC witness claimed the CAA "received an annual subvention of $200,000 from the Communist Party." He found this claim suspect, though: "[T]hat council members regularly squabbled over secretarial time or reimbursements of $5 or $10" makes this claim highly "unlikely." See: Carter, "Why I Support Dissent…," Ibid. According to Brenda Gayle Plummer, the CAA "received heavy funding from Communists and had significant Red participation." See: Plummer, *Rising Wind…*, Ibid., 158. It is unclear if she means individually or organizationally.

125. For a detailed analysis of Yergan's life, see: David Henry Anthony III, *Max Yergan…*, Ibid.

kept the organization afloat" and was considered one of the CAA's "leading figures at the height of... [its] influence"[126]; this was high praise, especially since Hunton's co-workers included Robeson and later Du Bois and Louise Thompson Patterson.[127] As others have written, CAA "activities and impact increased significantly after 1943" when Hunton joined the staff,[128] as he "transformed the Council...from an information provider to a mass organization."[129] Undoubtedly, "1943 marked a major turning point" for both Hunton and the CAA, as the "day-to-day work and policy was thereafter carried out" by Hunton,[130] who was considered "Robeson's right-hand man."[131] As Hollis Lynch writes, Hunton was "quite, radical and brilliant...the council's administrative and intellectual mainstay." Further, he was the "key staff person"[132] and the CAA's "most tireless worker."[133] Additionally, during the final years of its existence – due to the political repression Robeson and Du Bois faced – the CAA was "practically a one-man organization," as Mrs. Hunton recalled.[134]

Alphaeus still found time to mentor young activists, though. When SNYC leader Esther Cooper was elected as a delegate to the first World Youth Conference – which founded the World Federation of Democratic Youth – held in London in November 1945, she reached out to both Hunton and Du Bois for advice; she wanted to be "as informed as possible on the colonial question and youth movements in Africa and Latin America." That Hunton

126. Campbell, *Middle Passages...*, Ibid., 337 and Meriwether, *Proudly We Can Be Africans...*, Ibid., 61

127. For more on Thompson Patterson, see: Keith Gilyard, *Louis Thompson Patterson: A Life of Struggle for Justice* (Durham: Duke University Press, 2017)

128. William Minter and Sylvia Hill, "Anti-apartheid solidarity in United States-South Africa relations: From the margins to the mainstream," in *The Road to Democracy in South Africa, Volume 3, International Solidarity, Part II* (Unisa Press, 2008, South African Democracy Education Trust), 754

129. Allyson Nadia Field and Marsha Gordon (eds), *Screening Race in American Nontheatrical Film* (Durham: Duke University Press, 2019), 119

130. Von Eschen, *Race Against Empire...*, Ibid., 20

131. Francis Njubi Nesbitt, *Race for Sanctions: African Americans against Apartheid, 1946-1994* (Bloomington: Indiana University Press, 2004), 5

132. Gerald Horne, *Black & Red...*, Ibid., 114 and Horne, *W.E.B. Du Bois: A Biography* (Santa Barbara: Greenwood Press, 2010), 159

133. Plummer, *Rising Wind...*, Ibid., 157

134. Hunton, *Alphaeus Hunton...*, Ibid., 90

was considered as knowledgeable as Du Bois is telling; further, *New Africa* was then the "single most important source of information and enlightened opinion on Africa" and was regularly used by the SNYC in "its leadership training courses." Fortuitously, Esther Cooper ended-up chairing a panel in London on "colonies and self-determination."[135] Hunton would also have a profound influence on Charlene Mitchell, who in the early-1970s internationalized the campaign to free Angela Davis and later led the National Alliance Against Racist and Political Repression.[136]

Hunton and the CAA established and maintained contact with and aided Black liberation movements and leaders, partly as an accredited UN observer.[137] However, by 1948 it became increasingly evident that the ruling class hoped to contain African American civil rights discourse and activism safely within the bounds of liberal Western capitalism. Hunton and other Black Communists, like Ferdinand Smith, Claudia Jones, Benjamin Davis, Jr., and William L. Patterson were pushed aside to make room for those willing to acquiesce to reflexive anti-communism. Hunton, and his allies were hounded, harassed, imprisoned, and deported.

Despite the repression, as an organization that practiced international solidarity in a multiplicity of ways, the CAA under Hunton's leadership not only organized what amounted to "canned food drive[s] on behalf of hungry Africans,"[138] it merged humanitarian efforts with political activism geared towards Black liberation. Like the Civil Rights Congress [139] and the International Workers Order,[140] among other Communist-led organizations, the CAA saw its role as both advocacy and activism.

* * *

135. Munro, *The Anticolonial Front...*, Ibid., 81-82 and Swindall, *The Path To The...*, Ibid., 88

136. William Minter, Gail Hovey and Charles Cobb Jr. (eds), *No Easy Victories: African Liberation and American Activists over a Half Century, 1950-2000* (Africa World Press, 2007), http://www.noeasyvictories.org/interviews/int04_mitchell.php and Pecinovsky, *Let Them Tremble...*, Ibid.

137. Edward O. Erhagbe, "Assistance and Conflict: The African Diaspora and Africa's Development in the Twenty-first Century," *Africa Development*, Vol. XXXII, No. 2, 2007, 32 and Hunton, *Alphaeus Hunton...*, Ibid., 63

138. Campbell, *Middle Passages...*, Ibid., 339

139. Horne, *Communist Front...*, Ibid.

140. Zecker, *"A Road to Peace and Freedom...,"* Ibid.

In August 1943, Hunton wrote his first editorial for *New Africa*, the CAA's newsletter. "Millions of dollars worth of American war goods sent to Africa," as well as the "tens of thousands of American soldiers on African soil…[are a] measure of our country's new relation to the African continent and people," he emphasized. During a time of cataclysmic war, Hunton saw the shipping of goods and the deployment of soldiers as positive. "The purpose of this new relation is to defeat Hitler, of course, and that is the best possible reason for it." To Hunton and the CAA, the "winning of the war is still our first great task, and to it all our energies must be devoted." However, he continued, "As a part of the effort and as an inspiration for that effort, we shall, with the African people, think and plan and work for a new day for Africa." Even at this stage in the war, with victory still two years away, Hunton was cautiously optimistic; Hitler and Mussolini had been driven from the continent, though, a Second Front in Europe would not open for roughly another year. "The defeat of Hitlerism, the overthrow of Fascism and Nazi power offer the greatest possibility for a new day for Africa," he added. Hunton also called for the "application of the Atlantic Charter to the life of the African people" once the war was over. At this point, he saw "America's new relations to Africa" as pragmatic and constructive, a reflection of his overall optimism that the war-time alliance would persist, and that the role of the developing UN would grow. He saw "an Africa free from the heavy handicap of undemocratic rule," i.e., post-war colonial subjugation. "This is the perspective of the [CAA] for winning the war and supporting plans for a new Africa. We believe we can count on millions of Americans to join us in this program," he concluded.[141]

Shortly after the opening of the Second Front, the CAA issued a statement: "The Allied invasion represents a blow not only for the liberation of Europe but for the freedom of all mankind from the yoke of fascism. Africans and other colonial peoples throughout the world are sure to hail the invasion…African troops have been fighting in Italy and will doubtless see action in France. Africans are sharing in the Allied surge toward victory. The Council on African Affairs is confident that the democratic forces of the

---

141. Alphaeus Hunton, "Editorial," *New Africa*, Vol. 2, No. 1 (August 1943)

world will guarantee their share in the fruits of that victory."[142] Still a year from the triumph over fascism, Hunton and the CAA had reason to hope.

Domestically, Hunton continued to see Roosevelt and the New Deal coalition as the best path forward for African Americans and other peoples of color. In a July 1944 editorial, he blasted the "short-sighted, reactionary, and dangerous Americans-for-America spirit" of the "foreign policy section of the Republican platform." To Hunton, the "outlook of the Republican Convention was backward toward the Hoover era of 'rugged individualism' and imperialism." Conversely, the "world is moving forward toward the era of international collaboration and democracy forecast at Teheran," where Roosevelt, Churchill, and Stalin met. "The American Negro and his brothers in Africa and other colonial areas know that the best way and only way of realizing their full rights lies in marching forward together with all those mighty forces and millions of peoples who are headed toward a world governed by new principles – new principles which are being forged in the process of destroying fascism," Hunton concluded.[143] Hunton's outlook on Teheran was representative of most Communists at that time; the CPUSA had officially dissolved itself in May 1944 and reorganized as the Communist Political Association.[144] Like other Communists, Hunton was optimistic the war-time alliance would continue in the post-war period. Unfortunately, once the mutual fascist enemy was defeated, the alliance broke. Hunton, and those like him, became the new enemy, sacrificed on the altar of reflexive anti-communism.

Hunton also focused on the role of women in Africa. The September 1944 issue of *New Africa* included photos that provided "a small glimpse of the part African women today are playing in the war effort and in the life of their country." Hunton wrote that he would have liked to have "included…pictures of the teachers, farm workers, all the others in various fields of employment, who are demonstrating

---

142. "Council Acclaims Second Front Invasion – On D-Day, June 6, the Council on African Affairs issued the Following statement," *New Africa*, Vol. 3, No. 6 (June 1944)

143. Alphaeus Hunton, "Editorial," *New Africa*, Vol. 3, No. 7 (July-August 1944).

144. In 1945, shortly after the conclusion of World War II, the CPA was itself dissolved and the CPUSA was rechartered. Browder was expelled. See: Ryan, *Earl Browder…*, Ibid.

the capabilities of African women...In Africa as in America, the war has provided new opportunities for the women to come forward." He noted Liberia's voluntary women's military corps, the Ethiopian women's "social welfare and health service program," as well as the role of South African women in the "trade union movement and in mass organizations such as the African National Congress." Reflecting 1940s gender norms, Hunton continued: "Upon the African woman will rest a considerable part of the post-war task of bringing the benefits of modern education, health, nutrition, and housing standards to the untaught, ill-fed, and disease-stricken millions." Hunton clarified, though; to him, women were equal partners in the post-war effort to rebuild and improve living standards. "No mass campaigns for the improvement of social services in Africa can be successful unless the African women, convinced that the programs are genuinely in the interests of their families and communities, make the campaigns *their* campaigns." In short, the "women of Africa, given the necessary funds, technical assistance, and opportunity, will play an indispensable part in winning freedom and equality for the African," as elsewhere.[145]

Increasingly, Hunton began to focus on a post-war world, and what it might hold for colonial peoples. In March 1945, he wondered, "Will there be some effective method of international cooperation for the advancement of colonial peoples toward freedom?" To him, "it comes down to this: Are we going forward, or are we going back to the kind of world which gave rise to World Wars I and II – a world of international economic warfare, with every nation for itself; a world of power politics; a world of quick profits and long breadlines, high investment interest and wasted resources; a world of insecurity, hunger, and war?" As far as Hunton was concerned, "Colonialism and imperialism will go when that kind of world goes." He called for "*a world of collective security.*" He argued that the Crimea Conference, "together with the Bretton Woods agreement and the Dumbarton Oaks proposals, confirmed the determination and sincerity behind the pledge of international cooperation given...at Teheran. We are on the threshold of a new world order of democratic collaboration," he argued; his optimism, perhaps, got the best of him. Hunton emphasized the potential

---

145. Alphaeus Hunton, "Editorial," *New Africa*, Vol. 3, No. 8 (September 1944). *Italic* in original.

of the San Francisco UN Conference; he did not want the UN to become "another ineffectual League of Nations." "While continuing to press for the abolition of imperialism and colonialism in the making of the peace, let us remember that the successful establishment of the basic instruments of world cooperation...is the basic task of the hour."[146] It wasn't that colonial peoples should wait; it was that they would have a more effective vehicle to advocate for independence once the "basic instruments of world cooperation" were secured. Further, they would also have an ally in the Security Council, the Soviet Union, which proved to be the case.

Hunton also criticized "weaknesses" in the American colonial trusteeship plan at the San Francisco Conference. "The first is the failure to make the trusteeship system applicable immediately and uniformly to *all* colonial territories." For Hunton, if the "system is limited to the small fraction of colonies belonging to enemies in World Wars I and II," then some "native peoples would be in a better position merely because they had once been under enemy sovereignty." This, of course, left "unsettled the question of international supervision over colonies in general... [and] appears to make a concession to the nebulous principle of sovereign rights at the expense of collective security." The second criticism Hunton had was regarding the "composition of the Trusteeship Council." He called for "permanent seats" for the Soviet Union and China. "And, further, *there must be representation on the Council for the colonial peoples themselves,*" he added. "This is essential for winning their confidence in and support of the trusteeship program."[147]

As far as the CAA was concerned, "keeping the colonial question in the public spotlight and not pigeon-holed, as it has customarily been," was paramount. As such, the "the opportunity for carrying the solution of the colonial problem to a much higher level than that reached to date at San Francisco" was the immediate task. In a telegram to President Truman and Secretary of State Edward R. Stettinius, Paul Robeson was direct and to the point: "I am seriously disturbed by omission from the American proposal

---

146. Alphaeus Hunton, "Editorial," *New Africa*, Vol. 4, No. 3 (March 1945). *Italic* in original.

147. Alphaeus Hunton, "Editorial," *New Africa*, Vol. 4, No. 5 (May 1945). *Italic* in original.

of a forthright affirmation of our traditional American principle of freedom for colonial peoples...I respectfully urge our delegation to San Francisco...to give clear expression to and support the principle of full freedom within specified time for all colonial peoples." At this time, Robeson still had considerable influence; less than a year earlier, 12,000 people had gathered to wish the bass-baritone happy birthday; another 4,000 had been turned away. Hunton was just as critical but added a new dimension. He wrote, "it appears clear that the inadequacies of the United Nations' trusteeship plan, based upon the American proposals, must be attributed as much to the pressure of *forces right here in America*, as to the influence of imperialist interests abroad." The outcome of the UN trusteeship policy affected not only "the 750,000,000 people in the colonies; it directly affects the future peace and prosperity of America and the world," he added. "The forces of reaction," Hunton concluded, "must not succeed in depriving either us or the colonial peoples of the harvest of victory over fascism."[148] Hunton would not be deterred; he had his sights set on colonial independence and Black liberation.

*   *   *

In addition to his many CAA responsibilities, from July 1944 to January 1946 Hunton also wrote regular columns for the *Daily Worker*. His articles often highlighted Soviet socialism and its support for colonial independence. In July 1944, Hunton discussed a pamphlet published by the National Council of American-Soviet Friendship, of which he was a board member. The "common struggle against fascism" and the "strength of the Soviet Union... [has] made possible the clearing away of the rubbish of falsehood and slander about that country," propaganda that would intensify shortly after the war's end. "There has developed a widespread and genuine appreciation...of Soviet life," he wrote. For

---

148. "United Nations Colonial Policy Must Be Strengthened," "Council Urges Independence For Colonies," and Alphaeus Hunton, "Editorial," *New Africa*, Vol. 4, No. 6 (June 1945). *Italic* in original. Re Robeson's birthday, see: "Conference Urges International Action For African Progress," *New Africa*, Vol. 3, No. 5 (May 1944) and Duberman, *Paul Robeson...*, Ibid., 284-285. The CAA was more reserved than Duberman in its attendance estimate, claiming only 8,000 people assemble to honor Robeson.

example, "the way in which, within a quarter of a century, many millions of people of different races, creeds and cultures, illiterate, impoverished and degraded victims of exploitation" were quickly "raised to full social, economic and political equality." Importantly, this is a "record of achievement...of special interest to those who are thinking about the problem of abolishing colonialism and semi-colonialism in all areas of the postwar world,"[149] particularly African Americans and Africans then attempting to build solidarity across the Atlantic with the aid of the CAA.

"Yes, Africans today are learning and talking about the Soviet Union," he continued in another column. "With their increasing knowledge" of Soviet socialism and its successes, "African leaders are more frequently citing...the failure of the European colonial administration." Its inability "to provide any appreciable social advancement for the masses of Africans" was contrasted with the "remarkable success of the Soviet government in bringing social well-being and economic efficiency to millions" of people who had been "in a state of colonial serfdom." Hunton's use of the language of liberation is important; he is intentionally comparing colonial subjects in Africa and colonial serfs in the former Russian Empire in an effort to build solidarity between the Black and the Red. Hunton also called for an immediate end to an "outmoded system of imperialist exploitation and colonial tutelage."[150]

Like other Communists, Hunton was quick to point out the similarities between the racists at home and the fascists abroad. "The Hitlerite regime sought to prove that a super-race, a Herrenvolk [master-race], could rule the world." He speculated that white supremacists, "together with the anti-Communists and anti-Semites, propose to continue using Hitler's weapons and fighting Hitler's war even after Hitler is defeated," which unfortunately proved to be the case. Specifically, Hunton was then blasting the reactionary, racist Mississippi Senator Theodore Bilbo, who – along with his ilk – "are becoming more and more desperate in their efforts to stop the Negro's march toward full citizenship

149. Alphaeus Hunton, "Today's Guest Column: Textbook for Conference On Colonial Freedom," *Daily Worker*, July 20, 1944, 7

150. Alphaeus Hunton, "Today's Guest Column: People of Africa Learn From the USSR," *Daily Worker*, August 3, 1944, 7

rights."[151] By early September 1944, Hunton, along with numerous other "leaders of Negro organizations and trade unions" met in New York City to "map out plans for a mass non-partisan [voter] registration drive directed specifically to getting out the Negro vote" that fall, a vote that would aid African Americans in their "march" toward equality.[152] Domestically, Hunton continued, "The Negro is keenly aware of the stakes of freedom in this war." As African Americans reach a "higher level" in the struggle for equality, partly through the ballot box, they also "develop a closer relationship to the struggles of other oppressed peoples," he argued. Like the CAA's organizational and educational work, Hunton's *Daily Worker* columns focused on building international solidarity.[153] He called for "a new vision and policy of cooperation" in colonial Africa, one based on equality and liberation, not racism and subjugation. "To insure that deeds and not promises are the order of the day for colonial peoples, and to insure that America plays its full part in accomplishing the deeds, Americans have their job cut out for them in the coming elections," he concluded.[154] Hunton repeatedly connected the prospects for Black liberation in Africa with domestic electoral results.

"As in our own South, there is a growing recognition that the fight for Negro rights is an integral part of the fight for democratic rights in general," Hunton emphasized in another *DW* column. As discussed above, Communist leadership of the NNC, SNYC, the CAA, and the CRC – and a few years later, Sojourners for Truth and Justice and the National Negro Labor Council,[155] among other formations – centered the struggle for equality as a key component of the struggle for democracy.[156]

151. Alphaeus Hunton, "Today's Guest Column: 'Back to Africa' Cry Is Levelled Against Teheran," *Daily Worker*, August 17, 1944, 7

152. "Map Nonpartisan Drive For Negro Registration," *Daily Worker*, September 2, 1944, 5

153. Alphaeus Hunton, "Today's Guest Column: Negro People Concerned With Africa's Future," *Daily Worker*, August 24, 1944, 7

154. Alphaeus Hunton, "Today's Guest Column: Role of U.S. Elections In Future of Colonial Peoples," *Daily Worker*, September 14, 1944, 7

155. Alphaeus Hunton, "Today's Guest Column: South African Native Labor Movement Growing," *Daily Worker*, October 5, 1944, 7. For more on STJ and the NNLC, see: Gore, *Radicalism at the Crossroads...*, Ibid.

156. For more on the question of "centrality," see: Johnson, "The Communist Party and the African American Question," in Pecinovsky (ed), *Faith In The*

Like his comrade Thelma Dale, a Howard University graduate, SNYC leader, and national secretary of the NNC,[157] Hunton was already thinking ahead, pondering peace-time reconversion jobs for African Americans. He wondered if "the employment gains we [African Americans] have made" during the war would be "maintained and extended" during the peace? Organized labor, he added, needs to "plan concretely for safeguarding the job status of Negroes as part of the larger task of maintaining democratic employment standards for all workers." Unfortunately, this task proved considerably more difficult with the passage of the Taft-Hartley Act in 1947, the coming Red Scare, and the purging of Communists from the U.S. labor movement. Again, Hunton focused on the international impact of domestic politics, and added, "the economic future of the Negro and the strength of the labor movement, when victory has been won, hinge on whether this country continues to play its proper role in developing and realizing a program of international collaboration for promoting a peaceful economy of abundance, world-wide in scope." Like other Communists, Hunton was optimistic that the war-time alliance with the Soviet Union would continue. This alliance, he wrote, coupled with "increased industrial and agricultural production" equaled peace and jobs. "In such a program lies the only real promise of security for the Negro and all other workers in America, as well as of liberation for peoples throughout the world from the chains of colonialism and feudalism."[158]

Masses..., Ibid. In 1948, CPUSA leader William Patterson wrote, "He who has the leadership of the Negro people for equal rights, has the leadership of the whole American movement for constitutional liberties, civil and human rights...There is no problem, no issue, no project...that takes priority over the Negro question." See: Horne, *Communist Front...*, Ibid., 330. Of course, other Communists may have disagreed with this formulation, particularly Communists of other ethnicities. For example, see: Enrique M. Buelna, *Chicano Communists And The Struggle For Social Justice* (Tucson: University of Arizona Press, 2019); Horne, *Fighting In Paradise...*, Ibid.; and Pecinovsky, *Let Them Tremble...*, Ibid. (chapter 5 on Native American CPUSA leader, Judith LeBlanc)

157. Gore, *Radicalism at the Crossroads...*, Ibid. and Thelma Dale, "Reconversion And The Negro People," *Political Affairs*, October 1945

158. Alphaeus Hunton, "Today's Guest Column: Negro People Going Forward With Roosevelt," *Daily Worker*, November 2, 1944, 7. For more on Taft-Hartley and the purging of Communist-led unions from the CIO, see: See: Stepan-Norris and Zeitlin, *Left Out...*, Ibid.

Hunton made many comparisons between racists in South Africa and segregationists in the southern U.S. He noted the "growing tension…[as] reactionary forces have attempted to block the Africans' increasingly organized efforts to gain justice." As would also become a common feature in newspapers and TV stations in the U.S. in the 1950s and 1960s, "disciplined and orderly" demonstrations in South Africa were likewise being "deliberately provoked…[with] tear gas." The "South African counterparts of the Ku Klux Klan, Christian Front and other pro-fascist forces," were responsible for the violence, Hunton emphasized, not peaceful demonstrators seeking equality. To Hunton, "discrimination whether in this country, Africa or elsewhere, is incompatible with any genuine concept of world security," a theme he repeatedly articulated. In short, a "real and lasting victory over fascism" required that the emerging United Nations "erase this evil [of racism] wherever it exists."[159]

By early 1945 Hunton was optimistically writing of the coming end of WWII, the "finis to fascism." He called for "a worldwide system of prosperity and peace," a call that would ultimately prove elusive. He also chastised Western leaders as they continued to "talk of 'trusteeship' and 'preparing backward peoples for the management of their own affairs,'" which were little more than "modern paraphrases of 'the white man's burden.'" To Hunton, unanswered were the "practical questions of HOW and WHEN" colonial peoples would gain freedom; "vague promises" were no substitute for "conscientious and systematic planning…[if] the democratic forces of the world" were to win "a real New Year and New Deal for the hundreds of millions of colonial peoples."[160]

Hunton also criticized liberal forces in South Africa unwilling to work with Communists. "The weakness of the progressive forces in South Africa" isn't due to a "lack of program or lack of influence and following among the masses of the people." Rather, it was a result of "too much factionalism and division among those who should be fighting together. The Labor Party, for

159. Alphaeus Hunton, "Today's Guest Column: Johannesburg Riot Reflects a World Problem," *Daily Worker*, November 9, 1944, 9

160. Alphaeus Hunton, "Today's Guest Column: Colonial Peoples Look Forward as 1945 Opens," *Daily Worker*, January 4, 1945, 7

example, will not collaborate with the Communist Party because of the latter's unqualified stand against all racial discrimination." There, as in the United States, he continued, "the only way to lick reaction is through the united strength of all those on the side of democracy and progress," including Communists.[161]

Hunton frequently sparred with apologists for imperialism in his columns, too. George S. Schuyler, an African American *Pittsburgh Courier* columnist, for example, "peddles his subversive poison...[his] made-in-Berlin propaganda...[which] specializes in redbaiting, parading before his readers every conceivable slander against the Soviet Union and against Communists." To Schuyler, "a dangerously large percentage of so-called thinking Negroes has swallowed the red propaganda," an explicit acknowledgement of the continued potency of Black militancy comfortable with red allies. Approvingly, Hunton quoted another *Pittsburgh Courier* columnist, Liu Liang-mo, who also shared a disdain for Schuyler. "Hitler's and Japan's last trump card is to split the unity of the United States with anti-communism and anti-sovietism [sic], and it looks like Mr. Schuyler is doing his best...to serve the purpose of our common enemy," a tactic many in Washington would soon emulate. Schuyler also attacked Black support for Roosevelt in the 1944 elections and paternalistically urged "really intelligent, informed" African Americans "interested in racial welfare" to vote for Norman Thomas and the Socialist Party, "to which the only alternative is ultimate slavery." "There you have it," Hunton exclaimed! "There couldn't be a better illustration of how the ultra-left and the ultra-right travel the same road of reaction." He likened Schuyler to Westbrook Pegler, a white conservative journalist who spent much of his career attacking unions, the New Deal, and Roosevelt.[162] According to Hunton, both sought to weaken democracy in a failed attempt to destroy Communists.

In his analysis of the April-May 1945 San Francisco United Nations meeting, Hunton criticized the American, British and French proposals regarding the post-war colonial "trusteeship

---

161. Alphaeus Hunton, "Today's Guest Column: Two Letters From South Africa," *Daily Worker*, February 8, 1945, 7. The CPUSA shared this experience as well, especially in the South, where it insisted upon interracial meetings, marches, and rallies. For example, see: Kelley, *Hammer And Hoe...*, Ibid.

162. Alphaeus Hunton, "Today's Guest Column: The Westbrook Pegler Of Negro Journalism," *Daily Worker*, March 8, 1945, 7

problem." The Soviet delegates, on the other hand, "made the more specific and far-reaching proposal of 'progressive development toward self-government and self-determination, with active participation of the peoples of these territories having the aim to expedite the achievement of national independence.'" This was a goal Hunton continued to support. To Hunton, the "wording used in the revised draft of the American plan...fails to match the Soviet point of view" and was "even a qualification," a constraining "of the original American formula." Apparently, this was "a concession to the wishes of the British" then preparing a "conveniently-timed" announcement of "plans for self-government in Burma." Complicating matters, however, was the lack of evidence, "for the very good reason that it can't be found," that the Burmese people "are satisfied with the self-government plans as proposed" by the British delegates. To Hunton, "A fundamental principle is at stake in this issue: It is no mere quibble over words." Former colonial peoples "cannot be said to be truly self-governing unless and until they have the right to independence," a reality then eluding the American, British and French delegations. Clearly, "withholding the right of independence makes the concept of self-determination, upon which the Big Five have already agreed, absolutely meaningless," Hunton argued. He urged action. "The American people should insist," he concluded, "that their delegates...adhere to this policy in working out the final decision regarding trusteeship arrangements."[163]

Hunton did not ignore South Africa; he called "all the fulsome adulation" bequeathed upon Gen. Jan Smuts, the prime minister of the Dominion of South Africa, while in San Francisco, "wearisome, if not nauseating." He wrote that it would "be difficult to cite a better instance of these evils [racist and fascist oppression coalescing] than the notorious case of South Africa itself." Smuts and the South African regime represented a "postwar fascist threat" where "8,000,000 non-white peoples and a large section of the white workers as well, are kept enslaved."[164] Conversely, he praised the SACP as "the only political party in South Africa

163. Alphaeus Hunton, "Today's Guest Column: Hull Defined The Solution," *Daily Worker*, May 24, 1945, 11
164. Alphaeus Hunton, "Today's Guest Column: A Voice from South Africa," *Daily Worker*, July 6, 1945, 12

which stands foursquare for the abolition of the entire system of exploitation," namely colonialism, imperialism, and capitalism buttressed by racism. Despite the "cold shoulder" they received, Communists continued to build a "united front,"[165] thereby planting seeds resulting in their leading role in ending white minority rule and building a coalition government headed by the ANC.

Perceptively, Hunton recognized in their attempt "to block the march of millions of colonial and semi-colonial peoples toward freedom and progress, the imperialist powers are promoting, not good will, but an ever-increasing and explosively dangerous volume of ill will." Imperialist powers "aim at a 'peace' with all the old special privileges of race, nationality and class remaining intact,"[166] he concluded. South Africa was a case in point. In one of his final *Daily Worker* columns South Africa was considered "one gigantic concentration camp" where the Pass Laws restricted all "freedom of movement" of the Black majority.[167]

*   *   *

In July 1945, the CAA published a statement by Dr. A.B. Xuma, President-General of the African National Congress, "summarizing the oppressive conditions" of life in South Africa. According to Xuma, the South African Native Policy reduced the Black majority to "abject poverty, ill health and ignorance." He laid out the political, economic, industrial, criminal, and educational components of white minority repression. Politically, the Black majority "have no right of franchise to elect members of various legislative bodies…Having no vote they have no voice in Government affairs." Economically, they "have no inherent right to own, purchase, lease, let, or rent land without the consent of the Government. For them land ownership and occupation is limited, restricted and discouraged." Further, they are "compelled" to live on "Native Reserves," where they "pay rent" to the Government. Industrially, they are "excluded from skilled trades and

---

165. Alphaeus Hunton, "Today's Guest Column: Why Imperialists Get South Africa's Help," *Daily Worker*, December 13, 1945, 7

166. Alphaeus Hunton, "Today's Guest Column: Thanksgiving Milestones," *Daily Worker,* November 22, 1945, 7

167. Alphaeus Hunton, "Today's Guest Column: 11 Badges of Serfdom in South Africa," *Daily Worker*, December 20, 1945, 7

occupations and they are doomed to low starvation wages. Their trade unions are not recognized and registered by the Government, hence breach of contract and a strike for them are criminal offenses...Thus they have no legal collective bargaining powers." As far as crime, "Of all Africans convicted annually, less than 5% are convicted for serious crimes." And education, according to Xuma, "Africans are well over 90% illiterate. The State has neither recognized the claim of every normal African child to be educated nor has it assumed full responsibility for the financial burden...As a result only less than 40% of the African children of school-going age can be accommodated for the most elementary schooling."[168] The racist white minority intended to keep the African Black majority in a permanent condition of servitude.

In the August-September issue of *New Africa*, Hunton tempered "the boundless expression of joy over the victorious end of the war against the fascist axis [sic]," and noted the "sober anxiety concerning the problems of peace with which, in all their hard and grim reality, the world is now face to face." African American equality and colonial liberation were both on his mind, as was the continued plight of Black South Africans. He feared some people were too eager for things to "just get back to normal," hoping "things will work out all right." For "the Negro worker in America 'normal' existence means discrimination, menial jobs or no job at all. For the Negro worker in Africa's colonies 'normal' existence means serfdom, ignorance, poverty and disease. There is a great deal to worry about," he added, "if no better prescription than that can be found for the problems of peace."[169] Perhaps, a recently cancelled broadcast on "Negro veterans' job rights" was fresh on Hunton's mind. Though "the Army had prepared and okeyed [sic] the script," the War Department and Columbia Broadcasting, Co. cancelled the program "with the explanation that such themes were not to be dealt with." According to Hunton, "Another item has been added to [the] record of discrimination against Negro troops." He demanded that the program be broadcast as scheduled. "The War Department owes at least that

168. Dr. Xuma Sends Statement On S. African Native Policy," *New Africa*, Vol. 4, No. 7 (July 1945)

169. Alphaeus Hunton, "Editorial," *New Africa*, Vol. 4, No. 8 (August-September 1945).

much to the Negro soldiers for their part in winning the victory." The NNC, the Negro Labor Victory Committee, and the United Wholesale and Warehouse Employees union, among others protested the cancellation.[170]

In short, Hunton was not about to let the jubilation of peace distract him from the privation of millions of African Americans nor the subjugation of tens of millions of Africans. If, as he noted in *New Africa*, "Mankind's future depends today, above all, upon the United States," then he wasn't optimistic. "As the world's most powerful nation this country can, if it adheres to the principles of collective security, perform the same kind of magnificent service in winning the peace as it did in winning the war." Ominously, though, he warned, "There are some powerful and influential people, however, who favor the idea of America taking what she wants and dictating what the rest of the world may have." The scholar-activist, then, asked, "Which policy do you favor? Don't tell us. *Tell your government*."[171] Hunton educated and agitated for justice.

Throughout its existence, the CAA focused on the repressive South African regime. Also, in the August-September issue was a short article on a 2,000 person march in Cape Town protesting the Pass Laws, "the African's badge of bondage." Another article highlighted the annual conference of the National Council of African Women.[172] A month later, the CAA reported on the killing of six African activists near Johannesburg; police "assaulted and opened fire upon [the] crowd" outside of a beer hall, killing four men, and two teenage children. Additionally, 87 women and 21 men were arrested "on charges of public violence." The protesters were demonstrating the "prohibition against the brewing of 'Kaffir beer' in African homes," which is "typical of the government's repressive measures practiced against the Bantu population." African homes are "raided by the police without the slightest regard for elementary civil rights," it was added. During

---

170. "Explain Radio Ban, Army Told," *Daily Worker*, August 24, 1945, 3

171. Hunton, "Editorial," *New Africa*, Vol. 4, No. 8 (August-September 1945). *Italic* in original.

172. "Campaign Against Pass Laws Continues In South Africa," and "South African Women Hold Annual Conference," *New Africa*, Vol. 4, No. 8 (August-September 1945)

the first three months of 1945, 35,000 Africans were "arrested *weekly* for violation of this law."[173]

Another article was titled, *"FASCISTS ON THE MARCH,"* and noted, the "anti-Negro, anti-Jew, anti-labor forces in South African politics, [were] permitted to hold a propaganda congress." Remarkably, no one was killed "when thousands of anti-fascists including soldiers and women clashed" with Nationalist Party supporters, though several Black South Africans were injured protesting a ceremony honoring General Jan Smuts. Additionally, the council reported on a "scheme" then "under consideration by the South African government's Social and Economic Planning Council whereby a public utility corporation 'sponsored' by the government would organize 60,000 African youth, aged 14 to 19, into service units, under European supervision for farming and industrial work." Apparently, this "scheme" would compel parents to "enter into a five year service contract with the corporation on behalf of their sons, thus presumably making the whole thing perfectly legal and binding on the youth, should they prefer not to complete their five years 'matriculation.'" Enrollees were promised "'vocational and scholastic' training. What, when, and how much is not clear, for the scheme calls for all costs of the corporation, which will include a board of directors, general manager, and administrative and technical staff, to be paid out of the earnings of the youth," who would be paid "5c per day for the first year, 16c per day for the second year, 20c for the third, 25c for the fourth, and finally 30c in their last year." Of course, part of the wages would be "deferred during the period of service, a larger amount annually as the wage increases," to supposedly be "handed over" once the full five years of service was completed. "However, the interest on this deferred pay as well as the difference between wages charged the employers and the wages given the youth will go to the corporation."[174]

Hunton also pushed the United States to advocate for democracy in South Africa. He pointed to President Truman's October 12 Navy Day address; Truman said, "We believe that all peoples who

173. "South African 'Justice' – Six Africans Killed By Johannesburg Police," *New Africa*, Vol. 4, No. 9 (October 1945). *Italic* in original.

174. "Fascists On The March," "Africans Mauled At Welcome To Smuts," and "Regimented Child Labor Planned For South Africa," *New Africa*, Vol. 4, No. 10 (November 1945)

are prepared for self-government should be permitted to choose their own form of government by their own freely expressed choice, without interference from any foreign source. That is true in Europe, in Asia, in Africa, as well as in the Western Hemisphere." Hunton noted, "There is unfortunately a basic and oft-repeated fallacy in the President's formulation...but as a statement of general principle it transcends anything which the leaders of the British, French, Dutch or other imperial powers have had to say on the right of colonial peoples to self-government." However, he cautioned, we would do "well to pause and consider that imperialism wears many dresses and colonialism is only one of them." Unlike the European empires, the U.S. had few actual colonial possessions; its unseen economic interests were vast, however, and continuing to expand; this was what worried Hunton. On the issue of self-government, Hunton continued, "it is not a question of whether peoples 'are prepared for self-government.' The fact of being human in itself implies the capacity and necessity of self-government. *The real question is when and under what circumstances the imperial powers will be prepared to yield self-government to their colonial subjects.*" To Hunton, the "answer" depends to a very considerable extent upon the foreign policy which the United States itself *practices* rather than professes."[175] These probing insights proved prophetic.

*   *   *

Hunton and the CAA didn't just report on what was happening in South Africa and elsewhere, nor did they neglect the activist components of their organizational mission. In January 1946, for example, 4,000 people attended a CAA sponsored meeting at Abyssinian Baptists Church (image 3) to aid the "4,000,000 starving women and children in the Union of South Africa."[176] "[E]very available inch of space" was jammed, the *Daily Worker* reported, as "10 tons of canned food and $1,730 in hard-earned money" was collected. Paul Robeson said, "freedom for the oppressed black peoples of South Africa is inseparable from the struggle for freedom everywhere – in China, or India, or our

---

175. Alphaeus Hunton, "Editorial," *New Africa*, Vol. 4, No. 10 (November 1945). *Italic* in original.

176. "Meeting Aids South Africans," *New York Times*, January 8, 1946

own South."[177] Hunton agreed and optimistically noted in his weekly *Daily Worker* column, "Harlem will start the New Year, appropriately enough, with a demonstration of support for the oppressed victims of imperialism across the sea." The goal was to "collect a mountain of canned food and substantial funds for the relief…[of] famine-stricken Africans." Hunton saw "great wealth in South Africa's modern cities." But the "African's life is one of poverty, hunger and disease." Due to the colonial theft of their lands, "Nine out of 10 African children are undernourished," while in "some areas the infant mortality rate is over 60 percent." To Hunton, "chronic starvation" was a deliberate policy directed against Africans "in the land of gold and diamonds," which is "how the system of imperialism works."[178]

Roughly one month earlier, in a December 1945 *Daily Worker* column, Hunton wrote, "Outside pressure upon the South African government…must be developed." The CAA, he continued, is "the only organization in this country thus far to bring the starvation crisis in South Africa to the attention of the American public." The CAA "has constantly sought to mobilize such [public] pressure," he added.[179] In a *New York Times* letter-to-the-editor, Hunton presented "a few facts…regarding the status of African people in the Union of South Africa." He decried the "deplorable health conditions and extremely high death rates," as well as the separate and unequal investments in education. He wrote, the "present per capita expenditure for the education of the white child is about forty times that for the African child." To Hunton, the logic of racism was simple. The "denial of adequate health, educational and other social services to the African majority is the determination of the white ruling class of that country to keep the Africans from attaining a status of economic, social or political equality," to keep them subjugated. "The sole blame for the Africans' failure to become fully integrated in modern culture rests upon the European," he concluded.[180]

---

177. Helen Simon, "4,000 Give Food, Urge Liberty for Africans," *Daily Worker*, January 9, 1946, 8

178. Alphaeus Hunton, "Today's Guest Column: Harlem Rallies to Aid Famine-Stricken Africa," *Daily Worker*, January 3, 1946, 7

179. Alphaeus Hunton, "Today's Guest Column: Hunger, Disease, Fascist Repression – South Africa," *Daily Worker*, December 6, 1945, 7

180. W.A. Hunton, "Progress in South Africa," *New York Times*, May 17, 1947

4,000 Give Food, Urge Liberty for Africans

By HELEN SIMON

The 4,000 who jammed every available inch of space at Abyssinia Baptist Church Monday night did more than launch a famine relief campaign for starving Africans. They expressed their conviction, as Paul Robeson put it, that freedom for the oppressed black peoples of South Africa is inseparable from the struggle for freedom everywhere —in China, or India, or our own South.

Robeson, voicing pride in his own African ancestry, illustrated in deep-noted song the high level of culture achieved by the African people. He told of his own childhood and youth—the hunger he had known, the speed-up of the brickyard where he worked at 13; he spoke of his father who escaped three times from slavery—and said to the 4,000,000 Africans who have asked for help: "I know what it is to starve and labor."

His listeners understood too. Most of them were Negroes, deeply hurt by oppression, discrimination. They gave generously 10 tons of canned food and $1,730 in hard-earned money for more food which the Council on African Affairs will ship to Africa.

Marian Anderson, tall and dignified, said, "I am thoroughly interested in the African people, and I think that whatever we can do is still too little."

So very much is needed, as Dr. Wulf Sachs, Russian-born visitor from South Africa, bore witness. Dr. Sachs, who is editor of The Democrat, progressive South African magazine, said bitterly that black Africans are victims of "extreme virulent fascism."

What makes their position even worse than that of Negroes here, he explained, is that discrimination there is embodied in law. It is illegal NOT to oppress. The starvation from which the many suffer, he said, is "human-made." Black Africans have never been permitted to develop their hand or brain; new restrictions on their freedom of movement, employment, organization are constantly being decreed.

Rev. Ben Richardo Richardson, associate editor of The Protestant, made a forceful appeal.

"The Africans need more than food," he declared, "They need to know how to overthrow the system that brings drought year after year. The enemy is the system of capitalism, whereby some grow strong and fat and greasy at the expense of the rest of us. We can reach over into Africa and share their miseries because to a great extent their miseries are our miseries."

The Jewish people were represented at the rally by Rabbi Max Felshin, of Radio City Synagogue, who linked the first stirrings of people's struggle in Africa with the freedom movements of Indonesians, Chinese, Indians, Jews.

Responsibility of the World Federation of Trade Unions and of labor everywhere to strike out for African freedom was highlighted by Josh Lawrence, representing the National Maritime Union.

Others spoke—Dr. Max Yergan and Dr. Alphaeus Hunton of the Council on African Affairs, which sponsored the meeting; Rev. Adam Clayton Powell Sr. and Father Shelton Hale Bishop; Judge Hubert T. Delaney, H. P. Osborne, of the West Indies National Council, and

MARIAN ANDERSON

PAUL ROBESON

Mrs. Lida C. Broner, who read a moving letter from South Africa about the famine.

Sgt. Eugene List was enthusiastically greeted when he made a surprise appearance and played two piano selections.

The gathering addressed a vehement protest letter to Gen. Jan Christian Smuts, Prime Minister of South Africa, and also urged the United Nations Organization to take steps to enforce its creed of human rights in South Africa.

What's On

RATES: What's On notices for the Daily and The Worker are 85c per line (4 words to a line—5 lines minimum).
DEADLINE: Daily at 12 Noon. For Sunday—Wednesday at 4 p.m.

Tonight—Manhattan

Italians Demonstrate For 'Bread and Work'

IMAGE 3: *Daily Worker*, January 9, 1946. Courtesy of *People's World*.

This was a tremendously busy time for Hunton. Like Robeson and Du Bois, he kept to a hectic schedule. Along with his CAA responsibilities elevating consciousness regarding racist oppression and starvation in South Africa, he also organized with the American Labor Party and spoke at their early 1946 "Negro

History Week" event.[181] In April 1946, he was one of 750 delegates attending the Win the Peace Conference held in Washington, D.C.; it was organized just one month after British Prime Minister Winston Churchill made his infamous Fulton, Missouri "iron curtain" speech initiating the Cold War[182] (a second Win the Peace Conference was held in Manhattan in June).[183] Hunton also challenged Secretary of State James Byrnes; he wrote, Churchill and Byrnes "hate and fear the principles of democracy and freedom for which the Soviet Union stands...The all-out campaign of slander against the Soviet Union must be stopped." The "voice of the Negro people as a whole, who want to work in friendship and cooperation with our Soviet ally, must make itself heard – loudly and quickly,"[184] he emphasized, while urging domestic action for peace as the tide turned toward Cold War.

Additionally, unlike Churchill, whose racism is now well-known,[185] the CAA was still focused on the plight of starving children in Africa; Hunton shared the stage with Pete Seeger, among others, at the Hotel Granada on May 6 to continue to raise awareness, while also reporting on the Win the Peace Conference.[186] In late May, the council organized "Broadway stars [to] make special appeals on behalf of...famine stricken South Africans." "Six radio programs during ten days," featuring Kenneth Spencer, star of Show Boat, Betty Garrett, star of Call Me Mister, Canada

181. "ALP Event to Mark Negro History Week," *Daily Worker,* February 5, 1946, 2

182. Rob F. Hall, "750 Delegates Open Win-Peace Parley; Sen. Taylor Hits War Clamor," *Daily Worker,* April 6, 1946, 2. For more on Churchill, the "iron curtain" speech, and the Cold War, see: Fraser J. Harbutt, *The Iron Curtain: Churchill, America, And The Origins Of The Cold War* (New York: Oxford University Press, 1986). According to Harbutt, "The Fulton address was a brilliant exercise in political prophecy. Like some master architect, Churchill laid out, in a necessarily general but easily recognizable form, much of the future shape and character of the Cold War." Harbutt, 184

183. "Civic Leaders Sponsor Win-Peace Conference," *Daily Worker,* June 22, 1946, 5

184. "Negro Press Doubts Byrnes," *Daily Worker,* April 7, 1946, 13

185. Richard Toye, "Yes, Churchill was a racist. It's time to break free of his 'great white men' view of history," *CNN,* June 10, 2020, https://www.cnn.com/2020/06/10/opinions/churchill-racist-great-white-men-view-toye-opinion/index.html and Priyamvada Gopal, "Why can't Britain handle the truth about Winston Churchill," *The Guardian,* March 17, 2021, https://www.theguardian.com/commentisfree/2021/mar/17/why-cant-britain-handle-the-truth-about-winston-churchill

186. "Hear Report on 'Win The Peace' Conference," *Daily Worker,* May 1, 1946, 4 (advertisement)

Lee, star of On Whitman Avenue, Judy Holliday, star of Born Yesterday, among others, participated in the CAA sponsored "Stars Radio Appeal."[187]

Just a few weeks later, CAA filled Madison Square Garden with at least 15,000 people calling for Big Three (U.S., Great Britain, and USSR) Unity for Colonial Freedom (image 4). The council not only protested the Truman administration's drive toward Cold War, it linked peace to colonial independence.

Robeson told the assembled activists, "The imperialists' 'Stop Russia' cry" must be "drowned out by the voice of the American people demanding Big Three unity for colonial freedom." To Robeson, "'Stop Russia' really means stop colonial independence, stop Europe's new democracy, stop labor unions, stop Negro organization and voting." Of course, Africa "is a major prize which the imperialist covet and which we, the anti-imperialists, must defend," he added. The Communist Councilman, Benjamin Davis, Jr., noted, "Only the Socialist Soviet Union...has spoken out for the freedom of Africa."[188]

Just days before the rally, the New York State Communist Party issued an appeal to its then considerable membership urging maximum participation. They noted, the rally "will be a blow for the freedom of the teeming millions of black peoples of Africa, [and] a blow for the freedom of the 14,000,000 Negro people in America. Hence, all anti-fascist America, Negro and white, must work for the success of the rally." The World Federation of Trade Unions endorsed the rally[189] ; Indian National Congress leader and soon-to-be Prime Minister of India, Jawaharlal Nehru, sent greetings, as well.[190] Dr. R. T. Bokwe, of the African Food Fund in a wire to Robeson, said, "hopes once raised by [the] Atlantic and UN charters [were] now dashed to the ground by starvation and repressive discrimination laws in South Africa." He called for "international pressure on the undemocratic government."[191] Max Yergan told the audience,

187. "Stars Radio Appeal for So. African Famine relief," *Daily Worker*, May 28, 1946, 11

188. "Africa Wants Freedom, Says Paul Robeson," *Daily Worker*, June 7, 1946, 12

189. "CP Hails June 6 Negro Rally As Blow For Peace," and "World Labor Body Backs Garden Rally," *Daily Worker*, June 3, 1946, 2

190. "Nehru Greets Rally on Colonial Freedom," *Daily Worker*, June 1, 1946, 2

191. "Africans Send Plea to Garden Rally Tomorrow," *Daily Worker*, June 5, 1946, 12

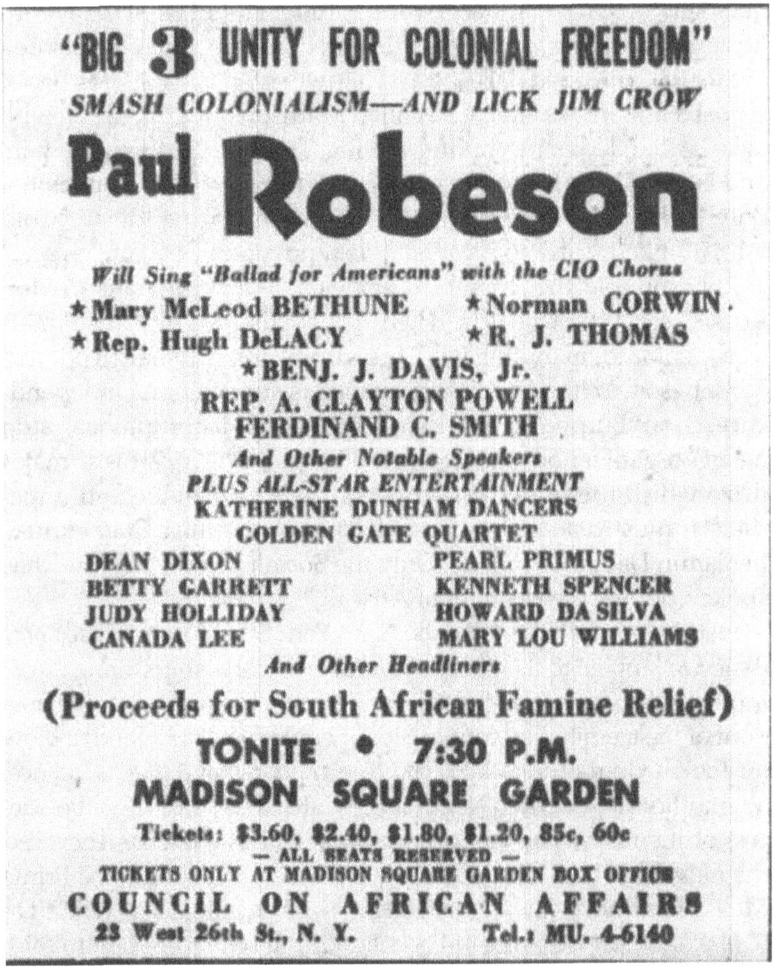

IMAGE 4: *Daily Worker*, June 6, 1946. Courtesy of *People's World*.

"colonial imperialism stands indicted before the bar of world opinion today." He called "upon all Americans" to demand that "colonialism – that bankrupt, plundering and wasteful system of the past – be done away with" and be replaced by "a new relation amongst the peoples of the earth [sic] characterized by dignity." Unfortunately, the political winds had already begun to shift. According to the *New York Times*, the CAA was nothing more than a "Communist-controlled organization supported mainly by Negroes,"[192] which highlighted

192. "Colonial Empires Assailed In Rally," *New York Times*, June 7, 1946

two converging realities: one, that the ruling class tacitly confessed Black militancy comfortable with red allies was a potent political force; and two, that the emerging Red Scare would soon focus laser-like on Communist-led organizations like the CAA and CRC to the detriment of African American equality, Black liberation, and socialism.

Undeterred, Hunton and Eslanda Goode Robeson[193] became regular fixtures at the UN, lobbying against South African Prime Minister Smuts' attempt to annex South-West Africa. CAA members attended sessions of the UN's Ad Hoc Committee on Non-self-governing Territories, the Trusteeship Council, and General Assembly; they distributed literature prepared by the CAA, and personally lobbied members of the Trusteeship Council. While the CAA was successful in stopping the annexation, the U.S. voted with South Africa; the racist regime would later "incorporate the mandate territory through the South Africa Act of 1949." Additionally, Hunton and Goode Robeson worked "behind the scenes" to shape an anti-racist resolution presented by India, challenging South Africa's "right to exclude people of Indian descent from voting." Hunton and the CAA organized "a letter-writing campaign" to Truman, the U.S. State Department, and the U.S. delegate to the UN supporting India's call for sanctions.[194] To Hunton, Black liberation and national liberation were linked; consequently, he attacked white supremacy in all of its manifestations.

The CAA also coordinated actions with, for example, the African National Congress. Hunton urged that "Negroes and progressive whites...must insist that our government stop giving aid in the form of money, guns or in any other form to uphold the white supremacy program" of the racist regime in South Africa. He likened the Malan government to "the same kind of white supremacy rule...[some] are trying to enforce in our own South."[195]

Increasingly, the CAA-ANC relationship defied the prevailing winds of the Red Scare and Hunton sought to bring the

---

193. For more on Goode Robeson's international solidarity, see: Annette K. Joseph-Gabriel, "Feminist Networks and Diasporic Practices: Eslanda Robeson's Travels in Arica," in Keisha N. Blain and Tiffany M. Gill (eds), *To Turn The Whole World Over: Black Women And Internationalism* (Urbana: University of Illinois Press, 2019)

194. Nesbitt, *Race for Sanctions...*, Ibid., 7

195. "Showdown in Africa," *The Worker*, April 6, 1952, 6

anti-apartheid struggle into popular consciousness. The council organized, and Hunton "presided" over, a Harlem rally of 5,000 people in April 1952 that featured Robeson, Congressman Adam Clayton Powell Jr. (D-New York), Charlotta Bass, William L. Patterson, Louis Burnham, Doxey Wilkerson, and Claudia Jones, among others, to coincide with the ANC's Campaign of Defiance of Unjust Laws. At the rally Robeson linked African American equality with Black liberation and said, "If The South African people win some freedom, we'll win some freedom." Claudia Jones emphasized international unity; "...we have to have the unity of all working people to win the fight here and in Africa." Hunton declared that it is the "aim of the Council to develop a united front of all the groups interested in aiding African freedom."[196]

After the rally, the CAA picketed the South African consulate. The police responded quickly, allowing "only two pickets at each entrance of the building." After a visit to the 35th St. precinct by the CRC and Furriers Joint Board, the restriction was lifted, and a permit was granted for 100 people to picket. Hunton urged more unions, like the Furriers, to support the fight against apartheid.[197]

The council also started a petition drive in support of the ANC – with a goal of collecting 100,000 signatures. Hunton called for "redoubled efforts...to broaden the petition drive...[and] translate into concrete and effective action the widespread bitterness and indignation of Americans, particularly black Americans, over the rampant racist barbarism" in South Africa. "Police violence is rampant," he noted in a July letter to CAA supporters calling for an "EMERGENCY CONFERENCE" on the crisis. To him, "the outcome of this heroic and historic struggle...holds the answer of freedom or slavery, life or death, for the ten million African and other darker peoples in South Africa." "More than this," the Defiance Campaign "is the test of whether fascist racism and fascist aggression and war are to be spread northward engulfing the whole continent," which would "certainly...be felt by the Negro people in the United States and the West Indies, and by colonial and subject peoples of other lands." Pointedly, he added, "Fascism in South Africa is a direct

196. John Hudson Jones, "So. Africa Rallies Fight Racial Laws: Harlem Rally Cheers Africa Freedom Struggle," *Daily Worker,* April 7, 1952, 1, 6 and "Africans Rally For Freedom To Robeson's Songs," *Daily Worker,* April 13, 1952, 2

197. "Win Right To More Pickets At So. African Consulate," *Daily Worker,* April 9, 1952, 3

threat to the struggle to preserve and extend our own democratic rights in America. It represents another serious peril to the cause of world peace. We are morally obligated to DO SOMETHING to aid the struggle of our brothers and sisters," he concluded before inviting recipients to the Emergency Conference, which "will seek to develop concrete plans for mobilizing...the fullest possible support for the people's fight against fascist tyranny in South Africa." Over 8,000 men, women, and children were incarcerated in South Africa during the Defiance Campaign; the CAA set a goal of raising $5,000 for their legal defense. Within ten days of Hunton's letter, on July 24, the petition drive was launched at the Conference attended by more than 60 African American and white religious, union, civic, and peace organizations from New York, Philadelphia, and Boston. The CAA's legal defense fund, petition drives, and campaigns to free political prisoners in South Africa foreshadowed the free Nelson Mandela campaigns that emerged years later,[198] as well as the anti-apartheid divestment movement, a campaign partly initiated and led by Communists such as Henry Winston, Charlene Mitchell, Anthony Monteiro, and the National Anti-Imperialist Movement in Solidarity with African Liberation founded in 1973.[199]

Just as television sets were becoming a staple of American households, the CAA sought to use film as an educational medium. In late-1951/early-1952, the council began screening the documentary *South Africa Uncensored*, a "raw and gritty" film with "firsthand testimonial footage of the appalling conditions endured" by Black South Africans under apartheid. The film "portrays the filth in black shantytowns lacking proper sewage systems," the segregation of public spaces, and the "vile white

---

198. Pope, *Exploring the Parallels...*, Ibid.; Nesbitt, *Race for Sanctions...*, Ibid., 19-20; and UMass-Amherst, Special Collections, W.E.B. Du Bois Papers, Box 136: Series 1, 1A: Letter from Hunton, July 14, 1952

199. Pecinovsky, *Let Them Tremble...*, Ibid., 201-208. For example, the African American Communist, trade union leader, and St. Louis Alderman (Ward 22) Kenny Jones would lead the divestment movement on a local level, while other Communists such as Henry Winston, Angela Davis, and Anthony Monteiro would help lead the divestment movement on a national level through NAIMSAL. Jones, a leader in the St. Louis chapter of the Coalition of Black Trade Unionists (which was largely led by CPUSA members), nearly came to blows with the St. Louis Mayor in 2010 when he was fired as director of the Civil Rights Enforcement Agency over support for another Communist then running for office. The author met regularly with Jones.

leisure spectacle of enjoying forced fisticuffs between black workers,"[200] a sport reminiscent of the brutal practice stemming from slavery.[201] The "film's aesthetics reflects the source footage's clandestine and illicit provenance," which was secretly obtained, as both the U.S. government and the South African regime south to minimize the brutality of life under apartheid. Narrated by Robeson, the film's ending "juxtaposes images of discrimination and police violence in Harlem as a rhetorical mirror for its intended U.S. audience." Apparently, the CIA feared the impact the film might have and requested funds to procure it, of which only one copy is known to exist.[202]

*   *   *

The CAA did not confine its activism to the struggle for African American equality and Black liberation. It also protested the emerging war in Korea and sponsored rallies calling for Hands Off Korea where prominent Communists, such as Benjamin Davis, Jr., and Ferdinand Smith spoke. At a July 1950 rally, Robeson declared, "we want no war and there will be none." "All over the world we will impose the peace," he cried.[203] Like other Communist-led groups, such as the Congress of American Women and the Women's International Democratic Federation, the CAA connected the U.S. military assault on Korea with the

---

200. Field and Gordon (eds), *Screening Race in American...*, Ibid., 121

201. See: Gerald Horne, *The Bittersweet Science: Racism, Racketeering, and the Political Economy of Boxing* (New York: International Publishers, 2021)

202. Field and Gordon (eds), *Screening Race in American...*, Ibid., 119-121 and "South Africa Uncensored," National Museum of African American History & Culture, https://nmaahc.si.edu/object/nmaahc_2012.79.1.5.1a?destination=edan-search/collection_search%3Fedan_q%3D%252A%253A%252A%26edan_fq%255B0%255D%3Dp.edanmdm.indexedstructured.name%253A%2522Beveridge%252C%2520Tee%2522%26op%3DSearch. Apparently, *South Africa Uncensored* was seen in the same light as *Salt of the Earth*; funds to procure both films were requested in the same CIA memorandum. Field and Gordon (eds), 120. Also, see: James J. Lorence, *The Suppression of Salt of the Earth: How Hollywood, Big Labor, and Politicians Blacklisted a Movie in Cold War America* (Albuquerque: University of New Mexico Press, 1999)

203. "Robeson At Korea Rally," *New York Times*, July 4, 1950

fight against colonial occupation.[204] Shortly thereafter, Hunton asked Du Bois to draft a statement "expressing the point of view of progressive Negro America on the Korea crisis"; the statement would "be issued on behalf of the Executive Board of the Council...[and] mailed immediately to about 500 Negro leaders throughout the country for their endorsement." Central to the draft, as far as Hunton was concerned, was that the "foreign intervention of what began as a Korean civil war must be stopped immediately." Hunton also emphasized that the crisis should be discussed within "the larger framework of the struggles for national self-determination in the whole of Asia and Africa, [and that] unilateral American action, with or without the support of a U.S. dominated United Nations must give way to a general settlement based upon decisions of a genuine United Nations organizations which includes the Soviet Union and the People's Republic of China."[205]

By August, Madison Square Garden refused rental to the CAA "pending action on the Mundt-Ferguson Communist-Control Bill," which was then in Congress.[206] Though the Bill would not become law, the damage was done. The Red Scare and fast emerging Cold War were already beginning to suffocate civil liberties. Communists like Hunton would soon be sacrificed to make room for civil rights activists like Randolph who were willing to acquiesce to liberal anti-communism in exchange for a retreat from Jim Crow. Regardless, Hunton, Robeson, and the CAA "denounced the Garden's actions as a denial of free speech and the right of assembly." They also called for pickets to protest the Garden's decision, which around 100 people took part in.[207] Additionally, Hunton led a delegation to visit Garden officials that included Henry Foner, of the Furriers Union, C.B. Baldwin, of the Progressive Party, Nat Ross, of the New York CRC, and Louis Thompson

204. Armstrong, "Gita, Betty, and the Women's International Democratic federation...," in Pecinovsky, *Faith In The Masses...*, Ibid.

205. UMass-Amherst, Special Collections, W.E.B. Du Bois Papers, MS 312: Letter from Hunton to Du Bois, July 7, 1950

206. "Rally In Garden Barred," *New York Times*, August 29, 1950

207. "Robeson Backers May Picket Garden In Protest Against the Ban on Meet," *New York Times*, September 2, 1950

Patterson, among others.[208] Afterward Hunton commented, "It is no accident that a progressive Negro organization [the CAA] and a great Negro leader like Paul Robeson, have [both] been made the first target of the proposed police state legislation."[209] Both – Robeson and the CAA – exemplified a still potent Red-Black alliance. Across the Atlantic, a similar trend was taking shape; Mandela and the ANC-SACP alliance were likewise targeted.[210]

Hunton put the need for international solidarity succinctly in a response to a letter he received that spring. "Jim-Crowism, colonialism and imperialism are not separate enemies, but a single enemy with different faces and different forms," he wrote. He urged the letter writer: "If you are genuinely opposed to Jim-Crowism in America, you must be genuinely opposed to the colonial, imperialist enslavement of our brothers in other lands."[211] Hunton was rearticulating a theme he would add to and expand upon for the remainder of his life. To him, African American equality, Black liberation, and socialism were interconnected and mutually reinforcing.

That November, Hunton was named treasurer of the "national 'Freedom Fund' to encourage and support" organizations and activities that fought for "the full equal citizenship status" of African Americans; the CAA and the National Negro Labor Council, as well as Robeson's *Freedom* newspaper were all recipients of the Fund. The announcement coincided with the printing of the introductory issue of *Freedom*, on whose editorial board Hunton served.[212] As Lindsey R. Swindall argues, *Freedom* "conjoined the primary impulses of both" the SNYC and the CAA "by wedding left-wing analysis of the battles for domestic civil rights with global campaigns for colonial self-determination." *Freedom*'s "uniquely intergenerational group of contributors," many

---

208. "Madison Sq. Garden Denied to Council On African Affairs," *Daily Worker*, September 3, 1950, 2

209. Hunton, *Alphaeus Hunton…*, Ibid., 82

210. Horne, *White Supremacy Confronted…*, Ibid. South Africa passed the Suppression of Communism Act in 1950.

211. William Minter, Gail Hovey and Charles Cobb Jr. (eds), *No Easy Victories: African Liberation and American Activists over a Half Century, 1950-2000* (Africa World Press, 2007), http://www.noeasyvictories.org/select/01_hunton.php

212. "'Freedom Fund' Set Up For Negro Struggle," *Daily Worker*, November 20, 1950, 5

from the South, challenges the argument that Communists and their allies, especially among youth, continued a retreat initiated in 1948 with the first Smith Act indictments. The paper "carved out a space for a progressive [even, pro-Communist] voice"; it "challenged the definition of freedom during a period of intense domestic repression and warmongering overseas."[213] Of course, Hunton and the CAA were part of a long tradition of peoples and movements dedicated to redefining freedom in the fabric of American society.[214]

In *Freedom*'s introductory issue, Hunton noted, "the continuing and expanding freedom struggles" of Asian and African nations, including the "victory of the Chinese people." This "contraction of the imperialists' 'free world'" has caused the "most reactionary minority of the American people," the U.S. ruling class, to change tactics, to advance "from its role of silent partner of the Western European imperialist powers, content with arming and financing their wars against the colonial revolutionaries, to that of aggressive leadership and active participation in those wars." Hunton quotes a leader of the African liberation movement: "'The cold war against the Soviet Union and the democratic countries and peoples of the world is already a hot war as regards the colonial people,'" it was said. As far as Hunton was concerned, the strategy of reflexively violent anti-communism was a dead-end. He argued, "the many-sided efforts to sell anti-communism to the people of that continent [Africa] have also failed." Hunton concludes his article by approvingly quoting Gabriel d'Arboussier, leader of the African Democratic Union: "All the anger of the reactionaries against the Soviet Union is also directed in other forms against the colonial peoples. The latter have learnt, thanks to these reactionaries, that there is a natural alliance between the country of socialism and the oppressed people of the world."[215]

In spring 1951, Hunton expanded upon his initial *Freedom* article and highlighted both U.S. financial support for the "fascist government" of South Africa and the hypocrisy of "American

213. Swindall, *The Path To The...*, Ibid., 160

214. For example, see: Philip S. Foner (ed), *We, the Other People: Alternative Declarations of Independence by Labor Groups, Farmers, Woman's Rights Advocates, Socialists, and Blacks, 1829-1975* (Chicago: University of Illinois Press, 1976)

215. Alphaeus Hunton, "'for fundamental freedoms for all': Status of Colonials Key to World Peace," *Freedom*, November 1950, 6

liberal opinion." He noted the shock and outrage when the U.S. government granted loans to "Dictator Franco of Spain" and even "more dismay" when "money and arms" were "squandered on Chiang Kai-shek" in China. However, "these same liberal circles have displayed little or no concern about the recent $80,000,000 loan" to South Africa. He noted that "big American bankers provided $30,000,000 of the recent loan and advanced another $10,000,000" in 1949 as "a token of interest" in the "land of gold, diamonds and rampant racism." To Hunton, Truman's insistence that "We" hold Africa, really translates into: "...Africa, its resources and people, must remain the property of the Western world to be freely exploited in the future as in the past, only more intensively and systematically." Further, when anti-communists speak of "preserving" the Free World "they mean maintaining the freedom to exploit other peoples." Specifically, in South Africa this means "eight million Africans are forced to labor at slave wages, under slave conditions, completely disfranchised, restricted by pass laws, crowded into Jim Crow ghettos poverty-stricken and disease-ridden beyond belief, denied freedom of assembly and every elementary human right." In short, he concluded, "American wealth and the American government have joined hands with South Africa's reactionary ruling circles in the effort to preserve this vicious system of exploitation."[216]

In the February 1952 CAA *Spotlight On Africa* newsletter, Hunton attacked the coalition of "imperialist over-lords" led by the United States, but noted resistance was mounting. He added, the CAA has "long foreseen...[the] explosion of national resistance to foreign domination" as evidenced by the emerging Black liberation struggles then taking shape in Africa. To Hunton, the CAA's "job – more urgent and important today than ever before – is to help make the [domestic] opposition" to U.S. imperialism more "organized, vocal and effective...[to] do the job which today requires doing." To that end, *Spotlight On Africa* was to be published twice monthly. Hunton wanted "to provide a digest of up-to-the minute news, and interpretation of what's behind the news, concerning the progress of the African peoples." He also urged CAA activists to "enlist hundreds of new members,

---

216. Alphaeus Hunton, "American Trusts Bolster South African Racists," *Freedom*, March 1951, 6

and scores of representative organizations, especially among the Negro people" in this effort. As he put it, CAA needed to "publish and disseminate more information in order to shatter the iron curtain of silence and hypocritical lies intended to conceal the drive for super-profits and war preparations in Africa and other enslaved lands"[217]; his comment was a less-then-veiled jab at Churchill's "iron curtain" speech. In a letter to Du Bois, however, Hunton acknowledged that the "sheer physical labor involved in preparing and mailing" *Spotlight On Africa* "twice a month is quite a strain...but I am convinced that, with all of its shortcomings, it will pay dividends if we can keep it coming out regularly." He also noted that the newsletter was mailed to about 3,000 readers.[218] Ultimately, though, the Red Scare would take a major toll on the CAA making its work increasingly difficult, and eventually its existence untenable.

*   *   *

In 1948, Max Yergan – CAA's former executive director-turned FBI informant, who was suspended for "mal-feasance, mis-feasance, and non-feasance," as it was eloquently put[219] – decided to exact revenge on the CAA by "fully co-operating...[and] supplying the FBI with information that would fuel the Bureau's relentless persecution"[220] of both the CAA as an organization, and its principal officers – Hunton, Robeson, and Du Bois – as individuals. Yergan would later tour Europe and Africa defending U.S. foreign policy. He became an "extreme right-wing crusader," a vocal apologist for apartheid South Africa.[221] Doxey Wilkerson

---

217. NYU, TAM 347, Box 13, Folder 52: *Spotlight On Africa*, CAA Newsletter, February 1, 1952 (Vol. 1, No. 1)

218. UMass-Amherst, Special Collections, W.E.B. Du Bois Papers, MS 312: Letter from Hunton to Du Bois, April 2, 1952

219. *William Alphaeus Hunton Papers...*, Ibid.

220. Anderson, *Eyes Off The Prize...*, Ibid., 164, 165

221. Minter and Hill, "Anti-apartheid solidarity in United States-South Africa relations...," Ibid. and "South African Leaders Blast Max Yergan," *Freedom*, October 1952, 1. *Freedom* quotes Nelson Mandela: "I was struck with the fact that Mr. Yergan made no attempt to meet the non-European leaders and discuss the defiance campaign with them direct[ly]...His visit to South Africa seemed to me to be very suspicious and Africans are asking if he didn't come here on a mission from the United States Government." Yergan's trip was called an "Uncle

had warned party leaders as early as November 1947 that Yergan had begun to "shift with the winds."[222] His concern proved well founded. Yergan had fired Wilkerson from the *People's Voice*, where he served as editor; Robeson resigned as a columnist in protest.[223] The situation escalated quickly. Herbert Aptheker, then serving on the CAA executive board, wrote that Yergan was removed as CAA executive director due to his inability to explain "very serious financial irregularities" and that it was only after his "financial irregularities" had been exposed that he turned to professional red-baiting.[224] According to David Levering Lewis, a CAA "audit disclosed large discrepancies in [Yergan's] expense accounts." Unknown to Hunton, Robeson, and Du Bois was Yergan's anti-communist about-face; according to Lewis, Yergan had already "decided to walk into FBI headquarters in Manhattan and change creeds."[225] Yergan calculated (correctly, as it turned out) that few would care about his misappropriation of funds if he claimed Communists were trying to subvert the CAA.

At a five-hour February 1948 CAA executive board meeting, Yergan declared that the CAA was not "identified with any partisan ideology." According to Robeson, Yergan's comment emboldened "red-baiters and would not help the Council" as it struggled to fight off the anti-communist civil liberties assault. In late-March, Yergan accused Robeson, Wilkerson, and Hunton of trying to gain control of the CAA. He told reporters, "this minority group" was part of an "unprincipled Communist-led effort to seize the organization, [its] prestige and property." How Robeson could seize a group he helped found, fund, and led was left unanswered. Regardless, the meeting "marked a decisive

---

Tom mission..." by *Freedom* editors. Also, see: Dr. Z.K. Matthews, "An African Leader Exposes Max Yergan," *Freedom*, June 1953, 10. As Grant writes, "...Yergan's new-found anticommunist credentials meant he was free to move between both countries." Even the otherwise moderate NAACP would chastise Yergan. Grant, *Winning Our Freedoms Together...*, Ibid., 46

222. Duberman, *Paul Robeson...*, Ibid., 330

223. Swindall, *The Path To The...*, Ibid., 137

224. Herbert Aptheker, *History and Reality* (New York: Cameron Associates, Inc., 1955), 119 and Gilmore, *Defying Dixie...*, Ibid., 436-437

225. Lewis, *A Biography...*, Ibid., 680-681. Apparently, Yergan also tried to blackmail Frederick Vanderbilt Field's wife as well. She initially found him charming and charismatic; their relationship may have "been a factor in the Fields' recent separation and divorce," Lewis writes.

defeat for Yergan" who abruptly left after being censured for his "financial transactions." Yergan claimed the split was due to the council's support of the Henry Wallace presidential ticket, a campaign backed by Communists. This was "completely contrary to the facts," as Robeson put it: "No such proposal whatever, either directly or indirectly, has been made at a Council meeting or by an officer of the Council." Robeson also noted Yergan's "serious mismanagement of financial affairs" and that he was "sharply" censured. Thereafter, Yergan and two supporters attempted to elect "a new set of officers to replace everyone except himself," while also unilaterally removing 23 leaders from the CAA's governing body. According to Robeson, Yergan had "resort[ed] to public red-baiting in an effort to cover up his own retreat from genuine struggle on behalf of African freedom and against imperialist oppression." Further, Yergan's actions were "highly reprehensible and dictatorial." The "familiar Communist bogey" was an attempt to evade "the real issues of policy, functioning and finances of the Council," Eslanda Goode Robeson added. To her, "the relevant, question of a normal, detailed financial report," was met "with the irrelevant answer, Communism." On May 28, the CAA "business affairs" became "more tangled than ever," as the *New York Times* put it. Yergan then claimed that Hunton and Wilkerson broke into his office, a dubious claim; the CAA executive board had "suspended [him] from his position" as executive director on May 26.[226]

226. "African Affairs Unit Avoids Partisanship," *New York Times*, February 3, 1948; George Streator, "Rift In Negro Unit Is Laid To Leftists," *New York Times*, April 6, 1948; "Hammond Balks At Rift," *New York Times*, April 8, 1948; "Battles Left Wing For Groups Office," *New York Times*, May 29, 1948; Duberman, *Paul Robeson...*, Ibid., 331-333; and UMass-Amherst, Special Collections, W.E.B. Du Bois Papers, Box 118: Series 1, 1A: Announcement from Robeson/statement from CAA Board, April 6, 1948; Letter from Robeson regarding postponing April 21 Executive Board meeting, April 15, 1948, Open letter from Eslanda Goode Robeson to members of the CAA, April 17, 1948, and Letter from Hunton to Council members, no date (c late-May/early-June, 1948). Re Robeson's help founding and funding the CAA, as well as his and Hunton's ties to the CPUSA: Eslanda Robeson recalls in an April 17, 1948, letter to CAA supporters discussing with Yergan the formation of the CAA: "I therefore gave him [Yergan] a check for three hundred pounds to help found such an organization [the ICAA], thereby becoming, he said, the first contributing member. I was able to interest Paul Robeson in the idea, and he became an enthusiastic supporter of the work." Further, "Max

By 1949, Louis Thompson Patterson had joined the CAA staff as organizing director, bringing with her years of IWO experience[227] and more ammunition for those like Yergan who claimed the CAA was nothing but a Communist front. That Hunton spoke at the Progressive Party's July 1948 Philadelphia Convention,[228] where Wallace's endorsement was ratified, likely served as further proof.

Regardless, Hunton saw Yergan's political turn as part of a larger Cold War assault on civil liberties. Just as the waters had begun to calm in the CAA with Yergan's removal, Hunton turned his attention to defending Du Bois, who had recently been expelled from the NAACP, the organization he helped to found. In a September 1948 letter to Arthur B. Spingarn, the association's president, Hunton spoke "simply as a rank and file member." He castigated the "top leadership" due to the treatment of Du Bois and noted that he wished to "regretfully request cancellation of my membership" to the NAACP in protest. [229]

Hunton also defended his CPUSA comrades, who in July 1948 were charged with advocating the overthrow of the U.S. government by force and violence. In an August 1949 letter to the *Daily Worker*, Hunton and Louis Burnham noted that the "odious legal proceeding" against the CPUSA's top leadership threatened civil

---

Yergan has not – until now – ever challenged the political opinions of Paul Robeson, Alphaeus Hunton, George Marshall, Doxey Wilkerson, Ferdinand Smith… He, along with the general public, has always known what the political opinions of these men were and are." She also noted that it was not any of her business if "my fellow members on the Council are Communists," and she reminded Yergan that it was at his home where she "first met [CPUSA leader] Earl Browder; this very well-known Communist was the guest of honor." Re funding of the CAA: Of course, the 1950 revocation of Robeson's passport had a "disastrous" impact on the CAA. The cancellation of hundreds of concerts around the world, "cut off the flow of funds from Robeson, the group's principal fund-raiser and benefactor." See: Nesbitt, *Race For Sanctions…*, Ibid., 22. In his biography of Du Bois, Lewis notes that Frederick Vanderbilt Field "bankrolled the CAA…" Lewis, *A Biography…*, Ibid., 680. Apparently, Robeson and Field were the two largest individual funders of the council.

227. For more on Thompson Patterson and the IWO, see: Gilyard, *Louis Thompson Patterson…*, Ibid. and Zecker, *"A Road To Peace And Freedom…,"* Ibid.

228. UMass-Amherst, Special Collections, W.E.B. Du Bois Papers, Box 118: Series 1, 1A: Letter from Hunton to CAA members, July 26, 1948

229. UMass-Amherst, Special Collections, W.E.B. Du Bois Papers, MS 312: Letter from Hunton to Spingarn, September 14, 1948

liberties for two reasons. First, it "violates the basic American principle that guilt must be an overt act and not an opinion," which would "destroy the right of political advocacy…[an] indispensable" right especially for African Americans "if we are to win our long and painful struggle for full freedom and equality." Second, they continued, the "trial by judge [Harold] Medina bears the stench of the lynch-dominated court which daily convict Negroes in the South of 'crimes' they have never committed." "In the fight which the Negro people are waging for their lives in the midst of unprecedented and mounting lynch terror in the South they need the support and fraternal cooperation of every progressive force in America including the Communists." Hunton and Burnham concluded, "The record will show that the fight for the freedom of the Communists is a fight for their right to fight for the rights of Negroes."[230] This neglected statement is profound and articulates an ideological formulation that centers the struggle for African American equality as essential to the fight for democracy. To Hunton, the role of Communists was to *both* defend *and* expand democracy, especially among people of color.

Later that month the assault intensified. On August 27 in Peekskill, New York, "a howling mob of assailants brutally attacked those assembled with the idea of claiming the scalp of the star of the show: Robeson." Considered "a turning point," the concert, organized to support the CRC, was viciously assaulted by about 1,000 racists, anti-Semites, veterans, and anti-communists, a witch's brew of pro-fascist forces emboldened by the growing Red Scare. Hundreds of concertgoers were injured. The attack "escalated into a full-blown riot, and organizers had to cancel… the benefit concert before it started." William L. Patterson likened the assault as "almost the great day of American fascism." To him, the "murderous imitators of Adolf Hitler" made a mistake in attacking Robeson, and what he stood for – Black militancy comfortable with red allies. "The great lesson of *Peekskill* is that the American people have the will to fight back and the power to smash tyranny and fascism," he added. At this point, Patterson and his comrades were still hopeful they could beat back the rising tide of repression. Days later, Robeson held another concert;

---

230. Alphaeus Hunton and Louis Burnham, "'Fight for 12 Is Fight for Negroes,'" *Daily Worker*, August 9, 1949, 5

concert goers were attacked again as they left. Of course, the CRC was blamed for "deliberately inciting disorder," all part of their "Communist strategy" to sow racial and religious hatred.[231]

In a memo written on-behalf of the CAA, Hunton called for an "open letter to President Truman expressing our demand that there must be no more Peekskill outrages." In detail Hunton described "a mob [that] resorted to lawlessness and violence... With police conspicuously absent, the mobsters barricaded the roads leading to the concert grounds, beat up men, women, and children...shouting obscene, anti-Negro, anti-Semitic epithets... and made a bonfire of the literature, music, and camp chairs for the concert. Meanwhile, on a nearby hill, a KKK cross flamed." After reciting the events, Hunton noted: "What happens next depends on you and other Americans." The CAA "is taking action on this matter," he continued, "because it regards what happened at Peekskill as the most threatening sign of emerging fascism in the United States which has thus far made itself visible." He warned, "Unless we all act together to protest against this danger, we face the complete fascist suppression of the Negro people, other minorities, and all individuals and groups which speak out for the protection of our constitutional liberties, for full and equal rights for all peoples, and for peace." He then urged that the enclosed letter be sent to Truman.[232]

A month later, Hunton angrily and concisely expanded on earlier comments when he told an audience in Philadelphia, "The people who are afraid to raise their voices and take a forthright stand in the fight for civil rights are only creating a quicker opportunity to have their own heads chopped off."[233] Undeterred, Hunton doubled down. In late December, he and Marxist philosopher Howard Selsam, among others, spoke at a National Council of American-Soviet Friendship sponsored symposium on Stalin –

---

231. Horne, *Paul Robeson...*, Ibid., 121-124 and Joel Feingold, "Remembering Peekskill," *Jacobin*, June 22, 2017, https://jacobinmag.com/2017/06/peekskill-riots-woody-guthrie-paul-robeson-anticommunism. Patterson's quote comes from his Introduction in Howard Fast, *Peekskill USA* (New York: Civil Rights Congress, 1951), 7-9. *Italic* in original.

232. UMass-Amherst, Special Collections, W.E.B. Du Bois Papers, MS 312: Letter from Hunton to Du Bois, September 16, 1949

233. "Robeson to Speak In Philadelphia," *Daily Worker,* October 6, 1949, 6

"The Man and His Work."[234] Despite the harassment he and his comrades faced, Hunton did not let up. In February 1950, he lectured at Camp Unity's Freedom Theatre Negro History Week closing program, which presented "Fighters for Freedom, a story of the Negro's contribution to the building of the United States." It was noted in the event program, "Dancing will follow" the speakers.[235] Even during the Red Scare Communists knew how to lecture and let-out, though by summer 1950 the CAA was running a deficit and lacked the funds to print *New Africa*.[236] Hunton, however, found other avenues for his internationalism; for example, the November issue of *Soviet Russia Today* included an essay by Hunton on the USSR and colonial independence.[237]

In a spring 1950 CAA pamphlet titled *Africa Fights for Freedom* (image 5), Hunton went on the offensive and sarcastically noted that the "would-be exploiters of Africa have left just one thing out of their precise calculations and pat blueprints – the *people* of Africa. The 180 million of them are rising, organizing and fighting with increased strength to break the chains, and this spells the nemesis of colonial exploitation in the last continent left to the imperialist gang." He added, with "guns from the United States, [the] arsenal of world imperialism…[a] brutal war of repression [is being waged] against the African people in a desperate effort to postpone their V-A Day." The scholar-activist also explored the complexity of fighting colonialism where a Western-style capitalist economy did not yet exist. He added new context to the then emerging revolutionary situation in Africa. Throughout his writings, Hunton rejected a rigid Marxism rooted in the primacy of the working class. "Among the common characteristics of the African liberation movements," he wrote, "first to be noted is that it is the middle-class intellectuals – lawyers, business men [sic], journalists – who constitute the main leadership." However, he was careful to reconcile this seeming contradiction to Marxism-Leninism. "Africa has no class of wealthy and powerful indigenous land-holders and industrialists…therefore, at the present stage, the basic demands

234. "Forum Tonight On Stalin By 4 American Scholars," *Daily Worker,* December 20, 1949, 8

235. "Unity Theatre Affair To Hear Marcantonio," *Daily Worker,* February 2, 1950, 5

236. Swindall, *The Path To The…*, Ibid., 149

237. "Can These People Be Planning War? [advertisement]," *Daily Worker,* November 12, 1950, 6

IMAGE 5: *Africa Fights For Freedom*, March 1950. Courtesy of Longview Publishing Co., Inc.

of the African middle class are in harmony with those of the workers and peasants," he clarified. Later, however, he added, organized labor "spearheads the national liberation movement in the colonies, spurring the middle-class leaders and their organizations forward and showing through example how to fight the monopoly exploiters, the real enemy." There is a certain ambiguity in Hunton's writing. In some instances, he places "middle-class intellectuals" at the center of his analysis, while in other places the labor movement is emphasized. For example, he likened colonial workers as "the shock troops of the liberation movement," who along with the peasants, women, youth – and the Communists – were engaged in a life or death struggle. Further, to Hunton, the "imperialists are caught in their usual dilemma: they demand more and more black labor yet struggle desperately to prevent the development of a black proletariat," though one cannot be created without the other. Throughout, Hunton articulated the dialectical relationship between Africans, African Americans, the Chinese, the Vietnamese, and other colonial peoples fighting for liberation. "The African people are on the side of democracy and world peace," he concluded, a peace based on equality and liberation.[238] The *Daily Worker* called the pamphlet "valuable, [and] fact-packed," and noted that it "tells how the Truman government and Wall Street have teamed up to convert Africa into a military base for a third world war, and to squeeze billions of profits out of the enslaved African mine and plantation workers."[239] Though he was no-longer writing for the *Daily Worker*, Hunton was still a regular fixture in the CPUSA's press.

By the early-1950s, the House Un-American Activities Committee would focus its civil liberties assault against Robeson,

238. Alphaeus Hunton, *Africa Fights for Freedom* (New York: New Century Publishers, March 1950)

239. Robert Friedman, "Book Parade: Six New Valuable Pamphlets on Africa, Peace, Mundt Bill, German Re-Nazification," *Daily Worker*, July 7, 1950, 11

Du Bois, and Hunton, and their main political outlets, the CAA and the CRC; both organizations had been branded Communist fronts. In August 1950, Robeson's passport was revoked,[240] in February 1951 Du Bois was indicted as a foreign agent,[241] and by July 1951 (image 6 and 7) Hunton had started a six month jail sentence – and was placed in a segregated federal prison – for "refusing to divulge" the names of CRC bail fund contributors[242]; his defense attorney was Mary M. Kaufman, a prosecutor in the Nuremberg War Crimes trials against Nazis. She charged, the outlawing of the fund and the imprisoning of the fund trustees "strikes at the very root of the constitutional right to bail."[243] Shortly thereafter, supporters tried to post bail for Hunton and the other CRC trustees; the government insisted on knowing the source of the funding. The intimidation tactic worked; sponsors backed out. "Nobody wanted to be publicly smeared as a 'supporter' of Communism."[244]

---

240. "In 1950 Robeson was offered his passport on the condition that he refrain from criticizing the U.S. government abroad and sign a so-called noncommunist affidavit." Characteristically, Robeson refused both. See: Grant, *Winning Our Freedoms Together...*, Ibid., 83. Although Robeson was never actually "charged with any crime," a government attorney defended the passport revocation in March 1953. He said, "...in view of the applicant's frank admission that he has been extremely active politically on behalf of independence of the colonial peoples of Africa...the diplomatic embarrassment that could arise from the presence abroad of such a political meddler, traveling under the protection of an American passport is unimaginable." See: Nesbitt, *Race for Sanctions...*, Ibid., 21. Also, see: Horne, *Paul Robeson...*, Ibid.

241. Horne, *Black & Red...*, Ibid. Numerous individuals and organizations came to Du Bois' defense, including the NAACP, which had ousted him as a leader just a few years prior. "World Protests Mount On The Indictment of Dr. DuBois," *Daily Worker,* July 25, 1951, 2

242. Russell Porter, "Bail of 14 Reds Voided Again; New Bonds Required Today," *New York Times,* July 17, 1951; Mary Helen Washington, *The Other Blacklist: The African American Literary and Cultural Left of the 1950s* (New York: Columbia University Press, 2015), 140; Plummer, *Rising Wind...*, Ibid., 191; Von Eschen, *Race Against Empire...*, Ibid., 137; Russell Porter, "Dashiell Hammett And Hunton Jailed In Red Bail Inquiry," *New York Times,* July 10, 1951; and "Judge Revokes Bail of 14 Reds: Must Get New Money Or Go to Jail," *The Pittsburgh Press,* July 16, 1951, 2

243. Tim Wheeler, "Mary M. Kaufman, a people's lawyer, dies at 82," *People's Weekly World,* September 16, 1995, 17 and Harry Raymond, "Jail 15 Again As Court Bars CRC Bail Fund," *Daily Worker,* July 12, 1951, 1,

244. Carter, "Why I Support Dissent...," Ibid. Carter added, "It was precisely to resist this totalitarian idea that my great-uncle went to prison."

Hunton and his comrades were not alone, though. Solidarity came from all corners. Perhaps, throwing a little salt in the wound was the goal when the All China Federation of Labor, "representing 5,000,000 Chinese workers," expressed indignation at the "arbitrary jail sentences" of Hunton, Dashiell Hammett, and Frederick V. Field, Hunton's CRC bail fund co-defendants. The All China Federation noted, "The prosecution...is in violation of the American Bill of Rights and is part of a plot for a new world war against world peace."[245] Closer to home, the Furriers Joint Council, as well as Locals 101, 110, 115, and 125, issued a joint statement "lauding" Hunton and the bail fund trustees, while also damning the "violation of constitutional rights"; the Joint Council also called for Hunton to be pardoned.[246] It wasn't just Communist-led unions, such as the All China Federation and Furriers, that were fed-up with the civil liberties assault; Joseph D. Keenan, retiring head of the AFL's Labor's League for Political Action, told the Federation, "I am not afraid of Communism... but I am afraid of these rightists who will sneak into power on us...[They] are fooling around with fascism like a doctor fooling around with dope, hoping they can control it."[247] Apparently, the opiate of fascism was a powerful, addictive to those doing the bidding of the ruling class. Du Bois composed a letter calling for Hunton's pardon and soliciting prominent African Americans to sign-on; he optimistically noted that Hunton's "imprisonment is so obvious a miscarriage of justice that I believe our appeal for pardon has a reasonable chance of success."[248]

Regardless, the CRC, a legal defense organization, then managed about $770,000 in donations, as well as a list of about 6,500 donors; Hunton served as one of its bail fund trustees.[249] In

245. "China Unions Hit Jailing Hunton, Hammett, Field," *Daily Worker,* July 25, 1951, 2. The Chinese military had delivered a decisive blow to U.S. armed forced in Korea in fall 1950 forcing an ideological and military retreat.

246. "Fur Locals Hit Jailing of Bail Fund Trustees," *Daily Worker,* July 30, 1951, 2 and "Fur Dressers Urge Pardon For Dr. Hunton," *Daily Worker,* September 27, 1951, 3

247. "Top AFL Official Tells Convention Fascism, Not Communism, Perils U.S.," *Daily Worker,* September 27, 1951, 3

248. UMass-Amherst, Special Collections, W.E.B. Du Bois Papers: MS 312: Letter from Du Bois, August 8, 1951

249. Horne, *Communist Front...*, Ibid. and Horne, *Black Revolutionary...*, Ibid, 138; Russell Porter, "Judge Seizes Bail Of 4 Fugitive Reds; Its Donors Sought," *New York Times,* July 4, 1951; Peter Kihss, "Red Bail Jumpers Wreck Fund, State

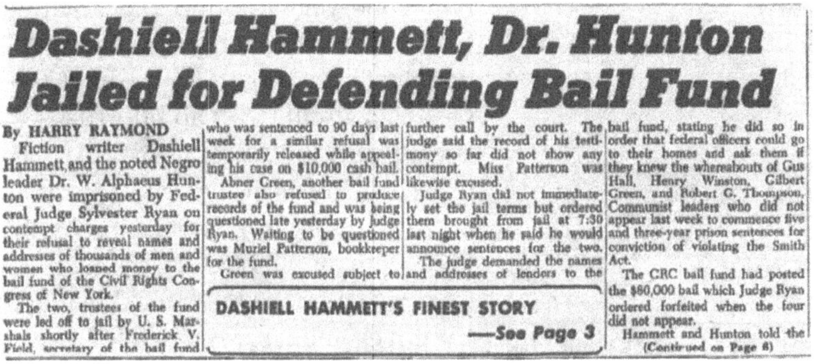

Dashiell Hammett, Dr. Hunton Jailed for Defending Bail Fund

By HARRY RAYMOND

Fiction writer Dashiell Hammett, and the noted Negro leader Dr. W. Alphaeus Hunton were imprisoned by Federal Judge Sylvester Ryan on contempt charges yesterday for their refusal to reveal names and addresses of thousands of men and women who loaned money to the bail fund of the Civil Rights Congress of New York.

The two, trustees of the fund were led off to jail by U. S. Marshals shortly after Frederick V. Field, secretary of the bail fund who was sentenced to 90 days last week for a similar refusal was temporarily released while appealing his case on $10,000 cash bail.

Abner Green, another bail fund trustee also refused to produce records of the fund and was being questioned late yesterday by Judge Ryan. Waiting to be questioned was Muriel Patterson, bookkeeper for the fund.

Green was excused subject to further call by the court. The judge said the record of his testimony so far did not show any contempt. Miss Patterson was likewise excused.

Judge Ryan did not immediately set the jail terms but ordered them brought from jail at 7:30 last night when he said he would announce sentences for the two.

The judge demanded the names and addresses of lenders to the bail fund, stating he did so in order that federal officers could go to their homes and ask them if they knew the whereabouts of Gus Hall, Henry Winston, Gilbert Green, and Robert G. Thompson, Communist leaders who did not appear last week to commence five and three-year prison sentences for conviction of violating the Smith Act.

The CRC bail fund had posted the $80,000 bail which Judge Ryan ordered forfeited when the four did not appear.

Hammett and Hunton told the

(Continued on Page 8)

DASHIELL HAMMETT'S FINEST STORY

—See Page 3

IMAGE 6: *Daily Worker*, July 10, 1951. Courtesy of *People's World*.

summer 1951, Donald H. Aiken, deputy superintendent of banks, questioned Hunton and other CRC trustees about the defense fund during a state banking inquiry. Aiken claimed his inquiry was not politically motivated. "We are interested only in violations of the banking law," a dubious claim.[250] Like the International Workers Order, which was then being dissolved,[251] the CRC's books were beyond reproach; that the CAA, CRC, and the IWO all catered to the needs of African Americans, and other people of color, meant they had to go.[252] Additionally, the court hinted at recalling Hunton and the other defendants to "ask them the same questions they had previously refused to answer," thereby threatening possible additional contempt charges.[253] According to Illinois Communist Party leader, Gil Green – who, along with Gus Hall, Henry Winston, and Robert Thompson, had been bailed out by the CRC and

takes Over to Liquidate," *New York Times*, April 15, 1952; and "Red's Bail Fund, frozen by Court," *New York Times*, May 6, 1952

250. Russell Porter, "Red Bail Trustees Also Defy State," *New York Times*, August 1, 1951, and "State Ends Query Of 4 On Red Bail," *New York Times*, September 12, 1951

251. Zecker, *"A Road To Peace And Freedom…,"* Ibid. and Author J. Sabin, *Red Scare in Court: New York Versus the International Workers Order* (Philadelphia: University of Pennsylvania Press, 1993)

252. For more on the IOW's approach to African Americans and other people of color, see: Edward L. Nelson, "N.Y. Threatens Low Cost Insurance for Negroes," *Freedom*, July 1953, 7 and Robert Zecker, "'Faith In The Masses': The International Workers Order," in Pecinovsky (ed), *Faith In The Masses…*, Ibid.

253. "Fields Loses Appeal On Contempt term," *New York Times*, December 4, 1951

IMAGE 7: Dashiell Hammett and Alphaeus Hunton in handcuffs as they are taken into custody in July 1951. Bettman Collection / Getty Images.

had gone underground precipitating the inquiry into the bail fund – HUAC wanted "to cripple the entire [CPUSA] bail-raising effort,"[254] an effort largely spearheaded by African American radicals like Robeson, Du Bois, Hunton, and Patterson. In December 1951, the CRC delivered its historic petition *We Charge Genocide* to the United Nations; the government's ire intensified; it was again humiliated for its civil liberties hypocrisy as the brutality directed against African Americans was apparent for the world to see.[255] That Hunton in late January 1952, received a standing ovation at a 2,500 person labor symposium when he "read the resolution endorsing the Genocide petition to the United Nations," meant his jailing was an abject failure; that the assembled unionists "called for work stoppages, boycotts, demonstrations and delegations to Washington" to protest lynching, added to the government's disappointment.[256] Resolute, by spring 1952 Hunton, the CAA, and CRC were collaborating in the annual New York May Day parade by mobilizing "America's largest single Negro community [Harlem]" around the theme "Stop Genocide at Home and Colonialism Abroad." The CRC demanded "an end to government-inspired Genocide against the Negro people," while the CAA demanded the "immediate freedom of all African colonial and semi-colonial nations."[257]

Unfortunately, Attorney General Nathaniel L. Goldstein forced the CRC to turn "over the list of fund contributors" to the FBI in the "interest of national security." Grace Hutchins, author of the groundbreaking *Women Who Work*, fellow Communist, and

254. Gil Green, *Cold War Fugitive: A Personal Story Of The McCarthy Years* (New York: International Publishers, 1984), 97

255. See: Horne, *Communist Front*, Ibid. and Horne, *Black Revolutionary...*, Ibid.

256. "2,500 At Genocide Rally Hail Work Stoppage Bid," *The Worker*, January 20, 1952, 4

257. "Harlem To March On May Day Against Genocide Here, Abroad," *Daily Worker*, April 29, 1952, 3

women's rights activist, became the "single trustee" of the CRC fund as it was being liquidated. She told reporters, she was "outraged and horrified." "In doing this," she declared, "the Attorney General has violated the confidential status of the fund records and exposed to possible persecution and harassment innocent people who did no more than exercise their constitutional rights in defense of a paramount constitutional right – the right to bail."[258] Ironically, the court's ruling took place just before the 1952 July 4th celebrations.

Communists and their allies were not silenced by the witch hunt, though. In the December 7, 1951, issue of the *Daily Worker* a notice was printed on the cover celebrating Hunton's coming freedom and informing readers of a small delegation that planned on meeting him at LaGuardia Airport, which included his wife, Robeson, and Du Bois (the moment was professionally captured by Inge Hardison; that photo now graces the cover of this volume).[259] In January 1952, 500 people filled the banquet hall at the Hotel Brevoort in New York to greet Hunton, his co-defendant Dashiell Hammett, and Abner Green, the executive secretary of the American Committee for Protection of the Foreign Born. The banquet sponsored by the CRC, "paid tribute" to the bail fund trustees who had been released from federal prison on December 24, 1951. Invoking the American democratic heritage, Mrs. Angie Dickerson, CRC assistant secretary, told the audience, "These men were not summer soldiers, or sunshine patriots…on the month of our Declaration of Independence, Hammett, Hunton, Green, and [Frederick V.] Field – these great Americans – stood firm, knowing the grey walls of prison faced them." Like other Communists, Hunton reaffirmed his commitment to the Bill of Rights and civil liberties. "We are in this fight to defend the right of Americans to have bail, reasonable bail," he emphasized. The CAA leader also noted that "the right to have legal counsel without having them persecuted and sent to jail for fighting for the rights of their clients" was essential in a free, democratic society.[260]

---

258. "Reds' Bail Fund Will Go Back to Donors, Who Will be Disclosed Only to the F.B.I.," *New York Times*, July 1, 1952

259. "Dr. Hunton to Be Welcomed Back On Sunday," *Daily Worker*, December 7, 1951, 1

260. "500 At Banquet Pay Tribute To Courageous CRC Bail Fund Trustees," *Daily Worker*, January 28, 1952, 8

In a January 1952 *Freedom* editorial, Dorothy Hunton reflected on what Alphaeus' imprisonment had meant to her. Initially angry, sad, and alone, she wrote, "I was suddenly shocked into the realization that I was not at all the person I had thought I was. In fact, I discovered I had the same weaknesses that I had so often pointed out in others. The heavy blow almost smothered me for a while." However, like other victims of Red Scare political repression, she relied on a small network of support and began to see her and Alphaeus' persecution in "proper focus," as part of "the people's forward march toward freedom and peace." She and Alphaeus had taken their "place at the side of all those men and women – especially among my own people, the Negro people – who are determined, whatever the personal cost, to make this a decent world in which to live." To her, "this understanding brings with it not only an abiding sense of personal freedom, but also a sense of great responsibility to one's fellow men. There is much work to be done, and few there are who are willing to serve. But serve we must, if we wish to be free," she added. To Hunton, the persecution became transformative and empowering. "He [Alphaeus] saw what was happening to me, how I found myself. As I was proud of what he had done in defense of his ideals, so I am thankful to be able to say, that he too was proud of the new wife that this experience gave him." Ultimately, the persecution they faced hardened their resolve. Boldly, they counted the "hardship of our separation not as a punishment and loss but as an opportunity and gain."[261]

Political repression had the opposite effect on Hunton's sister Eunice Carter, New York's first African American assistant district attorney credited with helping to "take down one of America's most notorious mob bosses," Charles 'Lucky' Luciano. "She wanted to be a judge. That was really an ambition of hers." It never happened, though. "Interestingly, Eunice didn't blame race. She didn't blame gender. She blamed her brother." Though

261. Dorothy Hunton, "Where are YOU Hiding? – A Present-Day Sojourner Truth Finds 'An Abiding Sense of Personal Freedom,'" *Freedom*, January 1952, 4. *Freedom* would print/reprint a number of articles highlighting the impact the anti-communist Red Scare would have on family members and friends of Communists. For example, see: Eslanda Goode Robeson, "I Know a Communist," and "'Afro' Speaks On Hounding Of Jacksons," *Freedom*, March 1952, 4-5

"they reconciled a little bit" they "never saw each other again before they died."[262]

Despite the repression, imprisonment, and family estrangement, Hunton did not skip a beat. The February issue of *Freedom* included a scathing critique of the inauguration of the Liberian President William V.S. Tubman, "who has opened up Liberia, as no one else has, for the full and exclusive benefit of American exploitation." Hunton added, before Tubman "Liberia meant only Firestone and rubber to most Americans. Today it also means a big business-operated iron ore concession exploited for the benefit of Republic Steel Corp." Ominously, Tubman's inauguration also meant "a permanent military-naval-air base strategically located on Africa's west coast." As Hunton put it, "Yes, Liberia today looms pretty large in America's global interests." Tubman, undoubtedly, "assured his foreign friends that he would guarantee protection for their investments," which he did as dictator until his death in 1971. Hunton and the CAA asked the members of the "official U.S. delegation" about opposition presidential candidate Didwho Twe, who was "barred from the ballot and forced to flee the country for his life."[263] It is unclear if Hunton or the CAA received a reply.

Amidst all his CAA activity, his journalism, and more, Hunton also found time to lecture at the Frederick Douglass Educational Center, which opened its doors in spring 1952. "Harlem's new school for Liberation," also included courses from Lloyd Brown, Alice Citron, Lorraine Hansberry, and Doxey Wilkerson, among others. The Education Center offered a "children's program," which included music, art, dancing, and "social subjects." It also sponsored a Harlem Music Festival and Dance in the Golden

---

262. "How Eunice Carter helped take down one of America's most notorious mob bosses," *CBS News*, October 20, 2018, https://www.cbsnews.com/news/eunice-carter-black-lawyer-who-took-down-one-of-americas-most-notorious-mob-bosses/. The *Daily Worker* early in her career reported on Carter's work and accomplishments and considered her one of the "most progressive leaders in Harlem"; it is unclear if Carter welcomed this coverage. For example, see: "Mayor Claims Report Lost," *Daily Worker*, April 8, 1936, 1 and Ben Davis, Jr., "James W. Ford 'Frederick Douglass of 1936,'" *Daily Worker*, September 26, 1936, 2

263. W.A. Hunton, "Liberia's Exploiters Hail Tubman's Inauguration," *Freedom*, February 1952, 3

Gate Ballroom.[264] In early April, Hunton organized a week-long informational picket outside the South African Consulate in solidarity with the ANC's Defiance Campaign.[265] By fall 1952, he urged "increased pressure" on the U.S. delegation to the UN to take a "positive stand" against the racist policies of the Malan government. The apartheid regime was "attempting to use not only increasingly harsh repressive measures, such as barring meetings, [imposing] curfews, etc., which the people resent, but is also ordering the police to shoot to kill." A general strike of 15,000 workers had recently crippled the South African coastal town of Port Elizabeth after the police murder of "freedom fighters" demanding an end to segregation. Hunton also called for the ANC to be heard at the UN "so that the full truth of the situation may be heard."[266]

By January 1953, Hunton, Robeson, and Du Bois, along with Charlotta Bass, Mary McLeod Bethune, William L. Patterson, Esther Cooper Jackson, among others, celebrated at the first annual National Committee to Defend Negro Leadership gala. The "defense of Negro leaders...[is] one of the most important causes of this historic time," Robeson told the gathering. The gala presented citations to African American leaders, including Hunton, "who have fought for democracy and peace in the face of attacks." Some, such as Henry Winston and Roosevelt Ward, Jr., among others, were not present due to Smith-McCarran Act persecution. Herbert Aptheker addressed the group, and noted, "a persecuted people will have persecuted leaders."[267] Du Bois, Robeson, and Hunton exemplified this fact.

Camaraderie at the gala notwithstanding, the persecution was real and according to Robeson, the CAA – like the CRC – was "involved in a fight for its life." However, he wrote, we "must defend it and its work – against prosecution under the McCarran

264. "Frederick Douglass School Opens Its Doors in Harlem," *Freedom*, March 1952, 2 and "The Frederick Douglass Education Center," *Daily Worker*, March 26, 1952

265. "Urge Turnout At South African Consulate Here," *Daily Worker*, April 11, 1952, 3

266. "Strike in South African City Protest Murders By Police," and "Ask Protests On Slaying," *Daily Worker*, November 11, 1952, 1-2

267. Robert Friedman, "Annual Citation Awards Set Up for Negro Leaders," *Daily Worker*, January 13, 1953, 8

(thought control) Act." "This fight," he told his friend Ben Segal, "means heavy legal expenses," which required "substantial assistance" from donors. "It is true that the going is rough," Robeson concluded, "by deliberate design of the enemy,"[268] an enemy determined to crush what Robeson, Du Bois, and Hunton, as well as the CRC's Patterson, exemplified: Black militancy comfortable with red allies. In an early October 1953 letter, Hunton informed CAA supporters of the "great expense of money and time" the McCarran Act had already cost the council. However, he noted that it was "in the larger area of public opinion and action, and not simply in the courts, that the battle must be waged and won." Therefore, the CAA endorsed a "Call for a People's Conference to Fight the McCarran Law Prosecution and McCarthyism." Optimistically, he concluded, the conference had the potential to be the "spear-head of a truly effective campaign of the American people to defend their democratic heritage."[269]

As the Red Scare intensified, Alphaeus – like Dorothy, Robeson, and Du Bois – refused to cower. Instead, he went on the offensive. He reminded *Freedom* readers of the "oneness of the struggle of black people in every land against racist oppression." He noted the treatment of three different men of color in three different lands. The first was a 24 year-old Nigerian in London training as a fireman who was either "above the maximum age," below the "minimum physical standards," and – by the way – "recruiting has been temporarily suspended." Any and every excuse was given to keep the Nigerian out of the profession. The second example was in Nigeria, where a leader of the liberation struggle was charged with sedition and imprisoned. The prisoner reported that Black inmates were denied "toilet soap… [and were] compelled to act as personal servants and 'night-soil' men for the white prisoners," while white inmates were supplied with cigarettes, socks, bath towels, boots, and sandals. The third example, from Jamaica, was on the "storm of protest" after Rev. Amos Carnegie, a Jamaican, "was beaten up and thrown off a bus by a white man in Georgia…for refusing to sit in the back seat of

268. NYU, TAM 681, Box 1, Folder – Correspondence: Robeson, CAA: Letter from Robeson to Ben Segal, October 29, 1953, and November 10, 1953

269. UMass-Amherst, Special Collections, W.E.B. Du Bois Papers, MS 312: Letter from Hunton to Du Bois, October 2, 1953

the bus"; this was about two years prior to Rosa Parks' historic protest in December 1955. The Jamaica Youth Movement protested outside the American consulate, and sent a letter stating: "The very fact that your government has taken no official steps to punish such an unlawful act, assures us that these outrages are condoned officially." Hunton, the scholar-activist, then connected these seemingly disparate acts to the "new laws to establish fascist dictatorship" in South Africa and called on *Freedom* "readers and friends" to write the UN Secretary General and the U.S. delegation to the UN to demand action.[270]

One month later, Hunton protested the barring of Bishops Frederick Jordan and Howard Primm of the African Methodist Church from going to South Africa to "preside over an estimated 150,000 AME members there." Apparently, the irony was lost on the South African ruling class as they blocked people of faith from practicing their religion, a claim regularly hurled at Communists. To Hunton, this was "an affront to the million member AME church, to the entire Negro people in the United States and to all American citizens." Further, it was an "indication of the lengths to which the Malan racists will go in their efforts to stop the rising tide of African resistance." This was in stark contrast to the warm reception Max Yergan had received in South Africa just a few months earlier. Ostensibly, the racist apartheid regime's "official explanation" for the ban is that the AME was affiliated with the ANC. Perhaps in a veiled reference to Yergan, Hunton added, "Negro Americans have not been welcome in South Africa unless they were servants, either domestic or official," of apartheid.[271]

Conversely, when Black South Africans, such as Z.K. and Frieda Matthews, came to the United States the CAA promoted the links between African American equality and Black liberation, and shared work around the ANC Defiance Campaign. Hunton and Du Bois discussed inviting a "selected group of friends to spend an evening at your home [Du Bois'] in February to meet the Matthews and contribute to the South African cause."

---

270. Alphaeus Hunton, "Jim Crow Wins 3 Bouts As UN Group Bides Times," *Freedom*, March 1953, 9

271. Alphaeus Hunton, "State Dept. Winks At Malan Church Ban," *Freedom*, April 1953, 1 and "South African Leaders Blast Max Yergan," *Freedom*, Ibid.

Hunton said Matthews "welcomes the idea."[272] The South African comrades also wrote a number of articles for the African American press "calling for African independence" and an end to apartheid; these and other activities gained the attention of the South African government and set in motion "a diplomatic tug-of-war aimed at the immediate return" of the ANC activists.[273] Like Yergan, the Matthews were wanted in South Africa, but for different reasons; whereas Yergan had become an apologist for the racist regime – and was therefore able to travel freely – the Matthews were vocal opponents of apartheid, which meant they had to be confined and sidelined, like Robeson, Du Bois, and Hunton.

Domestically, Hunton and the CAA still faced continued harassment by the Department of Justice because they were "the one organization in America which for more than a decade has been consistently exposing South African racism and enlisting American support for the struggles of the oppressed in that country." Hunton and the CAA pondered if the ongoing attacks levied against them were just another example of "Washington's friendly regard for South Africa's white supremacy rulers?" Taking direct aim at the McCarran Act it was noted that the Act was designed to enforce conformity. "In a free country we punish men for the crimes they commit but never for the opinions they have," the CAA approvingly quoted President Truman in his veto of the McCarran Bill. "But not so in this age of McCarthyism," it was added,[274] illustrating how emboldened the far-right had become.

Hunton was also concerned about the spring 1953 jailing of Jomo Kenyatta, and his allies in the Kenyan African Union. "The so-called suppression of terrorists is only a fig leaf to cover the wholesale robbery of the Kenya African tribes," he wrote.[275] Kenyatta agreed; during his sentencing he said, the real goal was "to strangle the Kenya African Union – the only African political organization which fights for the rights of the African people."[276]

272. UMass-Amherst, Special Collections, W.E.B. Du Bois Papers, MS 312: Letter from Hunton to Du Bois, December 1, 1952

273. Grant, *Winning Our Freedoms Together...*, Ibid., 76-79

274. "Answers Brownell Attack: African Council Charges Govt. Supports Colonial Oppressors," *Freedom*, October 1953, 6

275. "Robeson Calls For Protests On U.S. Aid To Imperialist Terror In Africa," *Daily Worker*, April 22, 1953, 2

276. "Let Africans Speak for Africa!," *Freedom*, June 1953, 5

At a CAA conference to establish a Kenyan Aid Committee, Hunton hit on a similar theme. Far from "subversive," the council, he said, "compiled and made public information exposing the imperialists' terror against Africans," as well as "the penetration of U.S. capital into Africa." Reflecting on McCarran Act persecution, he added: "We deny that this is subversive. On the other hand we believe it is in the best interests of all the people of our country to support the African people in the fight for freedom." Once again linking domestic and international struggles for equality and liberation, Hunton concluded, "The time has come in world affairs today...when we Negroes and others in this country will have to take their stand on the great issues coming to a head in Africa," namely Black liberation.[277]

In a 1953 CAA pamphlet titled *Resistance Against Fascist Enslavement In South Africa,* Hunton continued to pull on this thread, specifically linking fascism in South Africa with racist repression domestically. In the postscript he wrote, "there are some who may say that we have enough to do in cleaning up *our own* backyard; it is perhaps not quite as ugly as South Africa, but still surely bad enough. True. There IS a big job to be done in defending and winning our rights here at home." He added, "But can we separate the problem of Jim Crow in America from the problem of Apartheid in South Africa? Can the octopus of racism and fascism be killed by simply cutting off *one* menacing tentacle?" As a Marxist, a materialist, he looked for the economic motives behind racist repression. "Prejudice pays profits – to the few," he added. "Apartheid in South Africa pays big dividends to the few – not only in that country and in Britain, but also in the United States of America," a partial reason for the attacks levied against the CAA, as it stood alone in educating, organizing, and mobilizing popular sentiment against both Jim Crow and Apartheid despite the Red Scare attacks hurled at it. "Check down the list of this country's biggest corporations and you'll find practically all of them doing business – and an expanding business – in South Africa," he continued; U.S. Steel, Bethlehem Steel, Kennecott Copper, the Aluminum Co.

---

277. "African Council Says U.S. Foreign Policy Hinders Drive of Africans for Freedom," *Freedom,* April 1954, 3 and "Kenya-Aid Committee Set Up at Meet Here," *Daily Worker,* April 26, 1954, 6

of America, International Nickel, Union Carbide and Carbon, Eastman Kodak, among others, had operations there. He noted, "Ford opened its first plant in South Africa in 1925, and General Motors came on the scene the next year." Then came International Harvester, Chrysler, Packard, U.S. Rubber, Goodyear, Firestone. On and on, "and – of course – Coca Cola, to name just a few." This was just the tip of the iceberg, though. "To the direct operation of these American corporations in South Africa, one has to add the indirect control exercised by American finance... over a large section of that country's gold and diamond mines and secondary industries through New York-London-Johannesburg capital mergers such as the Anglo-Transvaal Consolidated Investment Company and the Anglo-American Corporation of South Africa." In conclusion Hunton asked, *"How much farther is the Government of the United States prepared to go...in helping to maintain in power a fascist regime which the peoples of the whole world condemn? Do Profitable investments and strategic raw materials have priority over the freedom, the rights, the very lives of the millions of human beings in South Africa whose skins are not white? Again we ask, how much of the blood of South Africa's oppressed black people is on America's own hands?"*[278]

Dissatisfied, Hunton quickly mobilized for sustained action. In a May 18 letter to supporters, Hunton reported on the "Working Conference in Support of African Liberation." He noted, "some 114 delegates and observers" were present, though he "would have liked many more, particularly from the trade unions and churches." He emphasized, "we did not come together just to talk and listen – the Conference was not an end in itself, but simply the means toward planning and organizing to expand and strengthen the work of the Council." To him, "the decisions reached there" were "the common property of all who stand for African freedom." He urged recipients to "study carefully" the "attached documents," a proposal for a Kenya Aid Program and the Declaration in Support of African Liberation. Though he was a scholar, action was key. "We would like you to discuss these with others," he

---

278. Alphaeus Hunton, *Resistance Against Fascist Enslavement In South Africa* (New York: Council on African Affairs, 1953), 48-62. *Italic* in original.

concluded, "in the church, trade union, professional, civic or fraternal organizations to which you belong."[279]

Hunton's ability to juggle multiple campaigns, issues, and demands was staggering. That August, he was again focused laser-like on South Africa and the ANC's Congress of the People. He noted, "50,000 volunteer organizers are being recruited to carry forward the mobilization for the Congress" and that everyone "over 18 is expected to take part in the election of representatives to attend the People's Assembly." The immediate task was to "conduct a nation-wide campaign of education and enable all citizens – through hundreds of meetings, house to house canvassing, and group discussions – 'to speak for themselves, and to state what changes must be made in their way of life, if they are to enjoy freedom.'" This education and organization culminated in the Freedom Charter, "the South African People's declaration of human rights, which every civilized South African will work to uphold and carry into practice." Hunton also noted the increased repression faced by the ANC and its allies. "The right of freedom of assembly is being increasingly trampled," he wrote. For example, the Cape ANC permit to hold "its annual conference...contained the provision that police detectives be allowed to attend all sessions and take notes." Additionally, that June "police armed with automatic weapons burst in upon an Anti-Apartheid Conference in Johannesburg attended by 1,200 delegates." Names and addresses of those present were taken to further intimidate participants. The "hounding and persecution of leaders of the people's resistance...have risen to new heights." Hunton added, "telephones are regularly tapped" and activists were "trailed wherever they go." He likened the persecution faced in South Africa under the Suppression of Communism Act to the repression faced by Communists and their allies domestically. He noted, "516 men and women including 53 trade union officials had been 'named' by the 'liquidator,'" which was "somewhat like the U.S. Attorney General's arbitrary listing of over 250 organizations as 'subversive,'" including the CAA. Hundreds of South Africans were "served with Government notices prohibiting them from holding office...from traveling freely...and from

---

279. UMass-Amherst, Special Collections, W.E.B. Du Bois Papers, Box 141: Series 1, 1A: Letter from Hunton to CAA supporters, May 18, 1954

attending any gatherings for two years, under pain of a maximum three-year imprisonment term." It was "in the face of such persecution that the Congress of the People is being organized," he emphasized.[280]

*   *   *

In the face of repression – domestically and internationally – Hunton remained defiant, though CAA donations dwindled; the climate had shifted so dramatically that Du Bois in a letter to Hunton requested that he "not acknowledge" the name of a "friend of mine" who had contributed financially.[281] Nonetheless, in 1954 the CAA turned the tables and put McCarthyism on trial. Like the NNC years before, theatrics were used to garner public support. Hunton testified at a "public trial" called by the New York Trade Union Veterans Committee, a group of trade unionists and World War II veterans who came together to discuss the growing "menace of McCarthyism and what they could do to combat it." The trial was held at St. Nicholas Arena on West 66th Street. The Arena, better known for its boxing matches, would now be at the center of a different kind of pugilistic battle. Hunton – along with other union and community leaders – testified against the Wisconsin senator's attacks on democratic rights. As 5,000 people filled the arena and another 2,000 filled a separate, overflow hall, Hunton took the witness stand. He said, "It is my conviction that Senator [Joseph] McCarthy, as the agent and co-conspirator of the most corrupt and pro-fascist elements in America" intends to "stifle all expression of opposition to the imperialist, Jim-crow [sic], status quo." Hunton, no stranger to the witch-hunt, said the level of repression exacted upon Blacks and reds depends on the actions of the American people. "The people – and only the people – can stop fascism from coming to America," he concluded.[282] After all he had been through over the past ten years, Hunton still had faith in the American people.

---

280. Alphaeus Hunton, "Despite Malan Terror – South Africans Organize Congress of the People," *Freedom,* August 1954, 1, 4

281. UMass-Amherst, Special Collections, W.E.B. Du Bois Papers: MS 312: Letter from Du Bois to Hunton, March 2, 1954

282. Hunton's speech is printed in Albert E. Kahn, *McCarthy On Trial* (New York: Cameron & Kahn, 1954)

In October 1954, Hunton was subpoenaed to appear before the federal grand Jury. He held out hope that legal counsel would be able to "quash the subpoena or secure limitation of the documents requested, or at the least get a postponement of the returnable date." The assault on the CAA climaxed in 1955 when the grand jury ordered the organization to "turn over all of its correspondence for the last decade." The government argued that the CAA violated the Foreign Agents Registration Act due to its work with the ANC. Financially crippled, the council, "on Hunton's recommendation, dissolved itself rather than release the records"[283] and face, as Horne put it regarding the 1951 CRC hearing, "the prospect of tireless inquisition."[284] Hunton argued, government harassment made continuing the CAA untenable.

Even as the cumulative years of government harassment and repression weighed on Hunton as an individual – and the CAA as an organization – he used whatever means available to him to continue challenging white supremacy and racist oppression. In the January 1955 issue of *Freedom*, Hunton reported on a heated debate at the UN regarding a commission to investigate "the racial situation" in South Africa. He noted, the U.S. delegate "saw no useful purpose the Commission could serve and would therefore oppose its continuance." Moreover, he "did not think it proper for the U.N. to single out South Africa or any other specific country for consideration of the question of respect for human rights." Apparently, each nation should be allowed to govern as they saw fit, unless, of course, they chose socialism. Hunton reported that this "let-South Africa-alone approach" was met with "indignation and impatience" by most of the UN. The Indian delegate condemned the South African government as "brutal Hitlerite Nazis with their insane notions of Race Superiority." The hypocrisy of the U.S. delegate was also criticized. Judge Jose Ingles, from the Philippines, "effectively demolished the argument" that the UN could not establish a commission on South Africa by reminding the delegates that Australia had called

283. Campbell, *Middle Passages...*, Ibid., 339; Von Eschen, *Race Against Empire...*, Ibid., 143; Hunton, *Alphaeus Hunton...*, Ibid., 91; and UMass-Amherst, Special Collections, W.E.B. Du Bois Papers, MS 312: United States, District Court (District of Columbia), Subpoena, October 7, 1954, and letter from Hunton to Du Bois, October 4, 1954

284. Horne, *Black Revolutionary...*, Ibid., 138

for the creation of such a commission to address human rights abuses in Bulgaria, Hungry, and Rumania, and that "this action had been supported by the same delegations which now denied the competence to deal with the same problem in South Africa." The same delegation, it was added, "had also backed the creation of a 'Commission on Forced labor'" in the Soviet Union. According to Hunton, "Only our government, together with the colonial powers and a small group of nations which are on the U.S. dole, opposed the aroused sentiment of the peoples of the world."[285]

Hunton tackled the question of segregated education, as well. In another *Freedom* article titled "In South Africa Education For Slavery Is Government Plan," he likened Southern Dixiecrat Jim Crow laws and resistance to integration to the South African Bantu Education Act. Some have "prophesied," he wrote, "that the die-hard Dixiecrats, after trying every conceivable and 'inconceivable' means of subverting the [1954 Brown vs. Board of Education] Supreme Court decision against segregated schools, may even reach the point of advocating" for secession in South Carolina, Mississippi, Georgia, and Louisiana. As outlandish as that seems, Hunton carried the discussion forward: "a logical proposal – that is, from the point of view of both the Dixiecrats and their racist kith and kin in Africa – would be to have the seceding states become the fifth (overseas) province of that other U.S.A., the Union of South Africa." To Hunton, the racist Senators James Eastland and Herman Talmadge "couldn't ask for anything nearer to their hearts desire than the Jimcrow [sic] system of education for slavery that has been conceived and enacted" in South Africa.[286] Fortunately, Communists – like Lee Lorch, who along with his wife in September 1957 accompanied the Little Rock Nine as they sought entry into that city's Central High School amid threats by white supremacists, segregationists, and KKK members[287] – and civil rights activists in the U.S. and in South Africa were determined to

285. Alphaeus Hunton, "U.S. Upholds Shame of Oppression In South Africa," *Freedom*, January 1955, 5

286. Alphaeus Hunton, "In South Africa Education For Slavery Is Government Plan," *Freedom*, March 1955, 4, 8

287. Author interview with *People's World* managing editor C.J. Atkins, a friend and student of Lorch's. "He [Lorch] was a member of the CP of Canada here and confirmed to me that he was indeed in the CPUSA before he left the U.S." Email correspondence in author's possession. Also, see: Horne, *Black & Red...*,

break down racist barriers. Hunton continued, as part of the Act school time "is to be sliced in half with two shifts, 8 to 12 a.m. and 11 a.m. to 2 p.m. – as an economy measure." To further cut costs, "daily cleaning, care and maintenance of grounds 'must be carried out by the pupils themselves.' It need not be added that teachers' salaries are cut to a minimum and bear no relationship to the salaries of white teachers of white children." Hunton called the Act a "state controlled system of African indoctrination," designed to prepare students to "satisfy the needs" of their "segregated community and such else as to qualify him for manual labor." However, he optimistically added, the Act would not stem "the rising demand for African liberation…one of the things to be discussed at the important Asian-African Conference to be convened at Bandung, Indonesia next month."[288] Just as he did with his *Daily Worker* columns, Hunton's journalism in *Freedom* continued to link domestic readers to the international struggles against racism and apartheid, colonialism and imperialism, U.S. militarism and reflexively violent anti-communism. Thanks to Hunton, the CAA, and *Freedom*, "a two-way transatlantic exchange persisted," even during the darkest days of McCarthyism.[289]

*   *   *

The American-based Caribbean activist Herman P. Osborne would later write, Max Yergan and those like him "wrecked [the CAA]…and in so doing strengthened the hands of reactionary forces in this nation that eventually sent into exile and death" both Du Bois and Hunton.[290] Though they never cowered, the combined weight of McCarthyism, the Smith and McCarran Acts, FBI harassment, and intimidation, cast a "blanket of fear and suspicion…[that threatened to smother] all free democratic expression," Hunton concluded.[291]

Ibid., 218-219 and David Margolick, "Lee Lorch, Desegregation Activist Who Led Stuyvesant Town Effort, Dies At 98," *New York Times*, March 1, 2014

288. Hunton, "In South Africa Education…," Ibid.

289. Munro, *The Anticolonial Front…*, Ibid., 135

290. NYU, TAM 132, Box 112, Folder 4: Letter from Herman P. Osborne, April 15, 1973

291. Robeson, *Here I Stand*, Ibid., 128

"Paradoxically," the CAA "was disbanded at a promising moment for anticolonial movements on the world stage."[292] In spring 1955, representatives from 29 African and Asian nations came together in Indonesia to demand self-determination and independence. The Bandung Afro-Asian Conference [293] attendees claimed to represent "nearly a billion and a half people" in the decolonizing world. In the May 1955 *Spotlight on Africa* newsletter, Hunton wrote, the conference "reflected the determination of Asian and African peoples at this stage of history to be done with Western dictation, guidance or 'tutelage.'" Decolonizing peoples were determined "to think for themselves and decide their own destiny." Hunton also criticized the small "anti-Communist faction" in Bandung, which included his one-time ally Congressman Adam Clayton Powell, Jr., who was then "capitalizing on anti-communism and hunting headlines." He noted that "their attempt to picture 'Communist colonialism' as a greater present danger than Western colonialism" was a "favorite theme of the U.S. State Department." It has "the double value of focusing attention on what the Soviet Union and China are alleged to be doing while diverting attention from the expanding economic colonialism of the United States itself and from the colonial regimes, particularly in Africa, still retained by the European imperialist powers, allies all of them of the United States in its 'free world' crusade." Fortunately, as Hunton put it, "the forces of unity prevailed over the agents of disunity."[294]

According to Hunton, the Bandung Conference "had a tremendous impact on all sections of the Negro people." For Black Americans "the Conference had a special significance derived from their identification with the subject peoples in other lands and especially Africa," an identification born out of "a common experience of oppression and common striving for freedom." The domestic African American press agreed with Hunton's assessment. The *Baltimore Afro-American* called the conference a "clear challenge to white supremacy," as well as the U.S. government's "split personality approach to colonialism." The *Boston Chronicle*

---

292. Swindall, *The Path To The…*, Ibid., 154

293. Lee, *Making A World After Empire…*, Ibid.

294. Niebyl-Proctor Marxist Library: *Spotlight on Africa*, May 1955 (XIV, 5) and Swindall, *The Path To The…*, Ibid. Interestingly, the theme of "Communist colonialism" would be used by some segments of the New Left in the 1960s and 1970s.

recognized Bandung as "an anti-imperialist conference," noting that "its formation strikes a blow at imperialism all around the globe." The Oklahoma *Black-Dispatch* editorialized, "We think it is about time that Western society awakens and does not set at naught the activities of a conference representing more than half the people on the globe. It is true these peoples are representatives of the colored race, but when they meet, as they are for the first time…they become like bees. Their sting can be terrible." The L.A. *Herald-Dispatch* saluted the conference and hoped that "the American Negro will learn a lesson from this historic meeting." Hunton agreed and added, African Americans should "derive greater strength from the knowledge of the kind of world colored peoples in other continents are trying to build."[295]

Hunton saw Bandung as a sign of a shift in the world balance of power precipitated by ascendant socialism and its embrace of self-determination and national liberation movements, including Black liberation in Africa. "If the Bandung Conference represented a new alignment of world forces, a fresh outlook toward achieving a world of equality, cooperation and peace among nations and peoples," then "the Negro people should be among the first in the United States to respond and orientate their thinking, organization and action in the new pattern," a pattern the ruling class was loath to welcome. African American "interest in what transpired at Bandung must not be allowed to wane [or] to die," he argued. Additionally, they must wield "their influence to place the Government of the United States on the side of the world's oppressed instead of their oppressors… [and] their proper place, along with all other sections of progressive America, at the side of the colored majority of mankind who have declared their determination to work together for PEACE."[296] The CAA sponsored a report-back discussion that featured Eugene Gordon, a "Negro journalist" who attended the Conference, as well as Eslanda Goode Robeson, Doxey Wilkerson, and Hunton, among others. It was noted by Gordon, "the Indonesian people knew all about discrimination against Negroes in the U.S. before I got there."[297] As discussed in the Introduction, Indonesia would soon become a major

295. *Spotlight on Africa*, May 1955 (XIV, 5)

296. *Spotlight on Africa*, Ibid.

297. "Newsman at Bandung Says Asia 'Knew All About U.S. Negroes,'" *Daily Worker*, June 8, 1955, 2

Cold War casualty; the hopes and dreams expressed at Bandung were drowned in an anti-communist tsunami of blood.

* * *

To the CAA "the internationalization" of the Black freedom struggle meant civil rights at home and Black liberation abroad. It meant "material support" for independence activists and striking trade unionists in Nigeria, "unequivocal" support for the Land and Freedom Army in Kenya, the Mau Mau,[298] as well as direct aid to the ANC, among other examples. The Nigerian Trades Union Congress in a letter to the CAA, wrote, "To know that we have friends at the other end of the Atlantic is comforting and inspiring in our struggle for freedom from want and heartless exploitation."[299] As Hunton recalled, the CAA "was not content to function simply as an information agency. It sought to translate knowledge into action,"[300] which partly explains why it was maligned so viciously. In another letter, a white South African trade union leader thanked the CAA for its support and noted, "Progressive forces all over the world must take steps to see that South Africa does not become the Nazi Germany of the African continent."[301] Hunton committed his life to ending the fascist apartheid regime.

The CAA promoted a "fundamental linkage" between the struggle for African American equality and the "fate of colonized peoples in Africa," thereby fostering a degree of internationalism largely absent from the civil rights organizations that would emerge after the near destruction of the domestic Communist left. Penny M. Von Eschen put the matter thusly, "U.S. government prosecution of activists such as Robeson [and Hunton] and the CAA, fundamentally altered the terms of anticolonialism and effectively severed the black American struggle for civil rights from the issues of anticolonialism and racism abroad." Gerald Horne forcefully articulates a similar sentiment. The emerging

298. Pope, *Exploring the Parallels...*, Ibid. and Nesbitt, *Race for Sanctions...*, Ibid.

299. Alphaeus Hunton, "Today's Guest Column: Trade Unionism in Nigeria," *Daily Worker*, September 28, 1944, 7

300. Robeson, *Here I Stand...*, Ibid., 127

301. Alphaeus Hunton, "Today's Guest Column: Two Letters From South Africa," *Daily Worker*, February 8, 1945, 7

civil rights organizations, even those connected to Dr. Martin Luther King, Jr., "did not have the international ties of the CRC, nor the global reach of the CAA, which amounted to a net loss for African Americans and their allies."[302] This is a qualitative loss the repercussions of which are still being felt to this day. In short, the CAA was the "most visible, vocal and vibrant African-American organization" supporting colonial liberation in the 1940s and 1950s. Its "tactics, objectives and problems" were later "inherited" by diasporic activists of the 1960s and 1970s.[303]

Hunton spent 12 years of his life building and leading the CAA. With its dissolution, he was unemployed, blacklisted, and diligently looking for work that would allow him to, in the words of his wife, "keep his self-respect and [his] sanity."[304] Hunton straddled optimism and despondence during this period. He was fortunate to have "temporary employment," which provided "a weekly paycheck with my name on it for the first time in a long time." But he also lamented the fact that it also left him "little or no free time" for continued research or writing. However, he noted some "new opportunities" and political openings; he was jubilant about the "presentation of the Du Bois bust at the Schomburg Library" celebrating his friend's pioneering work.[305]

In 1957, Hunton published *Decision In Africa: Sources of Current Conflict* (image 9). Du Bois called it a "brilliant exposition of the structure of the new imperial order in Africa and of the role of American capital, private and public, in underwriting it." In the Foreword, Du Bois praised Hunton's scholarly work. "I know of no one today who has a more thorough knowledge and understanding of that continent [Africa]" than Hunton. This was high praise indeed, as Du Bois was considered "the most eminent of African scholars."[306] In a December 1956 letter to Hunton, Du Bois

---

302. Pope, *Exploring the Parallels...*, Ibid.; Von Eschen, *Race Against Empire...*, Ibid., 3; and Horne, *Paul Robeson...*, Ibid., 150

303. Erhagbe, "Assistance and Conflict...," Ibid.

304. Hunton, *Alphaeus Hunton...*, Ibid., 94 and Campbell, *Middle Passages...*, Ibid., 339

305. NYU, TAM 134, Box 3, Folder 8: Letters from Hunton to Morford, February 11, 1957, and May 11, 1957. Dorothy Hunton deposited Alphaeus' papers at the Schomburg Library in 1985.

306. Hunton, *Decision In Africa...*, Ibid., 9 and Wilkerson, "William Alphaeus...," Ibid.

called *Decision In Africa* "a most valuable piece of work"; his only criticism was that "it is overloaded with facts. But that is a fault which I can forgive."[307] The *Pittsburgh Courier*'s review noted that *Decision In Africa* painted "a sorry picture of a continent being systematically and ruthlessly robbed" and added that "it is difficult if not impossible to controvert Mr. Hunton's thesis."[308] The *Daily Worker* noted, it was a "major work on a subject of deep interest," which "seeks to give the American reader an understanding of the freedom movements which are sweeping the continent from Capetown to Suez."[309] To Hunton, the project was a labor of love, though it was only read by a handful of Americans. In a new edition, Timothy V Johnson called Hunton's book a "under-recognized work of economic and political scholarship" that is still relevant today. The "key question" Hunton posed, "how does Africa develop given the context of its past exploitation," is still "germane," he concluded.[310]

Hunton dealt with issues "avoided by other writers," specifically the corporate interest in continuing colonialism. In a letter to a colleague he wrote, "The book is now out, and reviews will be appearing this month. Now comes the task of getting people to buy it and read it." While Hunton could not "afford any large-scale advertising" and he did not expect the book to "hit the best-sellers list," he was "convinced that a quite sizable audience...exist[ed] and can be reached if a few" colleagues and comrades "personally assume responsibility" for talking it up among friends, co-workers, and allied organizations. "If I receive your consent," Hunton continued, "I would like to forward as quickly as possible three, five, ten books – whatever you specify."[311] Richard Morford accepted Hunton's challenge and wrote to the leadership of the National Council of American-Soviet Friendship, noting that the former NNC and CAA leader "has given

307. UMass-Amherst, Special Collections, W.E.B. Du Bois Papers, MS 312: Letter from Du Bois to Hunton, December 14, 1956

308. P.L. Prattis, "The Angry Truth," *Pittsburgh Courier*, January 11, 1958

309. "Books: A New Book on Africa by Dr. Alphaeus Hunton Out Soon," *Daily Worker,* April 25, 1957, 7

310. Alphaeus Hunton, *Decision In Africa...* (New York: International Publishers, 2021). Quoted from Johnson's Foreword in the new edition.

311. NYU, TAM 134, Box 3, Folder 8: Letter from Hunton to Mr. Holman, November 14, 1957

unremitting attention, through many years, to developments in Africa, encouraging in every practicable way the struggle of the black men and women of Africa for freedom and equality. I do believe," Morford continued, "the wide circulation of his book is a worthy project."[312] Hunton thanked Morford for his support, adding that seven people replied, nine books were sold, and five were taken "on consignment." Hunton then urged that the book be brought to "the attention of Negroes not associated with the left," as their support was needed more than ever.[313]

In a September 1957 letter to Du Bois, Hunton wrote that another colleague had "offered to help in the distribution and sale of my book with a project similar to that which he worked out with you." Apparently, even Du Bois had had to rely on grassroots, word-of-mouth, personal networks during this time, as Hunton cautiously offered to "drop by, rather than [ask him] to commit the information to paper." Hunton was careful not to endanger his and Du Bois' mutual contacts; the FBI had close tabs on both men and were eager to grow their list of suspected Communists or Communist sympathizers. Regardless, Hunton was "glad" to stop by and visit his friend. He also joked about the pressures of writing and publishing *Decision In Africa* under such trying conditions: "I can now understand why some people have only one child and write only one book," he wrote. "I hope you and Shirley like the jacket design," he concluded to his mentor.[314] Though locked out of the academic mainstream, Hunton and his small network – which happened to include Du Bois and Robeson – pressed on.

Written 15 years before Walter Rodney's classic *How Europe Underdeveloped Africa*,[315] *Decision In Africa* brought a Marxist analysis to the plunder of the continent, while highlighting a path

312. NYU, TAM 134, Box 3, Folder 8: Letter from Morford to Friends of the National Council of American-Soviet Friendship, December 10, 1957

313. NYU, TAM 134, Box 3, Folder 8: Letter from Hunton to Morford, January 7, 1958

314. UMass-Amherst, Special Collections, W.E.B. Du Bois Papers, Box 146: Series 1, 1A: Letter from Hunton to Du Bois, September 11, 1957

315. For one contemporary example of the continued relevance of Rodney's text, see: Giovanni Vimercati, "The Persisting Relevance of Walter Rodney's 'How Europe Underdeveloped Africa,'" *Los Angeles Review of Book*, April 18, 2019, https://lareviewofbooks.org/article/the-persisting-relevance-of-walter-rodneys-how-europe-underdeveloped-africa/

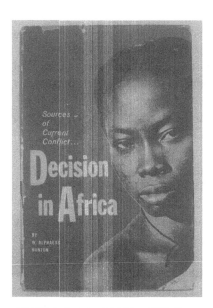

IMAGE 8: *Decision In Africa*, 1957. Courtesy of International Publishers.

toward independence aided by ascendant socialism. Hunton argued, "the peoples of Asia, the Middle East and Africa" were no-longer forced to "bend the knee by economic strangulation, for they now have an alternative to Western markets in the socialist sector of the world." He approvingly quoted Walter Lippman: "The emergence of the Soviet Union as a competitor is one of the great historic events of our times." Hunton continued, "The *kind* of assistance given [by the Soviet Union] is of more significance than the quantity of it." Further, since the "socialist countries do not normally make direct money loans," developing countries "do not have the problem of heavy interest rates or of being restricted to spending the money as the lender directs." Often "assistance takes the form of barter transactions that will enable the counties to industrialize themselves," thereby eliminating dependence on foreign markets and high interest rates. That ascendant socialism "came forward and offered economic assistance to the independent peoples of Africa…[with] trade deals and technical knowhow," put imperialism back on its heels. Cold War commentators insisted that the "offer of assistance" itself was a "threat to Africa and the 'free world.'" Hunton dug deeper, though. As he saw it, "what worries Washington is not so much the interests of the prospective recipients of Soviet aid as its *own* interests." World imperialism "fears…the weakening or loss of its *exclusive* controlling influence…it fears giving these countries the chance to make choices and decisions of their own." This fear, coupled with racism, was at the heart of the domestic Red Scare and international Cold War. Hunton added, that this "expression reflects the attitude (either unconscious or deliberate) of one talking about inferior people who *can't know* which way to go but must be pulled this way or that," lest their interests not align with imperialism. That these issues, like the 1956 nationalization of the Suez Canal, "could not be summarily resolved in the old ways of Western coercion and force, even though attempted, is proof of existence of a new equation of world power." Ascendant social-ism was strategically positioned to force concessions on behalf of independence and self-determination, African American equal-ity, and Black liberation. That imperialism was "desperate and degenerate" was not lost on Hunton. "If the West's ideological and economic weapons cannot keep the African obedient to its dictation, will deadlier weapons be used…all in the name of sav-ing Africa from Communism," he asked?[316] For American policy makers, reflexively violent anti-communism, brute force, and mass murder were the answer.

Perhaps unsurprisingly, Hunton does not mention the Khrushchev revelations documenting Stalin's crimes against the Soviet peo-ple and socialism.[317] Published one year after the Soviet premier's so-called "secret speech," which rocked the world Communist movement and caused further damage to the CPUSA's shrink-ing membership, *Decision In Africa* instead focuses on ascendant world socialism and its role in bolstering national liberation. As Gerald Horne argues,[318] many African American Communists,

316. Hunton, *Decision In Africa…*, ibid., 218-229. *Italic* in original.

317. Some CPUSA members supposedly fell victims to Stalin's purges, too. For example, see: Denise M. Lynn, *Where Is Juliet Stuart Poyntz?: Gender, Spycraft, and Anti-Stalinism in the Early Cold War* (Amherst: University of Massachusetts Press, 2021). Though Poyntz went missing in 1937 (it is doubtful Hunton ever met her), this example – repeated ad nauseum *and* without evidence – among others was used to justify post-war Red Scare repression, thereby laying the foundation for an anti-communist narrative that would serve to undermine the American left for decades. Understandably, Hunton, Robeson, and Du Bois, among others, refused to become props in the anti-communist crusade. Soviet supported anti-colonial, national liberation solidarity was an inspiration particularly to Black Communists like Hunton. As Munro put it, "For Robeson, red baiting and economic unfreedom were what fascism was; organizing across the color line, confronting empire, and coexisting with the USSR were how to fight it." See: Munro, *The Anticolonial Front…*, Ibid., 88. Though Munro is reflecting on Robeson's SNYC Southern Youth Legislature speech in 1946, there is no evidence to suggest that Robeson, Hunton, etc., fundamentally altered their perspective post-1956.

318. For example, see: Horne, *Black Revolutionary…*, Ibid, 156. Horne writes, "Since the Negro comrades had fewer illusions about the beneficence of the United States and a keener recognition of the need for global pressure to alleviate

were less susceptible to the Khrushchev revelations; capitalism was born of slavery and genocide, they reasoned, and continued to proffer from colonialism and Jim Crow; conversely, world socialism was a strategic and powerful ally. The revelations seemed to have no impact on Hunton's closest allies, Robeson[319] and Du Bois. Though not yet a CPUSA member, Du Bois was "publicly unmoved"[320]; Shirley Graham, went so far as to rationalize Stalin's excesses as necessary, earning her a rebuke from the pro-Soviet *New World Review*.[321] Hunton sought and received modest support from the National Council of American-Soviet Friendship with the promotion of *Decision In Africa*; he welcomed the publication of the book in the Soviet Union and Eastern Europe and accepted an invitation to travel there in the late 1950s and early 1960s, apparently without hesitation. A number of

---

the plight of African Americans, they were more disposed to aligning with Moscow," despite the revelations.

319. While Duberman notes, "few black members left the Party, preferring to read Khrushchev's revelations as a sign of renewed hope," he adds that it "would be the calculus of phony heroics to claim – as some of Robeson's intimates do – that the Khrushchev report had no impact on him. Such an interpretation would reduce a great hearted man to a wooden warrior. He was, demonstrably, mortal – susceptible to disappointment, weariness, despondency – if anything, more susceptible than most, given his enormous capacity for empathy. He did, however, make the decision not to comment on his reactions to anyone, instead maintaining silence and outward equanimity..." Admittedly, Duberman adds, we can only guess at Robeson's response to the revelations. As he put it: "There is no evidence that Robeson either disputed the accuracy of Khrushchev's revelations or discounted reportage of them in the Western press as exaggerated. His reaction *probably* – this must remain a 'best guess,' given the lack of concrete evidence – fell into the middle ground of disappointed acceptance: disappointment that the socialist experiment in which he believed had been derailed by the acts of an unsound leader, acceptance (and continuing faith) that in the long run the derailment would prove temporary and that socialism, still humanity's best hope, would triumph." See: Duberman, *Paul Robeson...*, Ibid., 416-417, 437. In short, Duberman provides no evidence for his ability to see into Robeson's mind; so, he speculates. It should be added, the CAA had just been forcibly dissolved, Robeson had just lost an appeal on his passport case, and he was still recovering from prostate surgery, all factors that may also have left him depressed. Regardless, by mid-August 1958 Robeson – now able to travel – was back in Moscow, where he was greeted by roughly 120,000 people. See: Horne, *Paul Robeson...*, Ibid., 170

320. Lewis, *A Biography...*, Ibid., 699

321. Gerald Horne, *Race Woman: The Lives Of Shirley Graham DuBois* (New York: New York University Press, 2000), 225

white Communists, such as Hunton's comrade in the campaign to integrate the Glenn L. Martin Aircraft Plant, George Meyers, noted in retrospect, "I joined the Communist Party because of the class struggle in the United States...That's why I never had any problems about all these foreign ups and downs."[322] Interestingly, subscriptions to the CPUSA's theoretical journal *Political Affairs* increased by over 2,000 readers during fall-1957/spring-1958, challenging the notion that Communists saw nothing but decline in the post-1956 period; despite the revelations and the repression, the journal remained "a significant site of anticolonial politics," as John Munro argues.[323] Regardless, Hunton seemed unphased by the revelations; however, thousands did leave the CPUSA during this time, including Hunton's good friend Doxey Wilkerson.[324] In short, like Robeson and Du Bois, Hunton doubled down and continued to see the Soviet Union as a bulwark against colonialism, imperialism, and war.

In 1958, Hunton attended the All-African People's Conference in Accra, Ghana, the first convergence in Kwame Nkrumah's Pan-Africanist campaign for continental unity. Though he was considered subversive in the U.S., while in Ghana Hunton was "treated like a visiting dignitary."[325] In an interview published that November in *The Worker*, he reflected on the tremendous pace of revolutionary change enveloping the continent. It was noted that Hunton was "Scholarly and calmly confident" and that *Decision In Africa* was "already a classic." Hunton defiantly said, "Africa will not wait...and the people of Africa will not wait for the white man to grant them freedom." He was asked, "Is the United States really a 'colonial' power in Africa?" Hunton's response: "It is to be remembered that Wall Street is the creditor of the old colonial, European powers...No longer able to raise loans in the London market for the exploitation of African resources, they come here.

---

322. Frederick N. Rasmussen, "George Aloysius Meyers, 86, Communist Party member," *Baltimore Sun*, October 21, 1999

323. Munro, *The Anticolonial Front...*, Ibid., 113-114.

324. Wilkerson also disagreed with the CPUSA's position on self-determination and the Black Belt. See: Johnson, "The Communist Party and the African American Question," in Pecinovsky (ed), *Faith In The Masses...*, Ibid., 168 and Bruce Lambert, "Doxey Wilkerson Is Dead at 88; Educator and Advocate for Rights," *New York Times*, June 18, 1993

325. Campbell, *Middle Passages...*, Ibid., 340

America holds the purse strings." He added, "Political freedom in Africa is an immediate prerequisite to economic independence and advance." Hunton also emphasized that, Africa was "in a transitional stage and world events, assuming the tempo of Soviet aid and assistance will grow, will eventually mean less dependence [on] western investments and more freedom for African nations to plan the type of economy they desire." Like all Communists, he saw socialism as ascending and permanent, as part of a world historical process that then seemed irreversible. Socialism, to him, was the "general direction of history. Sooner or later Africa too will have socialism," he continued.

When asked about Nkrumah's visit to the United States, Hunton replied that he had come to "build better relations with the Negro people of America and the cause of African freedom... that Negro freedom here and African freedom are not separable." Hunton was also asked about the NAACP and its reluctance to fight for freedom in Africa. According to *The Worker*, Hunton gave a rueful, perceptive smile and answered: "The Left should make this [the links between African American equality and Black liberation in Africa] a central part of their program and not leave the field to the bourgeois." Of course, with the badgering and forced dissolution of Hunton's CAA, an important lesson was learned by the NAACP regarding the permissible boundaries of domestic discourses on civil rights, equality, and liberation. Regardless, as Hunton noted, "That is one of the reasons I wrote [*Decision In Africa*]...Though there are a number of books, more or less objective, they failed in my estimation to bring home to American readers our direct stake in African affairs. Big Business sees its direct stake," he added astutely. Hunton was personally responsible for selling roughly 1,000 copies of the book.[326]

In an April 1959 *Political Affairs* article, Hunton expanded upon his *Worker* interview. He wrote, "the African people, inspired by a new high level of confidence, determination and unity reflected at the Accra Conference...will persist in their struggle for full equality

---

326. "'Africa Will Not Wait': An Interview with Dr. Alphaeus Hunton," *The Worker*, November 2, 1958, 8, 9, 11. Given the Red Scare anti-communist context in which it was published, it is unlikely *Decision In Africa* found much of an audience domestically outside of the Communist-affiliated left.

and freedom even if they have to fight alone."[327] Fortunately, they did not have to fight alone. Ascendant socialism "provided support as a genuine expression of its commitment to African liberation from European colonialism," as Dennis Laumann argues.[328] This reality is increasingly apparent now, three decades after the collapse of socialism in Eastern Europe. Further, the "CP-affiliated wing of the anticolonial front," of which Hunton was a central figure, "maintained and developed analyses of the very themes of racism, sexism, [and] empire that would prove so captivating to the 1960s left."[329] By the early-1960s, Communists would embark upon wildly successful college and university speaking tours, packing auditoriums with tens of thousands of students[330]; they often connected the struggles between African American equality, colonialism, national liberation, and ascendant socialism, themes that seemed to resonate.

While in Accra, Hunton met with the director of the Institute on African Studies in Moscow who informed him that *Decision In Africa* had been translated into Russian and would soon be published in the Soviet Union. Hunton was invited to speak there and receive modest royalties for his book, an example of socialism's commitment to African American equality and Black liberation, as well as its support for revolutionary movements and their cadre. By 1961, *Decision In Africa* had been published in East Germany, Hungary, Romania, and Bulgaria. That summer, Hunton and his wife were again invited to the Soviet Union, this time for "a complete medical checkup." For Hunton, the tireless worker, this was not a vacation; radio and press interviews, university lectures, and other speaking engagements were arranged throughout Eastern Europe.[331] Despite the hectic schedule, the

---

327. Alphaeus Hunton, "Central Africa and Freedom," *Political Affairs*, April 1959

328. Dennis Laumann, "A Soviet View on Southern African Liberation Movements," *Journal of African History*, Vol. 52, Issue 3 (Nov. 2011), 414

329. Munro, *The Anticolonial Front...*, Ibid., 118. To Munro, the CPUSA accomplished a tremendous amount despite the lack of internal democracy. As he put it, "Stalinism deadened democracy within the CP, yet much of the most meaningful postwar antiracist and anticolonial work was carried out under Party banners." Munro, 119

330. Pecinovsky, "Far From Marginal...," in Pecinovsky (ed), *Faith In The Masses...*, Ibid.

331. Hunton, *Alphaeus Hunton...*, Ibid., 96, 104-105, 121-124

trip was "a tremendously bracing and invigorating tonic." In all, Alphaeus and Dorothy spent seven weeks in the USSR, Bulgaria, Rumania, Hungary, and East Germany. While abroad, Hunton attended William Z. Foster's funeral, an "event to remember"; he also caught-up with Paul and "Essie" Robeson, who were preparing to go back to London.[332]

*   *   *

Central to Hunton's analysis of Black liberation was the question of political power. "The winning of political power is everywhere recognized as the first and fundamental requirement for African advancement." Africans "will be satisfied with nothing less than democratic self-government," he wrote in a February 1950 issue of *Masses & Mainstream*.[333] Hunton saw his life's work – especially his time with the CAA – as an expression of this idea. He was a domestic combatant in an international conflict for political power, African American equality, Black liberation, and socialism. Without reservation, Hunton criticized the "coalition of imperialist and pro-imperialist forces in the U.N. attempting to push aside" Patrice Lumumba, the first democratically elected prime minister of the Republic of the Congo. Lumumba was deposed by the dictator Joseph-Desire Mobutu in 1961 – with the aid of the CIA. That Lumumba "unquestionably enjoys the widest support among the Congolese" only added to the outrage when he was executed by firing squad. "It is a shame upon the United Nations! It is an insult against the Congolese and Africans generally," Hunton exclaimed.[334] As Hunton feared, "brute force" was used to roll back the gains then being made by national liberation movements, a scenario that would be repeated multiple times. However, to Hunton's comrade James Jackson, Lumumba's murder was an indication of weakness; it "constitutes but one bloody deed in the grand scheme of the imperialist powers

332. UMass-Amherst, Special Collections, W.E.B. Du Bois Papers, MS 312: Letter from Hunton to W.E.B. and Shirley Graham Du Bois, November 20, 1961

333. Alphaeus Hunton, "Upsurge In Africa," *Masses & Mainstream*, February 1950

334. Meriwether, *Proudly We Can Be Africans...*, Ibid., 227 and Emmanuel Gerard and Bruce Kuklick, *Death In The Congo: Murdering Patrice Lumumba* (Cambridge: Harvard University Press, 2015)

to thwart the march of the colonial masses toward freedom and independence. From Cuba to the Congo the arch-imperialists are trying desperately to shore up their crumbling colonial holdings." As socialism ascended, "colonial robber barons and imperialist bloodsuckers" became increasingly desperate. Just as "the hanging of John Brown foreshadowed the death-knell of chattel slavery," the murder of Lumumba "will summon new and mighty forces into the struggle to wipe out the last remnants of the bloody colonial system," he wrote.[335]

In 1960, Hunton emigrated to Guinea, the "first of France's colonial subjects in Africa to declare boldly for independence," which as he put it, continues "to point the way toward the creation of a new Africa, an Africa no longer subservient to or dependent on the imperialist powers of the West." The people of Guinea were taking "a giant step out of the mire of colonial stagnation toward a solidly based modern economy," he wrote in the first issue of *Freedomways*. Hunton also noted the substantial "backing from the Soviet Union, China, and other socialist countries" to finance Guinea's Three Year Plan. Why did they support "independent Guinea," he asked? His answer: The "offer of help" came from "a spirit of friendly cooperation – without strings." Later, he elaborated. "The West insists on its own terms for doing business with Guinea; the socialist countries agree to terms that are mutually satisfactory to *both* parties to the contract." With Marxist insight, he also analyzed the "elimination of feudal barriers to the development of political democracy," where "the institution of chiefs, themselves vassals of the colonial rulers, [were] officially abolished – another respect in which Guinea is unique among African states." Land formerly "held by the chiefs has become state property. It cannot be bought or sold or converted into hired-labor plantations; cultivation is either by the family or by the co-operatives and collectives." Hunton reported that "Guaranteed minimum wages and family allowances were greatly increased," as well, while "prices of the people's basic foods were reduced and kept low." These measures, among others, helped to eliminate extreme wealth disparity; "In

---

335. Jackson, *The View From Here...*, Ibid., 6. Interestingly, Hunton's "slave-born grandfather, Stanton Hunton...became a close confidant of John Brown when the raid on Harper's Ferry was being planned." See: Von Eschen, *Race Against Empire...*, Ibid, 57

the Guinean capital there is none of the ludicrous and shocking contrast of opulence and misery so prevalent in other cities. There are no fancy luxury-goods shops catering exclusively to a wealthy bourgeoisie. There are no large department stores stocked with all sorts of expensive imported items and run by French and British commercial trusts...You will not see in Conakry any pretentious buildings bearing the names of foreign banking, oil, and other trusts...And you will not hear any radio programs or see any billboard signs begging you to buy Coca-Cola or anything else." In Guinea, Hunton boldly, perhaps overly optimistically proclaimed, the "day is past where the poorer countries, for lack of any other source of aid, must obey the dictates of imperialist countries. Guinea is for all Africa, as Cuba is for all Latin America, a living demonstration that those nations which refuse to relinquish any fraction of their political or economic independence, can be sure of support from the socialist countries in their effort to rid themselves of the handicaps of colonialism." Hunton then invoked a word familiar to those who had read Karl Marx and Friedrich Engels' *Communist Manifesto*; he wrote, because "this is so and because the present day economic colonialists tremble at the possible consequences, they desperately strive to hide the truth about Guinea and Cuba behind a barrage of slander and absurdities."[336]

Hunton's optimistic view was not unrealistic. Black liberation in Africa, buoyed by ascendant socialism, was advancing on multiple fronts. Perhaps, Hunton was also jubilant about cosmonaut Yuri Gagarin, "from the first land of socialism," who on April 12, 1961,

---

336. Alphaeus Hunton, "Guinea Strides Forward," *Freedomways*, Vol. 1, No. 1 (Spring 1961), 22-31 and Mike Newberry, "A Talk With Editor Of 'Freedomways,'" *The Worker*, Sunday, June 18, 1961, 9. Here Hunton is making a somewhat veiled reference to Marx and Engels' comment in the *Communist Manifesto* (New York: International Publishers, 2014): "Let the ruling classes tremble at a communist revolution. The proletarians have nothing to lose but their chains. They have a world to win. Workingmen of all countries, unite!" As I have written elsewhere, with the triumph of the Bolshevik revolution in 1917, the formation of the Soviet Union and the corresponding emergence of Communist Parties throughout the world, the objective conditions were ripe for the working class to take full advantage of the general crisis of the capitalist system. For a brief moment in world history, the ruling class did in fact tremble. Though it may be difficult to imagine today, ascendant socialism compelled a retreat away from the most egregious aspect of capitalism and imperialism. Communists repeatedly returned to this theme. See: Pecinovsky, *Let Them Tremble...*, Ibid.

became the first "in the whole family of the human race" to break the barrier of Earth's atmosphere and ascend into space, as his comrade James Jackson put it.[337] Regardless, while in Guinea, Hunton felt as if he "was in the mainstream not only of African liberation forces but what was progressive globally." The whirlwind of change in Africa, coupled with his socialist convictions, provided Hunton with the intellectual and political freedom he was denied in the U.S., complicating our discourses on domestic Black civil rights. In Guinea, Hunton proposed to teach courses on, for example, *United Nations and African Administration* and *United States Policy in Africa and Problems of Pan-African Unity and Cooperation.*[338]

Shortly after returning from his 1961 Eastern Europe trip, Hunton excitedly wrote to W.E.B. and Shirley Graham Du Bois. Apparently, Alphaeus and Dorothy were unaware that the Du Bois' had planned to emigrate to Ghana and had been informed by "a mutual friend in Prague who had seen the Doctor [Du Bois] in Rumania... We were told that the move, to take place in Jan., was top-secret and should not be mentioned to a soul." Of course, they were "bowled over" by the October 1961 *Guardian* announcement "that you had already left for Africa." Hunton understood the need for secrecy, though, given the political repression both men had faced throughout their careers. "From all that I hear and read about the U.S.A. these days...I have not the slightest doubt that you acted wisely."[339] As a final thumb in the eye to U.S. imperialism, also in October 1961 Du Bois officially applied to join the CPUSA.[340]

Hunton also noted that it was "truly splendid that the direction [sic] of the Encyclopedia Africana has been offered to the Doctor – and even more splendid that he has accepted. My heartiest congratulations." While he was not "making any formal application at this point for a post on the project," Hunton did want to "say in all candor that if the Doctor thinks that I could be [of] some help and the circumstances permit it, I would consider seriously the question of moving from Guinea to Ghana" to work with Du Bois

---

337. Jackson, *The View From Here...*, Ibid., 111
338. Hunton, *Alphaeus Hunton...*, Ibid., 114, 118
339. UMass-Amherst, Special Collections, W.E.B. Du Bois Papers, MS 312: Letter from Hunton to W.E.B. and Shirley Graham Du Bois, November 20, 1961
340. Philip Bart, Theodore Bassett, William W. Weinstone, Arthur Zipser (eds), *Highlights Of A Fighting History: 60 Years Of The Communist Party, USA* (New York: International Publishers, 1979), 487-490

on the *Encyclopedia*. Teaching, "even in a place such as Guinea," has become "increasingly taxing," Hunton continued – and "I'm now fifty-eight." Additionally. His teaching responsibilities left him with "too little time and energy for what I want to do most, research and writing on African problems. You have already learned, or will soon, that when you work in Africa it is of paramount importance to conserve both time and energy." Hunton then noted that though his "teaching load" had been "reduced from 22 hours a week (last year's schedule) to 17," he still did not have time enough for intellectual pursuits.[341]

Shortly thereafter Hunton received a letter from Du Bois asking him to relocate to Ghana to help work on the *Encyclopedia*,[342] an invitation he was excited to accept.[343]

* * *

Hunton's ousting from Ghana after the 1966 coup did not tame his scathing critique of colonialism, neo-colonialism, and imperialism. He asserted, "colonial powers had yielded to popular self-government" in parts of Africa only to "strengthen their economic domination." He added that some leaders of "newly independent" African countries were nothing more than "the willing servants of their imperialist masters," as evidenced by post-coup Ghana.[344] In 1967, Zambian president Kenneth Kaunda invited Hunton to that country as his guest, where he worked on a history of the nationalist movement and wrote a column for *Mayibye*, the ANC's underground bulletin.[345] Hunton brought full-circle a

---

341. UMass-Amherst, Special Collections, W.E.B. Du Bois Papers, MS 312: Letter from Hunton to W.E.B. and Shirley Graham Du Bois, Ibid.

342. Hunton, *Alphaeus Hunton…*, Ibid., 126

343. Coupled with Hunton's excitement were more mundane and tedious tasks, such as securing a postal address or "some other forwarding address [in Ghana]…Prospects of our ever getting any mail that arrives here after we have left are extremely dim!" Hunton was also concerned with lodging and shipping "20 or so boxes of books (I'll leave some behind here), two filing cabinets, desks, three big trunks," etc. Ever the scholar, Hunton was concerned about his books and papers. UMass-Amherst, Special Collections, W.E.B. Du Bois Papers, Box 155: Series 1, 1A: Letter from Hunton to Du Bois, January 25, 1962

344. *William Alphaeus Hunton Papers…*, Ibid.

345. Hakim Adi, Marika Sherwood, *Pan-African History: Political Figures from Africa and the Diaspora Since 1787* (London: Routledge, 2003), 94

political life given substance with his initial work in the NNC 30 years earlier.

*   *   *

While in Africa, where there "is an openness, spacial as well as imaginative," Hunton watched as the civil rights movement back home grew in strength.[346] As one of the intellectual and organizational architects of the long civil rights movement, he never gave up on the struggle for African American equality or Black liberation in Africa. He understood the dialectical unity between the national and international qualities of these struggles. Black liberation and African American equality both "evoke memories of a common heritage, of the experience of centuries of struggle against racist oppression," CPUSA national chair Henry Winston wrote. Additionally, both are the enemy of U.S. capitalism, which "would never passively reconcile itself...[to] political independence in Africa or equality" at home. Though Hunton was now in Africa, his life's work embodied what Winston called a "special affinity between Africans and [U.S.] Blacks...who are struggling against oppression on the home grounds of U.S. imperialism – one of the most powerful sources of oppression in Africa."[347]

*   *   *

Diagnosed with pancreatic cancer, Hunton's appetite waned, and he grew increasingly weak and frail.[348] William Alphaeus Hunton died in Lusaka, Zambia on January 13, 1970. Kenneth Kaunda wept at his graveside.[349] Hunton lived his life in service to African American equality, Black liberation, and socialism. Writing to James and Esther Cooper Jackson shortly after Alphaeus' death, Dorothy Hunton noted, "I can't begin to tell you what a great consolation it has been to me in the darkest hours of my life to know

346. Alan S. Oser, "African Encyclopedia Still Alive, Scholar Ousted by Ghana Says," *New York Times*, January 29, 1967

347. Winston, *Strategy for a Black Agenda...*, Ibid., 11, 15

348. Hunton, *Alphaeus Hunton...*, Ibid., 171-174

349. Adi and Sherwood, *Pan-African History...*, Ibid., 94; Gerald Horne, "Introduction," in Pecinovsky, *Let Them Tremble...*, Ibid., xii; and "Alphaeus Hunton: Black scholar and freedom fighter," *Daily World*, July 3, 1980, 16

that Alphaeus and I have so many wonderful friends all over the world, and that he was deeply loved, respected and admired for his contributions to the betterment of the human race. Such a gentle soul, humble and kind, unassuming and tireless in his dedication to his work." She added solemnly, "It wasn't an easy life," but it was one dedicated in service to the "human family." "I will be coming home in the spring," she concluded. "Africa without dear Alphaeus holds no place for me."[350]

*   *   *

Considered "one of the most neglected African American intellectuals in studies of this period,"[351] partly a consequence of his life-long membership in the CPUSA, Hunton was nevertheless greatly admired within the African diaspora – like his good friends Paul Robeson and W.E.B. Du Bois. Charisse Burden-Stelly notes, Hunton "was one of the most important freedom fighters in modern history." As she put it, "Numerous organizations, publications, movements, and struggles benefitted from his deep knowledge of the African continent, steadfast commitment to ending colonialism and imperialism, protracted struggle to eradicate Jim Crow and apartheid, excoriation of fascism in its many forms, challenge to colonialism and corporate domination, and vision of a socialist world devoid of the violence and inhumanity wrought by capitalist exploitation.[352] Considered a "person with exceptional talent, rare personal integrity, a deep commitment to humanistic values, and an enormous capacity for hard work," Hunton was also modest, self-possessed, and tenacious. Doxey Wilkerson wrote in *Freedomways* shortly after his death: To Hunton "there was no contradiction between scholarly pursuits and full participation by the scholar in all aspects of humankind's

---

350. NYU, TAM 347, Box 8, Folder 5: Letter from Dorothy Hunton to Esther Cooper Jackson, February 8, 1970

351. Von Eschen, *Race Against Empire...*, Ibid., 57

352. Charisse Burden-Stelly, "Radical Blackness and Mutual Comradeship at 409 Edgecombe," *Black Perspectives*, July 16, 2019, https://www.aaihs.org/radical-blackness-and-mutual-comradeship-at-409-edgecombe/ and Hunton, *Alphaeus Hunton...* (New York: International Publishers, 2021). Quoted from Burden-Stelly's Foreword.

struggle for a better life,"[353] including the struggle for socialism. The *Daily World* (successor to the *Daily Worker*) commented that Hunton's passing was "an irreplaceable loss" to the struggles for African American equality and Black liberation.[354] CPUSA leaders Henry Winston and Gus Hall wrote that Hunton's "contribution and dedication to the advancement of national liberation, peace and socialism won [him] the admiration and comradeship of people in all parts of the world."[355] Herbert Aptheker called him "modest to a fault."[356] The *New York Times* obituary was considerably more reserved; it simply recognized Hunton as "an American authority on Africa."[357] A Friend of Hunton's from London – likely the last comrade to visit him as his health deteriorated – in a letter to the *Daily World*, added, that Hunton was a "modest but principled fighter for freedom – both in America and Africa."[358] Members of the Alphaeus Hunton College Teacher's Club of the New York Communist Party argued in a spring 1975 issue of *Party Affairs*, "Nothing is more important for the Party than work in educating our people about the theory and practice of socialism," a project to which Hunton devoted his life.[359]

In April 1943, while Hunton was making the transition from Howard University professor and NNC leader to CAA education director, *The Worker* noted, he is a "fine example of an intellectual that speaks the workers language,"[360] perhaps the highest praise possible for a Communist. As the political inquisitors questioned Hunton about the CRC defense fund in 1951, Du Bois wrote, "I have come to know this fine man very well." Du Bois called him, "Quiet, studious, conscientious and absolutely uncorruptible."[361]

353. Wilkerson, "William Alphaeus…," Ibid.

354. "William Alphaeus Hunton," *Daily World*, Thursday, January 15, 1970, 7

355. "W. Alphaeus Hunton, fighting scholar," *Daily World*, January 15, 1970, 9

356. Eric Foner and Manning Marable (eds), *Herbert Aptheker on Race and Democracy* (Urbana: University of Illinois Press, 2006), 232

357. "Dr. W.S. Hunton, Expert On Africa," *New York Times*, January 16, 1970

358. "Our readers say – Hunton's Concern For Encyclopedia," *Daily World*, February 13, 1970, 7

359. Alphaeus Hunton College Teachers Club, "Discussion of the Draft Resolution," *Party Affairs*, Vol. 9, No. 5 (May 1975), 37

360. "Negro People Are on the Move, Eastern Seaboard Parley Showed," *The Worker*, April 18, 1943, 8

361. Hunton, *Alphaeus Hunton…*, Ibid., 85 and UMass-Amherst, Special Collections, W.E.B. Du Bois Papers: MS 312: Letter from Du Bois, August 8, 1951

African-studies pioneer honored

DAILY WORLD — Thursday, July 3, 1980 — 16

The following are the remarks of Mrs. Dorothy Hunton, widow of Dr. Alphaeus Hunton, upon receiving the Trans-Africa special award honoring the scholar, presented on May 31, 1980 by former Rep. Charles Diggs, former chairperson of the House Foreign Affairs Subcommittee on Africa.

By Dorothy Hunton

Mr. Chairman, Congressman Diggs, friends:

Tonight is a very special occasion for me. As I scan this sea of faces, I am reminded of many meetings and rallies sponsored by the Council on African Affairs in the early/middle 30s and late 40s. But most of all, I remember the reception given for Alphaeus in December 1961 at Small's Paradise in Harlem. He had just been released from prison. It was an exciting experience, but also a sobering one. Exciting because Alphaeus was home after serving six months in the federal penitentiary in Virginia for contempt of court. As a trustee of the Civil Rights Bail Fund, he and three other trustees had refused to comply to a demand from the House Un-American Activities Committee to turn over their books with the names of contributors. McCarthyism ran extremely high, and the country was at its lowest ebb — red-baiting.

The occasion was sobering because new values, new friends, and new goals had emerged through the disruption of my life. No longer centered on a small, personal world, life became a universal challenge. A new dimension appeared living with Alphaeus. He taught me many things, among them patience and the wisdom to see oneself as his brother's keeper.

During those early days, the Council on African Affairs was like a small voice

Dorothy Hunton

crying in the desert, it was no easy task to spread abroad the true history and plight of the desperate millions in Africa. Few people had any knowledge whatsoever of the highly organised integrated system of African life and culture nor its great contributions in the realm of art.

Among many Blacks, there was a curious division in attitudes towards their history. They were at once ashamed and proud. Black certainly was not considered beautiful then, and few of us wanted to be associated with anything African, so ignorant were we of our roots.

The Council was the only organization of its kind that disseminated the correct information on Africa. Alphaeus labored intensely for 12 years as executive secretary to give the American people the true picture of that oppressed continent. But the McCarthy harassment continued to hammer away, and finally brought all activity to an end in 1955. Nevertheless, he continued to work at home, and in 1957, Decision in Africa was published.

An entire generation of Blacks who

know nothing about the efforts, the struggles, the heartaches of the organization that was started in 1937 by a small group of concerned individuals who were appalled by the disquieting news coming out of that last stronghold of colonialism. Paul Robeson was among that gathering and he became the chairman, a function he maintained to the bitter end.

For 17 years Alphaeus taught at Howard University before joining the Council, and you can be sure he was very active. Usually working quietly behind the scenes to make the wheels go round, he was particularly involved in the Teacher's Union, which he helped to organize, and the National Negro Congress, which played a tremendously important role in breaking down some of the dreadful conditions in which we lived.

How many young people today are aware of the many footsteps planted by the National Negro Congress? Footsteps in which they unknowingly stood through "Black Revolution" in the 60s. The push could not have been possible had not the groundwork been laid by many forerunners decades before Alphaeus was indeed one of them.

After publication of Decision in Africa there were no prospects of a meaningful job, it was rough. In 1960, however, at the invitation of Sekou Toure, President of Guinea, we went to that newly independent country to teach.

In 1962, Dr. W.E.B. DuBois, who worked closely with Alphaeus in the Council and was then living in Ghana, requested his contract release to work with him on the long awaited Encyclopedia Africana. On this immense project he devoted five years, laying the groundwork for a 10-volume history of Africa and setting up area committees in various sections of the continent. Then came the shocking coup that deposed Kwame Nkrumah.

One year later we were deported. A despicable, humiliating, unwarranted act from which Alphaeus never recovered. A quiet, reserved, undemonstrative person, always the meticulous scholar, he was a man of few words. Stunned and deeply hurt, denied the opportunity to continue his life's work for which he had given his all, he closed up. That was the beginning of the end for my beloved Alphaeus.

Given eight days to leave the country we had no choice but to return to the States. But after three months in New York we were back in Africa at the invitation of President Kenneth Kaunda of Zambia, who thought Alphaeus might be able to continue his work there. It was not possible. Three years later he died from cancer in 1970. The warm soul of the land he loved and devoted his life to help free received his worn out body.

Alone with Alphaeus in our lovely home in Lusaka, holding his icy, cold hand in mine as his last breath faded away, a deep, compelling conviction came over me that I must record his life. Crucial events in Black history had played an important part in it and should not be lost in the sands of time like much of our history in the past.

Three years of plowing through the intricate, untried path of writing was truly a labor of love. Many times, from sheer frustration I was ready to give up, the undertaking seemed too difficult. But one look at his picture which hung over my desk — his dark, brooding eyes looking down on me — always gave me courage.

The world, so full of confusion, upheavals and uncertainties, cries out for peace. Where shall we find it? Peace, like love, must start within oneself, then spread to the family, neighborhood, city, state, nation and around the world. Peace is the only thing that will save us. Let us send it out to all humankind and see it come back to us tenfold.

IMAGE 9: *Daily World*, July 3, 1980. Courtesy of *People's World*.

Nine years later, in a letter to Ishmael Flory, of the African American Heritage Association, Du Bois praised Hunton even more. He wrote: "Hunton is the kind of absolutely honest and unselfish scholar who is so apt to be trampled on and neglected in the present American world."[362] In a September 1962 correspondence with Hunton, Du Bois gently chastised his long-time co-worker and friend for too much humility. Hunton had left his name out of a "splendid" report he had written regarding the *Encyclopedia Africana*.[363] Du Bois' critique and comment is sound advice to scholars and activists who have too often left Hunton out of their analysis. Ten years after his death, on May 31, 1980, Representative Charles Diggs (D-Michigan), former chairperson of the House Foreign Affairs Subcommittee and staunch critic of

---

362. UMass-Amherst, Special Collections, W.E.B. Du Bois Papers: MS 312: Letter from Du Bois to Flory, April 16, 1960. For more on Flory, see: "Ishmael Flory, fighter for equality, 96," *People's World*, February 20, 2004, https://www. peoplesworld.org/article/ishmael-flory-fighter-for-equality-96/

363. Aptheker (ed.), *The Correspondence of W. E. B. Du Bois…*, Ibid., 459

South Africa, presented Dorothy Hunton the Trans-Africa special award posthumously honoring Alphaeus (image 9) as an internationalist and forerunner of the modern civil rights movement.[364] Like Robeson and Du Bois, Hunton's name should be revered, enshrined – in the struggle for African American equality, Black liberation, and socialism.

364. Hunton, "African-studies pioneer…," Ibid.

W. Alphaeus *Hunton's* Daily Worker columns, *1944-1946*

*   *   *

"Dr. Hunton Writes Guest Column," *Daily Worker*, July 20, 1944, page 3

During the absence from the city [New York] of Max Yergan*during the next few work weeks, his co-guest column will be conducted by Dr. Alphaeus Hunton.

Dr. Hunton is educational director of the Council on African Affairs. He is also in charge of the Council's publications, including its monthly paper *New Africa*, working closely with Dr. Yergan and Paul Robeson, Council officers.

Dr. Hunton was a member of Howard University in Washington, since 1926, before he came to work with the Council. In Washington, he was prominent in trade union and community work.

He is on the faculty of the Jefferson school and a member of the national board of the National Negro Congress. He is a frequent contributor to Negro progressive journals.

*   *   *

---

*For more on Yergan, see: David Henry Anthony III, *Max Yergan: Race Man, Internationalist, Cold Warrior* (New York: New York University Press, 2006)

179

"Today's Guest Column: Textbook for Conference On Colonial Freedom," *Daily Worker*, July 20, 1944, page 7

The experience of the common struggle against fascism and the national strength of the Soviet Union manifested in that struggle have made possible the clearing away of the rubbish of falsehood and slander about that country. There has developed a widespread and genuine appreciation of many of those aspects of Soviet life which form the basis of her national strength.

One thing which is attracting more and more international attention and interest is the way in which, within a quarter of a century, many millions of people of different races, creeds and cultures, illiterate, impoverished and degraded victims of exploitation under the old Russian Empire, were raised to full social, economic and political equality with the most advanced section of the population so as to form a strong, unified and closely knit federation of autonomous republics.

The record of this achievement, interestingly narrated in the pamphlet, "A Family of Nations," published by the National Council of American-Soviet Friendship, has been of special interest to those who are thinking about the problem of abolishing colonialism and semi-colonialism in all areas of the postwar world. A popular pamphlet entitled Soviet Light on the Colonies [sic], recently published by the Penguin Press in England, is having a big sale there. It is written by Leonard Barnes, an economist and colonial expert and also, incidentally, one of the charter members of the Council on African Affairs.

*   *   *

Significantly enough, the announcement of a colonial conference being held in London this weekend by the League of Colored Peoples carries the information that Mr. Barnes' pamphlet will be used "as our text-book." Dr. Harold A. Moody, president of the league,* says, "The very fact of what England has failed to

---

*For more on Moody and the League of Colored Peoples, See: Munro, *The Antico-lonial Front…*, Ibid., 54-56 and Von Eschen, *Race Against Empire…*, Ibid., 45-46, 50-51

do in Africa during these past 100 years, and what Russia has accomplished in these last 25 years, has come as a shock to the people of this country."

Prime Minister Churchill has maintained that self-government for Africans is not to be expected within any time "that it is reasonable or useful to foresee." If the same planless, laissez-faire, unprogressive colonial regime of the past is to continue in the postwar world, then he is perhaps right. But the people in British Asia, Africa and the Caribbean, as well as an increasingly large section of the British public itself, have a different outlook.

This progressive opinion has not been without its effect upon the British Colonial Office, despite the influence of the Churchill school of thought respecting the empire. No sweeping democratic reforms have yet been introduced in the colonies, but there is a decidedly fresh and up-to-date point of view expressed in the recent official report on "Mass Education in African Society." Reviewing the "startling successes" of educational programs of the Soviet Union, and also of China and Turkey, the report draws the conclusion that: (a) Literacy must be regarded "as the inevitable prerequisite for the political, economic and social advance of the whole people": (b) "the time factor is immensely important," and (c) "the uniting force in such a campaign is the enthusiasm of the people." The recommendations for the development of mass education in British Africa are based upon these three principles.

The Free French in their reexamination of colonial policies in Africa recently decided to send French missions to the Soviet Union.

And Henry A. Wallace, in his pamphlet, Our Job in the Pacific [sic], says, "Our example in the Philippines, together with Russia's enlightened treatment of Asiatic minorities, and any steps which China may take toward cultural and linguistic as well as political minorities, can bring tremendous pressure to bear on the whole colonial problem."

*   *   *

"Today's Guest Column: World Bank Plan Depends On Victory for FDR," *Daily Worker,* July 27, 1944, page 7

In addition to the Democratic Convention and the dramatic evidence that the Nazi war machine is having serious troubles within its high command as well as on the fighting fronts, another big news item of international importance last week was the successful completion of the international monetary conference at Bretton Woods, N.H. There was no fanfare and relatively little popular interest attached to the proceedings up at Bretton Woods, yet the decisions arrived at by the representatives of the 44 United and Associated Nations participating in the conference affect, as [Treasury] Secretary [Henry] Morgenthau said, "the most elementary bread and butter realities of daily life."

"What we have done," the Treasury Secretary said in summing up the results of the conference, "is to device machinery by which men and women everywhere can exchange freely, on a fair and stable basis, the goods which they produced through their labor. And we have taken the initial step through which the nations of the world will be able to help one another in economic development to their mutual advantage and for the enrichment of all."

Like the earlier United Nations Food and Rehabilitation Conference, the meeting which ended last Saturday was another milestone on the road of international collaboration in the spirit of Teheran. It brought nearer the prospect of rapid economic development of colonial and semi-colonial areas, of national and international prosperity based on an expanded world trade, and of that agreement and harmony on economic aims upon which world peace must rest.

*   *   *

That is the underlying meaning of the lengthy and complex articles of agreement in the plan for a $9,100,000,000 Bank for International Reconstruction and Development, and for an International Monetary Fund.

The Bank's main function is to guarantee long-term financial aid "at reasonable rates" to those countries that need it to develop their economic potentialities or to reconstruct their war-ravaged industry and agriculture.

Parallel with the Bank is the International Monetary Fund to stabilize postwar currencies. The Fund plan foreshadows an end to the sharp competitive practices of currency manipulation and depreciation, high tariff walls, unfair barter deals and restrictions on exchange. These are the things which in past history have hampered world trade and global economic progress, brought on depression and unemployment, and led to war.

The Bank's function will supplant the customary greedy and short-sighted practices of getting the quickest and highest possible returns on foreign investments. This it [sic] is which has accounted for the ruthless and inhuman exploitation of peoples in Africa, Asia, Latin America and other less advanced economic areas of the world. Agriculture and industry must be developed in these lands not, as in the past, for the profit of a handful of investors, but in order that the standard of living of the native peoples in these places may be raised: so that they can buy and consume more goods, and produce and sell more goods, thus contributing to world prosperity.

*　*　*

No one has stressed the urgency of this kind of postwar program for colonial and semi-colonial countries more emphatically than Earl Browder,* who, in his recent admirable guide to clear thinking in these times, "Teheran, Our Path in War and Peace," declares that "American industrialists and economists must, as a condition for the survival of their prevailing system, expand their concept of the foreign market by a thousand percent."

It is necessary to remember, however, that the World Bank and Monetary Fund schemes – and likewise other international

---

* In May 1944, the CPUSA officially dissolved under the leadership of Browder and re-associated as the Communist Political Association (CPA). However, in 1945, shortly after the conclusion of World War II, the CPA was itself dissolved and the CPUSA was rechartered. Browder was expelled. See: Ryan, *Earl Browder...*, Ibid.

agreements which will follow – must be approved by our government and other participating governments before becoming effective. We can expect the [Herbert] Hoover Republicans and other anti-Roosevelt forces to raise anew the old bogey about "the U.S.A. playing Santa Claus to the world." And that is just one more reason why it is imperative that Roosevelt be re-elected, and with him a Congress that wholeheartedly supports his views as to how to achieve collective security in the postwar world.

*   *   *

"Today's Guest Column: People of Africa Learn From the USSR," *Daily Worker,* August 3, 1944, page 7

As a kind of sequel to my column of two weeks ago in which I discussed the significant, new recognition being given in British, French and other circles to the applicability of Soviet experience to the colonial problems of Africa and other areas, I want to say something today about how the people of Africa themselves view this matter.

Yes, Africans today are learning and talking about the Soviet Union. An Allied Labor News Dispatch tells of African delegates participating in the Soviet Friendship Congress held in Johannesburg, South Africa, a few days ago. In an unprecedented action, these delegates were admitted to a "European Only" theatre to see a special preview of [the film] "The North Star."*

Some weeks ago, a parade of African troops, paying honor to Red Army victories, was held at Accra, capital of the Gold Coast, a British West African colony, once a main source of claves for America. As the black troops marched past the reviewing stand, upon which sat the Governor, paramount chiefs, and other African leaders, the Soviet flag was unfurled and the African military band played the new Soviet national anthem.

Symbolic of the new relations between Africa and the USSR, paralleling the closer ties between the continent and the USA, was the establishment early this year of full diplomatic relations by Ethiopia with the Soviet Union, and the presentation of a gift, a gold shield, from Emperor Halle Selassie to the Mayor of Stalingrad.

As the war has made the whole world smaller, so it has brought Africa closer to the great land of the Soviets, as well as to America. New airports and air routes across Africa from the west coast

---

* "The North Star" is a 1943 film about Ukrainian village resistance to Nazi occupation that favorably depicts guerrilla tactics and pro-Soviet collectivization. The film was initially universally praised and nominated for six Oscars. In 1947, the House Un-American Activities Committee cited the movie as an example of pro-Soviet propaganda. In 1957, the film was re-cut to remove idealized portrayals of Soviet collectivization and re-released as "Armored Attack." The re-released version concludes with a reference to the 1956 Hungarian Revolution.

to the east have made that continent a cross-roads between the Americas and the USSR.

*   *   *

With their increasing knowledge of the Soviet Power, African leaders are more frequently citing the contrast between the failure of the European colonial administration, during a half century or longer, to provide any appreciable social advancement for the masses of Africans under their rule, and the remarkable success of the Soviet government in bringing social well-being and economic efficiency to millions of heterogeneous peoples who 25 years ago were in a state of colonial serfdom comparable to that of the most "backward" Africans.

The editor of the West African Pilot, for example, points to the Soviet achievements in education in answering those who argue that "Nigeria would be unable to wipe out illiteracy within living memory." Stating that illiteracy had been reduced from 90 percent in Tsarist Russia to less than 10 percent today, he declares, "Nigeria can profit from the experience of Soviet Russia in the realm of education." Means must be found, he says, for making education for Africans free, compulsory, and universal.

*   *   *

Soviet ideas of collective agriculture and industrial enterprise find a ready understanding and appreciation among Africans. Prior to the coming of the Europeans and the consequent disruption of the traditional tribal life, the primitive communal system of sharing labor and property prevailed in African society. The land belonged to no individual but to the tribe or the village; no one who shared in the work went hungry. The introduction and spread of the capitalist wage-system has not been able to destroy this heritage. Communal practices still survive in the hinterland, and in the more advanced sections Africans have been able to develop, despite the economic handicaps of imperialism, some successful cooperative enterprises of their own in such fields as cocoa production.

Basically, a people cannot develop until they have a goal which is in their own interest and their own choosing. If the United Nations face the fact squarely and substitute a policy of cooperation on a plane of equality for the outmoded system of imperialist exploitation and colonial tutelage, Africans and other colonial peoples can advance rapidly, as the Soviet people have advanced, to assume their proper share of responsibility in a world of collective security.

* * *

"Today's Guest Column: America's Postwar Lesson in Phila. Strike Must Be Learned," *Daily Worker,* August 10, 1944, page 7

The immediate urgency and gravity of the problem of stamping out Jimcrowism [sic] struck this country last week with the impact of a thunderbolt. The shameful Philadelphia Rapid Transit walk-out* engineered by our home-grown fascists was not an attack upon the Negro; it was an attack upon the American government and the American people. There could have been no sharper and plainer warning of the danger which America and the world face if victory over fascism falls short of meaning victory over the doctrine and practice of "white supremacy." Neither could there have been any better demonstration of the effectiveness of a broad democratic policy backed up by the proper authority and forthright action as the means of achieving such a victory.

A New York Times editorial last Monday, in speaking of the great "spiritual and moral loss" entailed by the crisis in Philadelphia, asked, "What shall we say to the Negro fighting men? What shall we say to the Chinese, the Filipinos, the people of India and

---

*In August 1944, 4,500 white Philadelphia transit workers went on strike to protest the hiring of eight Black men to "positions previously reserved for whites." For six days trolleys and buses sat idle, as did "one of the country's leading wartime manufacturing centers," seriously affecting "the production of radar, heavy artillery, heavy ammunition, military trucks, bombs," and other war supplies. Thousands of African Americans and their allies protested to draw attention to the hypocrisy of fighting fascism abroad while Jim Crow prevailed at home. Pickets declared: "We Drive Tanks, Why Not Trolleys?" and "Race Discrimination Breeds Fascism." The strike ended after soldiers were called in. Months prior to the strike there had been a hotly contested and contentious organizing drive among the transit workers with three different unions vying for recognition. The then Communist-led CIO affiliated Transport Workers Union ultimately won the election; the more conservative AFL affiliated Amalgamated Association of Street and Electric Railway and Motor Coach Employees of America stayed silent on the question of race; the Philadelphia Rapid Transit Employees Union actively used racism and red-baiting as an organizing tactic, thereby stoking fears among the majority white union members. See: Dustin Waters, "Eight black transit workers got promoted. Thousands of white workers walked off the job," *The Washington Post,* June 15, 2020, and Maurice Isserman, *Which Side Were You On?: The American Communist Party During the Second World War* (Middletown: Wesleyan University Press, 1982), 143.

to others whom we needs as friends and allies but whose skins are of a slightly different color from that of most Americans?"

The answer given to these vital questions was: "All we can say, indeed, is that the United States Government, supported by the mass of enlightened opinion of this country, will not tolerate racial discrimination in the matter of war jobs." Very fine. But is that all? Such an answer can hardly satisfy the many millions here and abroad who are concerned about what kind of example the United States will set for the postwar world in the treatment of its own minority groups, and what kind of leadership this country will give to the United Nations in the framing of democratic policies for colonial and semi-colonial peoples.

The Times editorial does, indeed, declare that what happened in the City of Brotherly Love "ought to lead to an emphatic reaffirmation of human rights in this country." The sincerity of this laudable observation is brought into question, however, by the sentences immediately following in which the scope of "human rights" is limited "simply and solely" to the matter of "equality of economic opportunity." Is the Times so naïve as to believe that economic democracy can be achieved side by side with social and political discrimination?

* * *

The decisive manner in which the weight of federal authority was brought to bear in Philadelphia to uphold a decision of the Fair Employment Practices Committee points the way in which the government must attack racial discrimination all down the line. Congress must give permanent status and adequate authority to the FEPC so that postwar employment as well as war jobs may be open to all without discrimination, and it must adopt legislation to abolish the polltax [sic] and end Jimcrowism [sic] in all other areas of our social life. That is the will of the vast majority of the American people.

President Roosevelt established the FEPC in order to insure the full use of all available manpower in our war production program. That was a national necessity. Once the war is won, the world will face the pressing necessity of securing full production and full employment in order to win the peace. Somewhere between

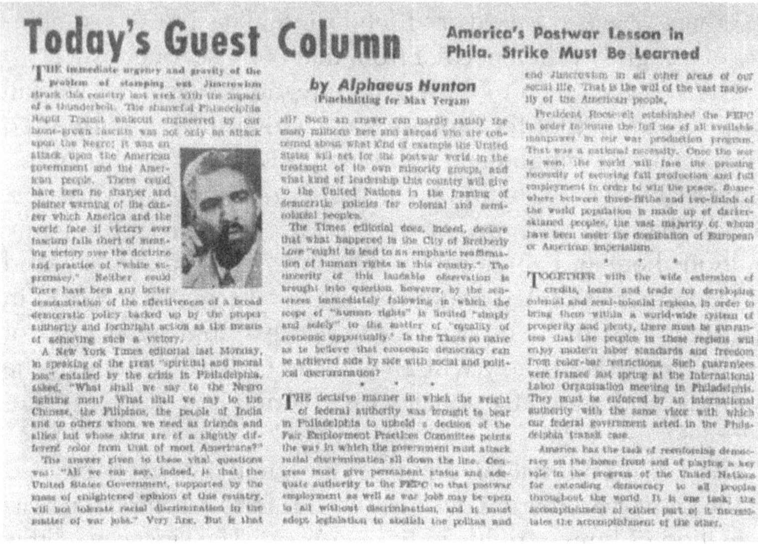

Today's Guest Column   America's Postwar Lesson In Phila. Strike Must Be Learned

by Alphaeus Hunton
(Pinchhitting for Max Yergan)

IMAGE 10: *Daily Worker*, August 10, 1944. Courtesy of *People's World*.

three-fifths and two-thirds of the world population is made up of darker-skinned peoples, the vast majority of whom have been under the domination of European or American imperialism.

* * *

Together with the wide extension of credits, loans and trade for developing colonial and semi-colonial regions, in order to bring them within a world-wide system of prosperity and plenty, there must be guarantees that the peoples in these regions will enjoy modern labor standards and freedom from color-bar restrictions. Such guarantees were framed last spring at the International Labor Organization meeting in Philadelphia.* They must be enforced by an international authority with the same vigor with which our federal government acted in the Philadelphia transit strike.

---

*In spring 1944, delegate from 41 countries met in Philadelphia and adopted the International Labor Organization's "Declaration of Philadelphia," which rededicated the organization to advancing workers' rights, human rights, and international economic planning.

America has the task of reenforcing democracy on the home front and of playing a key role in the program of the United Nations for extending democracy to all peoples throughout the world. It is one task; the accomplishment of either part of it necessitates the accomplishment of the other.

*   *   *

"Today's Guest Column: 'Back to Africa' Cry Is Leveled Against Teheran," *Daily Worker,* August 17, 1944, page 7

So Gerald L.K. Smith [anti-Semitic founder of the America First Party and 1944 presidential candidate] has joined Sen. Theodore Bilbo of Mississippi in advocating that American Negroes go "back to Africa." Perhaps we shall soon have Martin Dies denouncing the refusal of Negroes to heed this advice as evidence of "subversive influences" at work, and demanding still another investigation by Attorney General [Francis] Biddle.

The "back to Africa" proposal sounds ridiculous, and it is. But at the same time it is no laughing matter. It is no laughing matter to the Negro boys who are fighting abroad in order that they may come home to a better America. It is no laughing matter to the many millions of our darker-skinned allies who look to this war to bring to an end the practice of separating and differentiating between peoples according to race or color. The Hitlerite regime sought to prove that a super-race, a Herrenvolk, could rule the world. The advocates of "white supremacy" in America, together with the anti-Communists and anti-Semites, propose to continue using Hitler's weapons and fighting Hitler's war even after Hitler is defeated.

The Senator from Mississippi recommends that the Negro people seek security and equal opportunity not in America but in Liberia, the Negro republic on the west coast of Africa. The American First leader, Gerald Smith, goes him one better. He proposes that for the purpose of establishing a "homeland in Africa for the American Negro" – one excuse for imperialism is as good as another – this country should demand one million square miles of African territory from Great Britain and France in lieu of their war debts. Could Herr Goebbels himself have invented a better story to try to split the United Nations and alienate the African and other colonial peoples who are fighting with us?

*   *   *

Bilbo and Smith raise the cry of "Back to Africa" at a time when the southern reactionaries are becoming more and more desperate in their efforts to stop the Negro's march toward full citizenship rights. It has always been thus. The first proposal for transplanting American Negroes to Africa, a reliable historian tells us, was made by a white man in New Jersey in 1772 just after a slave revolt. The obvious intent of the proposal was to get rid of the more militant slaves and free Negroes. Gabriel's insurrection of 1800 and Nat Turner's rebellion in 1831 were both followed by new efforts toward stimulating migration to Africa. A colonization society formed in 1816 was sponsored and financed by southern slaveholders, including such men as [Senators] John Randolph and Henry Clay. These "Back to Africa" efforts during the slavery period were repeatedly denounced by David Walker, Frederick Douglass and other Negro leaders as intended only to sidetrack the emancipation movement.

The only African migration plan initiated by Negroes themselves which won any wide following among Negroes was the ambitious "Black Empire" scheme of Marcus Garvey in the early 1920's. The Garvey movement represented many things, but it represented one thing in particular: a widespread conviction among the Negro people at that time that they must seek their destiny alone.

World War I had brought a redivision of the colonial spoils among the victorious allies, with the German colonies in Africa being handed over to their new rulers in the form of mandates. In this country during the time of postwar readjustment a wave of terrorization and repression had broken out against the Negro to "put him back in his place" and he was isolated from the American labor movement and from American progressive forces in general. These were the conditions which engendered the Negro's conviction that he must stand by himself, and which made Garvey's "Black Empire" a meaningful symbol of freedom.

That was over 20 years ago. Gerald L.K. Smith and others of his kind are counting upon history repeating itself after this war. To recreate the conditions of the 1920's, it will be necessary for the United Nations to disintegrate, for Teheran to be forgotten, for Roosevelt and his policies to be defeated in November, and for the present close ties between the Negro people and the liberal white forces in America, particularly the CIO, to be suddenly

Today's Guest Column

by Alphaeus Hunton
(Pinchhitting for Max Yergan)

"Back to Africa" Cry Is Leveled Against Teheran

SO GERALD L. K. SMITH has joined Sen. Theodore Bilbo of Mississippi in advocating that American Negroes go "back to Africa." Perhaps we shall soon have Martin Dies denouncing the refusal of Negroes to heed this advice as evidence of "subversive influences" at work, and demanding still another investigation by Attorney General Biddle.

The "Back to Africa" proposal sounds ridiculous, and it is. But at the same time it is no laughing matter. It is no laughing matter to the Negro boys who are fighting abroad in order that they may come home to a better America. It is no laughing matter to the many millions of our darker-skinned allies who look to this war to bring to an end the practice of separating and differentiating between peoples according to race or color. The Hitlerite regime sought to prove that a super-race, a Herrenvolk, could rule the world. The advocates of "white supremacy" in America, together with the anti-Communists and anti-Semites, propose to continue using Hitler's weapons and fighting Hitler's war even after Hitler is defeated.

The Senator from Mississippi recommends that the Negro people seek security and equal opportunity not in America but in Liberia, the Negro republic on the west coast of Africa. The America First leader, Gerald Smith, goes him one better. He proposes that for the purpose of establishing a "homeland in Africa

for the American Negro"—one excuse for imperialism is as good as another—this country should demand one million square miles of African territory from Great Britain and France in lieu of their war debts. Could Herr Goebbels himself have invented a better story to try to split the United Nations and alienate the African and other colonial peoples who are fighting with us?

* * *

BILBO and Smith raise the cry of "Back to Africa" at a time when the southern reactionaries are becoming more and more desperate in their efforts to stop the Negro's march toward full citizenship rights. It has always been thus. The first proposal for transplanting American Negroes to Africa, a reliable historian tells us, was made by a white man in New Jersey in 1772 just after a slave revolt. The obvious intent of the proposal was to get rid of the more militant slaves and free Negroes. Gabriel's insurrection of 1800 and Nat Turner's rebellion in 1831 were both followed by new efforts toward stimulating migration to Africa. A colonization society formed in 1816 was sponsored and financed by southern slaveholders, including such men as John Randolph and Henry Clay. These "Back to Africa" efforts during the slavery period were repeatedly denounced by David Walker, Frederick Douglass and other Negro leaders as intended only to sidetrack the emancipation movement.

THE only African migration plan initiated by Negroes themselves which won any wide following among Negroes was the ambitious "Black Empire" scheme of Marcus Garvey in the early 1920's. The Garvey movement represented many things, but it represented one thing in particular: a widespread conviction among the Negro people at that time that they must seek their destiny alone.

World War I had brought a redivision of the colonial spoils among the victorious allies, with the German colonies in Africa being handed over to their new rulers in the form of mandates. In this country during the time of postwar readjustments a wave of terrorism and repression had broken out against the Negro to "put him back in his place," and he was isolated from the American labor movement and from American progressive forces in general. These were the conditions which engendered the Negro's conviction that he must stand by himself, and which made Garvey's "Black Empire" a meaningful symbol of freedom.

That was over 20 years ago. Gerald L. K. Smith and others of his kind are counting upon history repeating itself after this war. To recreate the conditions of the 1920's, it will be necessary for the United Nations to disintegrate, for Teheran to be forgotten, for Roosevelt and his policies to be defeated in November, and for the present close ties between the Negro people and the liberal white forces in America, particularly the CIO, to be suddenly and completely dissolved. Messrs. Bilbo and Smith, of course, would love to see all that happen. But I'm afraid they're in for a big disappointment.

IMAGE 11: *Daily Worker*, August 17, 1944. Courtesy of *People's World*.

and completely dissolved. Messrs. Bilbo and Smith, of course, would love to see all that happen. But I'm afraid they're in for a big disappointment.

*   *   *

"Today's Guest Column: Negro People Concerned With Africa's Future," *Daily Worker,* August 24, 1944, page 7

Although the American Negro, as we said in the column last week, rejects as an insult the "Back-to-Africa" mouthings [sic] of a [Senator] Bilbo or a [racist, anti-Semitic] Gerald L.K. Smith, that does not mean that he is indifferent to the future of Africa and its people.

Negro newspapers today carry more news of Africa than ever before, and there is no little discussion of what role the United States will play in Africa, of the future of Ethiopia and Liberia, of self-government for British West Africa, and of the need for drastic reforms in the Union of South Africa. Most widely discussed is the question of whether the claims of African and other colored peoples will receive proper representation and consideration at the peace conference.

All of this, of course, simply means that The Negro is keenly aware of the stakes of freedom in this war. Along with the higher level reached among the Negro people in their struggle for full rights in this country, there has developed a closer relationship to the struggles of other oppressed peoples. One widely circulated Negro weekly, for example, features columns on India, China, and Latin America, as well as news of Africa.

There is, however, one dangerous element still too often noticeable in the Negro's thinking about the darker peoples of the world. It is the tendency to view the problems as one of conflict between darker-skinned people in general and white people in general. This is the basis of the racial separatism advocated by Marcus Garvey and by the surviving remnants of his followers today. This is the basis of [conservative African American journalist] George S. Schuyler's cynical defeatism and his arguments for a long war as aiding the Negro's cause. Likewise, it is the basis of some recent prophecies of a third World War between the races.

The National Negro Congress has consistently championed the solidarity of Negro and white labor. The National Association for the Advancement of Colored people at its recent convention in Chicago gave convincing expression to this principle. These and other Negro organizations and inter-racial bodies, together with organized labor, must increase their efforts toward promoting clarity of thinking among both Negro and white Americans with respect to racial issues, not only in domestic affairs but in international affairs.

*   *   *

All enemies of the United Nations know that in narrow racial nationalism they have a fertile field in which to sow their seeds of division and discord. The doubts, suspicions, and outright lies voiced by a Norman Thomas [leader of the Socialist Party of America], a Gerald Smith, or a [Republican governor of New York] Thomas Dewey, as to the selfish, imperialistic schemes of the leading Allied powers, either individually or together, find an open ear among those who are already persuaded that the white world is arrayed against the colored world.

The influence of the defeatist forces among the Negro people and among white workers must be nullified by driving home in graphic and inescapable terms the realization that no nation or group of people can find security and democracy today outside of a framework of world-wide security and democracy in which all groups and nations work together for their mutual benefit.

The idea of a separatist "Back-to-Africa" movement is a reactionary pipe-dream, opposed to the objectives of the United Nations and opposed to the determination of the Negro people to win full democratic rights in this country to which they owe allegiance. Just as the struggle here will be won through the close collaboration and unity of the progressive forces in every section of the population, so the liberation and progress of the African people and other colonial subjects must come about through the concerted efforts of the United Nations, first in winning a decisive victory over fascism and, second, in building a new world of equality, justice and peace. The darker peoples in every land have helped in the winning of the war, and their full cooperation on a democratic basis will be essential in winning the peace.

*   *   *

"Today's Guest Column: Amsterdam News Echoes Dewey Defeatism," *Daily Worker,* September 7, 1944, page 7

It is time to do more than raise a critical eyebrow when a prominent Negro newspaper takes to echoing the defeatist line of the anti-Roosevelt and anti-United Nations press axis in this country. We refer to the Sept. 2 issue of the New York Amsterdam News – which, incidentally, is prominent among the minority of pro-Dewey Negro papers – containing a lengthy article by [journalist] A. M. Wendell Malliet on the Dumbarton Oaks conference. The article, in the style of a Hearst or Daily News editorial, is replete with suspicion – provoking questions, baseless speculations and undocumented assertions.

The Dumbarton Oaks conference, "in the opinion of some observers," Mr. Malliet says, presages the ordering of a world in which liberty for the small nations and oppressed peoples of the world, most of them are of the black, brown and yellow races, will be forced to do the will and obey the orders of the big and powerful nations." (Quoted as written.) Who are the unnamed "some observers?" Obviously, Thomas Dewey & Co., Norman Thomas & Co., and all the spokesmen of reactionary interests. If we believe these "observers," then we believe Hitler and Goebbels, who make precisely the same predictions.

Though Dewey gained nothing but embarrassment by his petty, partisan attack upon the current Washington parley in attempting to make an issue of the "rights of small nations," Mr. Malliet continues to sit astride this dead horse, whipping it for all he is worth. Without as much as mentioning the several explanatory statements by President Roosevelt, [Secretary of State] Mr. [Cordell] Hull and [Under Secretary of State and Chairman of the American delegation] Mr. [Edward R.] Stettinius about the conference, and without a word of reference to the principles upon which the conferees have agreed. He makes much ado about the "secrecy" of the parley, hints at "inside deals," and makes the wild charge that "every step taken so far (at the conference) has been in the direction of the traditional German policy of world rule and domination by the big and powerful nations."

*   *   *

In cheap journalism it has long been a habit of white chauvinism to paint a lurid picture of "the rising tide of color." Mr. Malliet reverses this and concocts a picture of the future which is just as lurid – and false. He warns that the "three greatest white nations" are scheming "to control the affairs and destinies of the world." Implicit here is the assumption that since the Soviet Union is a "white" nation, it will fall in with the plans (alleged) of America and Britain to further Anglo-Saxon domination of the world. Hence, in this distorted view, the colored races have as much to fear from the leading Allied powers (China, strangely, is not rated one of them) as from Nazi Germany (Japan in conveniently forgotten), since all alike are white and have the same aim of world domination.

*　*　*

I should like to remind Mr. Malliet, and others who think like him, of one point. It is that, apart from the absolute defeat of fascism, the first requisite of a New Deal in the various far-flung colonies and near-colonies is international agreement that there should and must be such a New Deal, followed by international collaboration toward accomplishing it. Who else can assure primary responsibility for developing such agreement and action except for principal Allied powers?

Democratic forces throughout the world, white and colored together, have the responsibility of giving unified support and constructive guidance to those who have the job of shaping a postwar world with guarantees of democracy and prosperity for all peoples.

*　*　*

"Today's Guest Column: Role of U.S. Elections In Future of Colonial Peoples," *Daily Worker*, September 14, 1944, page 7

British sensitiveness to American criticism of its colonial policies was again illustrated in the sharp and prompt reaction to the charges made by U.S. Ambassador William Phillips in his recently published letter urging action by the United States toward breaking the Indian deadlock in the interest of victory in the Pacific area. This sensitiveness is in part justified, since some of the American critics are better haters of Britain than they are friends of the colonial people. On one point of criticism, however, there can be no question. For India and the East, as well as for Africa, the West Indies, and other colonial areas, what is needed now is not further protestations of good intentions, but deeds.

British officials will no doubt respond to this by pointing to the efforts of the British Colonial Office to promote social and economic development plans in various colonies, and to the financial assistance being given to the colonies by the British government. This is all very true. But the fact remains that this planning for colonial advancement is on an extremely limited and piecemeal scale. It is left to the initiative of the governor of each colony to submit to the Colonial Office a 5 or 10 year plan of development. Few such plans, as might have been expected, have been received. And further, the maximum amount available from the British treasury to promote the economic and social progress of all the British colonies is $20,000,000 – an amount hardly adequate for British West Africa alone.

The need for an entirely new approach to this problem of developing the colonies through broad and systematically planned undertakings was strikingly impressed upon the British House of Commons recently. The speaker was Dr. Haden Guest, a member of Parliament and a leading British medical authority on the colonies. Calling for the adoption of not merely five-year plans but a 20-year plan on the Soviet model, Dr. Guest gave explicit and forceful expression to the increasing demand for application of Soviet experience to present-day colonial problems.

*   *   *

Stating that the social conditions which Soviet authorities had to cope with in Central Asia were "exactly comparable" to present day conditions in tropical Africa, Dr. Guest said: "By help and proper planning and the organizing of economic resources for their benefit the Soviet Union, out of people as primitive as those in Central Africa, made that mighty power of which we are now seeing the strength on the front against the Germans...In the populations of East and West Africa combined there are the human population and the natural resources available to create a great black population. We could do it if we had in this British empire the same vision as they had in the Soviet Union. We could in 20 years produce the same effects in that area as the Soviet Union has produced in the European parts of the Union in 25 years or so since the Soviet Revolution took place."

The accomplishment of such a revolution in colonial Africa as Dr. Guest pictures requires not only a new vision on the part of the British, but a new vision and policy of cooperation among all the governments which have political and economic interests in Africa. The effective planning and financing of broadly conceived development projects can only come through the kind of international agreement and collaboration which have characterized the United Nations conferences on rehabilitation and monetary problems. American leadership and participation in working out these new colonial policies is fundamentally necessary.

* * *

The question of whether this government will assume its responsibilities in this regard hinges on the question of whether the present administration's policies are upheld by the American people. The anti-administration forces have made their position clear. In his Louisville speech Mr. Dewey demonstrated the narrowness of his (or [the anti-New Deal former President Herbert] Hoover's) world outlook by his flippant crack about "an American WPA [Works Progress Administration] for all the rest of the world."

The arguments of "economy" and "states rights" used by the reactionary congressional coalition to knife the administration's reconversion plans for domestic security parallel the arguments of "national self-interest" and "national sovereignty" for wrecking world security proposals based upon international collaboration.

To insure that deeds and not promises are the order of the day for colonial peoples, and to insure that America plays its full part in accomplishing the deeds, Americans have their job cut out for them in the coming elections.

*   *   *

"Today's Guest Column: American Labor and the Colonial Postwar World," *Daily Worker,* September 21, 1944, page 7

The problems confronting the several labor conventions, to be climaxed by the CIO convention in November, are many and critical. Domestic problems, especially the question of how to guarantee postwar economic security for America, loom large. While it is essential for labor to deal fully and effectively with these home-front [sic] matters, I wish to suggest that it is likewise imperative for the trade unions to speak out more clearly and emphatically on matters of foreign policy than they have ever one [sic] before.

"Foreign policy, both political and economic," [CIO President] Philip Murray told American trade unionists in one of his addresses last year, "is as much our concern and can affect us as directly as the wages we are paid and the hours we work." The problem of insuring full employment and prosperity for American [sic] after the war is inseparably linked with the problem of furthering international cooperation toward building a worldwide system of economic security and democracy. Labor must simultaneously concern itself with domestic issues and questions of foreign policy as part of one common task.

*   *   *

In addition to postwar considerations, there are other immediately pressing reasons why organized labor in this country must today give due attention to foreign affairs. Present developments in India are once more approaching the showdown stage. The political crisis within that country will be sharpened by the impending all-out Allied assault against Japan. The duration of that campaign and its cost in human lives will depend very largely upon whether the Indian and other subject peoples of Asia are fully enlisted on our side of the struggle. And that in turn depends upon whether these peoples are given guarantees (not stale promises) that they are in fact and in truth fighting for their own freedom. CIO conventions and several of the major international unions have in the past repeatedly supported the demands of the Indian people. The present need is action toward speedily implementing the resolutions previously adopted.

If India is a pivotal problem for winning the war, Africa represents a key question in winning the peace. That great continent, the least developed in all the world, is fraught with dangers of imperialistic conflicts. The rapid development of Africa's great resources, already begun during the war, is a certainty. What is yet uncertain is whether that development will be to the advantage of the African people and in the interest of world-wide prosperity, or whether it will take the form of sharp competition between American trade and investment there, which has recently seen an immense increases [sic], and that of Britain and the other colonial powers in Africa. In view of the fact that Africa represents a critical testing-ground of International collaboration in which this country must play a leading part, it is to be hoped that the CIO will give to African problems attention and constructive action similar to that which it has manifested on Latin American affairs.

* * *

The forces of American imperialism backing Dewey's candidacy and striving to disrupt the continuing coalition of the United Nations are the enemies of American workers as much as of colonial and semi-colonial peoples. These reactionaries foresee no better world than that of Hoover's when workers and nations were "free" – free to starve.

In contrast with their dark prospect is the objective, as expressed by President Roosevelt, of "world-wide collaboration with the objective of security for all; of improved labor standards, economic adjustment and social security." The task of American labor, working in close cooperation with the democratic labor forces of all countries, is to exert maximum influence toward the shaping of a world which will no longer be one-third free and two-thirds slave. The time for American labor to apply itself to that task is now.

* * *

"Today's Guest Column: Trade Unionism In Nigeria," *Daily Worker,* September 28, 1944, 7

The prospect of raised living standards and large-scale industrial developments for "backward" areas of the world, in order to guarantee world-wide economic stability and prosperity, makes pertinent some consideration of the question of trade unionism in these "backward" regions. Having discussed last week the role of American trade unions in relation to present problems in India and postwar problems in Africa, I should like in this column and the next to sketch in some of the side of the picture, presenting a few facts about progress of trade unionism in two regions, British West Africa and the Dominion of South Africa.

War, even in the least economically developed countries, has meant a quickening of the tempo of production and the development of new industries. Supplying the new manpower needs means, especially in colonial or semi-colonial regions, shifting people from a primitive agricultural economy into an entirely new way of life. The new urban and industrial environment produces new social attitudes which supplant the old. The basis for working class organization and ideals is established.

Trade union development on any considerable scale among Africans has come about only in the recent years of the war. Its progress prior to the war was hampered by the outlawing of labor organization and the use of severe, repressive measures on the part of both employers and their friends in the government. The British Colonial Office, reacting to sharp parliamentary criticism of forced labor practices and inhuman conditions of work in many of the British territories, was forced eventually to institute reforms in the labor departments of the colonies. Consequently, within the last few years, Africans and other colonials have been trained and used as labor officers, and trade union organization in the territories, especially in the West Indies, West Africa and India, has advanced rapidly.

*   *   *

Nigeria in West Africa is representative of this progress. Working class organization in this colony reached a milestone a year ago when representatives of 36 trade unions met in the first convention of the Nigerian Trades Union Congress. Railway workers, mine workers, teachers, domestic servants, civil employes [sic] and office clerks were among those represented at that conference. African newspapers hailed the event and one editorial commented: "Gone are the days when the labor leader was officially regarded as a Bolshie [Bolshevik] and any person who preached the right of collective bargaining among workers was deemed to be a sedition-monger."

Last month the second meeting of the congress was held in Lagos. This time there were over 300 delegates representing 64 trade unions with a membership of over a half-million organized workers (the population of Nigeria is roughly 21,000,000).

* * *

The delegates discussed the question of women workers and their wages; resettlement of demobilized soldiers; rehabilitation of disabled veterans; health, housing and education of workers. The conference demanded rapid industrialization of the country, the nationalization of major industries and public services, and the establishment of a comprehensive state social interest plan comparable to that being formulated for Great Britain.

The TUC of Nigeria has extended an invitation to the Negro Labor Victory Committee of New York for a group of labor leaders from this country to pay Nigeria a good will visit. The Nigerian workers are looking forward eagerly to this event. The spirit behind their invitation is suggested by this sentence from a letter sent to the Council on African Affairs last year by the secretary of the TUC of Nigeria.

"To know that we have friends at the other end of the Atlantic is comforting and inspiring in our struggle for freedom from want and heartless exploitation."

* * *

"Today's Guest Column: South African Native Labor Movement Growing," *Daily Worker,* October 5, 1944, page 7

In common with other people all over the world, there is among the natives (of South Africa) a certain restlessness, particularly in the large urban areas. The natives are suffering from growing pains and this restlessness is a sign of their development as they emerge in a bigger world." This is what the Commissioner of Native Affairs told the South African Parliament a short while back. And the Commissioner has no great reputation for friendliness toward African aspirations.

The urbanized African worker in Cape Town, Johannesburg, Durban and other cities of the Dominion is becoming increasingly a force to be reckoned with as he builds his own labor organization and establishes closer ties with the powerful labor movement among the Europeans, the South African Trades and Labor Council. Expanded wartime production in this most highly industrialized section of Africa with its two million white people, a larger non-African population than even in French North Africa, has brought new strength and consciousness of that strength to the black workers and to the labor movement as a whole.

The African Mine Workers Union, the Non-European Railway Workers' Union and over 50 other African trade Unions with a membership approaching 100,000 are functioning throughout South Africa. These unions are run along sound democratic lines with elected African officers.

That the Negro worker in South Africa has been able to achieve any labor organization whatever is a remarkable fact. This is evident when one considers his deplorably low social and economic status, a condition forced upon him by the meanest provisions for education and other social services, by color bar legislation barring him from skilled employment, and by failure of the government to grant full trade union recognition and other democratic rights to African labor.

The official explanation of the government's efforts to keep the African worker down can be found In the Government Year Book of 1941: "It is generally admitted that the prosperity of South African trade and industry depends to a very great extent on an adequate supply of relatively cheap, unskilled non-European labor." This is the traditional South African economic policy. Today, however, it is being increasingly realized that the maintenance of the country's expanded wartime production necessitates raising the wages and living standards of four-fifths of the population, meaning the eight million Africans, so that there can be an adequate domestic market and purchasing power to buy the enlarged supply of goods.

The more progressive of the white trade unions have taken a strong stand against the many Jimcrow [sic] disabilities inflicted upon African and other non-European workers. As in our own South, there is a growing recognition that the fight for Negro rights is an integral part of the fight for democratic rights in general. The Communist Party of South Africa has been a major force in the development of this understanding. Several instances of notable interracial labor solidarity have come to light in recent months in the struggles for a higher minimum wage for unskilled workers, and for full bargaining rights and freedom of organization for African workers.

*   *   *

The forces of extreme reaction in South Africa, which make a fetish of racialism and are even now still openly pro-Nazi, are alarmed by these progressive developments, and they are plotting to ride into power on a wave of increased national disunity and discord after the war (exactly like their reactionary cousins over here). Company unions and other phony labor groups sponsored by fascist organizations like the Ossewabrandwag [an anti-British, pro-German organization that opposed South African participation in WWII] are being set up in an effort to undermine the bona fide trade unions. Further, in an effort to intimidate the organized African workers, mass arrests of hundreds of strikers have lately been instigated.

The South African equivalents of our poll-taxers and [Herbert] Hoover-[Thomas] Dewey Republicans are the enemy of both black and white workers in that country. In the near future will come the showdown test of whether organized labor and the liberal forces of South Africa, of whatever race and color, are strong enough and united enough to fight for and win the democratic prerequisites to prosperity for the country as a whole and a more abundant life for the vast majority of its Inhabitants.

* * *

Today's Guest Column

South African Native Labor Movement Growing

by Alphaeus Hunton

IN COMMON with other people all over the world, there is among the natives (of South Africa) a certain restlessness, particularly in the large urban areas. The natives are suffering from growing pains and this restlessness is a sign of their development so they emerge in a bigger world." This is what the Commissioner of Native Affairs told the South African Parliament a short while back. And the Commissioner has no great reputation for friendliness toward African aspirations.

The urbanized African worker in Cape Town, Johannesburg, Durban and other cities of the Dominion is becoming increasingly a force to be reckoned with as he builds his own labor organization and establishes closer ties with the powerful labor movement among the Europeans, the South African Trades and Labor Council. Expanded wartime production in this most highly industrialized section of Africa with its two million white people, a larger non-African population than even in French North Africa, has brought new strength and consciousness of that strength to the black workers and to the labor movement as a whole.

The African Mine Workers Union, the Non-European Railway Workers Union and over 50 other African trade unions with a membership approaching 100,000 are functioning throughout South Africa. These unions are run along sound democratic lines with elected African officers.

THAT the Negro worker in South Africa has been able to achieve any labor organization whatever is a remarkable fact. This is evident when one considers his deplorably low social and economic status, a condition forced upon him by the meanest provisions for education and other social services, by color bar legislation barring him from skilled employment, and by failure of the government to grant full trade union recognition and other democratic rights to African labor.

The official explanation of the government's efforts to keep the African worker down can be found in the Government Year Book of 1941: "It is generally admitted that the prosperity of South African trade and industry depends to a very great extent on an adequate supply of relatively cheap, unskilled non-European labor." This is the traditional South African economic policy. Today, however, it is being increasingly realized that the maintenance of the country's expanded wartime production necessitates raising the wages and living standards of four-fifths of the population, meaning the eight million Africans, so that there can be an adequate domestic market and purchasing power to buy the enlarged supply of goods.

The more progressive of the white trade unions have taken a strong stand against the many Jimcrow disabilities inflicted upon African and other non-European workers. As in our own South, there is a growing recognition that the fight for Negro rights is an integral part of the fight for democratic rights in general. The Communist Party of South Africa has been a major force in the development of this understanding. Several instances of notable interracial labor solidarity have come to light in recent months in the struggles for a higher minimum wage for unskilled workers, and for full bargaining rights and freedom of organization for African workers.

THE forces of extreme reaction in South Africa, which make a fetish of racialism and are even now still openly pro-Nazi, are alarmed by these progressive developments, and they are plotting to ride into power on a wave of increased national disunity and discord after the war (exactly like their reactionary cousins over here). Company unions and other phony labor groups sponsored by fascist organizations like the Ossewabrandwag are being set up in an effort to undermine the bona fide trade unions. Further, in an effort to intimidate the organized African workers, mass arrests of hundreds of strikers have lately been instigated.

The South African equivalents of our politicians and Hoover-Dewey Republicans are the enemy of both black and white workers in that country. In the near future will come the showdown test of whether organized labor and the liberal forces of South Africa, of whatever race and color, are strong enough and united enough to fight for and win the democratic prerequisites to prosperity for the country as a whole and a more abundant life for the vast majority of its inhabitants.

IMAGE 12: *Daily Worker*, October 5, 1944. Courtesy of *People's World*.

"Today's Guest Column: Willkie's Message – Choose Leaders Who Have Principles," *Daily Worker,* October 12, 1944, page 7

Wendell L. Willkie* will be remembered as an American who sacrificed himself rather than yield his principles to personal or party interests.

People in remote corners of the world – in Africa and in Asia – join in mourning the death of the man whose One World meant the abolition of imperialism and racial exclusiveness and the attainment of equal rights and equal opportunities for all peoples.

"It is not enough," Willkie said in an address last year, "merely to make safe the freedom of those peoples who are still free or even to restore freedom to the nations which have been conquered. If we want to lay the whole of the foundation which I believe is necessary in order for the world to have peace, then the peoples now living in mandates and colonies – of whatever nation – must also see that there will be room in the structure which we are building for them to attain eventual freedom."

The man who held such views could most certainly not be acceptable as a presidential nominee to the reactionary and imperialistic-minded leaders and backers of the Republican Party. They preferred a [famed ventriloquist] Charley McCarthy like Thomas E. Dewey. With a corporation lawyer of somewhat unsavory international connections as his adviser, Mr. Dewey opened his campaign by petty, partisan sniping at the Dumbarton Oaks conference. That fell flat. And so also did his not-so-clever attempt to get Willkie to join him in his attack upon the Roosevelt administration's world security aims. Since that fiasco, Dewey has had little to say on foreign policy. He has descended to the easier, simpler tactic of red-baiting and name-calling.

* * *

Although Wendell Willkie was not without certain errors in his judgments on foreign affairs, he was clear-sighted and steadfast on the central issue of our time, the necessity of developing

---

*Willkie died October 8, 1944.

genuine and effective international cooperation for maintaining world prosperity and peace.

It is today most appropriate that we recall a speech which Willkie made at Union College in Schenectady, New York, in 1942. Reviewing the election of 1920, when this country faced the problem of making a real peace after the first World War, Willkie told how [Warren] Harding, during his campaign, dodged and vacillated on the question of the League of Nations, immediately rejecting the League as soon as the election returns were in.

The American people in 1920, Willkie said, "were betrayed by leaders without convictions who were thinking in terms of group vote catching." And he warned that if this should happen again now, it would spell "sheer disaster." As though he foresaw clearly the choice which American voters would have to make today, Willkie said in that speech of two years ago:

"As citizens who may be called on to give your very lives to preserve your country's freedom, for God's sake elect to important office men who will not make a mockery of that sacrifice. Make sure that you choose leaders who have principles and the courage to state them plainly. Not men who examine each shift of sentiment and watch the polls of public opinion to learn where they stand. I beg of you, vote for straight-out men – not wobblers. This is no time for ambiguity."

There is no timelier message than that for Americans today. Now, during this [voter] registration period or what is left of it, we have the one crucial task of GETTING OUT THE VOTE – getting out the vote which will insure the reelection of President Roosevelt and the continuation of those administration policies of international cooperation out of which will come One World. By making this a record-breaking registration at the polls, Americans will be keeping faith with Wendell Willkie, with their country and Commander-in-Chief, and with the millions of downtrodden people throughout the world who are fighting on our side for a chance to live decently. GET OUT THE VOTE!

*   *   *

"Today's Guest Column: How World Economic and Social Council Would Work," *Daily Worker,* October 19, 1944, page 7

The decrepit and ineffectual League of Nations is dead, if not yet buried. A far stronger, abler United Nations organization has been born. Whether it will have proper nurturing and arrive at a healthy maturity is something that we – and the rest of the world – can determine better after Nov. 7.

Most of the discussion thus far on the Dumbarton Oaks agreement, the text of which was made public last week, has centered around the Security Council, which has primary responsibility for stopping aggressors, and the question of the voting privileges of its permanent members. This discussion has tended to obscure the importance and significance of the understanding reached with respect to the method of solving those international economic and social problems which are the underlying causes of war.

At Teheran, less than a year ago Roosevelt, Stalin and Churchill declared, "We seek the cooperation and active participation of all nations, large and small, whose peoples in heart and in mind are dedicated, as our own peoples, to the elimination of tyranny and slavery, oppression and intolerance."

At Dumbarton Oaks the representatives of the United States, the Soviet Union, Britain and China agreed that an international organization to be known as the United Nations "should facilitate solutions of international economic, social and other humanitarian problems and promote respect for human rights and fundamental freedoms." The Economic and Social Council is that branch of the United Nations, organization designated as directly responsible for the carrying out of this function, with the objective of "the creation of conditions of stability and well-being which are necessary for peaceful and friendly relations among nations."

* * *

It is important to note the way in which this council is to be organized, for this gives the clue to its probable representatives and effectiveness of action. It would serve under the authority of the General Assembly, which is made up of all the members of the United Nations organization, and would be composed of representatives of 18 of these member states. The states to be represented would be elected by the General Assembly for terms of three years, and each such state would have one representative with one vote. All decisions of this council would be by simple majority vote of those present and voting.

This arm of the United Nations organization would be empowered, among other things, "to make recommendations, on its own initiative, with respect to international economic, social and other humanitarian matters." It would establish various expert commissions to serve it, and it would act as the coordinating and clearing center for such bodies as the International Labor Organization, UNRRA [the United Nations Relief and Rehabilitation Administration] and the monetary agencies agreed upon at Bretton Woods.

*   *   *

If we may think of the organization's other arm, the Security Council, as the surgeon who is called upon to operate when necessary to prevent the outbreak or spread of international conflict, then we may regard the proposed Economic and Social Council as the doctor who prescribes for the patient so that his condition will not reach the stage where an operation is required.

The social and economic ailments from which the world at present suffers – and the cancer of colonialism is one of the gravest – call for the "doctor's" immediate attention. And that is why this country must give maximum support to President Roosevelt's demand for all possible speed in the approval and execution of these proposals for achieving worldwide security and a durable peace.

*   *   *

"Today's Guest Column: Negro People Going Forward With Roosevelt," *Daily Worker,* November 2, 1944, page 7

Negroes are asking, are the employment gains we have made in the last few years to be maintained and extended? Will the unity of the Negro people and organized labor continue and grow stronger?

The discussion of these questions at the recent convention of the United Federal Workers was extremely noteworthy for its frank and constructive character. It spotlighted the need for organized labor in general to plan concretely for safeguarding the job status of Negroes as part of the larger task of maintaining democratic employment standards for all workers during the transition from a wartime to a peacetime economy.

This is an important matter; it must be recognized as such by the rank and file of labor. But let it be also remembered that both the economic future of the Negro and the strength of the labor movement, when victory has been won, hinge on whether this country continues to play its proper role in developing and realizing a program of international collaboration for promoting a peacetime economy of abundance, world-wide in scope. That is what is at stake in this election.

Dewey, of course, has done plenty of talking about jobs and expanded production. But his remarks, as on all other issues, have been of that slippery, weasel-worded variety intended to please everyone and offend no one – especially not the [anti-New Deal] Col. [Robert] McCormicks, Herbert Hoovers and others of his imperialistic intentioned supporters. There's no question as to whom that progressive American industrialist, Henry J. Kaiser, was referring when he said, "I am not impressed by any candidate or any party promising jobs without telling how these jobs will be created."

President Roosevelt has not only repeatedly explained the HOW to the American people; he has gone about the business of converting principles into practice as speedily as possible. He can point to the record of actual accomplishment from the Moscow and Teheran decisions of last year down to the Bretton Woods and Dumbarton Oaks agreements.

In his masterly address at Chicago last Saturday night, the President once again emphasized the "cooperative measures" whereby the increased industrial and agricultural production of this country would be applied to promoting the well-being not merely of ourselves but of "the rest of humanity." This would mean, he said, that "the foreign trade of the United States can be trebled after the war – providing millions of more jobs." Such cooperative measures, the President pointed out, taking pains to remind the audience of the necessity of congressional approval, "provide the soundest economic foundation for a lasting peace, and that's what we want."

* * *

Yes, that is what organized labor wants, and that is why it is supporting Roosevelt. In such a program lies the only real promise of security for the Negro and all other workers in America, as well as of liberation for peoples throughout the world from the chains of colonialism and feudalism. It is because they cannot and dare not come clean on this central and crucial issue that the Republican spokesmen have resorted to mud-slinging and appeals to prejudice, and have attempted to divert attention to a number of phony issues. But they can't get away with it.

Next Tuesday, when they cast their ballots, the Negro people, along with all democratic Americans, will echo the determination of Franklin D. Roosevelt: "We are not going to turn the clock back. We are going forward, forward with the fighting millions of our fellow countrymen. We are going forward."

* * *

"Today's Guest Column: Johannesburg Riot Reflects a World Problem," *Daily Worker*, November 9, 1944, page 9

In scanning your newspaper last Monday morning, you probably did not notice or give much thought to a brief Associated Press dispatch telling of riots between Europeans and Africans in Johannesburg, South Africa, on the day before. Obviously, the Times' desk man wasn't too concerned about the item, for he headlined it "Capetown Riots Halted," confusing the origin of the cable with the place where the disturbance occurred, as stated in the first sentence. Neverthless [sic], it was an important story, meriting much more than the dozen lines given it.

The facts reported in the dispatch tell little or nothing. "The trouble arose," it says, "when a native was knocked down accidentally, police said. Natives stoned passing vehicles and the Europeans attacked the office of a native newspaper, they reported. Police charged the rioters, using tear gas."

Behind this accidental knocking down of a single African – if we accept that innocuous version of how the riots started – is South Africa's long history of gross discrimination and oppression, enforced by the white settlers' laws, against the eight million Africans and other non-European peoples in that British dominion. In recent months, as the Council on African Affairs has repeatedly pointed out and as I have mentioned in these columns, there has been a growing tension in the country as the reactionary forces have attempted to block the Africans' increasingly organized efforts to gain justice.

* * *

Through their trade unions and their people's organizations like the African National Congress, and supported by the Communist Party and a wide range of progressive elements among the Europeans, the Africans have pressed their demands for better working conditions and trade union recognition, for abolition of the pass laws, for better education. Johannesburg has been the scene of numerous mass expressions of these demands. Mammoth conferences have been held in Gandhi Hall, great crowds have assembled at meetings in Market Square, and thousands of Africans have marched in protest demonstrations through the main streets. In all cases these demonstrations have been disciplined and orderly.

This last point is important. For it seems quite probable, from the use of tear gas and other circumstances, that the riots in Johannesburg occurred during one of those street demonstrations and were deliberately provoked. Why? So that all public expressions of this sort by the Africans might be outlawed on the ground of protecting the public safety.

Who would most likely be responsible for these provocations? Clearly, the South African counterparts of the Ku Klux Klan, Christian Front and other pro-fascist forces which instigated the Detroit insurrection and the Philadelphia transit strike. There they are called the Ossewabrandwag and the Broederbond [a secret, exclusively Afrikaner Calvinist male organization]. And not far behind them are the Nationalist (opposition) Party and the Dutch Reformed (or much deformed) Church.

These forces, as the conservative Cape Times decently declared editorially, are leading the country along "the slippery path that leads downhill towards fascism and chaos." Furthermore, the government under the leadership of [Prime Minister] General [Jan] Smuts has itself encouraged this downward course by further entrenching and extending the Jimcrow [sic] system under the Native Laws Amendment Act.

The important thing is that race riots and racialism are not confined to the Union of South Africa, any more than they are confined to this country. The Dominion's influence extends over the entire continent of Africa, and it is a bad influence. It extends across the Indian Ocean to the people of India and the South Pacific, where we yet have a war to win.

Racial discrimination, whether in this country, Africa or elsewhere, is incompatible with any genuine concept of world security. If they are to achieve a real and lasting victory over fascism, the United Nations must individually and collectively erase this evil wherever it exists.

*   *   *

"Today's Guest Column: Liberia-U.S. Postwar Plans," *Daily Worker,* November 16, 1944, page 7

Liberia is Africa's front door for America. While all the rest of the world's least developed continent is bound directly or indirectly (as in the case of Egypt and Ethiopia) to Britain, France, Belgium, Portugal, and to Spain, Liberia's closest ties are with the United States. Africa's lone Negro-governed republic, slightly smaller in area than New York state, is closely linked with this country by geographic, historical and economic circumstances.

First, Liberia is the closest point in Africa to the Americas, 1,828 air miles from Natal, Brazil, and is thus of great strategic value in guarding the south Atlantic. Second, the republic was founded in 1847 by an expedition of freed Negroes from this county; it patterned its constitution, government and flag on this country's, and It has been able to survive as an independent nation largely by reason of our government's interest and support. And third, the biggest single investment made by American business in Africa is in the Firestone rubber plantations of Liberia, now producing about 35,000,000 pounds of precious rubber annually.

During the war, the ties between Liberia and the United States have been multiplied in many mutually beneficial ways. And now steps are being taken to consolidate these ties and guarantee their continuance after the war. This was made evident by the recent announcement that our Foreign Economic Administration would shortly send a mission of technical experts to Liberia, with the approval of that government. The mission is headed by Earl Parker Hanson, an explorer-engineer of wide experience, and sets something of a precedent for such economic missions in that it includes several Negro professional experts among its personnel.

* * *

The mission's objectives encompass the entire economic development of Liberia. Untapped deposits of gold, iron and other minerals will be explored for the first time. Means of developing and increasing the production of rubber, palm oils and other agricultural and timber resources will be studied. Much needed roads will be built. And a modern harbor will be constructed under the supervision of the U.S. Navy. The FEA is advancing the money, estimated at nine or ten million dollars, for this port construction and it will be repaid by the Liberian government out of commercial port revenue.

By the terms of the agreement regarding the construction of the seaport, the United States has the right to establish and operate naval, army and air installations "for the protection of the strategic interests of the United States of America in the south Atlantic." For the benefit of those American imperialists who are demanding bases, seized by force if necessary, all around the world, it should be noted that under the agreement, the United States "undertakes to respect, in the future, as in the past, the territorial integrity, sovereignty and political independence of the Republic of Liberia."

*   *   *

The three essential needs for the progress of Liberia – and for all similar undeveloped areas throughout the world – are technological assistance, capital and democracy – democracy in both internal affairs and international relations. The FEA mission to Liberia is representative of what can be done toward meeting the first two needs. But these measures will accomplish little of real value if the opportunity is not given for the whole population of Liberia, the two million native Africans as well as the more privileged few thousand Americo-Liberians who govern the country, to participate fully in the economic development program and to share fully in the benefits of that development. In Liberia this is a problem of urgently needed internal democratic reforms; in most other areas of Africa, it is the problem of making the change from colonial "tutelage" to self-administration and self-government.

*   *   *

Today's Guest Column

A New Deal for Colonial And Dependent Peoples

by Alphaeus Hunton

IMAGE 13: *Daily Worker*, November 23, 1944. Courtesy of *People's World*.

"Today's Guest Column: A New Deal for Colonial And Dependent Peoples," *Daily Worker*, November 23, 1944, page 7

As American organized labor meets in conventions this week, and when the delegates convene at the world labor conference in London* a few weeks hence, one of the many vital problems of postwar security to come before them will be that of promoting a New Deal for colonial and dependent peoples. In essence, that means furthering industrialization of all undeveloped countries,

---

*The World Labor Conference, which took place in London in February 1945, laid the organizational groundwork for the formation of the World Federation of Trade Unions, an international federation. Founded in October 1945, the WFTU would grow to represent 100 million workers. The establishment of the WFTU closely followed the San Francisco Conference which created the United Nations, and the WFTU included progressive and Communist-led unions, unions from Asia, Africa, and Latin America, as well as the All Union Central Council of Trade Unions of the USSR. During the Cold War, the WFTU was portrayed as an instrument of Soviet foreign policy. While CIO unions participated in the WFTU, the AFL did not. In 1949, the AFL helped found the International Confederation of Free Trade Unions, an anti-communist competitor to the WFTU.

and achieving full democratic rights for all peoples hitherto held in imperialist bondage.

Today the world is divided into two parts, unequal in size and in every other respect. The smaller of these parts, embracing the United States, the USSR, western Europe and some sections of the British Dominions, is highly industrialized and enjoys relatively high living standards. The other part, embracing nearly all the rest of the world including Asia, Africa, and Latin America, has an economy and living standards a hundred years or more behind the times.

The world's peace and economic stability cannot be won as long as this uneven economic development remains. Labor has the most vital stake in pressing for international agreements among the United Nations that will insure the raising of the socially and economically retarded two-thirds of the world up to the level of the more advanced one-third.

Why are the colonial and semi-colonial countries so far behind the rest of the world? Why are they spoken of as "backward areas"? The apologists for imperialism would have us believe that the explanation is in the inherent "primitive" character of the peoples in these territories. And this, incidentally, also gives them the right, so these apologists claim, to rule over these peoples.

The fallacy of this argument has been exposed time and time again by the findings of impartial students of anthropology, archaeology, and history. We have come to know that many of the things which we associate with modern civilization were a part of the culture of these so-called primitive peoples before America was discovered and when Europe was just emerging from feudalism.

*   *   *

No, the real explanation for the backwardness of colonial areas is to be found in the nature of colonialism itself. Colonialism is a synonym for social stagnation because colonies can only be profitable to a minority of foreign investors or immigrant settlers under conditions which are socially and economically disadvantageous to the native inhabitants.

The world's dependent and semi-dependent countries have in the past existed primarily as sources of raw materials is to be exported to and processed in the more advanced countries which dominated the dependencies. That is why manual labor and the most primitive methods of production prevail in the colonies – that is why poverty is the rule.

Further, production for export was concentrated upon materials which would bring the highest and quickest returns on investments. At one time Negro slaves represented the most profitable export commodity; later it was such things as gold, diamonds, copper, oil and rubber. Before this war, Africa, for example, produced 9 percent of the world's metals, which outsiders used, but only 3 percent of the world's agricultural products, which the undernourished Africans needed for their own use.

* * *

A retarded industrial development, shortsighted and selfish production for profit rather than for the needs of the people, restricted markets and discriminatory trade agreements, maintenance of a cheap and easily exploited labor force – these are the inevitable, essential characteristics of colonialism. And these same things spell international conflicts, depressions, and unemployment for the more advanced one-third of the world.

It is the task of American labor and world labor to give leadership in the correction of these evils and to help in building a new order of world-wide progress in place of the old imperialist regime of stagnation.

* * *

"Today's Guest Column: South Africa's Residence Law And the Reprisal of India," *Daily Worker,* November 30, 1944, page 7

It must be something of an embarrassment to Prime Minister Jan Christian Smuts and other prominent spokesmen of British Empire unity, especially now when the issues of empire vs. democracy is before the world for settlement, to have a quarrel break out between the Indian and South African governments over the question of racial discrimination. The discreet silence customarily maintained, in British official circles on the matter of South Africa's treatment of its non-European (non-white) population has been rudely shattered by the reprisal action of the Central Legislative Assembly of India placing restrictions upon the residence, trade, property and local franchise rights of white South Africans (except those from Cape Province) resident in India.

The immediate cause of this action was bitter resentment over the move by the South African government to enforce residential segregation upon the 300,000 Indians in Durban and other cities in the Transvaal and Natal provinces. The nearly 8,000,000 Africans who make up four-fifths of the Dominion's population have, of course, long been restricted to living in "reserves" and "locations." Similar restrictions apply to most of the 800,000 people of mixed racial stock called colored. The Indian Pegging Act passed last year would have made it illegal for Indians to own or occupy property in European residential areas. (In the United States residential "covenants," agreements among real estate operators, and other Instruments are used to segregate Negro residences.)

*   *   *

The great outcry raised against this discrimination made it necessary for the South African government to repeal the Pegging Act. Instead, with the cooperation of a few wealthy Indians who betrayed their people, a substitute agreement was reached, still banning residence, but establishing a Licensing Board by which Indian purchase of property might be controlled. But this failed to quiet the protests.

A warning from an influential pro-government newspaper, the Cape Times, as to the dangerous consequences of the discriminatory measure agains [sic] the Indians, was voiced as far back as last April. "It is a curious thing that the Dominion Party," an editorial said, "the one political party in this country which sets itself up as, before everybody else, the especial guardian of the 'Empire' as such, succeeds in doing so much mischief to the imperial cause. There can be no reasonable question that the recent Indian Pegging bill did more to upset inter-imperial relations than anything which has happened for a long time."

*   *   *

Just how much these relations have been upset and how far the rupture between India and South Africa will go remains to be seen. One may be fairly sure, however, that the reverberations of the present clash will be felt in some degree throughout the Empire. For the "color problem," with the rare exception of a New Zealand or Ceylon, is Empire-wide.

Underlying the immediate issue of Indian segregation and the disabilities and restrictions placed upon the entire non-European population is the reactionary hue and cry, heard also in Kenya and other parts of East Africa as well as in our own southern states, about "preserving white supremacy." In reality this means in Africa, just as over here, preserving the special privileges of a small clique of those white people who hold economic and political power.

At bottom this is a problem of class interest, not of race. That it is being increasingly recognized as such is proved by the fact that not only Africans and Indians but also a considerable number of white workers in South Africa are banding together to wage a common struggle in the Interest of democratic rights for all.

*   *   *

"Today's Guest Column: Trouble Spots in Africa And Some Soft-Soap Words," *Daily Worker*, December 7, 1944, page 7

As a sort of change of pace this week (assuming that some of you have been keeping pace with this column), we will do a hop-skip-and-jump on a few miscellaneous items of current relevance to the problem of building a United Nations world minus imperialism and race prejudices.

First, following up last week's column on the friction between the Indian and South African governments arising from discrimination against Indian residents in the South African Dominion, it should be mentioned that the London Times on Nov. 17 gave this matter editorial attention. The editorial gives, with apparent endorsement, a full statement of the arguments on the South African side. As for the other side, there is one sentence which makes non-committal mention of the fact that "consciousness of color" is "widespread" in South Africa, that "standards of living are sharply differentiated as between various racial elements," and that some South Africans "do not recognize India's changing position in the Commonwealth, its ever increasing political importance and its enormous economic potential."

With aloof impartiality, the Times calls on "Statesmanship on both sides to explore every means for an accommodation." It then states, "The dispute, in origin domestic, must not impede that intimate cooperation between the two countries in the economic sphere which is vital to the common war effort and to the interests of both in the defeat of Japan." That is indeed highly important and to the point. But the Times appears to be striving to localize the issue. Obviously, any impediment to the defeat of Japan affects the interests of all the United Nations.

*   *   *

Also deserving of attention is the rather significant pamphlet entitled First to Be Freed [sic], recently issued by the British Ministry of Information. It is about Eritrea and Somalia (Italian Somaliland), and contrasts the record of Italian fascist occupation of these colonies with that of the British military administration during the past two and a half years, since the Italian forces were expelled. The contrast presented is, of course, all to the credit of the British and the implications are obvious.

The pamphlet does not explain that these coastal territories once were a part of present land-locked Ethiopia, or that the majority of the inhabitants are culturally and ethnically related to the Ethiopians.

There has been no mention of it yet in any metropolitan daily, so far as I have seen, but a group of three Negro Americans representing the Negro Newspaper Publishers Association is at present touring various parts of West Africa.

While the trip is described as an "unofficial visit," the NNPA representatives are said to have been commissioned by President Roosevelt, following a conference of Negro newspaper publishers with the President last February, and to be working under the jurisdiction of the U.S. State Department, which arranged the tour. The first place to be visited was the Gold Coast, where African colonial administration is at its best.

The CIO convention resolutions dealing with racial discrimination and with the political and economic progress of colonial and semi-colonial peoples deserve the most careful study and widest discussion and support.

An excellent means of securing a full understanding of these problems and of what must be done toward solving them in our workaday world is by enrolling in the five-day course, 9 a.m. to 1 p.m., on the Negro and the Nation which is being sponsored jointly by the Carver School, 57 W. 125 St., the Jefferson School, 575 Sixth Ave., and the People's Voice. The course begins next Monday, Dec. 11. You can register for the course at either of the schools mentioned. How about it?

* * *

"Today's Guest Column: Greece and the Issue Of Colonial Policy," *Daily Worker,* December 14, 1944, page 7

The tragic and dangerous events which have lately occurred in Italy, Belgium and Greece – and Churchill's intervention policy which has given rise to them – have direct bearing on the colonial question. The man who said that he did not intend to "preside over the liquidation of the British Empire" would logically strive to retain or place in power in countries which lie along England's imperial life-line – Portugal, Spain, Italy and Greece – governments with which the British Empire has been in the habit of doing business.

Maintenance of the British Empire involves the maintenance of other empires. Hence, except with regard to Italy's former colonies, and in the joint Allied statement at the Cairo conference regarding Japan's empire, the British government during the war has carefully refrained from the slightest hint of any change in the pre-war status of the colonial world.

While conceding the desirability of regional collaboration in colonial matters on a purely consultative and advisory basis, the Colonial Office in London has thus far been very cool toward proposals of some form of international administrative responsibility for all colonial territories directed toward guaranteeing self-government. In maintaining the position of "holding our own," the British government has given the cue to other European colonial powers, including Italy, to do likewise.

Among those powers, France is the only one which has up to now given real evidence of realizing that colonial peoples, too, have stake in this war of liberation. The Dutch government-in-exile has made pronouncements of a new colonial policy, but it has yet to show that it means what it says. In contrast with the governments-in-exile which reposed safely in London, the leaders of French resistance, in order to survive and carry on the war, began applying a new progressive policy in French African territories even before the formal statement of that policy was issued at the Brazzaville conference in February of this year.*

* * *

The important point to note here is that it was the resistance forces, the democratic strength of France, which accomplished this change in the concept of the French empire, and which has brought about France's remarkably quick recovery as a ranking European power – notwithstanding Gen. Smut's gloomy prophecy of a year ago. These same democratic forces of resistance must now be permitted to come to the front in other European countries. That is the essential prerequisite for real postwar stability and security for Europe and the world – far more important than any momentary illusions of "law and order."

Our State Department has taken that stand. So also has the Soviet Union. And dark as the picture of British policy at the moment is, it must be remembered that the vote of confidence given Churchill last week by no means represented the British public's approval of that policy. Even the conservative London Times, after the confidence vote, continued to attack Churchill's position.

* * *

Everyone realizes that there are strong imperialist forces still active in Britain (and in the United States also). What is not generally understood is that these reactionary forces in England are able to gain some support in Parliament because of the belief that only by holding on to the empire and the special trade advantages thus afforded (fallacious though such thinking may be), can Britain compete with America in postwar trade. Only through frank discussion and settlement of this issue can we avoid further crises and set-backs.

---

*The Brazzaville Conference was a meeting of prominent Free French leaders held from January 30 to February 8, 1944 in Brazzaville, the then-capital of French Equatorial Africa. The conference, sponsored by the French Committee of the National Liberation, met to determine the role and future of the French colonial empire and to recommend political, social, and economic reforms.

The wisdom of President Roosevelt in urging the speediest possible realization of the Dumbarton Oaks proposals – not waiting for the end of the war – is today more evident than ever. The Teheran declaration still remains the guide-post of all democratic peoples. The Allies must continue to function together as as [sic] coalition with fullest consultation and agreement not simply on the strategy of the war and the specific problems of liberated countries but on the larger questions of the peace. Only as the larger questions – and that of colonies is one of them – are solved, will the day-to-day issues cease to loom repeatedly as grave crises.

*   *   *

"Today's Guest Column: Anglo-Ethiopian Relations In the Spotlight," *Daily Worker,* December 21, 1944, page 7

Ever since Mussolini's barbaric invasion of Ethiopia,* that nation has represented for Negroes in this country and throughout the world a symbol of their stake in the war against fascism. They have watched closely the subsequent history of Ethiopia, regarding that country as a kind of barometer of international policy. They hailed the liberation of Ethiopia and her emergence as a sovereign member of the United Nations. But they had misgivings about the role of Britain as Ethiopia's adviser, creditor and trustee under the terms of the Agreement and Military Convention signed between the two countries in January 1942.

These misgivings are now receiving explicit and acutely critical expression in some Negro newspapers as a result of the recent report of commentator Drew Pearson to the effect that Great Britain was planning to annex the two Ethiopian Provinces of Harrar and Ogaden, and that the Ethiopian Emperor had appealed to the United States to intercede.

* * *

Getting down to facts, Haile Selassie early this year presented to the British government certain proposals to be incorporated in the fresh Agreement between the two countries. No action was taken on the proposals. In May, the Emperor gave notice of termination of the Agreement, to become effective in three months·. A British commission was then dispatched to Addis Ababa to negotiate revision of the Agreement and Military Convention.

Under the terms of the 1942 agreement the British received the right, among other things, to maintain their own military administration over a section of the Ogaden Province.

The original reason for maintaining British troops in Ethiopia was, of course, one of military security. The London Times recently disclosed that the British now argue that military occupation must continue in order to safeguard the British-protected

---

*In October 1935.

Somalis who have grazing rights in Ethiopian territory. "The British authorities," says the London Times, "do not consider that conditions in Ethiopia are yet settled enough for British military administration in these areas to be withdrawn, as the Emperor desires."

*   *   *

Fortunately, the whole situation has now been clarified to a considerable extent. An announcement was issued two days ago by the British Information Service, indicating that an interim agreement between Ethiopia and Britain had been reached, breaking the stalemate which had existed since early May. According to the summary of the agreement released, Britain "surrenders the right to maintain military forces within Ethiopia, except such as are agreed upon by both governments to be helpful in maintaining order in certain border areas until the end of the war."

Other terms of the new agreement provide for the surrender of Britain's exclusive air rights in Ethiopia, of her operation of the Ethiopian-French railway to Jibuti, and of her precedence over other nations' advisers, the Ethiopian government being free to "choose any foreign advisers anywhere it wishes." This last point Is clearly a concession to the United States' increasing interest and influence in Ethiopan [sic] afafirs [sic] – an influence which promises well for the future independence and progress of Emperor Haile Selassie's kingdom.

Apparently, in withdrawing her priority rights in Ethiopia, Britain has also withdrawn her financial assistance to that country, since the report says simply that Britain will give "friendly consideration to any suggestion that Ethiopia may wish to make in the future" on this point. If this is true, it means that Ethiopia has decided to try to solve her serious economic problems through other wider channels than that of British support.

*   *   *

"Today's Guest Column: Colonial Peoples Look Forward as 1945 Opens," *Daily Worker,* January 4, 1945, page 7

While we're thinking at this New Year's time of how much longer it's going to take to write finis to fascism, let's remember that many millions of colonial peoples all over the world are thinking, as 1945 begins, not only of the end of the war but of the time when they can be free from imperialist domination. They understand that their liberation depends in the first place upon the defeat of the fascist enemy. But they know, too, that victory over the Axis will not of itself solve their problems.

For success in peace, as in war, there must be agreement and cooperation among the United Nations toward specific goals according to specified plans. This is indispensable in securing the economic and political progress of dependent peoples, as part of the task of developing a worldwide system of prosperity and peace. Colonial administrators, with extremely rare exceptions, have been notoriously lacking in specific goals and plans for the advancement of their governed subjects. This is not simply the fault of the individual administrators; it results basically from the stagnant character of the colonial regime.

Of course, there has long been much fine talk of "trusteeship" and "preparing backward peoples for the management of their own affairs." But these modern paraphrases of "the white man's burden" always evade the practical questions of HOW and WHEN. The implications of the planlessness of colonial administration up to the present are very aptly suggested by the editor of one of the daily papers published by Africans for Africans in Lagos, Nigeria:

"The colonial peoples are students in a school without a curriculum and under lecturers who are none too keen to admit that their pupils are, or ever will be, of age."

*   *   *

The old vague promises of "ultimate self-government" will not do today. As a British writer, Rita Hinden, says:

"It is no longer good enough to say, 'One day we will Africanize your administrative service – here are two appointments on account.' Instead, we must say, 'You will have 100 (or 500) African administrators in ten years – here are 100 scholarships for their training.' It is important to proclaim our intentions, but it is still more important to carry them out within a stated time limit – as irrefutable proof of our sincerity."

The time factor, with reference to both economic and political goals, is the essence of conscientious and systematic planning for the dependencies. Wendell Willkie expressed this idea without equivocation:

"It is the world's job," he said, "to find some system for helping the colonial peoples who join the United Nations' cause to become free and independent nations. We must set up firm time-tables under which they can work out and train governments of their own choosing."

* * *

One colonial territory (aside from the old Czarist empire now included within the USSR) to which a time-table of freedom was given – and adhered to – is the Philippines. Former Secretary Cordell Hull, speaking about the future of dependent peoples, on more than one occasion referred to this country's record of relationship with the Philippines as "an excellent example of what can be achieved." It is therefore to be expected that this government will stand for a United Nations policy of specific goals to be reached by dependent peoples within specific time limits.

If the democratic forces of the world, and particularly world labor, press for and win such a policy in 1945, it will mean a real New Year and New Deal for the hundreds of millions of colonial peoples.

* * *

"Today's Guest Column: The Candy Bar: A World Trade Problem," *Daily Worker*, January 11, 1945, page 7

Candy-eating Americans, who consume half the world's supply of cocoa, should be Interested in postwar trade arrangements concerning this tropical product. We grow no cocoa in the United States, and depend upon imports from West Africa, the West Indies and some South American countries. Before the war the British West African colonies produced almost two-thirds of the world's cocoa supply; today the figure is down to 55 percent, with the production in this hemisphere rising. Restrictions on shipping from Africa during the war account in large measure for the drop in production there; we have relied more and more upon cocoa sources nearer home. Several thousand tons of cocoa shipped here from Africa under reverse lend-lease have been devoted wholly to supplying our armed forces with candy.

All this explains why you do not see many chocolate bars on candy counters nowadays. Whether they will put in a reappearance after the war and whether the quality and cost will be radically changed from what we have been accustomed to brings up another one of the international trade problems which remain to be solved.

The British government focused attention on this matter when it issued a White Paper a couple of months ago proposing that beginning October 1945, organizations should be established by and responsible to the colonial governments of the Gold Coast and Nigeria (principal cocoa producing areas), to act as trustees for the producers. They would buy up the entire cocoa crop, prescribe the price to be paid the producers, and have full responsibility for marketing and sale. The proposals have been the object of criticism from three quite diverse quarters: from the African producers, from British commercial firms, and from American cocoa importers and chocolate manufacturers.

African objections are based upon previous and current experience with the system of controlled buying and marketing of their produce, whether by foreign commercial interests acting alone or in cooperation with local authorities or the Colonial Office in London. While the British West African Cocoa Control Board during the war period was piling up a profit of about $15,000,000 (held in reserve), the fixed price paid the African farmers was declining. At a conference held by the Council on African Affairs last year, an African from the Gold Coast, here on business, testified, "The farmers are paid two and one-half cents a pound for cocoa. It brings eight cents a pound in London, nine cents in New York. This is impoverishing the Africans."

The cocoa control organizations to be established would include only a minority of African representatives in the Gold Coast and would include them only in an advisory capacity in the Nigerian agency. This, the Africans argue, means an inadequate voice for those who grow this cash crop but are deprived of the profits from it.

*   *   *

British traders, on the other hand, regard the government proposal as an encroachment upon free enterprise. The smaller firms feel that the big interests like Cadbury Bros, and Lever Bros, will be favored and further dominate the market, while the big firms are not sure that the government agencies will not curtail their present high profits.

As for American traders and manufacturers, the Herald Tribune reported a few days ago that they were pressing our State Department "to discourage the British plan which they characterize as the opening wedge for hedging the postwar world with new and more thorny trade restrictions than the discriminatory international practices which grew up between the World War and the present war."

The issue appears to be one of American free access policy as against British imperial preference policy. International discussions on oil, rubber and other basic raw materials hinge on this same issue. Colonial cash crops like cocoa and sugar, even though they may not bulk as large in foreign trade as other more important commodities, nevertheless represent significant tests of our ability to work out a sound and just United Nations economic policy.

*   *   *

"Today's Guest Column: U.S. Foreign Policy And the Colonies," *Daily Worker,* January 18, 1945, page 7

Colonial peoples all over the world, who have looked particularly to this country and to the Soviet Union for leadership in eradicating imperialism and building a postwar world of democracy, will find their hopes strengthened by the contents of the recent letter of Secretary of State [Edward] Stettinius to Paul Robeson, chairman of the Council on African Affairs.

Replying to a communication from the Council signed by many representative leaders, recommending provisions to be incorporated in the Dumbarton Oaks plans for the advancement of Africa and other colonial peoples, Mr. Stettinius reaffirmed the statement of policy made by his predecessor, Cordell Hull:

"There rests upon the Independent nations a responsibility in relation to dependent peoples who aspire to liberty. It should be the duty of nations having political ties with such peoples, of mandatories, of trustees, or of other agencies, as the case may be, to help the aspiring peoples to develop materially and educationally, to prepare themselves for the duties and responsibilities of self-government, and to attain liberty. An excellent example of what can be achieved is afforded in the record of our relationship with the Philippines."

I think it is significant to note that the above statement was first made by the former Secretary of State in September 1943, and again repeated without any change in his memorandum of March 21, 1944 on Bases of the Foreign Policy of the United States, and is now for the third time restated. This repetition implies emphasis as well as consistency of position. Though it is a general statement, it nevertheless is an inclusive one. The last sentence of the statement, as I have mentioned before in this column, may be interpreted as an endorsement of the principle of putting specific time-limits upon colonial trusteeship.

*   *   *

"The Department of State recognizes the importance in world affairs of the problems of dependent peoples, in Africa and elsewhere," Mr. Stettinius said in his letter. "The government of the

United States realizes that the problems of the dependent peoples are of a unique nature, requiring special consideration and treatment. The appropriate divisions and committees of the Department of State are devoting serious attention to those problems with a view to devising practicable solutions which will insure the greatest tangible advancement possible and which will be based upon the fundamental principles of equitable and just treatment for all peoples."

Perhaps one of the most important implications of Mr. Stettinius' letter is that it demonstrates that our State Department, like President Roosevelt and his administration as a whole, is alert and responsive to the thinking of the democratic forces of this country. This is specifically exemplified in the Secretary's expression of appreciation of the Council's "constructive interest in the efforts now being made to assure a better world for all peace-loving peoples of whatever race, creed, or political status." It is the responsibility of every section of the American public to support the government's efforts along this line by every possible means.

*   *   *

While stressing the need for a sound and democratic colonial policy for the United Nations in the postwar period, it is at the same time necessary to see this question in the larger focus of international economic relations. Ever since Americans were colonial subjects of Great Britain colonies have been prized above all for their economic value. Hence voluntary relinquishment of claims to colonies can only be expected to come about as the guarantees are given that there is another and better way to achieve the same economic advantages. Within the framework of mutually beneficial economic agreements between this country and the other world powers, the international solution of the colonial question can be effectively worked out; without such agreements, noble declarations respecting the uplift and liberation of dependent peoples will remain simply far-off ideals.

*   *   *

"Today's Guest Column: British Guiana's Labor Delegate to the London Parley," *Daily Worker,* January 25, 1945, page 7

Little or no attention has been given by either the Negro press or the labor press to the fact that invitations to the World Labor Conference meeting in London week after next included labor groups not only in independent countries (with the exception of pro-fascist states like Spain and Argentina), but also in the various colonial territories. The London Conference in its democratic representativeness, will take practical cognizance of the fact that this is one world. In several respects this conference will, unquestionably, be history-making. For one thing it will be the first international meeting of such broad scope at which the colonial peoples have enjoyed a place and voice equal to that of other peoples in reaching decisions on various international problems, including, of course, the colonial problem. What better road to a people's peace?

Last Saturday afternoon I had the privilege and stimulating experience of meeting one of the colonial delegates who was stopping in New York en route to the London, Conference. He was Hubert N. Critchlow, one of the outstanding labor figures and popular leaders in the Caribbean and the executive secretary of the British Guiana Trades Union Council. (British Guiana is one of that small patch of colonies still remaining on the northern coast of South America, and linked geographically and otherwise with the West indies.)

In a crowded room up at Harlem's Hotel Theresa, this Negro pioneer in colonial trade unionism asnwered [sic] endless questions about the organized workers whom he represented – who they were, how many, what role they played in the colony, etc. Small in stature and of modest manner, he spoke quietly and deliberately, unruffled by the torrent of questions, emphasizing a point here and there which he especially wanted clearly understood – the point, for example, about there being no discrimination against Portuguese, East Indians or other non-Negro workers within the federation of trade unions which he heads.

*   *   *

Mr. Critchlow read from a copy of the resolutions which he is carrying to the London Conference, on behalf of the people of British Guiana. Two of the several points under the heading of Postwar Reconstruction are:

(1) "That the Atlantic Charter be made applicable to the whole world...(Including) colonies pending the attainment of their independence; and that the necessary legislation be enacted in all colonies to give effect to the principles of the Atlantic Charter.
(2) "That the prevailing low standard of living of the inhabitants of the Caribbean area calls for immediate creation of additional permanent industries in those colonies and the development on a large scale of the undeveloped South American colony of British Guiana...such capital as is necessary to be provided with the assistance of imperial funds so that the inhabitants may not be exploited but derive full benefit from the development."

*   *   *

I do not know to what extent the trade union organizations in the West Indies, Africa, and Asia will be able to provide the funds or – perhaps a greater obstacle – secure the sanction of government officials (British Guiana happens to have a liberal governor now) to send delegates to the London Conference. The All-India Trade Union Congress is certain to be represented, but other less powerful bodies may not be so fortunate. Even a strong organization of European workers like the South African Trades and labor [sic] Council could not get government approval of a visa for a Negro who was to be sent as one of the council's two delegates to the originally scheduled conference last June.

Such petty things, however, are insignificant trivialities in the larger picture of world economic developments. Even if some of Europe's statesmen will not yet admit it, it is nevertheless a fact that in order to survive today's world [they] must renounce colonialism, just as the world of a hundred years ago was compelled to renounce slavery. There is no other alternative to over-production and under-consumption – to universal economic ruin. The participation of colonial delegates in the World Labor Conference is a foreshadowing of the new world of democracy and equality of economic opportunity for all peoples which victory – genuine victory – must bring.

*   *   *

"Today's Guest Column: Disquieting British Views on the Colonies," *Daily Worker,* February 1, 1945, page 7

Except for Churchill's inept but bluntly frank declarations, there has been until recently a rather studied avoidance in British official circles of the general subject of postwar colonial policy. Now, however, a change is evident. With the realization that the United Nations must and will deal with this matter as part of the task of maintaining international security and peace, official and semi-official spokesmen of British colonial policy have begun to air their views.

The London Times on Jan. 10 had Colonial Tasks as the subject of its leading editorial, declaring significantly, "On Britain, with her exceptional record and responsibilities in the colonial field, rests the duty of giving a lead not only in administration but in thought" in shaping the future plans of the colonial powers.

In the same issue of this paper there was a long article by Lord Lugard (who shares top rank with Lord Hailey among Britain's most highly esteemed colonial authorities), under the title of A World Colonial Charter, in which, among other disquieting things, one finds the suggestion that "the present mandates have served their purpose and that annexation by the mandatories should now be recognized."

Especially indicative of the British government's current eagerness to have its colonial views placed in the public record was the recent visit to this country (after an inspection of the West Indies) of the Secretary of State for Colonies, Col. Oliver Stanley, and his address before the Foreign Policy Association in New York, Jan. 20.

*   *   *

He was aware, Col. Stanley told his American audience, that "there are many in this country who have a genuine and quite understandable desire to see us produce for the Colonial Empire some kind of charter which would give a universal blueprint and some kind of schedule which would give a universal timetable." But the problems were too diverse and complex for such a solution, he insisted (though members of parliament have more than once reminded him of the Soviet Union's successful experience in overcoming these same difficulties). The essence of his remarks was that the wisest policy was for the British colonial administration to continue to carry on its good work – which is a more polite paraphrase of Mr. Churchill's utterances on the Empire.

Lord Lugard's article follows the same line, except that he goes a step further and cites also the progressive tendency of other European colonial administrations, the French, Dutch and Belgian. He argues against any general international regulations for the colonies, and against any international commission for safeguarding the interests of dependent peoples. The latter, he says, "would introduce distrust and espionage destructive of local authority and responsibility," and "each responsible state can achieve the best results...if unhampered by rigid rules."

*   *   *

It is beyond my comprehension how this respected statesman, and he is not unique in his views, can uphold an obviously bankrupt laissez-faire procedure in colonial administration, and at the same time admit the fact that "it is mainly upon them (the colonial peoples) in their millions that success in the policy of 'expanding consumption and expanding production' depends for the rehabilitation of a shattered world."

It is necessary to decide, once and for all, whether the cake is to be kept or to be eaten! One can have unqualified imperial sovereignty or collective security, but not both together. Britain, for her own salvation, must join with this country and the other great powers in a concerted and coordinated effort to achieve a single and universal standard of decent living for peoples of every color in every land – which effort must include joint international responsibilities and agreed upon programs for the rapid economic and political advancement of all dependent peoples.

*   *   *

"Today's Guest Column: Two Letters From South Africa," *Daily Worker*, February 8, 1945, page 7

Since not much news out of South Africa, other than about Prime Minister Smuts, reaches the American public, I think it may be well to report on the contents of two letters lately received from correspondents in the South African Dominion. The letters both deal with the sharpening struggle between the democratic and reactionary forces in that land, and one of the main facets of that struggle – the issue of the rights of the 8,000,000 African, 250,000 Indian and 500,000 colored (racially mixed) peoples.

The first letter, from Dr. G. M. Naicker, chairman of the Anti-Segregation Council of Natal, concerns the campaign against Indian segregation, which was the subject of this column about two months ago, at the time when the Central Legislative Assembly of India sharply retaliated against the South African government's Indian discrimination.

The Anti-Segregation Council, Dr. Naicker writes, seeks to rally Indians in Natal, rich or poor, and unify the stand of all Indian organizations, including the influential Natal Indian Congress, against all measures of the government intended to limit the right of Indians to lease, buy or occupy any property.

The attempt to herd the Indians In South Africa into segregated areas, as has been done with the other non-white peoples, parallels the war-time flare-up of violent anti-Indian (as well as anti-Jewish and anti-African) agitation incited by the political demagogs and their followers.

The Indians have fought back, notwithstanding the waverings and compromises, of some of their leaders. Dr. Naicker tells of a huge mass meeting of 8,000 people held in Durban in early December. Such expressions of solidarity have forced the government to withdraw some of the worst features of the segregation measures. The issue, however, is far from settled.

In closing his letter, the Indian leader writes, "We want the people and the governments of the United Nations to strongly support the demands of the disfranchised Indians of Natal…We look to you for support."

* * *

The other letter, received a few days ago by the Council on African Affairs, is from a prominent white official of a major trade union in South Africa. It deals with the larger picture of conflicting interests in the country. "As a result of the very powerful reactionary and pro-fascist forces," the writer says, "the position of the millions of non-Europeans is becoming increasingly difficult." He cites as evidence of this, the Johannesburg riot which occurred in November.

He continues: "The internal progressive forces are, I am afraid, too weak to secure a change in policy, and the efforts of all external progressive forces will be of great service to the whole of humanity, including the masses of European people in South Africa. Progressive forces all over the world must take steps to see that South Africa does not become the Nazi Germany of the African continent."

* * *

The weakness of the progressive forces in South Africa, mentioned by the writer, is a weakness which comes not from lack of program or lack of influence and following among the masses of the people. It is a weakness which stems mainly from lack of unity. Though there has been marked progress made toward a united progressive front, there is yet too much factionalism and division among those who should be fighting together. The Labor Party, for example, will not collaborate with the Communist Party because of the latter's unqualified stand against all racial discrimination. In South Africa as in the United States, the only way to lick reaction is through the united strength of all those on the side of democracy and progress.

* * *

"Today's Guest Column: Crimea Conference Heightens Role of Negro History Week," *Daily Worker,* February 15, 1945, page 7

This Negro History Week has coincided with great and historic events which mark a new stage in the upward march of all humanity. But it is not the mere coincidence in time that is important. As [fellow African American CPUSA leader] Doxey Wilkerson pointed out so forcefully in his column on Monday, the basic lesson of the Negro people's history is that their progress and the progress of the nation as a whole have been and and [sic] are interdependent. The same is true of the liberation struggle of all colonial and oppressed peoples and the direction of general international economic and political developments.

Thus it is that this Negro History Week had special significance in view of the Allied military coordination now crushing the Nazi forces in a vise of steel, in view of the agreements reached at the Big Three Conference in the Crimea, and, finally, in view of the progress being made toward genuine international labor unity at the World Labor Conference in London.

The annihilation of fascism and the continued effective functioning of the United Nations coalition, strengthened by a united world labor movement, are the essential preconditions for what Churchill, Roosevelt and Stalin defined as "a secure and lasting peace which will, in the words of the Atlantic Charter, 'afford assurance that all the men in all the lands may live out their lives in freedom from fear and want.'"

*   *   *

It is interesting and pertinent to compare these present world developments, as they affect the Negro here and abroad, with events of a century ago when the struggle between slavery and advancing industrialism gripped the world and especially America.

England, the most industrially developed nation at that time, had been the first to abolish slavery, setting the Negroes free in its West Indian colonies in 1833. The Abolitionist forces in America, looked to England for help in their struggle, and they received much practical support, financial and otherwise. It is well known what a decisive role was played by British labor in its support of Lincoln and the North during the Civil War, counteracting the pro-slavery influence and aims of the British Tories.

Some interesting sidelights on the trans-Atlantic unity of democratic forces in that period are provided in the autobiography of the great Negro leader, Frederick Douglass. He tells with what immense enthusiasm he was received in England by great British anti-slavery leaders like Thomas Clarkson and by the people in general who heard his appeals during his first visit abroad just a hundred years ago.

To mention Just one Incident, there was the time when the great early Victorian champion of Irish freedom, Daniel O'Connell, introduced Douglass at a great public meeting as the "Black O'Connell of the United States." Said O'Connell, "My sympathy is not confined to the narrow limits of my own green Ireland; my spirit walks abroad upon sea and land, and wherever there is oppression I hate the oppressor, and wherever the tyrant rears his head I will deal my bolts upon it, and wherever there is sorrow and suffering, there is my spirit to succor and relieve."

For the rest of this Interesting and inspiring story of Douglass' experiences in England, I urge you to read the autobiography for

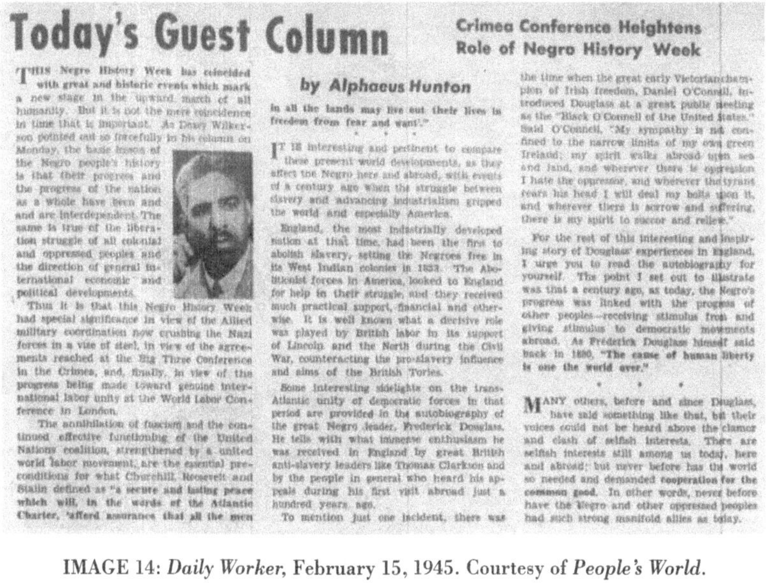

IMAGE 14: *Daily Worker*, February 15, 1945. Courtesy of *People's World*.

yourself. The point I set out to illustrate was that a century ago, as today, the Negro's progress was linked with the progress of other peoples – receiving stimulus from and giving stimulus to democratic movements abroad. As Frederick Douglass himself said back in 1880, "The cause of human liberty is one the world over."

*   *   *

Many others, before and since Douglass, have said something like that, but their voices could not be heard above the clamor and clash of selfish interests. There are selfish interests still among us today, here and abroad; but never before has the world so needed and demanded cooperation for the common good. In other words, never before have the Negro and other oppressed peoples had such strong manifold allies as today.

*   *   *

"Today's Guest Column: Pearl Buck Fails To See the Change," *Daily Worker*, February 22, 1945, page 7

In an article in the magazine This Month, Pearl S. Buck [the first American woman to be awarded both the Pulitzer and Nobel Prizes for literature], who has contributed greatly to the development of the One World concept, poses a rather curious question – curious because of the time at which it is asked. Miss Buck points "out that conquest and establishment of empire nave been the regular though unforeseen consequences of trade by the European powers with the peoples whom they now hold as dependents. In the light of this, she asks whether America, with its present eagerness "to trade everywhere in the world" may not, like England, France and Holland, "be building an empire without knowing it."

The trouble with this hypothesis is that it is unscientific, entirely on the level of abstract speculation. The conditions which made for imperialism yesterday will make for imperialism tomorrow only if tomorrow's world is a replica of yesterday's. Will it be? No doubt some advocates of the Century of American Imperialism would like it to be, but the march of events points to the contrary. Since she fails to mention them in her article, it would seem that Miss Buck either ignores or discounts the significance of Teheran, Bretton Woods, and Dumbarton Oaks. It seems that she does not realize that a program of world trade expansion is necessary not only for the security and employment of American workers and workers in other advanced countries, but also for the general levelling up of peoples in all countries to a plane of equality with the most advanced.

* * *

Miss Buck admits that "there is nothing intrinsically wrong with fair trade. Business properly conducted benefits both sides. But," she adds, "trade in the hands of the greedy, unchecked by law, uncontrolled by principles of justice, has resulted time and time again in empire." That is precisely the point. It is just that kind of trade which the United Nations intend to outlaw. We are on the road to international cooperation; the only alternative road is that of isolation, which in terms of today's world means simply imperialism.

Americans chose the first road in reelecting President Roosevelt. But the enemies of the administration – those who knowingly strive to erect an American empire on the basis of this country's preeminent economic power – have not given up the struggle to defeat the American people's will. That in essence is what the fight over Henry Wallace is about. That will be the test in what Congress does with the Bretton Woods agreement.

Wallace expressed the opinion of the great majority of Americans when he said back in 1942: "American peace – the peace-of the common man – must be translated into freedom everywhere... America is building a peace not based on imperialistic intervention. America will not have made her contribution until nine out of ten of the world's adults can read and write, until the children of the world can have at least a pint of milk a day, until education brings such a sense of responsibility that all the people of the world can be trusted to take part in democratic government."

*   *   *

I am sure Miss Buck backs such a goal for America. And if so, she must also necessarily approve of Wallace's and Roosevelt's objective of trebling America's foreign trade in order to help in bringing education, food and self-government to those who lack them throughout the world. By failing to distinguish between the opposite aims of the progressive and reactionary elements in this country, the author, unfortunately, has unconsciously aided the cause of reaction. For at this moment when the need is to rally public support for the administration's foreign policy, her forebodings about American imperialism will have the negative effect of spreading confusion and doubt in the public mind.

Yes, Miss Buck, Americans do want to trade everywhere in the world, but in a manner which the world has never before seen: on a basis of strict equity among all nations, and under just and democratic principles which will make for a unified world community in place of the old division of exploiters and exploited.

*   *   *

"Today's Guest Column: FDR's Conferences In Great Bitter Lake," *Daily Worker,* March 1, 1945, page 7

The conferences aboard the American cruiser in Great Bitter Lake (Suez Canal) at which President Roosevelt talked with King Farouk of Egypt, Emperor Haile Selassie of Ethiopia and King Ibn Saud of Saudi Arabia, reflect, like the decisions of the Yalta conference, the new determination of the United States to assume its full responsibility in grappling with problems in foreign lands which previously we have been content to let others assume as their burden. The President's discussions with the Middle East rulers signify that this country's Good Neighbor Policy is no longer to be limited to the Americas.

Reports of what was said between President Roosevelt and his royal visitors are, of course, fragmentary. The improvement of communications, particularly by air, and the desirability of closer relations and increased trade between the United States and the Middle East countries are mentioned as having been discussed. But more specific matters undoubtedly were included in the talks – such items as the disposition of Italy's African colonies, the question of air bases, the question of the Syrian-Lebanese demands for freedom from French mandate, the Palestine problem and the question of oil.

Without speculating on what may or may not have been said on these matters, we can say that the fact that our President took the opportunity of his presence in the Middle East to meet and talk face to face with the Egyptian, Ethiopian and Arabian rulers will help much toward solving these various problems. We hope that the result may also come from the conferences which Prime Minister Churchill had in Cairo with the Ethiopian emperor, the king of Arabia, the president of Syria and Egyptian leaders. Such friendly contacts between the leaders of the great powers and the statesmen of the smaller powers are needed to help smooth out the Dumbarton Oaks road to worldwide security and peace.

* * *

This is important. For, while the Crimea conference strengthened the coalition of the United States, the Soviet Union and Great Britain, the primary condition of postwar security, much remains to be done in strengthening the relations and establishing full confidence between the great powers and many of the smaller nations. And equally urgent, if not more so, is the job of establishing new relations between the great powers and their dependencies – which includes semi-colonial areas, protectorates, or just plain colonies.

If there is to be any success in bringing order out of the imperialist muddle, two things are absolutely necessary: the substitution of multilateral discussion and agreement in place of unilateral action, and the substitution of planning and working with dependent peoples on a basis of equality in place of the customary dictation to them by those who hold power. The first is necessary in order to avoid new and more bitter international rivalries; the second is necessary in order to avoid incurring the resentment or worse of subject peoples.

*   *   *

The conferences aboard the cruiser on Great Bitter Lake and the participation of colonial delegates in the World Labor Conference just ended in London, both set a new pattern of democratic relationship which must be developed between free peoples and dependent or semi-dependent peoples in the post-war world. It is appropriate and expedient that this new pattern should first be established at the top level of international planning. From there the pattern must be broadened and applied universally.

*   *   *

"Today's Guest Column: The Westbrook Pegler Of Negro Journalism," *Daily Worker,* March 8, 1945, page 7

George S. Schuyler is the Westbrook Pegler [an anti-New Deal, anti-union journalist] of Negro journalism. Practically every week through his two columns in the widely circulated Negro weekly, the Pittsburgh Courier, Schuyler peddles his subversive poison. The hacks in the pay of the Hearst-Patterson-McCormick gang have nothing on this Negro writer. He is against Roosevelt and all who support him, but hastens to the defense of the acknowledged fascist Lawrence Dennis* and outfits like Peace Now; he is "profoundly unconcerned about the outcome of the war," and the United Nations are merely something for him to sneer at.

Running true to the form of made-in-Berlin propaganda, Schuyler specializes in redbaiting, parading before his readers every conceivable slander against the Soviet Union and against Communists in this country and abroad. Quite revealing was his explanation given about a year ago to those readers who had condemned his identification of fascism and communism. "I purposely created this uproar," he said, "because I have noticed that a dangerously large percentage of so-called thinking Negroes has swallowed the red propaganda." So Mr. Schuyler sets himself up (or perhaps it isn't self-motivated), like King Canute, to make the tide recede.

But his real purpose, whether deliberate or not, goes much farther than simply attacking the Communists. Liu Liang-mo, who also writes a column for the Pittsburgh Courier, but of a decidedly different character, used that medium in the Feb. 24 issue to confront Schuyler with a whole series of his criminal allegations. Here are a few samples: "The Chinese Reds are pledged to an alliance of China and Russia against the U.S.A. and Britain if the Communists gain control of the Chinese government." "China ... is being divided between those two boon companions, Stalin and

---

* Lawrence Dennis, "arguably the 'brains' behind U.S. fascism," was born Black and spent his entire adult life passing for white. See: Gerald Horne, *The Color Of Fascism: Lawrence Dennis, Racial Passing, and the Rise of Right-Wing Extremism in the United States* (New York: New York University Press, 2006)

Mikado [the emperor of Japan]." "The ally (Russia) of today may be the enemy of tomorrow."

Says Liu Liang-mo, after reviewing this poisonous tripe: "Hitler's and Japan's last trump card is to split the unity of the United Nations with anti-communism and anti-sovietism, and it looks like Mr. Schuyler is doing his best in both his columns to serve the purpose of our common enemy."

*   *   *

The greatest menace of this writer is in his method of exploiting the Negro's grievances, such as discrimination in the armed forces, and the Negro's concern about the liberation of colonial peoples. At a time when Negroes, along with all other Americans, should be giving their fullest support to the establishment of a system of worldwide collective security – without which it is useless to hope for any improvement in the status of the Negro or colonial peoples – Schuyler says of what he calls the "Crime(a) conference" that "nothing surprising came out of it except the callousness with which the subject of colonies was ignored and the little countries of Europe made the victims of power politics."

*   *   *

What does Schuyler want? Well, it isn't hard to guess at the answers. A week after the elections last November, Schuyler gave vent to his irritation at the strong support which Negro leaders (and, incidentally, Negro people) had given in reelecting Roosevelt. He wrote: "As far as a capitalist party can be, the Republicans were right in the campaign...If Negro leaders had to take a capitalistic side, the GOP was the side, but if they were really intelligent, informed and interested in racial welfare, they should have urged their people to vote for Norman Thomas and the Socialist Party, to which the only alternative is ultimate slavery." There you have it! There couldn't be a better illustration of how the ultra-left and the ultra-right travel the same road of reaction.

Schuyler is a disgrace to Negro journalism, a danger to the Negro people and to the nation. He cannot be permitted to continue his slanderous and defeatist scribblings. A flood of letters of protest should be sent by all progressive-minded individuals and organizations to Mr. P. L. Prattis, executive editor of the Pittsburgh Courier, 2628 Centre Avenue, Pittsburgh 19, Pa. Schuyler must go!

* * *

"Today's Guest Column: What Future for the Mandated Territories?," *Daily Worker,* March 22, 1945, page 7

The Times and other U. S. papers have lately been carrying reports, as yet officially unconfirmed, of there having been some discussion or agreement at the Crimea conference on a new system of international trusteeship for the mandate territories, colonies formerly held by Italy and Japan, and perhaps other dependencies. There appears to be a general current of opinion in this country in favor of such a system. Across the Atlantic, on the other hand, both Churchill and [Charles] De Gaulle [chair of the Provisional Government of the post-war French Government] have recently made speeches in which the trusteeship idea was politely and indirectly but quite firmly rejected – at least as applied to the colonies or mandate holdings of their respective countries.

What lies at the basis of this apparent divergence of views? If we examine expressions of the sort made by Churchill and De Gaulle, we find that they are based upon:

(1) The insistence, sometimes sincere, that progress is being made and will be made, without outside aid or counsel (except perhaps as in such convenient and limited regional arrangements as the Allied Caribbean Commission), toward accomplishing the economic and social reforms – and, ultimately, the political reforms – which are acknowledged to be necessary.
(2) The belief that for Britain or France to maintain their place beside the United States and the Soviet Union as world powers, the retention of the economic advantages afforded by their imperial possessions is absolutely essential; and
(3) The fear that any relaxation of their own imperial controls would mean opening the door to American domination in their colonial markets.

*   *   *

With regard to the first point, it is of course true that as a consequence of this war, which unlike World War I has invaded the colonial world, the imperial powers on the Allied side have taken some forward steps in relation to their colonies. The steps taken, however, cannot be said to entail any thorough-going transformation in the economic status of the colonial peoples within the foreseeable future.

The two basic needs of the colonial areas everywhere are industrialization and the opportunity for the colonial peoples themselves to assume control of their own economic existence. And on these two points the imperial powers have said end done very little. Industrialization requires large scale capital investment and technical assistance, neither of which any European power will be able to spare immediately after the war, even if it desired to. Only the United States, through private enterprise channels, through agreements with other governments, or through the medium of the International Bank for Reconstruction and Development (Bretton Woods Plan) and other agencies can make a major contribution to the industrialization of the colonial world.

Without such a development program, in which the colonial peoples play their proper role, the colonial world, regardless of what other reforms may be granted, will remain what it has been – a narrowly limited market for cheap manufactured goods and a source of "cheap" raw materials. Such a prospect certainly spells disaster. For without a radical change from the usual colonial conditions of poverty and hunger, it will be impossible to achieve the expanded trade necessary to balance modern productive capacity and thus provide economic security on a worldwide scale.

* * *

America's role in this whole problem is the decisive factor. By its acceptance of the Bretton Woods plan, by lowering its tariff barriers, by entering into economic agreements on a fair basis with other nations, erasing the errors of the Chicago civil aviation conference, our government can allay the British fears that what we want is an expanded trade for America only.

* * *

"Today's Guest Column: Lippmann Sees Colonies Through Col. Blimp's Glasses," *Daily Worker*, March 29, 1945, page 7

Walter Lippmann chose the title "Pandora Box" for his Herald Tribune column of March 20 in which he discussed what ought – or more accurately, ought not – to be done about the colonial question at the San Francisco conference of the United Nations. You may recall that Pandora's box, given her by Zeus, held all of mankind's ills, which escaped when she opened it, while hope, also in the box, remained there. Of course, Pandora should have left the box alone.

The gist of Mr. Lippmann's column is that it would be wise for the San Francisco conference to do little, if anything, about the colonial problem. He would be satisfied if the United Nations merely assumed "limited power to create organs of consultation." The figurative title and the reasoning behind the column are both based upon a double fallacy: the assumption that the colonial peoples and the problems involving them are in a passive state, and that they will remain so as long as no attempt is made to do anything about them. That is what some British (and other) Tories would have us believe. Mr. Lippmann undoubtedly knows better. But for the purposes of his argument he has found it convenient to think and talk like Col. Blimp [a cartoon character identified by his walrus moustache known for being pompous, jingoistic, and stereotypically British].

Mr. Lippmann gives three reasons for keeping the lid down on the colonial question. The first reason is that the various colonial territories represent different problems, adding up to an exceedingly complex question which cannot be answered with any single solution. That, of course, is obvious. But it is equally obvious that one does not turn his back on a question simply because it is difficult.

Mr. Lippmann deliberately over-simplifies and distorts the program advanced by those who are calling for a colonial New Deal. He speaks disparagingly of "the assumption, now current, that the only right solution is to do what we are doing in the Philippines: that is, to prepare the colonial peoples for self-government, grant them independence, set them up as a new sovereign state and then clear out."

* * *

We do want to follow the Philippines example in setting a timetable for the abolition of the colonial status of every subject people, and we do want to allow (rather than "prepare") them to achieve self-government. As for what their new status shall be, that is something for the people themselves to decide. (Nowhere in his article does the author refer to the principle of self-determination.) They may, as in the case of India, decide on sovereign independence; they may choose some form of association with a stronger power (not necessarily the one which has governed them); or, as in the Caribbean and Africa, they may choose to federate themselves with other excolonial territories. In any event, these peoples will not wish to isolate themselves from the rest of the world; the imperialist exploiters are the only ones they want to "clear out."

Second, Mr. Lippmann acknowledges that those who govern dependent peoples are "accountable to the conscience of mankind," but he is opposed to the practical application of this principle by holding such governors legally accountable to the United Nations organization. Why? I quote: "It just is not in the cards to make the Governor of Alaska, the Governor General of Bermuda, or the Governor of Tunis legally answerable to an assembly in which Saudi Arabia, Iraq, Iran, Liberia, Ethiopia, Dominica, Haiti sit as sovereign judges." Is this a plea for Nordic Supremacy, or what?

* * *

The third reason is, I think, Mr. Lippmann's main one. Before we can properly settle the question of even the mandates and Japan's and Italy's colonies, he says, "it will be necessary to negotiate security pacts, in the Atlantic, the Mediterranean and the Pacific." For such pacts will determine who needs what sea and air bases in the colonies.

This point gives the key to what's fundamentally wrong with Mr. Lippmann's outlook. He has apparently failed to grasp the fact that Yalta and the San Francisco meeting represent the emergence of a new kind of world – a world of collective security. Mr. Lippmann's eyes are upon the past. He seems to be still thinking in the old terms of colonies as pawns in the imperialist game of power politics and spheres of influence.

* * *

"Today's Guest Column: Perspectives For Africa's Development," *Daily Worker*, April 5, 1945, page 7

The question frequently arises, in discussion on the future of the colonial peoples of Africa, as to whether when they have won self-government it may not be possible for them to leap the stage of capitalist development and advance rapidly from feudalism to socialism.

Such a question may appear to be rather academic in view of the circumstances that self-government is yet to be won. But the fact Is that in some sections of the No-Longer-Dark Continent one finds the educated minority of Africans themselves discussing it. I refer particularly to the British West African colonies of Nigeria, Sierra Leone, Gold Coast and Gambia with a total population of approximately 30,000,000.

In this, the most politically advanced section of subject Africa, the general conditions of colonialism, with the stifling of individual initiative and enterprise, have naturally blocked the development of any sizable middle class. But, on the other hand, the common struggle against the imperialist yoke has served to unite the workers in the towns and cities in these colonies (though the masses in the hinterland for the most part still remain separated into numerous feudalistic tribal units, carefully preserved by the British "indirect rule" system).

Unhampered by the presence and direct domination of European Immigrants and settlers, as in East and South Africa, the West African urban workers in their struggle have been able to achieve a high degree of organization.

*   *   *

These four British West African colonies were the only territories of that continent represented at the recent World Labor Conference in London by native African delegates. They represented a developing labor movement which embraces practically every strata of urbanized salaried workers from teachers, nurses and civil service employes [sic] to dock workers and unskilled laborers in the tin and gold mines. Even in their present early stage of development, the West African trade unions are a major progressive and unifying force among the people. And they are the most politically-developed and world-minded force. Their able leaders, men like Wallace Johnson, Edward Small and T. A. Bankole, gave clear evidence of this at the London Labor Conference.

Assistance in the development of the unions has been given by some of the British trade unionists who have been appointed labor officers in the colonial administration and who have tried to do an honest job. One of these men recently gave a lecture on The New Russia in a World Affairs Course, one of the adult evening classes conducted in a school at Lagos, the main city of Nigeria.

* * *

The speaker emphasized the similarity of conditions in pre-Soviet Russia and present-day Nigeria – the lack of industrialism, the prevalence of small and primitive individual farms and the widespread illiteracy, poverty and disease. "Then came Lenin." The rapid advancement of the country under socialism was described. The speaker explained how the Soviet people and the Red Army had been able to acquit themselves so gloriously in this war, and why Stalin was so respected and loved by all the

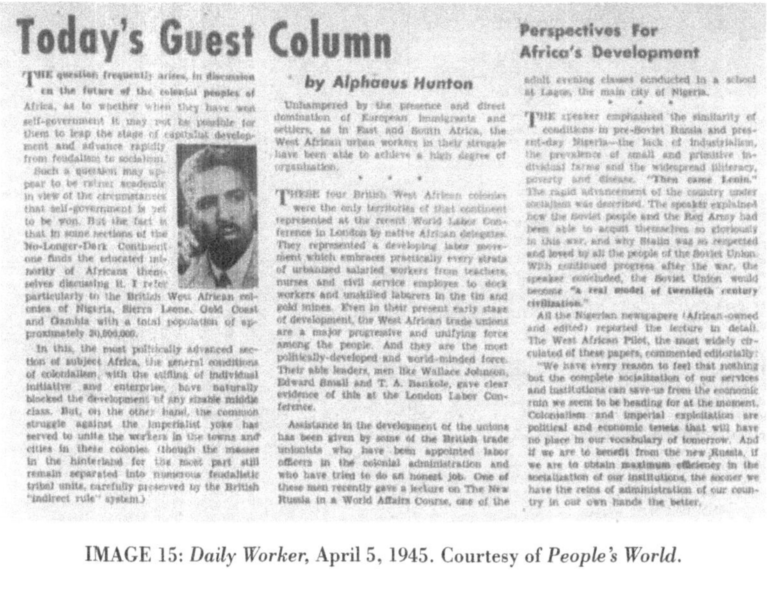

IMAGE 15: *Daily Worker*, April 5, 1945. Courtesy of *People's World*.

people of the Soviet Union. With continued progress after the war, the speaker concluded, the Soviet Union would become "a real model of twentieth century civilization."

All the Nigerian newspapers (African-owned and edited) reported the lecture in detail. The West African Pilot, the most widely circulated of these papers, commented editorially:

"We have every reason to feel that nothing but the complete socialization of our services and institutions can save us from the economic ruin we seem to be heading for at the moment. Colonialism and imperial exploitation are political and economic tenets that will have no place in our vocabulary of tomorrow. And if we are to benefit from the new Russia, if we are to obtain maximum efficiency in the socialization of our institutions, the sooner we have the reins of administration of our country in our own hands the better."

*   *   *

"Today's Guest Column: Self-Determination and Colonial Policy," *Daily Worker,* April 19, 1945, page 7

In April 1917, Stalin in his report on the national question stated: "The oppressed nations forming part of Russia must be allowed the right to decide for themselves whether they wish to remain part of the Russian state or to separate and form an independent state…The question of the right of nations freely to secede must not be confused with the question that a nation must necessarily secede at any given moment…I may recognize the right of a nation to secede, but that does not mean that I compel it to secede. A people has a right to secede, but it may or may not exercise that right, according to circumstances."

This is what we mean by the principle of self-determination.

Stalin's words of 28 years ago have important bearing on the present-day problems of what to do about the colonies. Stalin's words need recalling today because the current British, French and Netherlands proposals for the political advancement of their colonials, varied though their programs are, all have the common defect of ignoring the principles of self-determination. It is simply assumed that the colonial people and their territories will remain attached to Britain, or France, or the Netherlands, as the case may be.

* * *

The De Gaulle government, while holding views parallel to the British, has the advantage of having developed a more positive and constructive colonial policy, which it is apparently hastening, to apply. The April 1 issue of Free France, published by the New York office of the French Press and Information Service, defines the French goal as:

"A Federal Union of French nations, in which North Africa, Black Africa, Madagascar, and Indo-China, together with European France, would constitute so many federations with a very large measure of political and economic autonomy. Their respective populations would enjoy the rights of national citizenship, common to all. The latter would mean election to a Parliament sitting at Paris of two types of representatives: deputies in numbers proportional to the populations of the various federations, and deputies representing the nationalities."

This is splendid. The only question is whether that is what the masses of the people in each French colony (not merely the elite minority who have adopted the French way of life) really want. Are they to have the chance to accept or reject this form of government?

*   *   *

The article cites "the Russian federation" as an example of a similar political organization of heterogeneous peoples which has succeeded. Apart from the obvious territorial and other differences between the Soviet Union and the French Empire, there is a fundamental point which seems to have been overlooked. As was stated in the resolution on the national problem at the 10th congress of the Russian Communist Party in 1921, "Federation may be durable, and the results of federation real, only if it is based on mutual confidence and the voluntary consent of the countries constituting the federation."

No arrangements for the future of the colonial peoples, no matter how ideal they may be theoretically, can be successful if they are imposed from above without the voluntary acceptance of the people concerned.

The third principle of the Atlantic Charter is "the right of all peoples to choose the form of government under which they will live." President Roosevelt, whose sad loss the colonial peoples of Africa and Asia must feel no less keenly than do Americans, affirmed that "the Atlantic Charter applies not only to the parts of the world that border the Atlantic, [but] to the whole world."

*   *   *

"Today's Guest Column: San Francisco, 1945 And Paris, 1919," *Daily Worker,* April 26, 1945, page 7

The eyes of the whole world are on San Francisco [where 850 delegate representing 50 allied nations met to charter the United Nations; the UN would officially come into existence in October 1945 after China, France, the Soviet Union, the United Kingdom, the United States, as well as other signatories ratified the charter]. And one of the significant things about the conference [officially called the United Nations Conference on International Organization] which has just started is that the peoples of the world will be able to see what goes on there.

The provisions which have been made for the fullest possible press and radio coverage, for admission of the public to the meetings, and for the presence of consultants and observers representing various organizations all illustrate the marked difference between the present era and that of World War I – between the people's peace now taking shape and the "statesmen's peace" of 1919.

The San Francisco conference for the establishment of the charter of a general international organization is the logical outcome of the constantly increasing unity and solidarity of the United Nations, and primarily of the Big Three, which has been engendered by the common task of the defeat of fascism. The Paris peace conference, on the other hand, was the power-politics aftermath of a power politics war: the Allied statesmen there concentrated upon treaties and secret deals for maintaining or strengthening (so they thought) the power of their respective countries, while giving only perfunctory and formal consideration to Woodrow Wilson's principal concern, the drafting of the covenant of the League of Nations.

"It was a question of real-politik all day and League meetings only in the evenings," says one writer, describing the Paris conference. "One can still see President Wilson coming out at midnight from the commission which drafted the covenant, exhausted. At that time the League was predominantly American, its constitution elaborated in discussions at the American headquarters, its meetings largely inspired by American energy and staffed by American personnel."

*   *   *

The League of Nations, noble though it was in conception, was doomed from the beginning because it was based upon the illusion rather than the fact of unity of aim and purpose among the Allied powers. It represented a blueprint unrelated to reality, a bluepring [sic] drawn up by Allied statesmen who were interested in collective security only in so far as it did not interfere with their own scheme of national aggrandizement.

The fundamental differences between the structures of the old League and the new organization proposed at Dumbarton Oaks point to the genuineness of the present effort and concern for the establishment of a world instrument for the maintenance of security and peace.

Two differences stand out in particular: the provision for effective executive action by the most responsible nations, the permanent members of the Security Council; and the provision for coordinated planning and unity of action on the economic level.

There are other important structural differences. But the most basic differentiation between the League and the new institution being planned at San Francisco, it seems to me, lies in their genesis – the radically different conditions out of which they have developed.

*   *   *

No one, of course, alleges that there is unanimous agreement today among the various governments on all points regarding the postwar world. But no one can deny that there is a far wider basis of agreement than there is of disagreement. The successful prosecution of the war and the conferences which have led up to San Francisco are evidence of that fact.

Symptomatic of this basic agreement is the editorial warning given by the conservative N. Y. Times last Sunday regarding the question of American retention of Pacific bases: "The road to world order cannot be paved by jingo nationalism."

Out of a people's war will and must come a people's peace.

*   *   *

"Today's Guest Column: What Do Colonies Say Of Supervision Plan?," *Daily Worker,* May 3, 1945, page 7

One argument frequently advanced by the European imperial powers against international supervision of colonies, and which is fairly certain to be raised when this matter comes up at San Francisco, is that the colonial peoples themselves do not want such supervision. As this is a type of argument which on its face appears quite reasonable and high-minded – surely we don't want to impose something upon the colonial peoples against their will – it is well that we look into it a bit and see what it really represents.

In the first place, there is no evidence available that the majority of any colonial people either oppose or support the plan of international supervision, for the simple reason that they have never been polled on the question, any more than they have been polled with respect to what they think about their present administration.

Second, the statements of some colonial leaders on this point, upon which the government spokesmen base their argument, have to be interpreted in their full meaning in order that we may know just what it is they are opposed to. This opposition to international supervision is declared by the government spokesmen to mean a preference for remaining under the sole rule of the governing power. In practically all cases, however, it will be found that where opposition to international supervision has been expressed in the colonies or by colonial spokesmen outside the colonies, the alternative proposed is not a continuation of the existing external control but the achievement of self-government.

Thirdly, it must be borne in mind that the mandates system created by the League of Nations, which is the only form of international supervision the colonials know about, except for the recently established Anglo-American Caribbean Commission, has not been of any help in promoting self-government. Some of the Class A mandates have won their independence despite the League's authority. The Class B mandates (all of which are the former German colonies in Africa, divided among Britain, France and Belgium) and Class C mandates are no nearer self-rule than they were in 1919.

*   *   *

Colonial subjects, therefore, cannot be expected to look with approval upon any form of international supervision which is merely a duplication of the mandates system.

What the the [sic] minimum requirements of a satisfactory system of supervision? First of all, that the colonial peoples themselves should have a place and a voice in the top supervisory commission and at all levels of authority beneath it. Second, that the supervisory body establish a definite time-table of advancement to political self-determination for every colonial people. And third, that it be vested with the proper authority to hear direct complaints, make direct investigations, and exercise other powers in order to give real effect to a program of colonial advancement.

The mandates system met none of these requirements. If the colonial peoples were asked whether, short of immediate self-government, they would welcome this new form of supervision, with the United States, the Soviet Union and other democratic powers participating, I am certain that their answer would be overwhelmingly in the affirmative.

*   *   *

In his warmly applauded speech at the San Francisco Conference last Saturday, Gen. [Carlos P.] Romulo, representing the Philippines, struck an important note When he stated that "a billion faces" were turned hopefully toward the conference for help to become "not bystanders but collaborators" in the new international effort toward human welfare and advancement. This is the fundamental point which must be constantly kept in the foreground in relating colonial trusteeship plans to world security arrangements – the colonial peoples demand, and it is to our advantage to guarantee, that they be "not bystanders but collaborators" in winning the peace.

*   *   *

"Today's Guest Column: The U.S. Colonial Trusteeship Plan," *Daily Worker,* May 10, 1945, page 7

Exit the invincible (in 1941) German Wehrmacht! Two down and one to go!

The Nazi grand strategy, desperately acted out up to the very end, was to split the Allied powers, isolating the Soviet Union. It failed. And with it crumbled Hitler's sole hope of victory.

The war in the west is over. The war in the east gathers momentum. Meanwhile, in San Francisco – despite some bungling diplomacy and distorted press reports of a most unhelpful sort – the work continues of creating a permanent, indestructible coalition of the United Nations in order to preserve what has now been one-half won.

Very heartening was the announcement last Sunday of the wide area of agreement reached among the four inviting powers on proposed amendments to Dumbarton Oaks. And it did not escape your notice, I trust, that among the agreed-upon amendments was the Soviet-sponsored one for "protection of fundamental freedoms, self-determination and equal rights of peoples without regard to race, language, religion or sex."

It was agreed by the U.S., British, Chinese and Soviet delegates to include this principle in the statements of purposes of the General Organization (Chapter I), of the General Assembly (Chapter V) and of the Arrangements for International Economic and Social Cooperation (Chapter IX).

* * *

Also made public last Sunday was the text of the U.S. proposals for an international colonial trusteeship. There is no space to review these important proposals here (full interpretation and editorial comment on them are carried in the May issue of the bulletin of the Council on African Affairs). But I do wish to comment on one weakness of the proposals which it seems to me important to correct if we are to avoid the danger of disunity among the five major powers.

According to the American plan, the agent of the General Assembly in supervising all areas which come under the trusteeship arrangements (except the "strategic" areas, which come Under the Security Council's supervision) will be a Trusteeship Council. This would "consist of specially qualified representatives, designated (a) one each by the states administering trust territories; and (b) one each by an equal number of other states named for three-year periods by the General Assembly."

Now surely all of the Big Five should have permanent representation in this important body. Unity among them in dealing with the question of colonies is fundamentally necessary. At present only Britain and France, of the Big Five, hold colonial mandates. When the final peace terms are made, the United States will also most probably assume such mandates. But what about the Soviet Union and China?

*   *   *

To remove any doubts about their status on this Trusteeship Council, clause "a" in the passage just quoted needs revision to read: "One representative each from the United States, Great Britain, the Soviet Union, France and China, and from any other state administering trust territories."

One more point. As we have said many times in this column, to win the confidence and cooperation of the colonial peoples in the new trusteeship plan, it is essential that they have representation and voice in the international supervisory body. This, also, should the composition of the of the Trusteeship Council.

*   *   *

"Today's Guest Column: Colonial Issues Won't Be Solved by Strategic Bases," *Daily Worker,* May 17, 1945, page 7

About a month ago, two weeks before the San Francisco conference got under way, I sounded a note of warning in this column about the hue and cry arising over independent U.S. control of island bases seized from Japan. The noisy minority of imperialist reaction, abetted by some good-intentioned but misguided zealots for an "impregnable American defense system," is today attempting to make this issue of island bases the main ground of debate on the merits of the American proposals for colonial trusteeship.

If this kind of discussion is not soon squelched, it will of course, result in side-tracking agreement on any effective plan of international action for bringing progress and freedom to colonial peoples for the sake of world security. Not only that, it will lead in the exact opposite direction toward renewed imperialist rivalries.

This was made clear last week by Representative [Emanuel] Celler of New York, one of the few men in Congress who have spoken out on the right side of this question of Pacific bases. Pointing out that this country has no more right to special claims for national defense than do other countries, the Congressman asked:

"Are we to permit the world scramble to begin again? Under the Atlantic Charter we are pledged 'to seek no aggrandizement, territorial or otherwise.' Would not outright ownership or even sole trusteeship which has been translated by deed into outright ownership be a contravention of this basic principle recited in the Atlantic Charter? What dismal seeds of danger are we sowing thereby! Roosevelt could not rest in his grave with such vile hands tearing asunder his Atlantic Charter.

*   *   *

"The answer lies not in sole possession or sole trusteeship, but in international co-trusteeship with special accommodations for the needs of the country whose area is most vitally affected. The rights of visitation must be accorded all members of the United

Nations. Some compromise could be worked out as to Pacific bases where the United States might have unfettered control in military matters but we would have to respond to our co-trustees in all non-military matters.

"I would like to ask this question: against whom are we so busy protecting ourselves? I mean not only the United States, but Great Britain, France and Russia as well? Against each other? Are we starting a world peace conference in an atmosphere of mutual distrust? Are we putting our faith in international organization or into weapons of war, island bases for war and cordons sanitaire?"

There is nothing much I need to add to that statement.

*   *   *

The basic aims of the new trusteeship arrangements were set forth in the American proposals made public two weeks ago. Since then the Soviet delegates have proposed an important supplement, the expediting of "full national independence," to these aims. "The basic objectives of the trusteeship system," according to Soviet formulation announced last week, "should be to promote the political, economic and social advancement of the trust territories and their inhabitants and their progressive development toward self-government and self-determination,

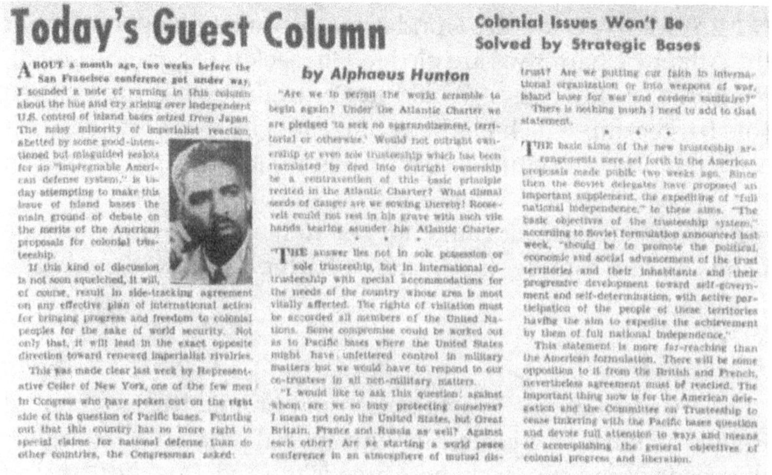

IMAGE 16: *Daily Worker*, May 17, 1945. Courtesy of *People's World*.

with active participation of the people of these territories having the aim to expedite the achievement by them of full national independence."

This statement is more far-reaching than the American formulation. There will be some opposition to it from the British and French, nevertheless agreement must be reached. The important thing now is for the American delegation and the Committee on Trusteeship to cease tinkering with the Pacific bases question and devote full attention to ways and means of accomplishing the general objectives of colonial progress and liberation.

* * *

"Today's Guest Column: Hull Defined The Solution," *Daily Worker*, May 24, 1945, page 11

The American delegation at San Francisco faces another crucial test of its adherence to or abandonment of policies established during Roosevelt's administration. This test is on the question of whether the limited objective of self-government or the guarantee of full independence should be the political aim of the proposed colonial trusteeship system. The British and French delegates insist on the former while the Soviet and Chinese support the latter. The U.S. delegation thus holds the pivotal position among the Big Five in the solution of this issue.

Let us review briefly what has happened on this question. The original American proposals, which provided the first basis of discussion of the trusteeship problem, called for the colonial peoples' "progressive development toward self-government." Although this formulation left many questions unanswered about the political future of the colonies, it did represent a marked advance over the aims of the old mandate system. Article XXII of the Covenant of the League of Nations, which provided for the establishment of mandates, used only the vaguest formulation of promoting the "well-being and development" of the peoples in the mandated territories.

The Soviet delegates, reacting to the American plan, made the more specific and far-reaching proposal of "progressive development toward self-government and self-determination, with active participation of the peoples of these territories having the aim to expedite the achievement of national independence."

* * *

However, the wording, used in the revised draft of the American plan embodying the results of discussion among the Big Five, not only fails to match the Soviet point of view but is even a qualification of the original American formula. The political aim in this "working paper," now being considered by the Committee on Trusteeship, reads: "To develop self-government in forms appropriate to the varying circumstances of each territory."

This clearly represents a concession to the wishes of the British. The conveniently-timed announcements of Britain's plans for self-government in Burma and of France's intentions toward Indo-China are, of course, intended to provide evidence of the sincerity of the self-government aim which these governments have insisted on. What is lacking – and for the very good reason that it can't be given – is evidence that the Burmese and Indo-Chinese peoples are satisfied with the self-government plans as proposed.

A fundamental principle is at stake in this issue: it is no mere quibble over words. A people cannot be said to be truly self-governing unless and until they have the right to independence. If they do not choose independence, that is their prerogative. But withholding the right of independence makes the concept of self-determination, upon which the Big Five have already agreed, absolutely meaningless.

* * *

There is no doubt about what the policy of the Roosevelt administration on this matter was. It was clearly set forth by Secretary of State Cordell Hull two years ago when he declared in the course of a definite statement of American foreign policy:

"There rests upon the independent nations a responsibility in relation to dependent peoples who aspire to liberty. It should be the duty of nations having political ties with such peoples, of mandatories, of trustees, or of other agencies as the case may be, to help the aspiring peoples to develop materially and educationally, to prepare themselves for the duties and responsibilities of self-government, **and to attain liberty** (my emphasis – A. H.). An excellent example of what can be achieved is afforded in the record of our relationship with the Philippines."

Not merely self-government but liberty is unequivocally stated here as our aim for colonial peoples. And citation of the Philippines further underscores the principle of independence within a definite stated time. The American people should insist that their delegates at San Francisco adhere to this policy in working out the final decisions regarding trusteeship arrangements.

* * *

"Today's Guest Column: Conversation In the Colonies," *Daily Worker*, May 31, 1945, page 7

There hasn't been any information available yet as to how the peoples in the far-flung colonial world are reacting to the trusteeship proposals now under consideration at San Francisco. But I can imagine something like the following conversation taking place somewhere in Africa and (with slight variations) elsewhere:

A: What's this I hear about the United Nations conference over in America? Seems they are planning to set us people in the colonies free – as Lincoln did the slaves in the Civil War.

B: Hold on, brother. Somebody's been kidding you.

A: What do you mean? I saw in the paper [Soviet Minister of Foreign Affairs Vyacheslav] Molotov told them in San Francisco that there must be full independence for the colonial peoples as the guarantee of international security.

B: Yes, but the British and French delegates balked at that. And the U.S. delegates, believe it or not, stood by them. They're willing to promise only self-government.

A: Self-government? Well, we've been hearing about that for a long time, at least from the British. Did they say when?

B: No, brother. They might possibly get around to that question when the trusteeship arrangements are agreed on for those territories which are voluntarily placed under the system by their controlling governments.

A: You mean the system won't apply to all colonies, and isn't even, compulsory for the old mandates, or the new areas taken over from Italy and Japan?

B: That's right. Not unless the countries that have those territories or get them in the peace settlement want to come under the trusteeship plan.

A: Looks to me like that's not going to do much for us. What about the territories here in Africa that Britain, France and Belgium got from Germany after the first World War?

B: They'll just go on keeping them, I guess. Gen. Smuts even had the brass to tell the conference that the Union of South Africa planned to annex the adjacent mandated territory of southwest Africa. But there doesn't seem to be much discussion at

San Francisco of any specific areas except some Pacific islands that the United States wants – for reasons of military security, they say.

A: And I always thought the United States stood for doing away with the colonial regime instead of extending it. Won't that mean that Britain will want to hold on to the Italian East African colonies now under their military occupation?

B: Very likely.

A: What about the Atlantic Charter? What about our having something to say about this business? We helped win the war, didn't we?

B: Well, you know that the British government wouldn't even let the Nigerian people send unofficial observers to San Francisco. But don't worry. There are plenty of people in America, white people as well as Negroes, who're no more satisfied than we are with this trusteeship business as it stands. And even plenty of people in Great Britain and France, too.

A: Well, it's sure time for them to speak up so that we will really get this peoples' peace that we've heard about so much and struggled so hard to win.

B: Yes, brother. But meanwhile we must go on strengthening organization and solidarity among ourselves. The Lord helps those that help themselves. Come on, let's get going.

* * *

"Today's Guest Column: Chinese Communist Interviewed by Negro Press," *Daily Worker,* June 7, 1945, page 7

Reporters out at San Francisco have commented on the fact that one of the least communicative of the leading figures at the UNCIO [United Nations Conference on International Organization] is Dr. T. V. Soong, chairman of the Chinese delegation, a man well-trained in the old school of diffident diplomacy. But when they talk with Tung Pi-wu, Communist member of the Chinese delegation, it's quite a different story.

Whereas the circumspect Dr. Soong has carefully sidestepped press questions regarding such controversial conference issues as racial equality and colonial freedom, Tung Pi-wu talked frankly and earnestly about these matters in an interview reported in the May 26 issue of the Chicago Defender, widely circulated Negro weekly. And an extremely interesting interview it is.

The 61-year-old Chinese Communist leader told his Negro interviewer that the people of China knew little about Negroes in America, and that most of what they heard came through sources not too sympathetic to colored Americans. But he emphasized that their knowledge of Negroes, as of other peoples outside China, was improving. He said that Langston Hughes was the most widely-read Negro writer in the Orient.

"Although they have experienced some Western chauvinism, Chinese people as a whole do not know very much about race prejudice in America," Tung stated. The Chinese Communists, of course, "don't tolerate race discrimination," he said, adding, however, that "in Chiang Kai-shek's area in China, minority groups are not treated as equals."

We would like to have had his reaction to Japan's much-touted "champion of the darker races" propaganda line. This apparently didn't come up in the interview, but we have a pretty good idea of what he would have said. That he had no use for doctrines of racial separatism was made clear in his observation on the fight against discrimination in America: "I believe American Negroes should unite with white groups who are progressive. Especially among the trade unions. The cultural and economic standards of all minority peoples must be raised. This will take time. But you will succeed." Sounds familiar, doesn't it?

* * *

Tung Piwu [sic] was sharply critical of the weak stand taken by the Kuomintang delegates on various critical issues during the earlier sessions of the conference, during which time he was practically ostracized by them. His subsequent pressure upon the Chinese delegation, which he promised to exert, is believed to have influenced the gradual strengthening of the Chinese stand on colonial trusteeship, the "right to work" amendment, and other issues on which the United States has been aligned with Britain on the wrong side against the Soviet Union and China.

Toward the end of the interview, Tung Pi-wu spoke quietly but seriously about the Communist armies of China, the government's blockade against them and their hard-won victories. "The only help we have had has come from the common peoples of the world," he said. "From Indians, Canadians, Negroes, Russians and even some Englishmen. We have had no help from any government. Is it any wonder we prefer to discriminate against fascist governments – and not against the common peoples of any race?"

* * *

If the Chinese are today learning more about American Negroes, as this great Chinese leader said, it is immeasurably more urgent that colored American [sic] learn more and do more about the problems of the Chinese people. The struggle for democratic rights is today worldwide in scope. In fighting for their own rights, Negro Americans must not lose sight of the fact that the reactionary elements in America which would hold them back are the very same ones which would support the anti-democratic Kuomintang regime against the Communist and other progressive forces of China. The fight against fascism, against reaction and imperialism everywhere in the world is one fight.

* * *

"Guest Column: The Charter and the Colonial Countries," *Daily Worker,* July 3, 1945, page 12*

The weaknesses in the World Charter drafted at San Francisco, especially with reference to colonial trusteeship, deplorable though they are, should not be permitted to weaken the Negro's support for the Charter as a whole. We must keep the larger perspective clear. The San Francisco Charter is not the end but merely the beginning of United Nations' planning for world security and peace. As such a beginning, a foundation stone of international cooperation on which to build, the Charter is an important and essential document.

Every means must now be utilized, therefore, to secure the Senate's speedy ratification of the Charter so that it may be implemented and clothed with substance and meaning as quickly as possible. Realizing they can't win with a frontal attack on the Charter, the [Democratic Senator Burton K.] Wheelers and [Republican Senator Author H.] Vandenbergs will resort to the more subtle technique of time-consuming delays and amendments. it [sic] is especially important for those who realize the shortcomings of the Charter to be on their guard against the latter strategy: attempts in the Senate to "improve" the Charter, though on the surface appearing laudable, can only have the effect of killing it.

The strengthening of the United Nations postwar program on colonies or any other problem cannot be accomplished by each of the fifty nations tinkering with the Charter prior to ratification. Rather it is through further decisions yet to be made by the major powers and through the actual application of the Charter to specific probelms [sic] that the means must be found for filling in the loop-holes and strengthening the weak sections of the Charter.

This applies especially to action on the colonies. It yet remains to be seen whether the old mandated territories and new ones resulting from this war will be brought under the trusteeship plan or will be in effect annexed by individual powers. It also remains to be seen what concrete guarantees and conditions will

---

*Note the slight name (from "Today's Guest Column" to simply "Guest Column") and page number change; no reason is given in the *Daily Worker* as to why. Hunton returns to the usual column name and page with the July 26 issue.

be required of those powers which place their territories under world organization supervision. Progressive public opinion, if adequately organized and effectively expressed in the United States, Great Britain, France, and other countries, can have a great deal to do in getting the correct determination of these and other still-to-be-settled questions.

The key test will be right here in the United States. As was made manifest in San Francisco, this country holds the decisive power for making the United Nations Organization either a weak and inneffectual [sic] instrument (and consequently a dangerous one, such as the League was) or a strong agency for general progress.

To get down to specifics, consider the demand for unilateral control of "strategic" areas in the Pacific (other areas throughout the world are also claimed) as though the U.S. alone had the job of maintaining world peace. It was this demand which was responsible for the extremely limited and dubious character of the American proposals on trusteeship. Far more attention and organized opposition to this thinly disguised program of imperialist expansion must be evinced by organized labor and other progressive forces in the United States.

The European powers will take their cue as to their colonial policies from the United States. It therefore rests with the most alert progressive elements in this country to recognize and live up to their responsibility for mobilizing public opinion so that our government will throw its influence on the side of self-determination and independence for all colonial peoples, as demanded by the Soviet Union and other anti-imperialist states. A serious and vigorous people's campaign toward this goal will counteract and negate the nationalist-imperialist currents which are finding too frequent expression today not only in Hearst and other such papers, but in the very halls of our Congress. This campaign must be undertaken simultaneously with the campaign for Senate approval of the World Charter, so that, once ratified, it will be properly implemented.

* * *

"Guest Column: A Voice from South Africa," *Daily Worker,* July 6, 1945, page 12

A bit wearisome, if not nauseating, was all the fulsome adulation during the San Francisco conference heaped upon that "elder statesman," Gen. Jan Smuts, Prime Minister of the Dominion of South Africa and Churchill's right-hand man in the game of imperial politics.

Gen. Smuts co-authored the Charter's "Human Rights" preamble (which pleased Vandenberg so much) and his speeches to the delegates were full of fine and noble generalities. But I failed to discover one word from the gentleman about the evils of imperialist aggression and oppression. It would be difficult to cite a better instance of these evils than the notorious case of South Africa itself (which even now plans to annex the neighboring mandate colony of Southwest Africa).

Although the conference is over, I think it not amiss for Americans to hear another and quite different voice from South Africa saying some of the things which the venerable Prime Minister failed to mention. The voice I refer to is that of Inkululeko, organ of the Communist Party of South Africa. I quote from the April 14 issue:

"The world expects and demands from San Francisco plans and decisions for a new world order; one which will guarantee to the common people of all lands that freedom from fear, want, insecurity and tyranny for which they believe this war is fought. The decisions of San Francisco must be political, rather than military. The United Nations have shown their unity against the common enemy of fascism. Can they retain that unity for the building of peace, progress and prosperity?

"If the seeds of future international conflict are to be avoided, certain truths must be frankly faced.

"The British colonial system, which keeps millions of people poor, backward and dependent, and which denies huge undeveloped markets to the rest of the world, must go. Otherwise the world will not know peace.

*   *   *

"The American capitalists must be restrained from embarking upon a policy of greedy, unchecked competition in the markets of the world. Otherwise there can be no long peace (my emphasis – A. H.).

"The practice of racial and national discrimination in Africa and elsewhere must go. It cannot continue in a free world.

"The people of all countries must enjoy democratic rights, including the right of self-determination.

"We are glad that South Africa will be represented at San Francisco. But the Union's delegation will be unrepresentative of the millions of people who are denied the right to elect the Union Parliament. At future conferences we must see that South Africa is represented not only by delegates from a government elected by one-tenth of the population.

"The majority of the people have the right to be heard at such conferences. Men like Dr. Xuma, Dr. Jabaru, Mr. Kotane and Dr. Nhlapo should be there. [These are Negro leaders, in the order named, of the African National Congress, the All-African Convention, Communist Party and African Teachers' Union – A. H.].

"It is the duty of the people of South Africa to see that they are."

And it is also the duty of the people of America, I would add. The Union of South Africa represents the same postwar fascist threat for Asia and Africa as Argentina represents for the Americas. We would be wise to keep our eyes upon the role of South Africa in that area of the world and upon the practices of the government whereby 8,000,000 non-white peoples and a large section of the white workers as well, are kept enslaved to the powerful mining interests (in which American capitalists, it should not be forgotten, have a big share).

* * *

"Today's Guest Column: Value of Rereading Dutt's 'World Politics,'" *Daily Worker*, July 26, 1945, page 7

I have just been re-reading R. Palme Dutt's* "World Politics: 1918-1936," published nine years ago, and I have found the experience so profitable that I want to urge all readers of this column to make or renew their acquaintance with this valuable Marxian study of the clash of Imperialist interests on the eve of World War II.

The book has an especially timely interest. It answers many of the important questions currently being discussed. Can or will monopoly capitalism reform itself? Can reliance upon an association of capitalist powers for collective security, even though the Soviet Union is a party to the association, be substituted for the effort of the masses of workers to achieve worldwide socialism? Or, in other words, can the working class permanently identify its interests with those of the bourgeoisie in the pursuit of the goal of collective security?

If there is any fuzziness In your thinking on these questions, there won't be after you've studied Dutt's World Politics [sic]. The book was written in the period of economic crisis and rising fascist aggression, when all progressive and democratic forces were endeavoring to forestall the impending world conflict by developing a united front policy among the anti-fascist powers. Though world fascism now faces destruction as a consequence of the united front policy which the capitalist powers were at last belatedly compelled to adopt in order to save themselves, there remains the basic economic fact underlying imperialist and fascist aggression – the fact of monopoly capitalism, developing at uneven rates among the different powers, demanding ever-expanding markets, and thus resulting in "the competitive conflict of the imperialist powers over the already divided world."

*   *   *

---

*Dutt was a leading member of the Communist Party of Great Britain, an intellectual and journalist, and early supporter of the National Negro Congress. See: "R. Palme Dutte [sic] Greets Negro Congress in U.S.," *Daily Worker*, January 11, 1936, 6

"These realities of imperialist relations," wrote Dutt, "have to be taken into account in estimating the possibilities of the line of collective security as a line of prevention of war. This does not mean that the line of collective security is therefore to be rejected as valueless. But it does mean that the line of collective security, the realization of which is dependent on the policies of imperialist governments, can never be a substitute for the Independent struggle of the masses of the peoples themselves in all countries for peace and against the policies of their governments driving to war. The central factor in the struggle for peace is the independent mass struggle, led by the working class, in unity with the peace policy of the Soviet Union. The strength of this factor will in practice also determine the degree of realization of the line of collective security.

"The positive value of collective security is not as a solution of the problems of imperialism, which from its nature it cannot attempt, but as a temporary method within the conditions of imperialism to delay the outbreak of war. The solution of the problems arising from the existing division of the world cannot be reached within imperialism.

* * *

"The final solution lies outside the conditions of imperialism, through unified world socialist organization, alongside complete national liberation (as exemplified on a regional scale in the Soviet Union), thus eliminating the questions of the division of the world, of colonies, of frontiers as expressions of power-groupings, of monopolies of raw materials, etc. Towards this final solution the mass struggle, led by the working class, against imperialism and against imperialist war, leads the way. The fight for collective security is only a temporary weapon in this struggle."

Dutt's book is a challenging reminder that, while taking the lead among the progressive forces of the world in securing the maximum good from the United Nations charter and Bretton Woods, the working class vanguard must not for a moment lose sight of its historic obligation of pressing forward toward the victory of socialism, toward the final and permanent victory over imperialist, fascist aggression.

* * *

"Today's Guest Column: Colonies Await Action By British Labor Cabinet," *Daily Worker,* August 2, 1945, page 7

Some 25 million people cast their votes in the British election. Taking no part in the election, but as directly affected by the results as dock workers of East London and coal miners in Wales, were the 460 million people who inhabit Britain's vast colonial empire of nearly 6,000,000 square miles. In deciding what sort of government they want to direct their own affairs, England's voters, incidentally, determine the kind of government that shall direct the affairs of the voiceless millions in the colonies. This time the wishes of the enfranchised minority in England coincided with the wishes of the subject majority in the colonial empire. The Tories, whose reactionary imperial policy was boldly and even arrogantly expressed by their leader Churchill, are out of office.

The great Labor Party victory has been cheered in India, in British Africa and in the British West Indies. The peoples in these lands followed the election campaign closely. A leading Nigerian newspaper (published by Africans), for example, conveyed the attitude of the people of British West Africa toward the election in these words:

"Knowing the political beliefs of the British Labor Party and appreciating what this body stands for, at least in principle, we cannot help but regard the utterance of the party through Major [Clement] Attlee 'to advance the standards of life of less developed peoples' of the empire as pregnant with hopes of a better future for us. We staunchly believe that nothing but a socialist government can raise us from the slough of despond to the bright sunshine of emancipation and all it stands for."

*   *   *

The British Labor government is, of course, not the kind of "socialist government" from which can come any new British colonial program remotely resembling the Soviet program for the former czarist empire. But one does have a right to expect that the stuffy old Colonial Office and the creaking colonial civil service apparatus will at least receive a thorough ventilating and overhauling, resulting in genuine colonial advancement. Labor members of Parliament have long been asking for this; they now have the chance to do the job themselves (the Labor Party's colonial policy for Africa, as stated two years ago, will be discussed next week).

The new government takes office at a time when there is desperate need for the quick solution of the question of Indian independence, and for honest and forthright dealings with other Asiatic and African people. As Leonard Barnes, the British colonial expert, wrote in the London Worker some months ago, "There is a crisis of confidence in the relations of the colonial people to Britain. They no longer trust the British – any of us – Right, Center or Left. It is the task of the Left to restore a measure of confidence."

* * *

The first step in that direction has been made by ousting [Leopold] Amery and most of his kind from Parliament, effectively demonstrating that such men do not represent the British people. To hold the confidence of the colonial peoples, the new government must proceed without delay to demonstrate in deeds that is [sic] is committed to new policies. It is the task of British labor now to see that this is done, to defeat every effort of reaction to block, sabotage or delay the carrying out of the clear mandate of the British electorate.

The labor government has responsibilities not only to the British people but to the peoples of every land where Britain's influence or dominion extends. The common people of England (or of America) can enjoy lasting economic security and democracy only to the degree that security and democracy prevail throughout the world.

* * *

"Today's Guest Column: Laborites' Statements On Colonial Policy," *Daily Worker,* August 9, 1945, page 7

"The Labor Party's Postwar Policy for the African and Pacific Colonies," a detailed 12,000-word report issued two years ago, gives a good picture of both the strength and weaknesses of the British Labor Party's stand on the colonies. As a forecast and measuring rod of what may be expected of the new people's government in Britain, this report, which was endorsed by the 1943 Labor Party convention, deserves a careful review.

We'll take up the creditable features of the report first. There are several positive and concrete proposals for the promotion of better health services, for the Improvement of education of all kinds and for all age groups, for the protection of colonial labor and the advancement of trade unionism in the colonies. The immediate abolition of the "Color Bar" system is called for, and eight specific measures for wiping out this system are listed.

Also commendable are the proposals for agricultural reforms in Africa, including a system of planned production to meet domestic consumption as well as export needs, and changes in colonial taxation and land policies which at present compel the Africans to leave their own land and work for the Europeans. There is, however, too much insistence that "agriculture is, and probably for some time will remain, the basis of economic life in all the African colonies." An extremely cautious attitude toward industrial development is expressed, except in the case of railways, which it is proposed should be developed by international action.

* * *

On the other hand, one of the most noteworthy points in the report is the promise to carry out in the colonies the program of nationalization of large-scale industry now at the top of the agenda of domestic reforms for Britain. Railways and mines in the colonies would be taken out of the hands of private ownership.

Says the report, "The exploitation of mineral wealth by private profit-making enterprise in Africa...has been detrimental to the economic and other interests of the natives, and in the future the object should be to bring it under state ownership and control everywhere."

These are some of the more outstanding positive features of the Labor Party's declaration of colonial policy. If put into effect with real determination, these various measures are bound to bring a radical change in the present miserable existence of the native population of British Africa – and are also certain to influence changes in the other French, Belgian, Portuguese, Spanish and Italian colonies in Africa, which are in even greater need of such reforms.

* * *

To make these plans work and to get maximum results in a minimum amount of time, the British Colonial Office must have much more centralized authority than it now has, and must be far more efficiently organized; the burdensome baggage of Col. Blimps in the Colonial Service, from governors on down, must be kicked out, and a new relationship of democratic cooperation with the colonial peoples, their mass organizations and leaders must replace the old imperialist dictatorship. The Labor Party, despite the handicap of some of its leadership on the right, should assuredly be expected to make far better progress along these lines than did or could the Conservatives.

All this is very well, you say, but what are all these reforms to lead to? What about self-government and independence for the colonial subjects? Well, that brings us to the negative side of the Labor Party's policy for the African colonies, which subject will have to be left for next week's column.

* * *

"Today's Guest Column: Laborites' Colonial Policy Can Be Changed," *Daily Worker,* August 16, 1945, page 7

The breath-taking sequence of events during this historic month, bringing the Japanese fascists to their knees,* has catapulted the world smack up against the problem of constructing the peace.

One big aspect of the problem of constructing the peace is this: "Since practically all territories suitable for imperial exploitation have already been partitioned and no imperial State is prepared to surrender any of its possessions peacefully, a dissatisfied 'Power' can only obtain a colonial empire by force, by dispossessing a possessor. That is why under present conditions the existing monopoly of colonial territories must always remain a potential menace to the peace of the world."

That succinct quotation is from the British Labor Party's 1943 report on its Postwar Policy for the African Colonies (a review of which I began in last week's column). Note that clause, "no imperial State is prepared to surrender any of its possessions

---

*On August 6, an American B-29 bomber dropped the first atomic bomb on Hiroshima killing at least 100,000 people; tens of thousands more would later die of radiation exposure. Three days later on August 9, a second atomic bomb was dropped on Nagasaki, killing an estimated 70,000 people. Six days later on August 15, Japan surrendered. Written during a time of cataclysmic war, there is no mention in the above article or in Hunton's other *Daily Worker* columns of the horrific toll the use of nuclear weapons had on Japanese civilians, nor is there a deeper analysis of the impact the use of atomic weapons might have on U.S. or Soviet geo-politics in the region. By late-August several African American newspapers, including the *Atlanta Daily World,* the *Chicago Defender,* and the *Baltimore Afro-America,* among others, had denounced the dropping of the atomic bombs. Langston Hughes, W.E.B. DuBois, and other Black leaders quickly began to protest. Many African Americans wondered why the atom bomb was used on the Japanese – a people of color – and not on the Germans? Additionally, by September 5, 1945, Wilfred Burchett's "The Atomic Plague" was published by the London *Daily Express* documenting the horrendous effects of radiation on Japanese civilians; by mid-September Hunton would have been aware of this article. For an analysis of the African American response to the dropping of the atomic bombs, see: Intondi, *African Americans Against The Bomb...,* Ibid., 12-16, 22. For an analysis of Burchett's first-hand account (as the first Western journalist to reach Hiroshima), see: Tanter, "Voice and Silence in the First Nuclear War: Wilfred Burchett and Hiroshima," *The Asia-Pacific Journal,* Vol. 3, Issue 8 (August 2005) and Burchett and Shimmin (eds), *Rebel Journalism...,* Ibid.

peacefully" – surrender them, that is, we presume, not only to another Power, but more to the point to the native peoples to whom they rightfully belong.

Was the Labor Party perhaps indirectly criticizing the Churchill's government's insistence upon holding on to the empire? No, it was simply recording what it regarded as an inescapable fact in international affairs. Thus it is that when it comes down to the question of self-government and independence for the colonies, there seems to be little to choose between Conservative and official Labor pronouncements.

In the statement under consideration, for example, we find the usual condescending references to Africans as "peoples of primitive culture," who are "not yet able to stand by themselves." Ignoring the political advancement and current popular demands in areas such as Nigeria and Gold Coast, the report holds that "for a considerable time to come these peoples will not be ready for self-government." There is the usual pledge to "train" the colonial subjects to rule themselves. But the Labor Party spokesmen are at least a little more candid than the Tories – near the end of the report is an inconspicuous one-sentence confession: "It cannot be said that any substantial advancement toward self-government is taking place."

The question of the hour in London's top circles is, of course, how to strengthen Britain's war-shattered position as a world power. Unfortunately, too many of the British Labor Party's bigwigs, in sharp variance with the more progressive rank and file of British labor, share the Tory conviction that maintenance and tightening of the colonial empire, with much greater utilization of its resources than hitherto, is Britain's only present salvation.

Are there any prospects, then, that the new Labor government of Britain will lend a hand in removing the menace to peace represented by "the existing monopoly of colonial territories"? Yes, I think there are.

First, the government must answer to the people, to the rank and file workers, who elected it to office. Second, the government is committed to a policy of close collaboration with the Soviet Union, the foremost champion of independence for colonial peoples. And third (as I should like to point out next week in concluding this topic), the British Labor government is committed to a program of genuine and effective international supervision

Today's Guest Column

by Alphaeus Hunton

Laborites' Colonial Policy Can Be Changed

THE breath-taking sequence of events during this historic month, bringing the Japanese fascists to their knees, has catapulted the world smack up against the problem of constructing the peace.

One big aspect of the problem of constructing the peace is this: "Since practically all territories suitable for imperial exploitation have already been partitioned and no imperial State is prepared to surrender any of its possessions peacefully, a dissatisfied 'Power' can only obtain a colonial empire by force, by dispossessing a possessor. That is why under present conditions the existing monopoly of colonial territories must always remain a potential menace to the peace of the world."

That succinct quotation is from the British Labor Party's 1943 report on its Postwar Policy for the African Colonies (a review of which I began in last week's column). Note that clause, "no imperial State is prepared to surrender any of its possessions peacefully"—surrender them, that is, we presume, not only to another Power, but more to the point to the native peoples to whom they rightfully belong.

Was the Labor Party perhaps indirectly criticizing the Churchill government's insistence upon holding on to the empire? No, it was simply recording what it regarded as an inescapable fact in international affairs. Thus it is that when it comes down to the question of self-government and independence for the colonies, there seems to be little to choose between Conservative and official Labor pronouncements.

In the statement under consideration, for example, we find the usual condescending references to Africans as "peoples of primitive culture," who are "not yet able to stand by themselves." Ignoring the political advancement and current popular demands in areas such as Nigeria and Gold Coast, the report holds that "for a considerable time to come these peoples will not be ready for self-government." There is the usual pledge to "train" the colonial subjects to rule themselves. But the Labor Party spokesmen are at least a little more candid than the Tories—near the end of the report is an inconspicuous one-sentence confession: "It cannot be said that any substantial advancement toward self-government is taking place."

THE question of the hour in London's top circles is, of course, how to strengthen Britain's war-shattered position as a world power. Unfortunately, too many of the British Labor Party's big-wigs, in sharp variance with the more progressive rank and file of British labor, share the Tory conviction that maintenance and tightening of the colonial empire, with much greater utilisation of its resources than hitherto, is Britain's only present salvation.

Are there any prospects, then, that the new Labor government of Britain will lend a hand in removing the menace to peace represented by "the existing monopoly of colonial territories"? Yes, I think there are.

First, the government must answer to the people, to the rank and file workers, who elected it to office. Second, the government is committed to a policy of close collaboration with the Soviet Union, the foremost champion of independence for colonial peoples. And third (as I should like to point out next week in concluding this topic), the British Labor government is committed to a program of genuine and effective international supervision of all colonies—something which the United States delegates helped defeat at San Francisco, but which may yet be realized—if we all, here and abroad, really work for it.

IMAGE 17: *Daily Worker*, August 16, 1945. Courtesy of *People's World*.

of all colonies – something which the United States delegates helped defeat at San Francisco, but which may yet be realized – if we all, here and abroad, really work for it.

*   *   *

"Today's Guest Column: Handling of Colonies Will Be Key Test," *Daily Worker*, August 23, 1945, page 7

The final answer to the question of how and by whom colonial territories taken from Italy and Japan shall be administered will be one key test of whether it's really peace we've won this time or just another temporary armistice as in 1919. Another division of spoils as after the last World War – no matter in what guise of respectability on grounds of "military security" it may be dressed – will mean another failure to establish a sound basis of peace. Only genuine international responsibility for such territories can make collective security a reality.

At the San Francisco conference no clear answer was given to this question, though at the special insistence of the U.S. delegation, unilateral control by a single power over any territory was made possible within the framework of the charter. At the Potsdam conference the Soviet Union recommended an international authority over such parts of Italy's empire as may be lost to her, but again no decision was reached, and It may be assumed that there was opposition to the recommendation from either or both British and American quarters.

Now our government has placed its cards on the table. Last Saturday a special subcommittee of the House Naval Affairs Committee submitted a lengthy report recommending that the U.S. maintain control over a vast chain of islands in the Pacific, including "specific and substantial rights" to American bases on islands belonging to other Allied powers as well as outright domination of Japanese-owned and mandated islands. These plans have been brewing in Washington for a long time. To date the progressive forces in America have paid far too little attention to this aspect of our foreign policy.

* * *

I'll defer comment on this House subcommittee's report to another time. The point I want to raise now is what sort of stand on this whole problem we may expect from the new British government. With the Soviet Union urging concerted international action in the colonial sphere and with the United States officially moving toward unilateral action, Prime Minister Attlee and his Labor colleagues are faced with a clear-cut issue.

As I mentioned last week, the British Labor Party in a formal statement on colonial policy made in 1943, while favoring the retention of national administration of colonies as at present, declared that "the mandate system in so far as it establishes this important principle of publicity and International supervision... should be extended to all backward colonial territories."

The statement goes on to define the powers of an International Colonial Commission which would give effect to this principle of collective supervision. It would give "international publicity to the measures taken (or not taken)" to advance the welfare and self-government of colonial peoples. It would entertain directoral [sic] petitions and "be a peripatetic inspectorate reporting, in consultation with the people, on the whole of the administration of each colonial territory."

*   *   *

The whole plan (I cannot describe it fully here) goes far, far beyond what was written into the trusteeship sections of the San Francisco charter. Though Major Attlee and his Labor colleagues may have done little or nothing at San Francisco to get their party's colonial program approved or to support the progressive Soviet proposals, they cannot now, with their election to power, escape responsibility for advancing that program.

If the British Labor Party means what it said in 1943, the British government will Join with the Soviet Union in demanding an effective system of international supervision of colonies which can be a vital instrument for maintaining world peace and bringing full freedom to colonial peoples.

*   *   *

"Today's Guest Column: Danger's in U.S. Pacific Policy," *Daily Worker,* August 30, 1945, page 7

About those Pacific bases. As you know a House Naval Affairs Sub-Committee a few days ago issued a lengthy report declaring that "the United States should take outright the Japanese mandated islands and the outlying Japanese islands" and secure "full title" to bases on other Pacific islands now owned by Great Britain, France, Australia, New Zealand, Portugal, Chile, and the Netherlands.

As Hanson W. Baldwin stated in the New York Times of Aug. 24, this report demonstrates "more than the re-emergence of imperialist thinking...its blunt tones will alarm some of our Allies, already worried by the possibilities of American economic imperialism."

What makes this report extremely ominous and a matter of national and international importance is that it is in line with the expressed policy of our administration. In his radio address to the nation of Aug. 9, President Truman said that "though the United States wants no territory or profit or selfish advantage out of this war, we are going to maintain the military bases necessary for the complete protection of our interests and of world peace. Bases which our military experts deem to be essential for our protection, and which are not now in our possession we will acquire. We will acquire them by arrangements consistent with the United Nations Charter."

* * *

Just what does that last sentence mean? Is it, as some thought, a promise that these bases will be placed under United Nations supervision? Hardly. The United States delegation at San Francisco took pains to guard against just that in the wording of the trusteeship provisions. Those provisions do not require any power to bring any territory under collective supervision.

All who support this policy of U.S. domination in the Pacific assert that it is for the protection of the United States. Protection against whom? They're not very explicit on that. But you may have observed that some of these same people have been outspoken champions of a "soft peace" for Japan. And you may have observed also that those who yell loudest for American expansion in the Pacific are the very same ones who say that we "cannot trust the Soviet Union."

In its editorial policy the New York limes cannot be relied upon to affirm today what it said yesterday. Nevertheless, four months ago on the eve of the San Francisco Conference, that paper said editorially: "On the political side the retention of all our present bases would justify the inference that we intended to police the whole world all by ourselves…Even the Pacific is not our responsibility alone. Many Australians and New Zealanders and hundreds of thousands of Chinese have shed their blood there fighting the Japanese (and the Soviet Union also entered the fight after this was written – A.H.). They have a stake in the Pacific as well as has the United States. And they should have a voice in deciding who holds what base.

*   *   *

"To abandon Guadalcanal and Tarawa and Guam and all the rest on V-J Day would be an absurdity that no one probably will propose. But for the United States to take the attitude that 'we won these and we intend to keep them' is just as absurd. It would be a tragedy if the pendulum that swung so far one way in the years immediately following the World War of 1914-18 should now swing as far in the opposite direction. The road to world order cannot be paved with jingo nationalism."

The only political and military policy which can safeguard the peace of America, especially in this new atomic age, is one in which the United States acts not independently but in concert and full cooperation with the other major Allied powers – and, above all, with the Soviet Union. It is this policy rather than that proposed by the House Naval Affairs Sub-committee which the American people must demand of their government.

*   *   *

"Today's Guest Column: Future of Italy's Former Colonies," *Daily Worker*, September 6, 1945, page 7

The news is that the U.S. State Department has been unable to decide which of two plans It should adopt for settling the fate of Italy's colonies in Africa – Libya, Eritrea, and Italian Somaliland, a total area of nearly 900,000 square miles with a native population of over 2,500,000. The question remains unsettled on the eve of Secretary [James F.] Byrnes' departure for the meeting of the Foreign Ministers' Council in London, where the drafting of the Italian peace treaty is the first order of business.

This situation is reminiscent of the State Department's protracted difficulty in getting final agreement on the colonial trusteeship proposals for the San Francisco Conference. Despite the numerous personnel changes, the department is evidently still suffering from a severe case of split personality.

According to James Reston, N.Y. Times reporter, one school of thought within the State Department, represented by James C. Dunn (who is accompanying Byrnes to the London meeting), favors letting Italy have her African colonies back. Not, mind you, out of any spirit of generosity or forgiveness toward Italy, but for the specific purpose of sidestepping the plan for joint allied supervision or administration of those colonies, as proposed by Stalin at the Potsdam Conference, thus preventing the Soviet Union from having any share in determining policy in the Mediterranean area and in Africa.

Supporters of this anti-United Nations and anti-Soviet policy warn against the "expansion of the Russian sphere of influence" into areas beyond Eastern Europe. What they have in mind, of course, is the protection and preservation of British and American imperialist holdings. These reactionaries unquestionably are filled with dismay at the prospect of the Soviet Union, with its aim of independence for colonial peoples, having anything to say about the government of Africa.

* * *

The other school of thought in the State Department, that group which is attempting to live up to the principles of the San Francisco Charter, wants to turn the Italian colonies over to the United Nations Organization to be administered by a commission representing the Big Four or the United Nations as a whole.

This group presents solid reasons for opposing the return of Italy's colonies to her: (1) because it is an unworkable as well as a bad policy to attempt to use Italy as a buffer against the Soviet Union; (2) because Italy's record as a colonial administrator has been among the worst; (3) because both Arabs and Ethiopians are opposed to Italian control; and (4) because the balance of power system contradicts all that the San Francisco Conference strove to achieve.

There is another angle to this problem not brought out in Reston's story. Far from entertaining any ideas about letting Italy have her African empire back, British officials contemplate bringing those colonies under permanent British control (they are now under British military Jurisdiction) – just as this government plans to take over Japanese holdings in the Pacific. The claim is that the Italian colonies are strategically situated along Britain's imperial "life-line" to India and the East. The plan to return Italy's colonies to her thus appears designed to shut out not merely the Soviet Union but – even more directly – America's chief capitalist rival, Great Britain.

*   *   *

And what about the views of the native population in the affected colonies? That's still another angle of the problem, which must be left over for next time.

But in the meantime, let's hope that progressive Americans will not be caught napping again on this issue as happened at San Francisco, when the cause of colonial independence was left for the Soviet Union to fight for almost single-handedly.

*   *   *

"Today's Guest Column: Sinclair Oil Lease in Ethiopia," *Daily Worker,* September 13, 1945, page 7

The 50-year lease announced last week, giving the Sinclair Oil Corp. exclusive control of Ethiopian oil, is a clear example of how "American big business, with the aid of government on the diplomatic level, is reaching out to consolidate its positions throughout the world," as the editorial of last Sunday's Worker pointed out.

The Sinclair deal marks a new chapter in Ethiopia's long struggle to preserve its independence as one of the three remaining states in Africa – about one-fifteenth of the continent – not directly ruled by foreign powers. The coastal territories of [Emperor] Menelik XI's greater Ethiopian empire were nibbled off little by little during the last century by England, France and Italy. And in 1935 what remained of Ethiopia was taken over by Mussolini and his fascists.

Since regaining his kingdom in 1942, Emperor Haile Selassie has been making great efforts to develop the country to the status of a modern power. Though handicapped by financial difficulties, he has been pressing forward the modernization of roads, communications, health and education. He no doubt looks to the new oil developments by the Sinclair Corp. to assist in raising the economic and social level of the country. The Liberian government had similar hopes when it permitted the Firestone Co. to establish a rubber monopoly in that West African republic. But it has not been the habit of such monopolies doing business in colonial or near-colonial countries to concern themselves with anything but maximum profits. Our next door neighbor, Mexico, learned that lesson and took steps as soon as she was able to reestablish Mexican ownershsip [sic] of Mexican resources.

* * *

In all likelihood the risks entailed in the Sinclair deal have been carefully considered by the Ethiopian Emperor, who learned a good deal about the ways of big power diplomacy from his experience in the League. There was not much room for voluntary choice in the matter. The Emperor was faced with the alternative of making concessions to American business in order to get U.S. diplomatic support, or of being forced to come under the British sphere of influence in East Africa. The latter would have meant the virtual impossibility of Ethiopia's regaining Eritrea, bordering the Red Sea, from Italy in view of Britain's own interests in that area. And further, it might have meant the loss of additional Ethiopian territory in the eastern Harrar and Ogaden provinces, now still under British military occupation – the very same area where the rich oil deposits are said to be located. In approving the Sinclair deal, therefore, the Emperor apparently chose what he regarded as the lesser of two evils.

*   *   *

That the Emperor was desperately struggling to get free of British domination, the cost of British aid in getting his kingdom back, was made clear by the terms of the revised Anglo-Ethiopian agreement signed last December. The new agreement deprived Britain of its prior position in the supervision of Ethiopian affairs, but it also cancelled out the possibility of Ethiopia getting any further large financial assistance from Britain. The Sinclair deal was the logical next step.

The announcement of the transaction, coming as it does on the eve of the London conference of Foreign Ministers, which will consider the Italian peace treaty and the question of Italy's African colonies, is bound to have an important bearing on the decisions on those matters and on the whole tenor of the conference. Just how much of a real United Nations peace the conference will be able to draft remains to be seen.

*   *   *

"Today's Guest Column: Trusteeship and The Italian Colonies," *Daily Worker,* September 20, 1945, page 7

Recent news from the Council of Foreign Ministers in London indicates that the colonial trusteeship provisions adopted at San Francisco may develop out of the stage of resembling a prettily-wrapped gift package with nothing inside. Reports, as yet not officially confirmed, state that a plan is being considered for bringing Italy's African colonies directly under the control of the Trusteeship Council set up by the San Francisco charter. The Italian colonies would thus become the first territories to fall within the jurisdiction of the new international authority. Self-government would become a near probability rather than a remote possibility in the territories.

This very promising development, naturally, does not meet with unanimous approval. Some of the opponents are sincere but misguided Italian patriots; most of the others, including several American commentators, are concerned less about Italy than about the maintenance of the old colonial imperialist system. These people advance two main arguments: (1) that international responsibility for colonies simply won't work, (2) that it Is unfair to penalize the emerging democratic Italy (now our ally) for the crimes of the fascist regime.

The answer to the first point is that the proposed plan, which is quite different from the mandate system under which in substance there was simply a redivision of German and Turkish colonies among some of the victors, has never been tried – certainly not with the Soviet Union as a participant (and that is what the imperialists fear most).

As for the second point, if the new Italy is truly democratic, it will not wish to keep Arabs and Africans in colonial subjection, and it might as well turn the job of emancipating them over to an international agency. Colonialism as practiced by a "democratic" power may be slightly less brutal than that of a fascist power, but it is none the less intolerable and dangerous to world peace.

*   *   *

A year ago, six prominent Italians, including [conductor] Arturo Toscanini, [journalist, literary critic] G. A. Borgese and [anti-fascist historian] Gaetano Salvemini, declared in a manifesto: "As Africa is not Italian, neither is she French, Belgian, Portuguese, nor Spanish, nor British...She belongs to her native peoples. The white man's burden, insofar as it is not a lie, must be turned over by the separate nations to a supernational organism assigning responsibilities and distributing rewards." Upon this basis they renounced the prospect of Italy demanding "even partial restoration of her African empire."

And just last week, Palmiro Togliatti, Italian Communist leader and Minister of Justice, condemned colonialism, described Italy's colonies as a burden, and proposed that the African territories should have self-government. Trusteeship, he said, should mean "quick passage to self-government."

It is not so much Italy's claims as Ethiopia's that are deserving of some attention and consideration by the Foreign Ministers' Council. Soon after he had regained his throne in 1941, Emperor Haile Selassie demanded the return of Eritrea and Italian Somaliland. "Before the Italian conquest," he said, "these territories were part of the ancient Ethiopian empire. We should like them returned to us."

*   *   *

When the British were struggling to oust the Italians from East Africa, the British military authorities, on the emperor's behalf, prepared and printed a proclamation which was showered by the thousands from RAF [Royal Air Force] planes over Eritrea. The proclamation called upon the native people to "join in the struggle at the side of your Ethiopian brothers. Let none of you be a tool in the hands of the Italians against your motherland of Ethiopia, or against our friends the English. Your destiny is strictly bound with that of the rest of Ethiopia."

A British intelligence officer wrote that Eritreans finding and reading this proclamation "were seen to kiss the seal, press it to their foreheads and weep. There were desertions backward and some to our lines. The Italians instituted the death penalty on anyone found reading our propaganda."

Was it only a "propaganda" stunt, then? The Ethiopians and Eritreans certainly did not think of it in that way. They are waiting to hear the London meeting's answer to Haile Selassie's demand.

* * *

"Today's Guest Column: The East Is Fed Up With Promises," *Daily Worker,* September 27, 1945, page 7

The American people are up in arms over what [General Douglas] MacArthur is doing in Japan. Deserving of the same public pro- test is what is happening in the territories liberated from Japan. The establishment of a real basis of peace in the eastern world depends as much upon, the achievement of freedom for the peo- ples of these liberated territories upon the conversion of Japan from caste rule to democracy. American policy – or more prop- erly, lack of policy – toward Indo-China, Malaya and the Dutch East Indies is a matter of vital concern. In these areas as in Japan those responsible for allied policy have been pursuing a course exactly opposite to the one necessary for the establishment of a real basis of peace.

With the notable exception of the recent Soviet-Chinese treaty of alliance, with its pledge of self -determination and independ- ence for earstern [sic] colonial peoples, events in the Far East have lately departed more and more from the principles set forth in the Atlantic Charter and at the Crimea and other allied confer- ences. In London, Paris and The Hague an unholy zeal is being displayed for the speedy return of the colonial areas overrun by the Japanese imperialists to their former European imperialist rulers. Meanwhile, in Washington, plans are afoot for the further penetration of American influence in the Asiatic sphere by taking over of some strategic islands from Japan.

And as for India, the touchstone of colonial independence in the east, a very disturbing and disappointing prospect is pro- vided by the British Labor government's stupidity and effrontery in dishing up once again, slightly warmed over, the same old rejected and discredited [Sir Stafford] Cripps' formula [a failed March 1942 effort to gain Indian support of the British war effort in exchange for promised independence].

* * *

Under the pretext of establishing "law and order," British and American military authorities have been making the liberated territories "safe" for the return of their former rulers. The infamous policy of Gen. [John R.] Hodge in permitting Japanese authorities to continue the administration of affairs in Korea has its parallel in other areas.

In the Dutch East Indies, for example, Japanese acting under British orders are holding down freedom-hungry Indonesians.

Japanese tanks and machine guns last week surrounded a mass rally of 10,000 people who raised the demand for the freedom of Java.

In Indo-China, martial law has been invoked and the British are shooting down Annamites in an effort to crush their struggle for freedom from French rule. Only a small fraction of the stories of these repressive measures gets told in the general press.

The issue of the liberation of India, Burma, Malaya, Indo-China and the Indonesian islands from imperialist domination received sharp and clear expression last week in the resolution adopted by the working committee of the Indian National Congress in convention at Bombay. Independence for the peoples of these lands, the resolution declared, was essential to avoid "sowing the seeds of a future war." In an editorial entitled "Number One Problem of Asia," the New York Times last Sunday commented on the Congress' resolution and acknowledged that it reflected "the aspiration of the great majority of the native peoples of southeast Asia and Oceania. It is a problem that must be solved to the satisfaction of these peoples if there is to be real hope for peace and progress in that area of the world."

* * *

The London Times, too, has likewise taken note of the importance of divesting the Japanese slogan of "Asia for the Asiatics" of its dangerous implications for world peace by making the slogan a reality. But when it comes down to the question of how and when the problem is to be solved, both papers flounder around in vague generalities. Says the New York Times, the solution "cannot come today, or next week, or next month." Or next year, or in the next decade?

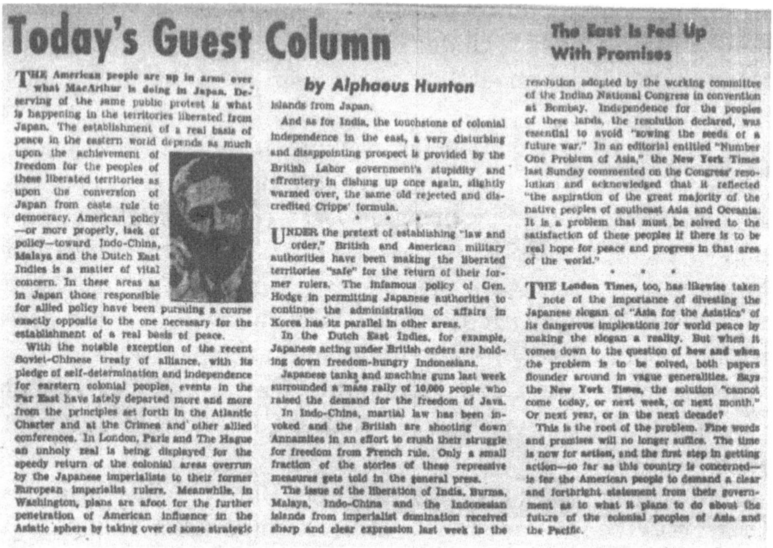

IMAGE 18: *Daily Worker*, September 27, 1945. Courtesy of *People's World*.

This is the root of the problem. Fine words and promises will no longer suffice. The time is now for action, and the first step in getting action – so far as this country is concerned – is for the American people to demand a clear and forthright statement from their government as to what it plans to do about the future of the colonial peoples of Asia and the Pacific.

*   *   *

"Today's Guest Column: The Negro's Stake in World Labor Congress," *Daily Worker,* October 4, 1945, page 7

It was extremely unfortunate, though entirely without deliberate intention, that no Negro member was included in the CIO delegation to the current Constitutional Convention of the World Trade Union Congress. However, this has in no sense detracted from the great interest which Negro organizations and labor are taking in the meeting. Two leading Negro weeklies have sent writers to Paris to cover the conference. The Negro recognizes the fact that this organization of world labor is the main hope of getting the kind of world that the common man, whatever his color, has fought a war to win.

As you perhaps read, the Negro Labor Victory Committee, National Negro Congress and the Council on African Affairs jointly sponsored the sending of Charles Collins, executive secretary of the first-named organization, to the Paris meeting. This sponsorship was broadened last week when several prominent Negro labor and civic leaders in New York joined in endorsing a statement to be submitted through Mr. Collins to the World Trade Union Congress.

The statement had as its main theme the responsibility which world labor has of uprooting colonial imperialism and all the "artificial barriers which now divide workers of different races." Unless this is accomplished, the statement said, labor "will fail in its efforts to win the security and freedom of any workers."

"As American labor has a direct responsibility for broadening the basis of democracy in the United States, so British labor, French labor, Dutch labor and the organized labor forces of every other imperialist power have a direct responsibility for extending democracy to the colonial peoples ruled by their respective governments. This responsibility must be fulufllled [sic] both through direct pressure by organized labor within each country – this should most certainly be effective especially in Great Britain at the present time – and through the collective influence and strength of the World Trade Union Conference.

"We earnestly hope that the Convention will fix responsibility on its general officers, and create, if necessary, a special agency to guarantee consistent and effective action…towards attainment of full national independence and security for the colonies, dependencies and subject countries."

* * *

The colonial workers' specific handicaps, including the color bar, forced labor, pass law system, and restrictions upon trade unionism, were pointed out in the statement. It was emphasized that there must be full support of the liberation struggle of colonial peoples, since democratic labor rights can only be achieved within a democratic political framework. The statement called special attention to the grave situation in Southeast Asia and the Pacific (and the signers at the same time telegraphed President Truman demanding that the United States not be a party to any coercive retoration [sic] of European colonialism in the Far East).

The labor delegates in Paris have already had the issue of colonial independence placed before them sharply by representatives from colonial areas. One of these representatives, S. A. Dange, president of the All-India Trade Union Congress, stated last week that though he "did not want to wreck the conference on political issues," it was necessary to take note of how American and British troops together with the Japanese were attempting to crush the national independence movements in many parts of the Far East.

"People who demand independence are being shot down," he said. "What is the attitude of the British, Dutch and French working classes? These are inconvenient questions, but labor must decide whether it will support the governments responsible for such things."

Negro Americans echo this Indian leader's questions. What will world labor do to combat the bold resurgence of imperialist forces? It is hoped that the present Paris Conference may provide some concrete answer.

* * *

"Today's Guest Column: Col. Blimp Counts His Rubber Profits," *Daily Worker,* October 11, 1945, page 7

How does the British ruling class (and I don't mean labor) react to the current Annamite and Indonesian struggles for independence? Have the old-school-tie gentlemen of Liverpool, London and Birmingham, who are so fond of talking about "the glory of the Empire," learned anything from the war? Are they perhaps a bit perturbed or conscience-stricken by the widespread revolts against European imperialism taking place in the Far East?

Suppose, for an answer, you take a look with me at the copy of the London Times for Sept. 19. What do we find?

Well, here on page 3 is a brief three-paragraph dispatch from Melbourne entitled "Annamite Opposition to French Rule." One sentence states that the Annamites in Saigon are "cooperating with the Americans even more than with the British, in the hope that American commercialism will displace French colonial imperialism." The article goes on to emphasize the Japanese aid given the Annamites and the "Communist tendencies" found among several of their parties.

Turning to page 4, we find another article about five times as long, almost a full column – and they pack a lot of type into a London Times column. Headline of this is: Rubber from Malaya – First 500 Tons – Prospect of Good Production.

"Ah!" says Lord Wigglesworth, settling back more comfortably in his chair at the club. "That's more like it! I say, Smithers, bring me another brandy."

We read: "The first shipment of Malayan rubber, about 500 tons, has left Singapore today." Many more thousands of tons of rubber and awaiting shipment. Yes, God's in his heaven and all's right with the British Empire.

We are told that the European interests in Malaya, members of the Rubber Growers Association, "have sensibly agreed to pool their interests, resources and profits until such time as a return can be made to the prewar company system."

* * *

The Japanese, it seems, didn't do much with the rubber, owing to shortage of shipping. They discouraged small-scale native production, "forcing the native owners to grow foodstuffs Instead" (no doubt, they had more to eat than when they were "permitted" to grow rubber for export).

More good news: the rubber estates "are in fairly good shape... At a rough estimate, at least nine-tenths of the Malayan rubber trees are undamaged." After more of this sort of inventory, we finally come to the human element in the business equation – the labor supply. Here the picture is not so bright. There is prospect of a labor shortage: "It may take time to reassemble those who survived the Japanese occupation."

The article goes on to speak about the prospects of tin mining in Malaya. Bemoaning the sad plight of the Malayan and Dutch refineries, in contrast with the large new Texas refineries handling Bolivian tin ore, the article concludes with the pious hope that (as in the good old prewar days when world tin was one of the most tightly cartel-controlled materials) "matters can once again be regulated on a worldwide basis with the minimum of friction."

*   *   *

If you're not already bored, we'll take just a glance at a long letter on page 5, same paper, same date, written by one Croft of the Empire Industries Association. He presents an elaborate plea, ornamented with some questionable trade figures and a great deal of righteous flag-waving for the maintenance of the British imperial preference system, whereby Britain during the depression period attempted to erect a Chinese Wall around the empire's trade.

Well, that's enough for one sitting. I think we have the answer to our opening questions. Some people learn easily; some learn the hard way; people like Lord Wigglesworth and our friend Croft never learn.

*   *   *

"Today's Guest Column: An Appeal for Cacchione And Baker in Brooklyn," *Daily Worker,* October 18, 1945, page 7

This is a period of important history. And whether it is a question of international politics or of a city election, it is the people, the workers, who determine the shape of history. This is worth remembering as we go into the home stretch of the New York election campaign. There are just 18 precious days left to do the job of getting out the vote which will guarantee the victory of Benjamin J. Davis, Jr., Peter V. Cacchione and other progressive people's candidates.

I want to talk about the election campaigns of two Brooklyn councilmanic candidates in particular—Peter V. Cacchione and Bertram L. Baker.

There have been disturbing reports that our campaign forces, especially over in Brooklyn, have been too few and too slow in getting into action. The pep and drive which two years ago gave Pete the highest number of first choice votes of any councilmanic candidate in the city has been lacking this year. This let-down, attributable perhaps to over-confidence or other psychological factors – but certainly not to any decline in Pete's top-flight record of achievement in the City Council – must be overcome. And quickly.

The failure to reelect Pete Cacchione – a possibility which must be frankly faced – must mean the personal shame and disgrace of every Communist Party member of Brooklyn. And more than that, it would mean a heavy and irreparable loss to all those for wrom [sic] and with whom Pete has labored as City Councilman – the trade unions, the Negro and other minority people, and all liberal and progressive forces in the borough. That must not happen!

In the final home-stretch drive of the Brooklyn campaign, a lot of lost ground must be made up in order to bring Pete home on top. It's up to every able-bodied one of us to shake a leg getting over to the campaign headquarters of his district – with as many workers as he can carry along – and get busy on the job that must be done. Let's do that now. Then there'll be no occasion for gloomy post-mortems on Nov. 7 about what ought to have been done.

As a Brooklynite myself, I'm also particularly concerned about the election of another councilmanic candidate from the home of the Dodgers – Bertram L. Baker. Brooklyn has never yet sent a Negro to the City Council – or to the state legislature either, for that matter. There have been well-qualified Negro candidates running in past elections, but they have failed to get the unified support of the Negro voters of all parties or adequate support on a boroughwide scale.

This year, in the candidacy of Baker, a Democratic nominee with ALP [American Labor Party] endorsement, there is an excellent opportunity of overcoming both these obstacles and of enabling the large Negro population of Brooklyn to send its own representative to the City Council – as it rightfully should. But it can only be done – as it was done and will be done again in Manhattan in electing Ben Davis – with the help of all the progressive forces of the borough.

Brooklyn must reelect Peter V. Cacchione and elect Bertram L. Baker. Greater New York needs two Negro Councilmen as well as two Communist Councilmen. So let's shake a leg! History is ours to make.

*   *   *

"Today's Guest Column: 'Soviet Light On the Colonies,'" *Daily Worker,* October 25, 1945, page 7

I've been reading a frayed, pocket-size, nondescript-looking paper-backed book which I borrowed from someone who got it from someone else who brought it over from London. The title is Soviet Light on the Colonies [sic]. The author is Leonard Barnes. It is by far the best book I have read on the subject of what the fight against colonial imperialism means at this present period of world history.

Barnes is an Oxford-educated Englishman who set out, after World War I, to find out about imperialism. With this purpose he worked for a time in the British Colonial Office and then spent seven years in Africa, without benefit of official status, as a settler and newspaperman. Later, in 1938, he visited the USSR. He is the author of a number of valuable studies of colonial questions, two of the most notable being The Duty of Empire [sic] (1935) and Empire or Democracy? [sic] (1939). Incidentally, he is also a charter member of the Council on African Affairs, headed by Paul Robeson and Max Yergan.

Soviet Light on the Colonies was published last year in England as a Penguin Special (288 pages, including index, at the amazing price of nine pence). I am told by the American branch of Penguin Books that it won't be available in the United States for another year. But we can't wait that long. Progressive forces here have urgent need of this valuable ideological weapon to aid them in the present fight against monopoly capitalism, colonial imperialism and fascism. One reason for my writing about a book that isn't readily available is to underscore the importance of finding some way of getting it circulated over here as quickly as possible.

* * *

Some books on colonial imperialism have merit in giving an accurate and clear picture of what's wrong in the dependent countries, but fail to show how the basic causation of these conditions lies in the workings of monopoly capitalism. Other books have merit in giving a Marxist analysis of modern finance capitalism and its general effects, but fail to show in concrete terms what it means in the lives of colonial peoples.

Barnes' Soviet Light [sic] combines these two virtues, an all too rare occurrence, and adds still a third – a full explanation of what Soviet socialist planning is and what it has accomplished for the many nationalities formerly enslaved in the Czar's colonial empire. The author accomplishes this difficult three-dimensional task by the clever device of having a Soviet citizen, Vova, travel about various sections of Africa, discoursing on the things that he sees and hears with the various colonial officials and others whom he meets along the way.

Vova remarks that the British, in their dealings with their dependencies, everywhere avoid administrative responsibility except insofar as this may be necessary to preserve and promote empire trade, the primary consideration.

This judgment is documented and reinforced over and over again in the course of Vova's journey. And at every point he contrasts the shocking waste, aimlessness and human degradation of the colonial regime with the systematic progress achieved in the Soviet Union by the application of the scientific principles of decolonization developed by Lenin and Stalin. The contrast is devastating.

*   *   *

And it has the essence of timeliness! What exasperates Vova most is that the British (and, by inference, all other imperial powers) cannot realize that they are complacently plodding toward disaster. The only alternative to economic chaos and more war, the only way by which democracy can really triumph over fascism, he urges repeatedly, is by ending colonialism through socialist planning.

"My stars," Vova exclaims, "if we could have 15 years in Africa, what a country we would make of it!" That is without doubt what was in Molotov's mind at the recent London conference when he astounded the British and Americans by proposing that the Soviet Union assume trusteeship over a certain part of the Italian colonies in Africa.

*   *   *

"Today's Guest Column: A Letter to The President," *Daily Worker*, November 1, 1945, page 7

Dear Mr. President:

I am one of the millions who sat at the radio listening to your Navy Day speech last Saturday afternoon. Like others, I was eager to hear what had been announced as a most important statement on our foreign policy.

There have been published comments on the speech from some Congressmen and other important figures, but I haven't yet seen any reports on what the man in the street thought about it (the volume of applause from your mammoth immediate audience in Central Park did not seem to register any too much enthusiasm, but that may have been a fault of radio transmission). I hope and presume you will be interested in trying to find out what Mr. Average Citizen thought of your speech. This letter may be of some small help in that direction.

Perhaps, as just an average citizen, I am rather naive, but I had expected that our chief executive would have dealt rather concretely with the most fundamental question of the hour: the effort toward achieving full understanding and cooperation among the Big Three, what difficulties were involved and what progress was being made.

I can't say that you clarified any of these questions for me, sir. You, of course, emphasized the need for "a policy of friendly partnership with all peaceful nations." But you failed to say what specifically was being done, or ought to be done, to realize that policy in action.

* * *

While you dealt in generalities in speaking about international cooperation, there was no lack of concreteness – even to the point of hurting someone's feelings – in your statements about the United States retaining "the greatest naval power on earth" and "one of the most powerful air forces in the world," "necessary bases for our protection" and embarking, if possible, upon a program of compulsory universal military training. Moreover, you were quite explicit about the United States retaining exclusive knowledge of how to make atomic bombs and other weapons.

All this military might, you stated, was desired "solely to preserve the peace of the world." But somehow, Mr. President, I had the impression that we were creating the United Nations Organization and seeking other means of international cooperation in order to preserve the peace of the world. Where do we stand? Are we for international cooperation or aren't we? Or are we, perhaps, for such cooperation on terms dictated by the United States as the dominant world power?

You warned against "the threat of disillusionment, the danger of an insidious skepticism – a loss of faith in the effectiveness of international cooperation" in this present atomic age. Who is guilty of fostering such dangerous doubts? Is it to be assumed that other nations will have utmost faith in the intentions of the United States when the United States clearly manifests its distrust of her allies by preparing to police the world single-handedly?

* * *

The 12-point statement of our foreign policy appeared to be sandwiched in between boasting of our military might, which I take to be the 13th and cardinal point of our foreign policy. The 12 points were in the main a restatement of the principles of the Atlantic Charter and Four Freedoms (aren't these documents mentioned any more in polite society?) with the addition of some implied anti-Soviet jibes.

As just an average citizen, it seems to me, Mr. President, that it is high time we stopped reiterating abstract principles, however noble, and began applying and practicing them. What, for example, is this government doing to promote a unified, democratic regime instead of civil war in China, or to permit the Indonesian and Indo-Chinese peoples to "choose their own form of government…without interference from any foreign source." I ask you.

* * *

"Today's Guest Column: Colonial Rulers Are Shy About Statistics," *Daily Worker*, November 8, 1945, page 7

When someone asks the size of the native population of Java, or Indo-China, or British West Africa, or some other colonial territory – or when someone asks what is the total population of all the colonies in the world – there will be as many answers given as there are persons asked. This is because the statistics of colonial population are about as accurate as Mr. [William Randolph] Hearst's "facts" about the Soviet Union.

It is safe to say that official census counts of colonial peoples are invariably short of the actual population figures. Official British government figures, for example, give the total colonial population as only some 60 or 70 million. Even adding India (which the British refuse to acknowledge as a colony), this would make for a total British colonial population of about 460 million. Half a billion or more is nearer the truth. The· Dutch claim the population of the East Indies to be only 61 million, but in current press stories the more accurate figure of 70 million is used. And so it goes with the other colonial powers.

The reason for talking about this question of colonial population is twofold: to emphasize the fact that such figures are at best only approximations, and to cite this inaccuracy as simply another instance of the inefficiency and aimlessness of colonial governments. It is important to remember that behind the bare statistics of population, startling though they are in their immensity, are the innumerable human lives which add up to the immense burden of poverty, disease and cultural backwardness which handicaps the rest of the world.

*   *   *

To make this question of population figures more concrete, I would like to quote part of an article from a progressive South African magazine, The Democrat. The writer remarks that no one should be surprised at the difficulties involved in getting an accurate picture of the size of the African population in South Africa, since "after all, if you haven't considered It worth while to make the registration of births, deaths and marriages compulsory among your native rural peoples or insist that their children go to school, you must expect snags when it comes to counting heads."

He continues: "Until we have compulsory registrations of all human beings – black no less than white – our census can only be a rough estimate of the native population. It is quite well-known, for instance, that in the Transkei during the 1936 census it was the habit of enumerators to visit a kraal, count all the thatched huts within sight, and multiply by five. That gave (he reckoned) the 'near enough' population of that particular area.

* * *

"Nor has the time come when we can expect to assess the ages of our native peoples with any great degree of accuracy. In the 1936 census the enumerators were confronted with 647 males and 765 females who claimed to be over 100. In Aberdeen there was a native who said he was 180 years old. A veteran at Ubombo (admittedly a lone spot with few distractions to pollute the simple mind) said he was 133; while at Kroonstad in the Free State there was one toothless black gentleman who said he was 130. Such claims have to be tested in the light of known facts, more especially the established figure of 45 as the average age at which South African native males die.

"The present rate of increase of the Bantu is about 2 percent, which means that in 35 years, approximately, they will have doubled themselves. Since it has already been officially declared that there never will be enough land for all the natives in the Reserves (there are already thousands of them landless) the prospect of squeezing a quart into an egg-cup (which is the the [sic] future task of the Native Affairs Department) is obviously one to defy all known laws of mathematics.

"If there is one thing which distresses government circles, it is a scientific approach to the natives."

* * *

"Today's Guest Column: Fate of Indonesia Signpost Of Future – It's Up to the People," *Daily Worker,* November 15, 1945, page 7

If the British or any other power were to launch a full-scale attack of warships, bombing planes and artillery against the native inhabitants of one of the Caribbean islands, Americans would be highly wrought up about it. Because this is happening across the Pacific, in Java, is it any less reason for Americans to be concerned?

True, the British surrender ultimatum and subsequent massacre in Surabaya* have brought forth a rising expression of protest in this country during the past few days. But this protest has not been wide or sharp enough to jar the administration (up to the time this was written) out of its silence-implying-approval of the dastardly British slaughter of Indonesians.

Why should Americans and the peoples of every other country be concerned about events in Java? Because that island is today the test of whether the imperialist powers have any solution other than brute force to offer in meeting the necessary radical adjustments of economic and political relations between themselves and those whom they govern as colonial "dependents" (just who is dependent on whom is a question we need not go into here).

The struggle of the Indonesians is the same as that of colonial peoples throughout Asia and Africa. The degree of intensity of the struggle varies in these countries, but the fundamental issue at stake is the same everywhere – freedom, freedom to live and order their own lives. The British, with the United States as silent partner, are backing up the Dutch in Indonesia because they know that the challenge to imperial domination there means

---

*The Battle of Surabaya was fought between British and British Indian troops and Indonesian nationalists as part of the Indonesian National Revolution (1945-1949) against the re-imposition of Dutch colonial rule. This was the largest single battle of the revolution and became a national symbol of Indonesian independence; Indonesia gained independence from the Netherlands in December 1949. It is estimated that 40,000 people, mostly civilians, were killed during the battle. See: Abdul Wahid, "The untold story of the Surabaya battle of 1945," *The Jakarta Post,* November 12, 2013, https://www.thejakartapost.com/news/2013/11/12/the-untold-story-surabaya-battle-1945.html

the weakening of imperial authority throughout the vast British Empire itself.

If brute force is to be the recourse of the imperialist powers for maintaining rule over their colonials, we may expect that brute force also will be used to silence the demands of under-paid and unemployed workers in this and other capitalist countries. The current sit-down strike of U. S. Steel, General Motors, Ford and other big monopolists is the domestic counterpart of American imperialism's efforts to bolster feudalistic and colonial regimes in China and the Eastern world. The road leading back to the colonial stagnation and economic depression of prewar days – the road which the dominant and most influential forces in this country appear to have chosen – has a signpost marked FASCISM.

* * *

Thus the Indonesians' struggle for freedom is as much our fight as it is theirs. This was the dominant note registered at the mass meeting in support of the Indonesians held last Sunday in New York under the auspices of the Emergency Committee for Indo-nesian Seamen. Letters and telegrams should be sent to the President and Secretary of State, demanding that this government repudiate the course which the British Commander in Surabaya, allegedly acting on behalf of the Allies, is pursuing. Moreover, contributions should pour in to help the Emergency Committee for Indonesian Seamen to carry on its work (checks payable to Max Yergan, Treasurer, 13 Astor Place, Room 605).

The leading role in fighting resurgent imperialism must be assumed by organized labor. American workers are at the present time naturally preoccupied with the problems of their own job status. But, as [CIO president] Philip Murray once said, "Foreign policy, both political and economic, is as much our concern and can affect us as directly as the wages we are paid or the hours we work." Australian and New Zealand trade unions, together with West Coast longshoremen under Harry Bridges and the National Maritime Union, have shown the way for labor to effec-tively oppose the imperialists by their practical action in halting the shipping of supplies, munitions and troops to the Dutch East Indies.

Today's Guest Column

Fate of Indonesia Signpost Of Future—It's Up to the People

by Alphaeus Hunton

IF the British or any other power were to launch a full-scale attack of warships, bombing planes and artillery against the native inhabitants of one of the Caribbean islands, Americans would be highly wrought up about it. Because this is happening across the Pacific, in Java, is it any less reason for Americans to be concerned?

True, the British surrender ultimatum and subsequent massacre in Surabaya have brought forth a rising expression of protest in this country during the past few days. But this protest has not been wide or sharp enough to jar the administration cup to the time this was written) out of its silence-implying-approval of the dastardly British slaughter of Indonesians.

Why should Americans and the peoples of every other country be concerned about events in Java? Because that island is today the test of whether the imperialist powers have any notion other than brute force to offer in meeting the necessary radical adjustments of economic and political relations between themselves and those whom they govern as colonial "dependents" (just who is dependent on whom is a question we need not go into here).

The struggle of the Indonesians is the same as that of colonial peoples throughout Asia and Africa. The degree of intensity of the struggle varies in these countries, but the fundamental issue at stake is the same everywhere—freedom, freedom to live and order their own lives. The British, with the United States as silent partner, are backing up the Dutch in Indonesia because they know that the challenge to imperial domination there means the weakening of imperial authority throughout the vast British Empire itself.

If brute force is to be the recourse of the imperialist powers for maintaining rule over their colonials, we may expect that brute force also will be used to silence the demands of underpaid and unemployed workers in this and other capitalist countries. The current sit-down strike of U. S. Steel, General Motors, Ford and other big monopolists is the domestic counterpart of American imperialism's efforts to bolster feudalistic and colonial regimes in China and the Eastern world. The road leading back to the colonial stagnation and economic depression of prewar days—the road which the dominant and most influential forces in this country appear to have chosen—has a signpost marked FASCISM.

* * *

THUS the Indonesians' struggle for freedom is as much our fight as it is theirs. This was the dominant note registered at the mass meeting in support of the Indonesians held last Sunday in New York under the auspices of the Emergency Committee for Indonesian Seamen. Letters and telegrams should be sent to the President and Secretary of State, demanding that this government repudiate the course which the British Commander in Surabaya, allegedly acting on behalf of the Allies, is pursuing. Moreover, contributions should pour in to help the Emergency Committee for Indonesian Seamen to carry on its work (checks payable to Max Yergan, Treasurer, 12 Astor Place, Room 605).

The leading role in fighting resurgent imperialism must be assumed by organized labor. American workers are at the present time naturally preoccupied with the problems of their own job status. But, as Philip Murray once said, "Foreign policy, both political and economic, is as much our concern and can affect us as directly as the wages we are paid or the hours we work." Australian and New Zealand trade unions, together with West Coast longshoremen under Harry Bridges and the National Maritime Union, have shown the way for labor to effectively oppose the imperialists by their practical action in halting the shipping of supplies, munitions and troops to the Dutch East Indies.

Let all the trade unions—rank and file as well as leaders—come forward, demonstrating the solidarity of white and non-white workers, of labor in the colonies with labor in the colony-holding countries, fighting together against imperialism. Rallying international labor to its responsibilities in the present struggle is especially the job of the World Federation of Trade Unions. Now is the time for that body to begin wielding its great power in the cause of democracy.

IMAGE 19: *Daily Worker*, November 15, 1945. Courtesy of *People's World*.

Let all the trade unions – rank and file as well as leaders – come forward, demonstrating the solidarity of white and non-white workers, of labor in the colonies with labor in the colony-holding countries, fighting together against Imperialism. Rallying international labor to its responsibilities in the present struggle is especially the job of the World Federation of Trade Unions. Now Is the time for that body to begin wielding its great power in the cause of democracy.

*   *   *

"Today's Guest Column: Thanksgiving Milestones," *Daily Worker,* November 22, 1945, page 7

It doesn't require any superior intelligence or special powers of discernment for one to be aware of how ironically out of place, how unseemly almost to the point of indecency have been the national holidays celebrated in this country during November in this year 1945.

One would have thought that the first Armistice Day and Thanksgiving after the end of World War II would be glorious and hallowe d occasions. There are those usual holiday orators who try to make believe that such is the case, but their high-flown rhetoric cannot dispel the bitter uncertainty and fear in people's hearts.

Yes, it is true; six years of a second world war are at last ended and fascism is militarily crushed; a United Nations Organization has been created; people's progressive governments are coming to the front throughout Europe; a World Federation of Trade Unions has been organized. Yes, all these and other great things have happened since Thanksgiving a year ago. And yet we know that these accomplishments are not in themselves the answer to what mankind needs, and must have. They are only the means, the essential first steps toward the answer.

*   *   *

To review, a little history, it was at Thanksgiving time in 1939, six years ago, that the first German planes bombed British soil.

At Thanksgiving time in 1942, the mighty forces of the Soviet Union had broken the siege of Stalingrad, and the doom of the fascist axis was sealed.

And it was a few days after Thanksgiving, 1943, that Marshal Stalin, President Roosevelt and Mr. Churchill Issued the memorable Teheran declaration (well worth rereading in these days):

"We express our determination that our nations shall work together in the war and in the peace that will follow.

"We recognize fully the supreme responsibility resting upon us and all the United Nations to make a peace which will command

good will from the overwhelming masses of the peoples of
the world and banish the scourge and terror of war for many
generations.

"We shall seek the cooperation and active participation of all
nations, large and small, whose peoples in heart and in mind are
dedicated, as our own peoples, to the elimination of tyranny and
slavery, oppression and intolerance."

*　*　*

It is the maintenance rather than the elimination of these social
evils which marks the open campaign for the preservation of
European imperialism and feudal dictatorship in the Asiatic
world undertaken by Britain, France, Kuomintang China and the
United States. These powers aim at a "peace" with all the old
special privileges of race, nationality and class remaining intact.
In attempting thus to block the march of millions of colonial and
semi-colonial peoples toward freedom and progress, the imperialist powers are promoting, not good will, but an ever-increasing
and explosively dangerous volume of ill will.

If Thanksgiving, 1946, is to be better than today, the march
of the people forward, Americans and other non-colonials side
by side with those in the colonies, must be unblocked. The fas-
cist-imperialist upsurge must be smashed by the united strength
of the forces of democracy.

*　*　*

"Today's Guest Column: A Hollander Put Finger On Indonesian Crisis in 1860," *Daily Worker,* November 29, 1945, page 7

The answer to imperialism's face-saving allegation that the Indo-nesian revolt was plotted by the Japanese as a mean trick against the allies was given 85 years ago. In 1860 a courageous writer who called himself Multatuli (a Latin pseudonym meaning "I endured much") published in Holland a book entitled Max Havelaar, or the Coffee Sales of the Netherlands Trading Company [sic].* In it he foretold what is happening today; there will inevitably arise, he said, a desperate, determined struggle to throw off "the sys-tem of abuse of authority, of theft and murder, under which the poor Javanese are crushed."

If you go looking up Max Havelaar, as I hope you will (an Eng-lish translation was published by Knopf in 1927), I must warn you not to be exasperated by the roundabout way in which the author develops his story. He says, "I make no apology for the form of my book," admitting that it "is a patchwork." His object was to get his book read, and by all sorts of people. The main part of it tells how a Dutch colonial officer, assigned to a pover-ty-stricken and corruption-ridden district of Java, tried to govern with honesty and justice, and in so doing found himself opposed and finally defeated by his superiors and the whole system of colonial government.

The following observation by Multatuli on the nature of official colonial reports applies equally well to the British, French and other colonial systems. Says the author:

"The Government of Netherlands India writes for preference to its masters in the motherland that everything goes well. The Residents [Dutch colonial officials in charge of given areas] like to report this to the government. The Assistant-Residents [in charge of divisions of an area], who in their turn receive hardly anything but favorable statements from their Controllers [over-seers, also

---

*In April 1999, the *New York Times* would recall this groundbreaking work as "…The Book That Killed Colonialism." See: Pramoedya Ananta Toer, April 18, 1999, https://www.nytimes.com/1999/04/18/magazine/best-story-the-book-that-killed-colonialism.html. Like *Uncle Tom's Cabin*, the article continues, *Max Havelaar* "was nothing less than earth-shaking."

Dutch], prefer, for their part also, to send no disagreeable tidings to the Residents, this an artificial optimism is born in the official and written dealings with affairs, contrary not only to the truth, but also to the opinion held by those optimists themselves, as that opinion appears whenever they treat those affairs orally, and – stranger still! – often even in contradiction of their own written reports.

"The Resident speaks in glowing terms of the flourishing trade, and asserts that in the whole province the greatest prosperity and industrial activity are to be observed. A little lower down, however, speaking of the slender means at his disposal for circumventing smugglers, he immediately wishes to remove the disagreeable impression that would be made on the government by the conclusion drawn that in this residency a good deal of customs duty must then be evaded. 'No,' he says, 'there is no need to fear this; little or nothing is smuggled into my residency, for… there is so little doing in these parts, that no one would risk his capital in commerce'!!!

*   *   *

"Where the population does not increase, the fact is attributed to to [sic] the inexactitude of the enumerations of previous years. Where the revenue from taxation does not rise, one counts it a merit: the intention is by low assessments to encourage agriculture, which is just now beginning to develop, and will soon – for preference when the writer of the Report shall have left the district – yield Incredible results. Where disturbances have taken place that cannot be concealed, they were the work of a few ill-disposed persons who in future need no longer be feared, as now there is general contentment. Where distress or famine has thinned the population, it was the result of crop-failure, drought, heavy rains, or something of the kind, but never of bad government…

"What improvement may be hoped with regard to so much wrong, if there is a predetermined purpose to twist and distort everything in those reports to the government? What, for instance, may be expected from a population which, by nature gentle and submissive, has for years upon years complained of oppression, when one Resident after another is seen to retire on furlough or pension, or called away to another office, without the slightest thing being done to redress the grievances under which that population is bowed down? Will not the bent spring in the end recoil? Will not the long suppressed discontent – suppressed in order that one may continue to deny its existence – at last pass to rage, to despair, to madness? Is there not in sight, at the end of this road, a Jacquerie [a revolt]?"

Yes, Multatuli, your warning of 85 years ago went unheeded, and we have now reached the end of the road in Java.

*   *   *

"Today's Guest Column: Hunger, Disease, Fascist Repression – South Africa," *Daily Worker*, December 6, 1945, page 7

The Union of South Africa, which must be classed with Spain and Argentina as one of the places where the job of liquidating fascism remains to be accomplished, rarely gets into the news except when Gen. Smuts makes one of his pompous pronouncements on international affairs. The fact that scores of people are injured in riots between Nationalist Party adherents and their anti-fascist enemies in the streets of Johannesburg, is not considered news in the Big Business press. Neither is the fact that African women and children are shot down for protesting against one of the innumerable repressive ordinances controlling the native population. Neither is the fact that acute starvation is at present threatening four million Africans segregated in South Africa's "native reserves" under conditions not very different from those in Germany's concentration camps.

Undernourishment and disease, which go along with poverty, have stalked the indigenous population of South Africa ever since the coming of the European. Starvation, a chronic and almost annual condition, reaches alarming proportions at periodic intervals. The land which formerly provided these people with the necessary sustenance now belongs to the foreign invaders. The Boer fanners have staked out thousands of acres for their cattle. And the British have laid claim to whatever lands that contained gold, diamonds, coal and other minerals.

With the labor of the African, the Europeans have converted South Africa into the most highly industrialized, productive and wealthy region of the entire African continent. And yet starvation stalks the Africans in their kraals. No better example than South Africa can be found to illustrate how capitalism and imperialism inevitably lead to poverty and hunger in the midst of of [sic] wealth and plenty.

As in the case of India's famine, starvation in South Africa is attributable directly to the land policy which in both cases spells poverty and backwardness for the masses and super-profits for a select minority. In South Africa, one-half of the 8,000,000 Africans (the white population numbers 2,000,000) exist in an area comprising only 13 percent of the whole country. In many of the districts the peasant farmers have no land whatever to till; the largest holdings do not exceed eight or 11 acres (the European farms average 2,000 acres). Drought, soil erosion and primitive agricultural methods all limit productivity of the Africans, but the root cause of their starvation is their landlessness and over-crowding in the areas where they are permitted to live.

*   *   *

Added to the land policy are the pass system, preventing the African from moving from place to place without the consent of government authorities and private employers, and the color bar, preventing him from securing skilled employment. By these instruments the European mine operators and farmers are able to maintain a ready supply of cheap African labor. The effects of this vicious system are reflected not only in the African's starvation and suffering but in the curbing of further industrial develop-ment and the limitation upon the purchasing power of the whole country. Even some of South Africa's business leaders are begin-ning to acknowledge the disadvantages of the repressive system. But instead of lifting the restrictions, the government is extending and reinforcing them.

Outside pressure upon the South African government – as upon the Argentine and Spanish regimes – must be developed. The Council on African Affairs, which has been the only organ-ization in this country thus far to bring the starvation crisis in South Africa to the attention of the American public, has con-stantly sought to mobilize such pressure. The South African Min-ister in Washington, Mr. H. T. Andrews, should be advised that Americans, while working to make democracy real in the United States, want Gen. Smuts and the South African government to contribute to world security and peace by cleaning up their own back yard, abolishing the land restrictions, pass laws and other discriminatory devices which serve to keep the African majority in subservience to the white minority in South Africa.

*   *   *

"Today's Guest Column: Why Imperialists Get South Africa's Help," *Daily Worker*, December 13, 1945, page 7

An understanding of South Africa's place in the anti-democratic line-up of nations is important not only in terms of knowing what goes on within the Dominion ruled over by Gen. Smuts, but also for comprehending the role South Africa has played and will play in the UNO [United Nations Organization] and international politics generally.

You may have noticed, for instance, what happened the other day when a test vote occurred in the UNO Preparatory Commission on a motion of the Soviet Union to guarantee the unqualified right of petition by colonial peoples to the UNO Trusteeship Committee for redress of grievances. When it came to counting heads for and against the motion – which fortunately carried – the Dominion of South Africa went along with Britain and the European colonial powers in trying to defeat it. South Africa, far more than any of the other Dominions, can always be depended upon to support British imperial policy. Smuts is now Attlee's right-hand man, just as he was Churchill's.

It is not simply that South Africa's economic interests are tied up to such a great extent with British capital. The line-up of political power in South Africa is likewise a vital reason why that Dominion will always be found supporting the reactionary side of any international question. The basic tenet of all major political parties in South Africa is the same. They all maintain the doctrine which Cecil Rhodes, the founder of the British empire in South Africa, proclaimed a half century ago when he said, "We must adopt a system of despotism, such as works well in India, in our relations with the barbarians of South Africa."

* * *

The two leading political groups in South Africa are the United Party led by Gen. Smuts and the Nationalist Party led by Dr. Malan. These two parties differ on foreign policy, with the Nationalists following an open pro-fascist line and keeping alive the old Boer versus British feud (as our polltax [sic] Congressmen over here are still fighting the Civil War). But on internal policy, in maintaining the African majority in a state of perpetual subjection, the two parties work in perfect harmony. This agreement on domestic policy is what is fundamentally important.

The South African Labor Party, which holds the balance of power in the government, sides with the United Party on foreign policy, and – except for occasional minority dissent – goes along with both of the other parties on domestic affairs. The Labor Party upholds the color bar because it conceives of this as a protection of the relatively high wage standard enjoyed by the (exclusively white) higher category of skilled workers.

The Communists are the only political party in South Africa which stands foursquare for the abolition of the entire system of exploitation of the non-European population – Africans, Asiatics and racially-mixed groups. The Communists tried in the 1943 elections to build a united front with the United and Labor parties in a fight against the Nationalist and other fascist groups. They got a cold shoulder. The Communists are a small though vocal minority in the political life of the country.

All liberal elements in the country, however, are now beginning to see the need for a united front against the increasing fascist threat. The Springbok Legion, an organization of ex-soldiers, and the Campaign for Right and Justice, people's organization in Johannesburg, are two of the leading groups seeking to mobilize unity in the anti-fascist ranks.

The latter organization recently secured over 40,000 signatures to a petition to Prime Minister Smuts calling upon the government to punish racial incitement as a crime; dissolve all organizations of the Nazi kind; ban private armies; expel all anti-democratic and anti-soldier elements from the public service, police and teaching; prevent any discrimination against the ex-soldier, and punish South Africa's quislings and war criminals. But Gen. Smuts has ignored the petition while continuing to appease those fascist elements against whom it was directed.

*   *   *

Today's Guest Column

11 Badges of Serfdom In South Africa

by Alphaeus Hunton

NON-WHITE people in the Union of South Africa often speak of that country as one gigantic concentration camp. Nowhere else in the world that I know of is freedom of movement of people so restricted as in the South African Dominion. The regulations there known as the Pass Laws are paralleled only by regulations which the Nazis brought into use against the Jews of Europe.

The Pass system originated in South Africa back in 1817 and has been developed over the years into an elaborate technique for controlling the entry and movement of Africans in the cities and for maintaining a supply of cheap African labor wherever it is desired. The Pass is the African's badge of serfdom.

Suppose a young African wants to leave the Native Reserve where he has grown up, and seek work in one of the cities. Our young African has heard about Passes, but in the Native Reserve areas he hasn't had to worry about them, because these are the only places in the country where passes are not required.

FIRST of all, he must have his Identification Pass, which must be renewed monthly and costs two shillings (40 cents). To leave the reserve, he must get a Trek Pass, and to buy a train ticket, he must also have a Travel Pass. That makes three of these things to start with. The District Commissioner, if he feels that this young African should remain where he is, will simply refuse to grant these passes.

Having reached the city, our African friend must immediately register and get a Six-Day Special Pass, the fourth pass, which allows him to seek work. He may get this renewed once, but if after 14 days he still is in the city and without a job, he will soon be picked up by the police.

Having found work, our young African must acquire his fifth and sixth passes to prove that he has a job: a Service Contract Pass and a Daily Laborer's Pass, both of which must be renewed monthly.

If he wants to visit someone who lives in another area or location (segregated quarters outside of the city), he must have his seventh and eighth passes, the One-Day Special Pass and the Location Visitor's Pass. If he must be out on the city streets after 9 p.m. (curfew time for Africans) he must have a Night Special Pass—the ninth pass.

Besides all this, he must also carry his Lodger's Permit, which costs between 30 and 50 cents per month and his Poll Tax Receipt Pass, which costs $4.00 or $6.00 annually, depending upon where he lives.

That makes 11 of these dog tags. There is also an Exemption Pass, exempting the bearer from carrying these other passes. But the number of Africans lucky enough to have these Exemption Passes was only 12,300 in 1940—out of a total African population of eight million.

IT GOES without saying that the African lives in constant fear of the police. If he cannot produce any of these passes when asked for by an officer of the law he gets thrown into a police van, spends the night in jail, and stands before the magistrate the next morning to receive a fine or jail sentence. In the one province of Transvaal, in which the two principal cities of Johannesburg and Pretoria are located, there were in one year 300,000 arrests under the Pass Laws.

For many years the Africans have been protesting against this humiliating and vicious Pass System, demanding its abolition. At present, the agitation for repeal of the laws is at its highest pitch. Yet the government is taking steps to extend and strengthen them. The Pass System, the Color Bar in industry, residential segregation, and political disfranchisement all serve to keep the black man in South Africa in subjection. For a more detailed picture of what Gen. Smuts' country really is, I would refer you to the monthly publication, New Africa, issued by the Council on African Affairs, 23 W. 26 St. (subscription $1 a year).

IMAGE 20: *Daily Worker*, December 20, 1945. Courtesy of *People's World*.

"Today's Guest Column: 11 Badges of Serfdom In South Africa," *Daily Worker*, December 20, 1945, page 7

Non-white people in the Union of South Africa often speak of that country as one gigantic concentration camp. Nowhere else in the world that I know of is freedom of movement of people so restricted as in the South African Dominion. The regulations there known as the Pass Laws are paralleled only by regulations which the Nazis brought into use against the Jews of Europe.

The Pass system originated in South Africa back in 1817 and has been developed over the years into an elaborate technique for controlling the entry and movement of Africans in the cities and for maintaining a supply of cheap African labor wherever it is desired. The Pass is the African's badge of serfdom.

Suppose a young African wants to leave the Native Reserve where he has grown up, and seek work in one of the cities. Our young African has heard about Passes, but in the Native Reserve areas he hasn't had to worry about them, because these segregated rural areas, where Africans are crowded together, are the only places in the country where are not required.

*   *   *

First of all, he must have his Identification Pass, which must be renewed monthly and costs two shillings (40 cents). To leave the reserve, he must get a Trek Pass, and to buy a train ticket, he must also have a Travel Pass. That makes three of these things to start with. The District Commissioner, if he feels that this young African should remain where he is, will simply refuse to grant these passes.

Having reached the city, our African friend must immediately register and get a Six-Day Special Pass, the fourth pass, which allows him to seek work. He may get this renewed once, but if after 14 days he still is in the city and without a job, he will soon be picked up by the police.

Having found work, our young African must acquire his fifth and sixth passes to prove that he has a Job: a Service Contract Pass and a Daily Laborer's Pass, both of which must be renewed monthly.

If he wants to visit someone who lives in another area or location (segregated quarters outside of the city), he must have his seventh and eighth passes, the One-Day Special Pass and the Location Visitor's Pass. If he must be out on the city streets after 9 p.m. (curfew time for Africans) he must have a Night Special Pass – the ninth pass.

Besides all this, he must also carry his Lodger's Permit, which costs between 30 and 50 cents per month and his Poll Tax Receipt Pass, which costs $4.00 or $6.00 annually, depending upon where he lives.

That makes 11 of these dog tags. There is also an Exemption Pass, exempting the bearer from carrying these other passes. But the number of Africans lucky enough to have these Exemption Passes was only 12,300 in 1940 – out of a total African population of eight million.

*   *   *

It goes without saying that the African lives in constant fear of the police. If he cannot produce any of these passes when asked for by an officer of the law he gets thrown into a police van, spends the night in jail, and stands before the magistrate the next morning to receive a fine or Jail sentence. In the one province of Transvaal, in which the two principal cities of Johannesburg and Pretoria are located, there were in one year 300,000 arrests under the Pass Laws.

For many years the Africans have been protesting against this humiliating and vicious Pass System, demanding its abolition. At present, the agitation for repeal of the laws is at its highest pitch. Yet the government is taking steps to extend and strengthen them. The Pass System, the Color Bar in industry, residential segregation, and political disfranchisement all serve to keep the black man in South Africa in subjection. For a more detailed picture of what Gen. Smuts' country really is, I would refer you to the monthly publication, New Africa, issued by the Council on African Affairs, 23 W. 26 St. (subscription $1 a year).

*   *   *

"Today's Guest Column: Trade Policy to Break Grip On Colonial Economy Needed," *Daily Worker,* December 27, 1945, page 7

With the British government, not without reluctance and misgivings, having approved the Bretton Woods plans and thus opened the way for the operation of new international monetary policies, the question now remains whether parallel policies can be worked out in the trade and commercial spheres in order to promote a stable world economy. Plans for an international trade conference next spring have been announced.

If that conference is to result in revised trade arrangements which will do away with the present division of the world into developed and slum areas, the latter in the great majority, one of the things it will have to deal with is the matter of cash crops produced in colonial and semicolonial countries for export.

The economy of such countries is unbalanced and steadily deteriorating; the producers of the crops eke out miserable earnings bearing no relation to the market price of their products, while the profits go to foreign corporations which control the purchase, export, and marketing of the products.

An organized and determined effort to crack this system is now being made by several hundred thousand cocoa farmers in the British West African colonies. They demand abolition of the government's control scheme and freedom to sell their own crops abroad. A delegation representing the farmers went to London. They failed to get an audience with the Colonial Secretary but have attracted wide attention and some sympathetic support in the British press.

*   *   *

Major grievance of the West African farmers is the unsatisfactory price paid them for their cocoa. The government offered $2.50 per 60 lb. load. In the face of indignant protests from the farmers, the offer raised to $3.00. But the farmers are holding out for $5.00 (25 shillings).

An editorial in an African newspaper published in the Gold Coast colony makes the following ironic observations on this price question:

"With the price (of cocoa) in New York at £80 ($320) per ton, even if the British price were £60 per ton, there should still be left a large and generous margin to enable our government to say:

"'Good farmers. You are poor. You need meat. You need health. You need schools. Also you need houses, and towns, and amenities and decent living conditions almost as good as our own people have in our own homes…

"'So, Good Farmers, now the power is in our hands as to what price you get, we're going to give it to you. Ill-bed fellows are ill-health, ignorance and poverty with a rich and free and intelligent Empire…

*   *   *

"'Therefore since we have been controlling your cocoa and its price for the duration of the [sic] and now that you and your sons have helped our Empire to get over that nasty business, we are going to be realists and men of feeling and sentiment. We wish to command that you have the price you want, 25 shillings a load of 60 lbs.

"'We are to you like the Genii in the story of Aladdin. We have only to wave a wand, to say the word, and riches and health and meat are yours. Hey, Presto! We wave the wand, we say the word. We command the price! Have it! Twenty-five shillings.'"

The point of this satire, of course, is the life-and-death control exercised by the British government, acting on behalf of British economic interests, over the existence of the African cocoa farmers. It is the same story with sugar farmers in the West Indies, rice farmers in Burma, and other cash-crop farmers in all alien-controlled countries. What is going to be done about it?

*   *   *

"Today's Guest Column: Harlem Rallies to Aid Famine-Stricken Africa," *Daily Worker,* January 3, 1946, page 7

Harlem will start off the New Year, appropriately enough, with a demonstration of support for the oppressed victims of imperialism across the seas. The victims upon whom special attention is being focused in this case are the people of that vast colonial continent, Africa.

I'm referring to the mass meeting to be held next Monday night, Jan. 7, under the auspices of the Council on African Affairs, at the Abyssinian Baptist Church on 137 St. Specific object of this meeting – and of a month-long campaign which the meeting will initiate – is to collect a mountain of canned food and substantial funds for the relief of four million famine-stricken Africans in the Union of South Africa. The campaign is being undertaken in response to urgent cables to the Council appealing for help from America. We've got to deliver!

As I remarked in this column some weeks ago in discussing the famine situation and other aspects of African life in the British dominion over which General Smuts presides, you will search in vain for information on such matters in the Big Business daily press. Talk about freedom of the press! The Times' idea of news that's "fit to print" doesn't include such items as the following from South Africa:

"Syalamba – we are starving. You can say that I, Noxgoweni, the headman, say WE ARE STARVING."

"We have lost so many cattle that many Africans will never get milk for the rest of their lives."

* * *

How does it happen that half the African population of the South African Union is faced with starvation? Land-hunger is the answer.

During the 19th century the Boer settlers and the British colonists pushed the Africans back farther and farther into the country, herding them into smaller and every smaller areas. By trickery and theft, but mainly by might of European guns over

African spears, the white invaders took away the African's land. The Boers staked out their thousand-acre cattle farms; the British staked out their claims to diamond fields and gold mines.

Though they fought a bitter war at the end of the century, and the Boers yet resent the political dominance won by the British, the primary and common concern of both European groups is to keep the Africans, who outnumber the Europeans four to one, "in their place." The land theft has been sanctified by law. Legal statutes now designate a mere one-eighth of the country as "Native Reserve Area", and all Africans not in the employment of Europeans must remain in these areas.

Thus it happens that these restricted "reserve areas" are crowded with half the African population, those not working on European farms, in the mines, or in the cities (and by law they cannot hold skilled jobs). There is not enough land in the reserves to support the primitive subsistence economy of the people. Crops are meagre and there is not enough grazing land for cattle.

*   *   *

There is great wealth in South Africa's modern cities, but in the reserves the African's life is one of poverty, hunger and disease. There is food aplenty in the cities, but in the reserves there is no money to buy any food and not enough is produced to go around. Nine out of 10 African children are undernourished. Men leaving the reserves to go to work in the mines require a special diet before they can perform hard labor. In some areas the infant mortality rate is over 60 percent.

This chronic starvation condition reaches calamitous proportions in the reserve areas when, as happened this year, a severe drought occurs, killing off cattle and destroying the already inadequate crops. That is how it happens that people are today dying of starvation in the land of gold and diamonds, South Africa. That is how the system of imperialism works.

And that is why all df us – not only Harlem but all of New York – should turn out to the mass meeting next Monday night. That is why we should give liberally, individually and through organizations, to this cause of famine relief.

With Paul Robeson and [contralto] Marian Anderson heading the list of speakers, and with a powerful mass expression of solidarity with the cause of oppressed peoples, Monday night's meeting will be heard all the way to South Africa.

*   *   *

"Today's Guest Column: A Meeting in Harlem And the UNO Session," *Daily Worker,* January 10, 1946, page 7

Today in London the opening session of the Assembly of the United Nations Organization is taking place. Numerous problems, including the big question of trusteeship and colonies, will get an airing by the Assembly's delegates. The tone and character of their discussion on this question, as well as such other questions as atomic energy, procedure for settling the peace terms, and the matter of the representation of the World Federation of Trade Unions in the UNO will foreshadow whether or not this newly-born organization can truly become an instrument for international unity and cooperation for achieving security, peace and progress.

To leave this high plane of diplomatic intercourse for a moment, it might be mentioned that another kind of meeting took place last Monday night in New York's Harlem. It, too, was concerned with international unity and cooperation. Over 4,000 people, called together by the Council on African Affairs, brought tons of canned food and contributed over $1.500 for the relief of their brothers and sisters facing starvation in South Africa. This meeting was the common man's demonstration of international fellowship and good-will. And it was a great demonstration!

* * *

The various speakers, especially Paul Robeson and Josh Lawrence, made clear to the audience the way in which imperialism makes for hunger and want in all parts of the world and among all kinds of people, and how it is the job of the Negro to ally himself with all oppressed workers in the struggle for the achievement of their common security and liberation from exploitation.

The demand for the abolition of South Africa's own special brand of imperialist exploitation, which is one of the worst, was voiced by the assemblage in resolutions addressed to Prime Minister Smuts and the UNO. The latter pointed out the fact that one of the purposes of the UNO is "to achieve international cooperation in…promoting and encouraging respect for human rights and for fundamental freedoms for all without distinction as to race, sex, language or religion," whereas the Union of South Africa with its openly avowed policy of maintaining white supremacy violated this observance of the fundamental human rights and freedoms in principle and practice, in law and custom.

*   *   *

Notwithstanding the argument against "interference in the internal affairs of sovereign states" (which is closely parallel to the states' rights pleas made by the Bilbos and Rankins), the resolution called upon the UNO "to take such steps as may be necessary to insure the observance" of the rights and freedoms of all people without distinction as to race in the Union of South Africa.

Another point of the resolution directly pertinent to the unresolved question of what is to be done with the colonial mandates inherited from the League of Nations (South Africa holds such a mandate over the former German territory of southwest Africa) was the demand that the South African Union be barred from any trusteeship or other colonial control until that country's pass-laws, color bar, residential restrictions and other discriminatory practices have been abrogated.

If the Assembly of the United Nations Organizations is to be the international political forum of the common people of the world as our own Congress is (or should be) the forum of the American people, it is necessary for the masses everywhere to speak up and make similar representations to this international body.

*   *   *

"Today's Guest Column: Lenin's Warning On Opportunism," *Daily Worker,* January 19, 1946, page 7

It was a timely and important note that William Z. Foster* struck in his article on Leninism and [John Maynard Keynes] Keynesism [sic] in last Sunday's Worker. One of the principal aims of our study and propagation of Leninism, as he pointed out so clearly, must be to counteract the "many subtle and dangerous illusions as to exaggerated possibilities" embodied in Keynesism and New Dealism, which reformist illusions act as a "barrier to the movement for socialism."

While the American labor movement by and large has failed to distinguish between temporary and immediate reform objectives and the basic and inevitable goal of socialism, it is the reactionary labor leadership here and abroad that is mainly responsible for befogging this distinction and leading the forces of labor down blind alleys.

In [Lenin's] Imperialism, the Highest State of Capitalism [sic], written in 1916, Lenin pointed out the way in which labor may be led into supporting the imperialist system because of the failure to see that it is the central enemy of the working class. In his 1920 preface to that work, he spoke of the "labor aristocracy" which serves as "the principal social prop of the bourgeoisie."

To understand the role of the Bevins in Britain or of our own [president of the International Ladies Garment Workers Union David] Dubinskys and [the anti-communist AFL vice president]

---

*Foster replaced Browder after the latter's expulsion from the CPUSA. With early signs of the Cold War and Red Scare emerging, the CPUSA under Foster's leadership, took a left turn; Hunton's last *Daily Worker* column reflects this turn. Though his CAA activism remained broad-based and outwardly projecting, by the late-1940s and early-1950s the CAA – like the rest of the domestic Communist movement – was on the defensive. Communists would rebound somewhat in the early- and mid-1960s and 1970s. For more on Foster, see: Arthur Zipser, *Working Class Giant: The Life of William Z. Foster* (New York: International Publishers, 1981), James R. Barrett, *William Z. Foster and the Tragedy of American Radicalism* (Chicago: University of Illinois Press, 1999), and Edward P. Johanningsmeier, *Forging American Communism: The Life of William Z. Foster* (Princeton: Princeton University Press, 1994)

Matthew Wolls,* a rereading of Lenin's analysis of the relationship of the British labor movement to British imperialism is in order. He points out (New Data for Lenin's "Imperialism," pages 224-226):

"Imperialism has the tendency to create privileged sections even among the workers, and to detach them from the main proletarian masses. It must be observed that in Great Britain the tendency of imperialism to divide the workers, to encourage opportunism among them and to cause temporary decay in the working class movement, revealed itself much earlier than the end of the 19th and the beginning of the 20th centuries; for two important distinguishing features of imperialism were observed in Great Britain in the middle of the 19th century, viz., vast colonial possessions and a monopolist position in the world market. Marx and Engels systematically traced this relation between opportunism in the labor movement and the imperialist features of British capitalism for several decades.

"We thus see clearly the causes and effects, the causes are: (1) Exploitation of the whole world by this country [Britain]; (2) its monopolistic position in the world market; (3) its colonial monopoly. The effects are: (1) A section of the British proletariat becomes bourgeois; (2) a section of the proletariat permits itself to be led by men sold to, or at least, paid by the bourgeoisie.

"The distinctive feature of the present situation is the prevalence of economic and political conditions which could not but increase the irreconcilability between opportunism and the general and vital interests of the working class movement. Embryonic imperialism has grown into a dominant system; capitalist monopolies occupy first place in economics and politics; the division of the world has been completed.

"On the other hand, Instead of an undisputed monopoly by Great Britain, we see a few imperialist powers contending for the right to share in this monopoly, and this struggle is

---

*Woll is considered one of the most conservative of all major American labor leaders. For example, he denounced the 1935 Wagner Act, the National Labor Relations Act, which gave workers the legal right to form and join unions. Woll was also a mentor to expelled Communist turned red-baiter Jay Lovestone, who led CIA backed and funded "free trade unions." See: "Revised Labor Act Is Urged By Woll," *New York Times*, September 6, 1938, and Jeff Schuhrke, "Reckoning With the AFL-CIO's Imperialist History," *Jacobin*, January 1, 2020. For more on Dubinsky, See: Robert D. Parmet, *The Master of Seventh Avenue...*, Ibid.

characteristicofthewholeperiodofthebeginningofthe20thcentury. Opportunism, therefore, cannot now triumph in the working class movement of any country for decades as it did in England in the second half of the 19th century, But in a number of countries it has grown ripe, over-ripe and rotten, and has become completely merged with bourgeois policy in the form of social-chauvinism.'"

Today it is the United States which above all threatens the imperialist monopoly of Britain. American labor must not be permitted to follow the opportunist path travelled, with some notable and glorious exceptions, by the British labor movement.

* * *

"They Second Ben Gold's Motion: 'Fight for 12 Is Fight for Negroes,'" *Daily Worker*, August 9, 1949, page 5

Response continued to grow yesterday to Ben Gold's "motion," addressed to progressives, asking for contributions and pro- tests on behalf of the Twelve.* To "second the motion" means to pledge $1 a week to the defense, plus a letter of protest sent to the *Daily Worker*. Following are some of the replies:

Dear Ben Gold:
We are happy to "second" the motion to support the legal fight in the defense of the 12 leaders of the Communist Party.

This odious legal proceeding is a major threat to our liberties for two main reasons:

(1) It violates the basic American principle that guilt must be on overt acts and not on opinions; it seeks to destroy the right of political advocacy and thus endangers the fight [sic] of any American to differ with the government with respect to important political isues [sic]. For Negroes, the safeguarding of the right to protest, to oppose constituted authority, and to fight for social changes, is indispensable if we are to win our long and painful struggle for full freedom and equality.

(2) The conduct of the trial by Judge [Harold] Medina bears the stench of the lynch-dominated court which daily convict Negroes in the South of "crimes" they have never committed. Medina's admonition to the Hon. Benjamin J. Davis, Jr. to "be a good boy" and his summary remanding of Henry Winston, national organizational secretary of the Communist Party, to jail for the duration of the trial, would qualify him for a posi- tion in any police court in Georgia or Mississippi, the native states of these two Negro victims.

---

*For an excellent discussion of the Smith Act indictments, see: Somerville, *The Communist Trials and the American Tradition...*, Ibid. Also, see: Martelle, *The Fear Within...*, Ibid.

In the fight which the Negro people are waging for their lives in the midst of unprecedented and mounting lynch terror in the South, they need the support and fraternal cooperation of every progressive force in America including the Communists.

The record will show that the fight for the freedom of the Communists is a fight for their right to fight for the rights of Negroes. In these circumstances, we are privileged as Negro Amercans [sic] who will never be content with anything but unqualified freedom, to join Ben Gold's appeal, and to urge other Negro Americans and their organizations to join us with their dollars and their protests.

Louis Burnham and Alphaeus Hunton

About the Author

Tony Pecinovsky is the president of the St. Louis Workers' Education Society, a 501c3 non-profit organization. His articles have been published in the *People's World*, *St. Louis Labor Tribune*, *Alternet*, *Shelterforce*, *Political Affairs*, *Z-Magazine*, and *American Communist History*, among other publications. He is the author of *Let Them Tremble: Biographical Interventions Marking 100 Years of the Communist Party, USA* and editor of the collection *Faith In The Masses: Essays Celebrating 100 Years of the Communist Party, USA*; he is also a contributor to the *Encyclopedia of the American Left* (Third Edition, 2022). Pecinovsky regularly speaks on college and university campuses, and at various academic and activist conferences, including the Organization of American Historians, the Working Class Studies Association, Labor Notes, Labor Campaign for Single Payer Health Care, and the International Labor Communications Association, among others. He lives and works in St. Louis, Missouri and loves cats.

Bibliography

Abt, John J. and Myerson, Michael, *Advocate and Activist: Memoirs of an American Communist Lawyer* (Urbana: University of Illinois Press, 1995)

African Communists Speak: Articles and Documents from "The African Communist" (Moscow: Nauka Publishing House, 1970)

Allen, Robert L., *The Brotherhood of Sleeping Car Porters: C.L. Dellums and the Fight for Fair Treatment and Civil Rights* (Paradigm Publishers, 2015)

American Friends Service Committee (ed), *Anatomy of Anti-Communism* (New York: Hill & Wang, Inc., 1969)

Anderson, Carol, *Eyes Off The Prize: The United Nations and the African American Struggle for Human Rights, 1944-1955* (Cambridge: Cambridge University Press, 2003)

Andrew, Christopher and Mitrokhim, Vasili, *The World Was Going Our Way: The KGB and the Battle for the Third World* (New York: Basic Books, 2005)

Anthony III, David Henry, *Max Yergan: Race Man, Internationalist, Cold Warrior* (New York: New York University Press, 2006)

Aptheker, Herbert (ed), *The Correspondence of W. E. B. Du Bois: Volume III Selections, 1944-1963* (Amherst: University of Massachusetts Press, 1997)

———— Aptheker, *Mission to Hanoi* (New York: International Publishers, 1966)

———— Aptheker, *History and Reality* (New York: Cameron Associates, Inc., 1955)

Armstrong, Elisabeth, *Gender and Neoliberalism: The All India Democratic Women's Association and its Struggle of Resistance* (New Delhi: LeftWord, 2021)

Barrett, James R., *William Z. Foster and the Tragedy of American Radicalism* (Chicago: University of Illinois Press, 1999)

Bevins, Vincent, *The Jakarta Method: Washington's Anticommunist Crusade & the Mass Murder Program that Shaped Our World* (New York: Public Affairs, 2020)

Blain, Keisha N. and Gill, Tiffany M. (eds), *To Turn The Whole World Over: Black Women And Internationalism* (Urbana: University of Illinois Press, 2019)

347

Brodine, Virginia, *Red Roots, Green Shoots* (New York: International Publishers, 2007)

Bryant, Earle V. (ed), *Byline, Richard Wright: Articles from the DAILY WORKER and NEW MASSES* (Columbia: University of Missouri Press, 2016)

Buelna, Enrique M., *Chicano Communists And The Struggle For Social Justice* (Tucson: University of Arizona Press, 2019)

Bunting, Brian, *Moses Kotane, South African Revolutionary* (London: Inkululeko Publications, 1975)

Burchett, George and Shimmin, Nick (eds), *Rebel Journalism: The Writings of Wilfred Burchett* (Cambridge: Cambridge University Press, 2007)

Campbell, James T., *Middle Passages: African American Journeys to Africa, 1787-2005* (New York: The Penguin Group, 2007)

Chura, Patrick, *Michael Gold: The People's Writer* (Albany: State University of New York Press, 2020)

Davey, Elizabeth and Clark, Rodney (eds), *Remember My Sacrifice: The Autobiography Of Clinton Clark, Tenant Farm Organizer And Early Civil Rights Activist* (Baton Rouge: Louisiana State University Press, 2007)

Davies, Carole Boyce, *Left Of Karl Marx: The Political Life Of Black Communist Claudia Jones* (Durham: Duke University Press, 2008)

Debray, Regis, *Revolution in the Revolution* (New York: Grove Press, 1967)

Dennis, Michael, *Blood On Steel: Chicago Steelworkers And The Strike Of 1937* (Baltimore: Johns Hopkins University Press, 2014)

Duberman, Martin, *Paul Robeson: A Biography* (New York: The New Press, 1995)

Ellis, Stephen and Sechaba, Tsepo, *Comrades against Apartheid: The ANC & the South African Communist Party in Exile* (Bloomington: Indiana University Press, 1992)

Fanon, Frantz, *The Wretched of the Earth* (New York: Grove Press, 1963)

Feurer, Rosemary, *Radical Unionism In The Midwest, 1900-1950* (Chicago: University of Illinois Press, 2006)

Finkelman, Paul (ed), *Volume 1 – Encyclopedia Of African American History, 1896 To The Present: From The Age Of Segregation To The Twenty-First Century* (New York: Oxford University Press, 2009)

Fisher, Nick, *Spider Web: The Birth of American Anticommunism* (Urbana: University of Illinois Press, 2016)

Foner, Philip S. (ed), *The Bolshevik Revolution: Its Impact on American Radicals, Liberals, and Labor* (New York: International Publishers, 2017)

———— Foner, *Organized Labor & The Black Worker, 1619-1981* (New York: International Publishers, 1981)

———— Foner (ed), *We, the Other People: Alternative Declarations of Independence by Labor Groups, Farmers, Woman's Rights Advocates, Socialists, and Blacks, 1829-1975* (Chicago: University of Illinois Press, 1976)

Fowler, Josephine, *Japanese and Chinese Immigrant Activists: Organizing in American and International Communists Movements, 1919-1933* (New Brunswick: Rutgers University Press, 2007)

Frazier, Robeson Taj, *The East Is Black: Cold War China In The Black Radical Imagination* (Durham: Duke University Press, 2015)

Friedman, Jeremy, *Shadow Cold War: The Sino-Soviet Competition for the Third World* (Chapel Hill: University of North Carolina Press, 2015)

Gardezi, Hassan N., *Chains To Lose: Life and Struggles of a Revolutionary – Memoirs of Dada Amir Haider Khan* (University of Karachi, 2007)

Gasiorowski, Mark J and Byrne, Malcolm, *Mohammad Mosaddeq and the 1953 Coup in Iran* (New York: Syracuse University Press, 2004)

Gellman, Erik S., *Death Blow To Jim Crow: The National Negro Congress and the Rise of Militant Civil Rights* (Chapel Hill: University of North Carolina Press, 2012)

Ghodsee, Kristen, *Second World, Second Sex: Socialist Women's Activism and Global Solidarity during the Cold War* (Durham: Duke University Press, 2019)

Gilmore, Glenda, *Defying Dixie: The Radical Roots of Civil Rights, 1919-1950* (New York: W.W. Norton & Co., 2008)

Gilyard, Keith, *Louis Thompson Patterson: A Life of Struggle for Justice* (Durham: Duke University Press, 2017)

Gleijeses, Piero, *Conflicting Missions: Havana, Washington, and Africa, 1959-1976* (Chapel Hill: University of North Carolina Press, 2002)

Gore, Dayo F., *Radicalism at the Crossroads: African American Women Activists in the Cold War* (New York: New York University Press, 2011)

Gradskova, Yulia, *The Women's International Democratic Federation, the Global South and the Cold War: Defending the Rights of Women of the 'Whole World'?* (New York: Routledge, 2020)

Grandin, Greg, *Empire's Workshop: Latin America, the United States, the Rise of the New Imperialism* (New York: Metropolitan Books, 2006)

Grant, Nicholas, *Winning Our Freedoms Together: African Americans & Apartheid, 1945-1960* (Chapel Hill: University of North Carolina Press, 2017)

Green, Gil, *Cold War Fugitive: A Personal Story Of The McCarthy Years* (New York: International Publishers, 1984)

Hall, Gwendolyn Midlo (ed), *A Black Communist in the Freedom Struggle: The Life of Harry Haywood* (Minneapolis: University of Minnesota, 2012)

Haviland, Sara Rzeszutek, *James and Esther Cooper Jackson: Love and Courage in the Black Freedom Movement* (Lexington: University Press of Kentucky, 2015)

Honey, Michael K., *Going Down Jericho Road: The Memphis Strike, Martin Luther King's Last Campaign* (New York: W.W. Norton & Co., 2007)

Horne, Gerald, *The Bittersweet Science: Racism, Racketeering, and the Political Economy of Boxing* (New York: International Publishers, 2021)

———— Horne, *White Supremacy Confronted: U.S. Imperialism and Anti-Communism vs. the Liberation of Southern Africa from Rhodes to Mandela* (New York: International Publishers, 2019)

———— Horne, *Facing The Rising Sun: African Americans, Japan, and the Rise of Afro-Asian Solidarity* (New York: New York University Press, 2018)

———— Horne, *The Rise & Fall Of The Associated Negro Press: Claude Barnett's Pan-African News and the Jim Crow Paradox* (Chicago: University of Illinois Press, 2017)

———— Horne, *Paul Robeson: The Artist as Revolutionary* (London: Pluto Press, 2016)

———— Horne, *Black Revolutionary: William Patterson and the Globalization of the African American Freedom Struggle* (Chicago: University of Illinois Press, 2013)

———— Horne, *Fighting In Paradise: Labor Unions, Racism, And Communists In The Making Of Modern Hawaii* (Honolulu: University of Hawaii Press, 2011)

———— Horne, *W.E.B. Du Bois: A Biography* (Santa Barbara: Greenwood Press, 2010)

———— Horne, *Mau Mau In Harlem: The U.S. And The Liberation Of Kenya* (New York: Palgrave Macmillan, 2009)

———— Horne, *The Color Of Fascism: Lawrence Dennis, Racial Passing, and the Rise of Right-Wing Extremism in the United States* (New York: New York University Press, 2006)

———— Horne, *Red Seas: Ferdinand Smith and Radical Black Sailors in the United States and Jamaica* (New York: New York University Press, 2005)

———— Horne, *Race War!: White Supremacy and the Japanese Attack on the British Empire* (New York: New York University Press, 2004)

————— Horne, *Class Struggle In Hollywood, 1930-1950: Moguls, Mobsters, Stars, Reds, & Trade Unionists* (Austin: University of Texas Press, 2001)

————— Horne, *Race Woman: The Lives Of Shirley Graham DuBois* (New York: New York University Press, 2000)

————— Horne, *Fire This Time: The Watts Uprising and the 1960s* (Charlottesville: University Press of Virginia, 1995)

————— Horne, *Black Liberation / Red Scare: Ben Davis and the Communist Party* (Newark: Associated University Presses, 1994)

————— Horne, *Communist Front: The Civil Rights Congress, 1946-1956* (Associated University Presses, 1988)

————— Horne, *Black & Red: W.E.B. Du Bois and the Afro-American Response to the Cold War, 1944-1963* (Albany: State University of New York Press, 1986)

Hunton, Alphaeus, *Decision In Africa: Sources of Current Conflict* (New York: International Publishers, 2021)

Hunton, Dorothy, *Alphaeus Hunton: Unsung Valiant* (New York: International Publishers, 2021)

Intondi, Vincent J., *African Americans Against The Bomb: Nuclear Weapons, Colonialism, And The Black Freedom Movement* (Stanford: Stanford University Press, 2015)

Isserman, Maurice, *Which Side Were You On?: The American Communist Party During the Second World War* (Middletown: Wesleyan University Press, 1982)

Jackson, James E., *The View From Here: Commentaries on Peace and Freedom* (New York: Publishers New Press Co., Inc., 1963)

James, C.L.R., *A History Of Pan-African Revolt* (Oakland: PM Press, 2012)

Johanningsmeier, Edward P., *Forging American Communism: The Life of William Z. Foster* (Princeton: Princeton University Press, 1994)

Johnson, Howard Eugene with Johnson, Wendy, *A Dancer in the Revolution: Stretch Johnson, Harlem Communist at the Cotton Club* (New York: Fordham University Press, 2014)

Jones, Howard, *My Lai: Vietnam, 1968, and the Descent into Darkness* (New York: Oxford University Press, 2017)

Keeran, Roger, *The Communist Party and the Auto-Workers' Union* (New York: International Publishers, 1986)

Kelley, Robin D.G., *Hammer And Hoe: Alabama Communists During The Great Depression* (Chapel Hill: University of North Carolina Press, 1990)

Kersten, Andrew, *A. Phillip Randolph: A Life in the Vanguard* (Roman & Littlefield Publishers, Inc., 2007)

Lanzona, Vina A., *Amazons of the Huk Rebellion: Gender, Sex, and Revolution in the Philippines* (Madison: University of Wisconsin Press, 2009)

Laumann, Dennis, *Colonial Africa, 1884-1994* (New York: Oxford University Press, 2013)

Lee, Christopher J., *Making A World After Empire: The Bandung Moment And Its Political Afterlives* (Athens: Ohio University Press, 2019)

Lewis, David Levering, *A Biography: W.E.B. Du Bois* (New York: Holt Paperbacks, 2009)

Lewis, David Levering; Nash, Michael; Leab, Daniel J. (eds), *Red Activists And Black Freedom: James and Esther Jackson and the Long Civil Rights Revolution* (New York: Routledge, 2010)

Lightfoot, Claude, *Chicago Slums To World Politics: Autobiography of Claude M. Lightfoot* (New York: New Outlook Publishers, no date)

Lorence, James L., *The Unemployed People's Movement: Leftists, Liberals, And Labor In Georgia, 1929-1941* (Athens: University of Georgia Press, 2011)

────── Lorence, *The Suppression of Salt of the Earth: How Hollywood, Big Labor, and Politicians Blacklisted a Movie in Cold War America* (Albuquerque: University of New Mexico Press, 1999)

Luckhardt, Ken and Wall, Brenda, *Organize...or Starve: The History of the South African Congress of Trade Unions* (New York: International Publishers, 1980)

Lynn, Denise M., *Where Is Juliet Stuart Poyntz?: Gender, Spycraft, and Anti-Stalinism in the Early Cold War* (Amherst: University of Massachusetts Press, 2021)

Manjapra, Kris, *M.N. Roy: Marxism and Colonial Cosmopolitanism* (New York: Routledge, 2010)

Marcuse, Herbert, *One-Dimensional Man: Studies in the Ideology of Advanced Industrial Society* (Boston: Beacon Press, 1964)

Martelle, Scott, *The Fear Within: Spies, Commies, and American Democracy on Trial* (New Brunswick: Rutgers University Press, 2011)

Maxwell, William J., *New Negro, Old Left: African-American Writing and Communism Between the Wars* (New York: Columbia University Press, 1999)

Memmi, Albert, *The Colonizer and the Colonized* (Boston: Beacon Press, 1965)

Meriwether, James Hunter, *Proudly We Can Be Africans: Black Americans and Africa, 1935-1961* (Chapel Hill: University of North Carolina Press, 2002)

Minter, William; Hovey, Gail; and Cobb Jr., Charles (eds), *No Easy Victories: African Liberation and American Activists over a Half Century, 1950-2000* (Africa World Press, 2007)

Munro, John, *The Anticolonial Front: The African American Freedom Struggle and Global Decolonization, 1945-1960* (Cambridge University Press, 2020)

Murrell, Gary, *"The Most Dangerous Communist in the United States": A Biography of Herbert Aptheker* (Amherst: University of Massachusetts Press, 2017)

Naison, Mark, *Communists in Harlem during the Depression* (Chicago: University of Illinois Press, 2005)

Nelson, Bruce, *Workers on the Waterfront: Seaman, Longshoremen, and Unionism in the 1930s* (Chicago: University of Illinois Press, 1990)

Nesbitt, Francis Njubi, *Race for Sanctions: African Americans against Apartheid, 1946-1994* (Bloomington: Indiana University Press, 2004)

Nicholson, Philip Yale, *Labor's Story In The United States* (Philadelphia: Temple University Press, 2004)

Nkrumah, Kwame, *Class Struggle In Africa* (New York: International Publishers, 1984)

Parenti, Michael, *The Anti-Communist Impulse* (New York: Random House, 1969)

Parmet, Robert, *The Master of Seventh Avenue: David Dubinsky and the American Labor Movement* (New York: New York University Press, 2012)

Pecinovsky, Tony, *Let Them Tremble: Biographical Interventions Marking 100 Years of the Communist Party, USA* (New York: International Publishers, 2019)

——— Pecinovsky (ed), *Faith In The Masses: Essays Celebrating 100 Years of the Communist Party, USA* (New York: International Publishers, 2020)

Perlo, Ellen; Perlo, Staley; Perlo, Arthur (eds), *People Vs. Profits – Columns of Victor Perlo: Volume 1: The Home Front* (New York: International Publishers, 2003)

Perry, Imani, *Looking for Lorraine: The Radiant And Radical Life Of Lorraine Hansberry* (Boston: Beacon Press, 2018)

Plummer, Brenda Gayle, *Rising Wind: Black Americans And U.S. Foreign Affairs, 1935-1960* (Chapel Hill: University of North Carolina Press, 1996)

Pomeroy, William J., *The Forest: A personal record of the Huk guerrilla struggle in the Philippines* (New York: International Press, 1963)

——— Pomeroy, *Guerrilla & Counter-Guerrilla Warfare: Liberation and Suppression in the Present Period* (New York: International Publishers, 1964)

——— Pomeroy, *Apartheid Axis: United States & South Africa* (New York: International Publishers, 1971)

———— Pomeroy, *Apartheid, Imperialism and African Freedom* (New York: International Publishers, 1986)

Prashad, Vijay, *Washington Bullets: A History of the CIA, Coups, and Assassinations* (New York: Monthly Review Press, 2020)

———— Prashad (ed), *The East Was Read: Socialist Culture In The Third World* (New Delhi: LeftWord Press, 2019)

———— Prashad, *The Darker Nations: A People's History of the Third World* (New York: The New Press, 2007)

Riddell, John; Prashad, Vijay; Mollah, Nazeef (eds), *Liberate the Colonies: Communism and Colonial Freedom, 1917-1924* (New Delhi: LeftWord Books, 2019)

Robeson, Paul, *Here I Stand* (Othello Associates, Inc., 1958)

Robeson, Jr., Paul, *The Undiscovered Paul Robeson: Quest for Freedom, 1939 – 1976* (Hoboken: John Wiley & Sons, Inc., 2010)

Roman, Meredith L., *Opposing Jim Crow: African Americans And The Soviet Indictment Of U.S. Racism, 1928-1937* (Lincoln: University of Nebraska Press, 2012)

Rueda, Maria Alicia, *The Educational Philosophy of Luis Emilio Recabarren* (New York: Routledge, 2021)

Ryan, James G., *Earl Browder: The Failure of American Communism* (Tuscaloosa: University of Alabama Press, 1997)

Sabin, Author J., *Red Scare in Court: New York Versus the International Workers Order* (Philadelphia: University of Pennsylvania Press, 1993)

Savonen, Tuomas, *Minnesota, Moscow, Manhattan: Gus Hall's Life and Political Line Until the Late 1960s* (Helsinki: The Finnish Society of Sciences and Letters, 2020)

Schwenkel, Christina, *Building Socialism: The Afterlife of East German Architecture in Urban Vietnam* (Durham: Duke University Press, 2020)

Shubin, Vladimir, *The Hot "Cold War": The USSR in Southern Africa* (London: Pluto Press, 2008)

Solomon, Mark, *The Cry Was Unity: Communists and African Americans, 1917-1936* (Jackson: University Press of Mississippi, 1998)

Somerville, John, *The Communist Trials and the American Tradition: Expert Testimony on Force and Violence, and Democracy* (New York: International Publishers, 2000)

Stanton, Mary, *Red, Black, White: The Alabama Communist Party, 1930-1950* (Athens: University of Georgia Press, 2019)

Stepan-Norris, Judith and Zeitlin, Maurice, *Left Out: Reds and America's Industrial Unions* (Cambridge: Cambridge University Press, 2003)

Stevens, Margaret, *Red International And Black Caribbean: Communist In New York City, Mexico And The West Indies, 1919-1939* (London: Pluto Press, 2017)

Swindall, Lindsey R., *The Path To The Greater, Freer, Truer World: Southern Civil Rights and Anticolonialism, 1937-1955* (Gainesville: University Press of Florida, 2014)

Taylor, Clarence, *Reds At The Blackboard: Communism, Civil Rights, and the New York City Teachers Union* (New York: Columbia University Press, 2011)

Vine, David, *The United States of War: A Global History of America's Endless Conflicts, from Columbus to the Islamic State* (Oakland: University of California Press, 2021)

Von Eschen, Penny M., *Race Against Empire: Black Americans and Anticolonialism, 1937-1957* (New York: Cornell University Press, 1997)

Westad, Odd Arne, *The Cold War: A World History* (New York: Hachette Book Group, Inc., 2019)

Wieder, Alan, *Ruth First and Joe Slovo in the War Against Apartheid* (New York: Monthly Review Press, 2013)

Winston, Henry, *Strategy for a Black Agenda: A Critique of New Theories of Liberation in the United States and Africa* (New York: International Publishers, 1973)

———— Winston, *Class, Race and Black Liberation* (New York: International Publishers, 1977)

Woddis, Jack, *New Theories of Revolution: A commentary on the views of Frantz Fanon, Regis Debray and Herbert Marcuse* (New York: International Publishers, 1972)

Yordanov, Radoslav A., *The Soviet Union and the Horn Of Africa during the Cold War: Between Ideology and Pragmatism* (Lanham: Lexington Books, 2016)

Zecker, Robert M., *"A Road to Peace and Freedom": The International Workers Order and the Struggle for Economic Justice and Civil Rights, 1930-1954* (Philadelphia: Temple University Press, 2018)

Zieger, Robert H., *For Jobs And Freedom: Race And Labor In America Since 1865* (Lexington: University Press of Kentucky, 2007)

Zipser, Arthur, *Working Class Giant: The Life of William Z. Foster* (New York: International Publishers, 1981)